SOCIETY FOR NEW TESTAMENT STUDIES

MONOGRAPH SERIES

General Editor: G. N. Stanton

59

WOMEN IN THE EARLIEST CHURCHES

Women in the Earliest Churches

BEN WITHERINGTON III

Associate Professor of Biblical and Wesleyan Studies,
Ashland Theological Seminary, Ohio

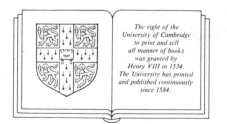

*The right of the
University of Cambridge
to print and sell
all manner of books
was granted by
Henry VIII in 1534.
The University has printed
and published continuously
since 1584.*

CAMBRIDGE UNIVERSITY PRESS

CAMBRIDGE
NEW YORK   NEW ROCHELLE
MELBOURNE   SYNDEY

Published by the Press Syndicate of the University of Cambridge
The Pitt Building, Trumpington Street, Cambridge CB2 1RP
32 East 57th Street, New York, NY 10022, USA
10 Stamford Road, Oakleigh, Melbourne 3166, Australia

First published 1988

Printed in Great Britain at
the University Press, Cambridge

British Library cataloguing in publication data
Witherington, Ben
Women in the earliest churches. — (Society
for New Testament Studies monograph
series).
1. Women and religion.   2. Church history
— Primitive and early church, ca
30–600
I. Title   II. Series
291'.1'78344   BL458

Library of Congress cataloguing in publication data
Witherington, Ben, 1951–
Women in the earliest churches.
(Monograph series / Society for New Testament
Studies; 58)
Bibliography: p.
Includes index.
1. Women in Christianity — History — Early church,
ca. 30–600.   2. Women in the Bible.   I. Title.
II. Series: Monograph series (Society for New Testament
Studies); 58.
BR195.W6W58   1988   270.1'0088042   87-24916

ISBN 0 521 34648 7

WS

CONTENTS

PREFACE

A portion of this work (parts of chapters 1, 4, and 5) exists in a somewhat different form in my doctoral dissertation, accepted by the University of Durham, England, in 1981. Again, I must express my gratitude to Professors C.K. Barrett (my advisor), J. McHugh, and A.T. Hanson for their assistance with my original thesis. In addition, I wish to thank Professor Graham Stanton for his help and suggestions when this new volume was being prepared.

Finally, I dedicate this work to women of faith engaged in the scholarly study of the New Testament material and the hermeneutical task of applying biblical texts to modern religious contexts. 'Apply the whole of yourself to the text; apply the whole of the text to yourself' (J. Bengel).

ABBREVIATIONS

Standard works

A-S	G. Abbott-Smith, *A Manual Greek Lexicon of the New Testament*.
BAG	W. Bauer, W. Arndt, and F. W. Gingrich, *A Greek-English Lexicon of the New Testament*.
BDF	Francis Brown, S. R. Driver, and C. A. Briggs, *A Hebrew and English Lexicon of the Old Testament*.
CIG	A. Boeckh, *et al.*, eds. *Corpus Inscriptionum Graecarum*.
CIL	Academiae Litterarum Regiae Borussicae, *Corpus Inscriptionum Latinarum*.
Danby	Herbert Danby, trans., *The Mishnah*.
DNTT	Colin Brown, ed., *Dictionary of New Testament Theology*.
IDB	G. A. Buttrick, ed., *Interpreter's Dictionary of the Bible*.
IDB Suppl.	*Interpreter's Dictionary of the Bible, Supplement*.
IG	Academiae Litterarum Regiae Borussicae, *Inscriptiones Graecae*.
Lampe, *PGL*	G. W. H. Lampe, ed., *A Patristic Greek Lexicon*.
LSJ	H. G. Liddell and R. Scott, rev. H. S. Jones, *A Greek-English Lexicon*.
Metzger, *TC*	Bruce M. Metzger, *A Textual Commentary on the Greek New Testament*.
MHT	J. H. Moulton, W. F. Howard, and N. Turner, *A Grammar of New Testament Greek*.
MM	James Hope Moulton and George Milligan, *The Vocabulary of the Greek Testament*.
Moule, *I-B*	C. F. D. Moule, *An Idiom-Book of New Testament Greek*.
NTAp	Edgar Hennecke, *New Testament Apocrypha*.
NTGNA	E. Nestle and K. Aland, eds. *Novum Testamentum Graece*.
ODCC	*Oxford Dictionary of the Christian Church*.
PGrenf.	B. P. Grenfell, ed., *An Alexandrian Erotic Fragment and Other Greek Papyri, chiefly Ptolemaic*.
POxy	B. A. Grenfell, A. Hunt, *et al.*, eds., *The Oxyrhynchus Papyri*.
PTeb	B. Grenfell, *et al.*, eds., *The Tebtunis Papyri*.
Robertson	A. T. Robertson, *A Grammar of the Greek New Testament in the Light of Historical Research*.
SIG	W. Dittenberger, ed., *Sylloge Inscriptionum Graecarum*.

Str-B	Hermann L. Strack and Paul Billerbeck, *Kommentar zum Neuen Testament aus Talmud und Midrasch.*
TDNT	Gerhard Kittel and G. Friedrich, eds., *Theological Dictionary of the New Testament.*
UBSGNT	Kurt Aland, *et al.*, eds., *The Greek New Testament* (United Bible Society).
Wettstein	Jacobus Wettstein, *Novum Testamentum Graecum.*
Zerwick	Maximilian Zerwick, *Biblical Greek.*
Zerwick-Grosvenor	Maximilian Zerwick and M. Grosvenor, *A Grammatical Analysis of the Greek New Testament.*

Series

BNTC	Black's New Testament Commentary
BZNW	Beihefte zur Zeitschrift für die neutestamentliche Wissenschaft und die Kunde der älteren Kirche
Budé	Paris: Société D'Éditions "Les Belles Lettres"
CGTC	Cambridge Greek Testament Commentary
FRLANT	Forschungen zur Religion und Literatur des Alten und Neuen Testaments
HGNT	Handbuch zum Griechen Neuen Testament
HNT	Handbuch zum Neuen Testament
HNTC	Harper's New Testament Commentary
HTKNT	Herder's Theologischer Kommentar zum Neuen Testament
ICC	International Critical Commentary
KEK	Kritisch-exegetischer Kommentar über das Neue Testament
LCL	Loeb Classical Library
MNTC	Moffatt New Testament Commentary
NCB	New Century Bible
NICNT	New International Commentary on the New Testament
NIGTC	New International Greek Testament Commentary
NPNF	Nicene and Post-Nicene Fathers
NTD	Das Neue Testament Deutsch
PNTC	Pelican New Testament Commentary
SBLDS	Society of Biblical Literature Dissertation Series
SBLMS	Society of Biblical Literature Monograph Series
SNTSMS	Society of New Testament Studies Monograph Series
ThHK	Theologischer Handkommentar
THKNT	Theologischer Handkommentar zum Neuen Testament
TNTC	Tyndale New Testament Commentary
UNT	Untersuchungen zum Neuen Testament

Journals

AER	*American Ecclesiastical Review*
AJA	*American Journal of Archaeology*
AJP	*American Journal of Philology*
AJT	*American Journal of Theology*
BA	*Biblical Archaeologist*

BAR	*Biblical Archaeology Review*
BeO	*Biblia e Oriente*
Bib	*Biblica*
BibLeb	*Bibel und Leben*
BJRL	*Bulletin of the John Rylands University Library of Manchester*
BR	*Biblical Research*
BSac	*Bibliotheca Sacra*
BT	*Bible Translator*
BTB	*Biblical Theology Bulletin*
BW	*Biblical World*
BZ	*Biblische Zeitschrift*
CBQ	*Catholic Biblical Quarterly*
CBR	*Christian Brethren Review*
CTJ	*Calvin Theological Journal*
CTM	*Concordia Theological Monthly*
EspV	*Esprit et Vie*
ET	*Expository Times*
ETh	*Eglise et Theologie*
ETL	*Ephemerides theologicae lovanienses*
EvQ	*Evangelical Quarterly*
Greg	*Gregorianum*
HR	*History of Religions*
HTR	*Harvard Theological Review*
Int	*Interpretation*
JAAR	*Journal of the American Academy of Religion*
JBL	*Journal of Biblical Literature*
JJS	*Journal of Jewish Studies*
JHS	*Journal of Hellenic Studies*
JETS	*Journal of Evangelical Theological Society*
JR	*Juridical Review*
JTNT	*Journal of the Theology of the New Testament*
JTS	*Journal of Theological Studies*
JTSA	*Journal of Theology for S. Africa*
KG	*Kathologische Gedänke*
LTQ	*Lexington Theological Quarterly*
LV	*Lumen Vitae*
MS	*Marian Studies*
NTA	*New Testament Abstracts*
NRT	*Nouvelle Revue Théologique*
NTS	*New Testament Studies*
NVet	*Nova et Vetera*
PalCler	*Palestra del Clero*
RB	*Revue Biblique*
RevExp	*Review and Expositor*
ResQ	*Restoration Quarterly*
RHE	*Revue d'Histoire Ecclésiastique*
RHPR	*Revue d'Histoire et de Philosophie Religieuses*
RJ	*Reformed Journal*

RSPT	*Revue des sciences philosophiques et théologiques*
RUO	*Revue de l'Université d'Ottawa*
SBL	*Society of Biblical Literature*
SJT	*Scottish Theological Journal*
TGl	*Theologie und Glaube*
TQ	*Theologische Quartalschrift*
TS	*Theologische Studien*
TSK	*Theologische Studien und Kritiken*
TynB	*Tyndale Bulletin*
TZ	*Theologische Zeitschrift*
USQR	*Union Seminary Quarterly Review*
VD	*Verbum Domini*
WTJ	*Westminster Theological Journal*
ZNW	*Zeitschrift für die neutestamentliche Wissenschaft*

INTRODUCTION

My previous monograph, *Women in the Ministry of Jesus*, concentrated on one particular kind of material in the New Testament, i.e., that which may well go back to the *Sitz im Leben Jesu*. This volume seeks to take the next step by looking at texts which give us clues about women and their roles in the earliest post-Easter communities. In order to have some sort of historical perspective, we will attempt to look at the relevant texts in what may roughly be called chronological order, realizing that the dates for various of the New Testament books are debatable. Thus, after the necessary background chapter we will deal with the Pauline material, including the Pastorals. Then we will examine the perspectives of the evangelists about women and their roles. In the concluding chapter we will move beyond the canonical period to glimpse how the various trends and trajectories of the New Testament period were followed or abandoned during the age of the ante-Nicene Fathers.

At this point it may be worthwhile to explain this book's *raison d'être*. In reading through the ever-growing literature dealing with women in the Bible, one is constantly confronted with able scholars who nonetheless come to the text with a specific agenda in mind, whether patriarchal or feminist. This is not surprising in view of the importance of the issue, but when the Bible is used to justify positions which are polar opposites one suspects that something has gone awry. Thus, for instance, on one end of the spectrum we hear of *The Inevitability of Patriarchy*,[1] and that women are not allowed to teach or preach in the Church in any authoritative capacity.[2] On the other end of the spectrum we hear of *Biblical Affirmations of Woman*[3] in which relevant biblical texts are divided up into 'positive' and 'negative' categories depending upon whether the author thinks they affirm or deny a feminist agenda.

We are also asked to choose between Paul as chauvinist or feminist.[4] These terms usually come to the fore when one is dealing

1

with crucial texts such as Gal 3.28. Thus, for instance, it has been maintained that this text is a 'magna charta' affirming a truly egalitarian agenda so far as social relationships are concerned.[5] On the other hand, it has also been argued that this is part of a baptismal liturgy that speaks only of one's position of equality in the eyes of God. If this is the case, then Gal 3.28 has no clear implications for social relationships.[6] One wonders if the categories of chauvinist and feminist are not so anachronistic that it becomes impossible to hear the various texts in their original historical contexts.

Either/or categories do not seem helpful when dealing with complex biblical material. Perhaps the very reason polar opposite positions seem able to claim support from the New Testament is because the material is by no means monolithic. What is needed, and what this study will try to bring to the discussion, is some balance and an attempt to deal with the variegated material without imposing twentieth-century categories on the texts. Of course, no one comes to the text without presuppositions, but this author has tried to let the text inform and reform his presuppositions so that it is the text that has the last say about the material.

A second reason for this study is the lack of detailed exegetical studies that deal with the gamut of the material rather than selected texts. This selective approach seems especially to have plagued the study of Paul's view of women. It is too easy to write off this or that text as a 'post-Pauline' interpolation or a contradiction to the earlier and more pristine views of Paul (or various of the other New Testament authors for that matter), when our knowledge of the original historical contexts is at best only partial. It is always *possible* that a creative thinker such as Paul may have changed his mind over the course of time about women and their roles. However, in view of the fact that Paul did not adopt diametrically opposed positions on other social issues during the time he wrote, it will require compelling evidence to warrant such a conclusion. This is especially so since all of the authentic Pauline letters come from a person with fourteen or more years of Christian experience behind him. In short, Paul's letters were written by a mature Christian who had had ample time to consider deeply the major issues of Christian faith and practice.

It may be gathered from all the above that a large portion of this monograph will be spent studying Paul. This is so not only because of the vast amount of relevant material in the Pauline corpus, but also because of the vast amount of controversy connected with it.

It is disturbing to notice various attempts to over-emphasize some material at the expense of the rest of the data. The whole of what an author says must be listened to carefully and repeatedly before that author is charged with inconsistency or a notable shift in thinking. To that end I have spent some twelve years now carefully studying and restudying the texts discussed in this book, and at various points I have had to revise my initial impressions of what the author meant. I have found it worthwhile to be as patient with the New Testament data as one should be with a colleague's work before drawing radical conclusions or charging a careful writer with inconsistency.

Finally, I wish to make clear that this exegetical and historical study is by no means exhaustive, and therefore no attempt is made to draw out all the theological implications of the material under scrutiny. Nor do I attempt the hermeneutical task of trying to answer whether and how this material may be used or applied in a modern context. In fairness to the historical givenness of the texts, I must insist that the text cannot and must not be used today to mean something radically different, or antithetical, to what the original author intended it to mean. Thus, it is disturbing to hear an excellent exegete say: 'Clearly, the patriarchal stamp of scripture is permanent. But just as clearly, interpretation of its content is forever changing, since new occasions teach new duties and *contexts alter texts*, liberating them from frozen construction' (italics mine).[7] If contexts are allowed to alter texts radically, then historical perspective is lost, as is the difference between exegesis and eisegesis. Thus, I have tried to allow the text to have its own say whether or not it was congenial to my own viewpoints.

It is hoped that this attempt at balance and breadth of exegetical coverage will reveal clues as to how views of women developed in the earliest period of Christian history. It appears that the New Testament evidence shows a definite tendency on the part of the authors addressing the earliest churches to argue for or support by implication the new freedom and roles women may assume in Christ. At the same time, the evidence indicates an attempt at *reformation*, not repudiation, of the universal patriarchal structure of family and society in the first century in so far as it included the Christian family and community. It is crucial to see that this reformation was to take place 'in Christ'. In the New Testament material there is no call to social revolution or the overthrow of a patriarchal society outside of the Body of Christ. *Reformation in community*, not renunciation in society, is the order of the day.

This significant, though not radical, reformation in community and affirmation of women was not quickly or universally accepted even in the Christian Church. When the author of Luke–Acts wrote in the last quarter of the first century these views still had to be argued for. The same is true even later when the final form of the Fourth Gospel appeared. Even a cursory review of post-New Testamental and pre-Nicene material suggests that, as problems arose with heresy, the resistance to both the *reformation* and *affirmation* mentioned above intensified. These are some of the major themes we will attempt to examine and document in this work.

1

WOMEN IN FIRST-CENTURY
MEDITERRANEAN CULTURES

No study of women in the NT can be undertaken without looking at the larger historical context in which the events of NT history transpired. In this chapter we will attempt to indicate what the prevailing attitudes about women, their status and roles, seem to have been in various places in the Roman empire before and during the NT era. We can only hope to mention selected portions of the relevant data, but it appears that the material presented is representative of the period.

One of the great difficulties in dealing with the material is that by and large we only get the perspectives of those who were authors and authoresses, except in the case of the inscriptional and epigraphal evidence. Thus, we are most often hearing the views of those who were educated, literate, and in a numerical minority. Nonetheless, the inscriptional and epigraphal evidence seems to confirm that the writers of the era, to one degree or another, reflected the largely patriarchal orientation of the culture. As we shall see, however, within the general patriarchal framework, women's status and roles varied from one sub-culture to another.

A. Women and their roles in Greece, Macedonia, Asia Minor, and Egypt

Within the general patriarchal framework, present to a greater or lesser extent in all of Greece's city-states and colonies from Homeric times through the age of the Roman empire, one finds a diversity of roles and views of women that goes beyond the confines of rabbinic Judaism. There was a great deal of difference, however, between being a woman in Sparta or Athens, and in Macedonia. Each area will be assessed on its own merits.

Women in Greece had varying degrees of freedom in their family situations, ranging from a very limited degree of liberty among upper-class Athenian women (especially in classical times) to a considerable amount of liberty among Spartan women and especially those who had already raised their families. Consider first the lot of Athenian women.

Athens was a city of contrasts in regard to the status and roles of women. It is impossible to generalise about their positions because, apart from common prostitutes and slaves, there were three categories of women: Athenian citizens, concubines (παλλακαί), and 'companions' or 'foreign women' (ἑταῖραι).

Concubines are probably the smallest and least important group for our discussion. They occupied the middle ground between legal wives and companions. Their relationship to an Athenian male citizen was recognized by law, and if the concubine was an Athenian citizen her children would be free, though not legitimate members of the family of her male partner. A man could legitimise his concubine's children if he chose to do so. Finally, concubines had no dowry and their main function was to care for the personal, especially sexual, needs of their male partners. In this way a male Athenian citizen could limit his legitimate heirs without limiting his sexual activities.[1]

It is fair to say that although female Athenian citizens were respected as wives and mothers in the classical period and afterwards, their position on the whole was little better than that of Jewish women in Tannaitic times. Certainly the women of Attica led a more sheltered and subordinate existence than women anywhere else in Greece.[2] It appears that Athenian men of the classical period retained many of the attitudes toward women that were common in pre-classical Greece.[3] By Hellenistic and Roman times these views were still in existence, though less strongly held because of the liberalising influence of Macedonian and Roman occupation.

Thucydides (c. 400 BC) spoke not only for his generation but also for those succeeding in Attica when he had his hero Pericles remark that the glory of the woman is greatest '... of whom there is least talk among men, whether in praise or in blame.'[4] Athenian citizen-women were married usually at fifteen or sixteen years of age, and up to this time they were said to have seen little of the world and inquired about nothing.[5] Once an Athenian citizen-woman married, she usually lived in a separate and guarded chamber, not unlike some upper-class Jewish women in Tannaitic times.[6] It may be doubted, however, that Athenian matrons were never allowed out of those chambers.[7] Citizen-women were appreciated chiefly as a proper means to a legitimate heir, and were shown little love by their

husbands. Herodotus tells us of an Athenian woman who preferred
to save her brother over her husband or children because only he was
an irreplaceable loved one.[8] Consider Euripides' portrayal of a
matron's domestic plight: 'Surely of all creatures that have life and
wit, we women are the most unhappy, who first must buy ... a
husband ... but gain for our lives a master!'[9] In contrast to Spartan
practices, Athenians severely limited a matron's rights to acquire or
retain any personal property apart from her dowry.[10] If one bases
one's views of a woman's position in Athens solely on the position
of Athenian citizen-women, one can well understand why Thales was
grateful '... that I was born a human being and not a beast, next a
man and not a woman, thirdly, a Greek and not a barbarian.'[11]

The foreign women or companions (ἑταῖραι) had no civic rights;
however, this meant also that they had few civic restrictions. They
were not allowed to manage public affairs, or to marry citizens, or
to usurp citizen-women's positions in the cults. Beyond this they were
allowed virtually a free hand.[12] It was common for an Athenian man
to have a companion who was not his wife.[13] James Donaldson
informs us that this included Plato, Aristotle, Epicurias, Isocrates,
Menander, and many others.[14] Because of the frequent sexual
liaisons involved in such a relationship, the term soon became
synonymous with courtesan.[15] Yet it would be wrong to assume that
these women were simply harlots. In order to be a good companion
for intelligent and important men, many of them studied the arts,
philosophy, and politics, and as a result they were said to be the 'only
educated women in Athens'.[16] We know that one companion came
to Socrates to learn how to obtain true friends in Athens, thus showing
that at least some companions had access to the philosophical
schools.[17] Aspasia of Miletus is said to have instructed Socrates in
affairs of the heart, and also to have opened her house to Sophocles,
Euripides, Phidias, and Socrates as a place for debate and discussion.[18] Perhaps we may detect Aspasia's influence on Socrates
when he expresses his views of women: 'Woman's nature happens
to be in no respect inferior to man's, but she needs insight and
strength.'[19] Companions were not banned from all the cults, for
there are known cases of some being initiated into the Eleusinian
mysteries as early as the fourth century BC.[20] This may be attributed
to the fact that the Athenians tried to raise the Eleusinian cult to the
status of the common cult of Greece.[21]

Plato's views on women are more than a little difficult to assess.
On the one hand the material in *The Republic* must be treated with

caution since much of it is included merely for the sake of debate.[22] There are certain indications, however, that Plato did at some point hold a somewhat 'enlightened' view of women and their roles, for he allowed at least two well-known companions to study in his academy.[23] Plato's most famous pupil, Aristotle, is more outspoken in his negative views than his mentor. Aristotle says quite bluntly, '... the male is by nature superior and the female inferior, the male ruler and the female subject.'[24] To this he adds, '... a man would be thought a coward if he were only as brave as a brave woman, and a woman a chatterer if she were only as modest as a good man; since even the household functions of a man and a woman are different – his business is to get and hers to keep.'[25] It is true enough that in the latter remark Aristotle is referring only to citizen-women, but the former statement is of a more categorical and all-inclusive nature.

If we seek a reason why the Athenian matron was in such a subordinate position during and even after classical times, perhaps the answer lies in the observation that at various points in its history Athens (as well as other parts of Greece and its colonies) was influenced in its social habits by the original customs of some of its eastern neighbors with whom it traded.[26] One must bear in mind that within its own social framework Athens was a city of contrasts in regard to women's positions and rights. On the one hand we have seen that Athenian matrons who had the rights of citizens and the right of legal marriages were in most other regards disenfranchised. On the other hand companions who had no civic rights or right to marry an Athenian citizen could be educated and become objects of much of the affections of Athenian men. It is not surprising, then, that in Athens there was a shrine built, not to the matrons, but to the companions and their patron goddess, Aphrodite.[27]

In regard to an Athenian woman's religious and legal status little can be said. The primary means of contact that a young woman had with the outside world was through her participation in various religious processions.[28] At seven she could carry the mystical box; at ten she could grind the flour for the patron goddess' cakes; and at fifteen she could carry the sacred basket.[29] None of this should cause us to overlook the fact that the practice of leaving unwanted daughters on a hill to die is known even into NT times.[30] Citizen-women were allowed to participate in some of the cults, but so were the companions. The one important matter in regard to a woman's legal status that needs to be mentioned is this: so far as the evidence goes, it appears that an Athenian citizen-woman was not allowed to be a valid witness in Athenian courts except possibly in homicide cases.[31]

If one takes a cursory glance at the reference to *Spartan* women in Greek literature it is possible to draw the erroneous conclusion that women were liberated to a great extent in that part of Greece. While A. Oepke is correct in saying that in comparison to Athenians, women in Sparta 'occupied a position of more freedom and influence in the Doric world', this is only a relative difference, for even Spartan women were not equal to their male counterparts.[32] Lycurgus set the pattern for the future of women's roles in Sparta when he set up certain eugenic laws. Thus, Donaldson remarks, 'All the legislation that relates to women has one sole object – to procure a first rate breed of men.'[33] The Spartans felt it necessary to educate and train women to be strong, brave, and resolute so that their sons would have a similar character, ideal for military service. From the earliest times Spartan women were involved in gymnastics, wrestling, festivals, rudimentary educational schemes, offering sacrifices, and, in general, they mingled freely and competed openly with men. This not only prepared them to be good mothers, but also afforded the men an opportunity to choose a proper mate.[34] The darker side of this selection process was that the weaker women would be detected in various contests and prevented from marrying for fear of weak children.[35] It is in light of the Spartan belief in eugenic principles that one should evaluate the relative freedom of Spartan women.

Women of Sparta are praised in the inscriptions for their prudence, discretion, and true love for their husbands (Sparta having virtually a monogamous society).[36] Usually, Spartan women did not eat with their husbands, most of whom were soldiers who ate with their regiments. Further, a woman's sons were taken from her when they were of age and ready for military instruction.[37] This left mothers with a great deal of free time, and they were allowed to do whatever they pleased within legal and moral bounds.[38] Some women, once they had been good mothers and with their husband's permission, occasionally played a role in public life.[39] That women of Laconia were involved in public building projects or activities in the general interest and were known to have held public office indicates that they had money and were able to avail themselves of what the law and their husbands permitted.[40] This is not to say that Spartan women were equal to Spartan men.

The divorce laws favored the men. Childlessness was a ground for a man to divorce his wife and take another. Perhaps most representative of a Spartan woman's true position and her famed fidelity are the following words spoken to a man proposing an illicit relationship. 'When I was a girl, I was taught to obey my father and I obeyed him. When I became a wife, I obeyed my husband; if then, you have anything just to urge, make it known to him first.'[41] The Spartan woman, like her Jewish counterpart, was subordinate to her father or husband, yet she had greater civil and property rights than a Jewish woman, and probably greater security also since polygamy was not a viable option in Sparta. In her freedom of movement and physical and educational training she compared favorably to a Jewess and also to an Athenian matron. Little or nothing is known of Spartan attitudes about women as witnesses. In regard to their religious position, as elsewhere in Greece, Spartan women often participated in the cults and had official roles.[42]

Of the family life or legal status of *Corinthian* citizen-women little can be said, but it is a reasonable conjecture that their position was even more significantly compromised than Athenian women since Corinth was infamous all over the Mediterranean as the city of courtesans and companions. Of the religious status of Corinthian women and women who lived elsewhere on the Grecian mainland (other than Sparta and Ionia) we have more information.

If companions were honored by a shrine at Athens, they were incorporated into the very fabric of Corinthian public life. Heracleia and Timaeus tell us that many of these companions were dedicated to prayer in the temple of Aphrodite for the salvation of Corinth from Persia. They were present regularly whenever the city offered sacrifices to this goddess.[43] Being a port city, Corinth may have been more lax morally than other parts of Greece, but its difference from Athens in the freedom it bestowed on its companions was a difference of degree, not kind. Both companions and free citizen-women were allowed to be devotees and administrants in some of the Corinthian cults.[44]

It appears that Corinthian citizen-women had greater freedom and earned greater respect than their Athenian counterparts. There were separate festivals involving sacrifices in which free-born Corinthian citizen-women participated and were honored.[45] These women were noted for their boldness as well, for at one point they defended a particular sanctuary against the attack of Spartan men.[46] It was not only Corinthian women who had vested interests and important roles in the religious cults. This was one of the few features of life that women from all over Greece shared in common.

On a small island off the coastal town of Troecenia in Argolis, a young girl served as an official in a temple of Poseidon. This is noteworthy because usually women were administrants only in the cults of goddesses.[47] Women were almost always the organs of divine inspiration and prophecy in Greece, and in the cult of Apollo only women were allowed to perform this office.[48] The prophetess of Apollo was called a Pythoness and was expected to be a free-born Delphian widow who faithfully had tended the fires and given oracles in her home region.[49] The mystery plays, and the agricultural and fertility rituals were almost entirely in the hands of women, since men frequently were excluded from such festivals.[50] Women also led the processions in the mysteries, though there was a male overseer.[51] In the cult of Despoina there were apparently places, such as Megalopolis, where women had free access to the cult while men could enter only once a year.[52] Women were prominent particularly in orgiastic rites, such as the Baccanalia, and served as maenads and thyads in the Dionysian cult.[53] Even young girls could be initiated into the Dionysian mysteries.[54] There were some cults, particularly of the male deities, where women were not given the same privileges as men. For instance, in the important cult of Zeus at Olympus women were allowed to ascend only to the 'prothysis', but men could ascend even to the altar.[55]

Despite all the above, Pseudo-Demosthenes, writing about 340 BC, seems to sum up adequately the common view concerning Greek women from Homeric to Roman times when he says, 'Mistresses (ἑταίρας) we keep for the sake of pleasure, concubines (παλλακάς) for the daily care of our person, but wives to bear us legitimate children and to be faithful guardians of our households.'[56] Though it is probable that Grecian women gradually gained more freedom during the Hellenistic and Roman periods, and it is likely that most Grecian women compared favorably to Jewish women in Tannaitic times, they compared poorly in status and position to women of neighboring Macedonia, Asia Minor, and Egypt.

The bulk of our evidence about the women of Macedonia and Asia Minor is inscriptional and relates mainly to women who were wealthy or of royal lineage. Nevertheless, the evidence is pertinent to our discussion because Lydia of Acts 16 is portrayed as a well-to-do business woman and she appears to have assumed an important role in the Christian community in her area. Such a special position and religious role was not uncommon for women in Macedonia or Asia Minor.

It is common knowledge among classics and NT scholars that many women in *Macedonia* from the Hellenistic period onward had a great deal of influence and prominence. The following statement is typical.

> If Macedonia produced perhaps the most competent group of men the world has yet seen, the women were in all respects the men's counterparts. They played a large part in affairs, received envoys, and obtained concessions from them for their husbands, built temples, founded cities, engaged mercenaries, commanded armies, held fortresses, and acted on occasion as regents or even co-rulers ...[57]

This is substantiated in the pertinent literature and inscriptional evidence.

Macedonian men frequently named cities after their wives because they admired and respected them. For instance, Thessalonica was named by Casander after his wife, Thessalonice, daughter of Philip.[58] In the same area we have evidence of a woman being given inheritable civic rights in order to honor her.[59] There were women politarchs in Thessalonica and in some inscriptions a metronymic takes the place of the usual patronymic.[60] We find a similar phenomenon in inscriptions from Beroea and Edessa.[61] Both men and women in Macedonia could be money earners for there are cases of tombs erected for a husband and wife paid for out of their common earnings.[62] Not only private admirers, but also public bodies, erected monuments to γυναῖκα ἀρετῆς.[63] Often we find inscriptions to Macedonian wives in which they are referred to in deferential and warm terms. Consider the following: τῇ φιλάνθρωπῳ καὶ γλυκυτάτῃ συνβίῳ or τῇ συμβίῳ καὶ κυρίᾳ μνείας χάριν.[64] Women were permitted to eat at the same table with their husbands and share in their activities.[65]

One must take into account such Macedonian queens as Arsinoe II and Bernice who ruled with distinction in Egypt, as well as such queens as Eurydice or Olympias who ruled in the homeland.[66] Their rising status and importance is evidenced by the fact that from Arsinoe II onward the queen's head always appeared on the coins with her husband. These queens were noted for their love of culture and were known to have written poems to famous personalities and to have corresponded with scholars, such as the physicist Strato.[67] These women set a precedent which was followed by such royal figures of Greek blood as Apollonia who was spoken of as a model of womanly qualities.[68] Apparently, these Hellenistic queens also had an influence on Macedonian women who were not of royal blood, for we are told: 'From the Macedonian courts (relative) freedom broadened down to the Greek home ...'[69] Women, such as Epicurus' pupil, Leontion, were able to obtain not only an education but also fame.[70] Some women founded clubs and took part in various social organizations.[71] Freedom and education in Macedonia, though available to all women in theory, in fact could be grasped by only a few who could afford not to work. Undoubtedly, most women continued in their traditional roles without education or mobility, but at least the door was opened in Macedonia, and this had a great effect on Asia Minor and Egypt as Hellenization spread to the east.

Asia Minor and the nearby Aegean Isles bear more resemblance to Macedonia than to Greece in the roles they allowed to women. Whether one looks in records of public office, charities, or cults, women appear as regular participants in large cities and small towns, both on the mainland and on the islands. There were *hierodulae* serving in the precincts of Artemis in Ephesus, and rigid rules of chastity were applied to them.[72] Stratonice, wife of Antiochus I, built and enriched many temples, such as the Temple of Apollos at Delos and Syrian Atargatis at Hieropolis.[73] As in Athens, women led the cult worship of Dionysus on the island of Kos.[74] On a shrine in honor of Agdistis in Philadelphia, Lydia, we read of 'The commandments given to Dionysus by Zeus granting access to sleep in his own house both to free men and women ...'[75] Nonetheless, even in the Dionysian cults of Asia Minor, the women who celebrated the rites had a male overseer to make certain that all was done properly.[76]

Women were allowed to hold public and cultic offices in Asia Minor which elsewhere were held only by men. There is an interesting statue of a woman official in Ternossos.[77] Aurelia Harnastia, according to one inscription, was a priestess of Hera, demiourgos (a high magistrate), and at one point even a chief priestess.[78] Aristodama, a priestess of Smyrna, was so well known that she was given honorary citizenship in Thessaly.[79] In regard to the disposing of property, a woman's dowry remained her own in Asia Minor, though a husband had a right to its use in a somewhat similar fashion to the Jewish practice. After her husband's death, a woman could do as she wished with her possessions.[80]

The prominence and rights of Asia Minor women are perhaps a result of the growth and spread of the cult of Isis into the region from Egypt where women were allowed unprecedented freedom. A further factor was probably the Hellenization of Asia Minor during and after the time of Alexander. Donaldson is surely correct when he says:

> Especially in Asia Minor did women display public activity. Their generosity took the most various forms even to bestowing considerable sums on each citizen in their own cities. They erected baths and gymnasia ... presided at the public games or over great religious ceremonies ... and they paid the expenses incurred in these displays. They also held priesthoods and several of them obtained the highest priesthood of Asia – perhaps the greatest honor that could be paid to anyone.[81]

Markus Barth begins his discussion of women in *Egypt* in this fashion: 'The patron saint of the Egyptian women's movement was Isis. With the spread of the Isis cult and other mystery religions went the fact (and eventually the right) that women gathered for worship without men.'[82] This statement is supported by such sayings as: 'Thou gavest to women equal power with men.'[83] 'I am Isis, I am she whom women call goddess. I ordained that women should be loved by men; I brought wife and husband together, and invented the marriage contract. I ordained that women should bear children and that children should love their parents.'[84] Here was a deity who understood the plight of women, for Isis had been both wife and mother, and had suffered loss. This is why Isis, and not Athena or Artemis, could be called 'the glory of women'. It was in Egypt that this cult originated as but one manifestation of a general Egyptian attitude that a woman should be accepted as a man's equal in most respects.

We find evidence of this attitude in the cult of Amon in which women had offices and were called 'god's wife' or 'god's worshipper'.[85] Diodorus remarks that because of the example of Isis, Egyptian queens had more honor than kings, and that among the common people wives ruled their husbands.[86] More likely, it is the general status of women in Egypt that accounts for the cult of Isis, not the converse. There is excellent evidence that even many centuries before Christ, Egyptian women were juridically equal to men for the most part, except during the periods when Egypt reverted to a feudal society.[87] Evidently, there was improvement in an Egyptian woman's legal rights as time went on, especially in the matter of marriage, divorce, and property rights.[88]

Greek women in Egypt still needed a guardian in most situations involving legal matters, whereas Egyptian women did not.[89] There are many examples in the papyri of women in Egypt who were buyers, sellers, borrowers, lenders, or initiators of divorce.[90] It is likely that in most cases it is the affairs of native Egyptian women that are being recorded. Egyptian women were as liable as men to pay taxes, and even Greek women could petition the government for support or help.[91]

We have mentioned the importance of the Macedonian princesses, Bernice and Arsinoe II, who ruled in Egypt.[92] These women were only the first in a long succession of Greek queens who ruled in that country. In 51 BC the most famous of all Egyptian queens, Cleopatra, came to the throne. She was capable and ambitious; she disposed of all her rivals and succeeded in winning both Julius Caesar and Mark Antony. In Egypt there had long been a tradition that a daughter, if she was the eldest child, was the only legitimate heir.[93] Thus, the existence of Cleopatra and the Hellenistic queens in general is not entirely a result of the influence of Macedonian ideas or Hellenism. Certainly the power of Egyptian women in royal circles during the decline of the Ptolemies is indicated by the fact that a daughter and sister could succeed to the throne by birthright.[94] Nowhere else in the Mediterranean was this possible during this era. The influence of this growing presence of women in Egypt is evidenced in phenomena as diverse as the cults of Isis, Hellenistic queens, Egyptian marriage contracts, and perhaps some of the more misogynous writings of Philo who seems to be reacting against his non-Jewish environment. The cult of Isis had an especially dramatic impact on Rome and its women, as we shall see.

How then are we to evaluate the place of women in Greece and its Mediterranean settlements and neighbors? Clearly, the patriarchal framework continued to exist from antiquity through the Roman period in all the areas we have examined, though with decreasing male dominance as we move from Athens, to Sparta, to Macedonia, to Asia Minor, to Egypt. When women were priestesses in the Greek world, it was usually in the cult of a goddess, not a god, and this perhaps tells us more about women's separation from men than about their autonomy or equality with men. For the most part in the Greek-speaking world, with some companions and rich or royal women as notable exceptions, Plutarch's statement that education is only for free men holds.[95] It remains to be seen whether Rome offered women brighter hopes than Greece.

B. Women and their roles in Rome

In his important study on Roman women, J.P.V.D. Balsdon remarks, 'At no time did Roman women live in the semi-oriental seclusion in which women lived in Greece.'[96] Nonetheless, this scholar adds, 'Complete equality of the sexes was never achieved in ancient Rome because of the survival long after it was out of date of a deep-rooted tradition that the exclusive sphere of a woman's activity was inside the home ...'[97] Both of these statements are fundamentally correct; thus, we would do well to remember that we are not measuring Roman women's freedom by any other yardstick than the relative one of how they fared in comparison to their female contemporaries in the Mediterranean world. To anticipate our conclusions, Roman women compared favorably to their Athenian or Palestinian counterparts; however, there is reason to question whether or not they were better off than women in Macedonia, Asia Minor, and Egypt. Our examination of Roman women's roles in the family, the cult, and their status as witnesses, teachers, or leaders is crucial. It appears likely that the Gospel of Mark is addressed to a Roman Christian community,[98] and the historical background helps to illuminate such texts as Mark 3.34–35, 5.33–34, 10.12, and 15.41.

As was the case in various parts of Greece, one has to specify a class or group of Roman women when discussing whether or not they were freer than Greek women. If one is discussing the Roman matron, then she appears in most regards to be freer, better educated, more highly respected, and more influential than matrons of the Greek mainland. On the other hand, though there were prostitutes in Rome, we do not find the phenomenon of educated companions in any significant numbers in the Eternal City. Because of the paucity of evidence, we will be able to say little about the women of the plebian and slave classes. Thus, we will mainly be limited to an examination of Roman women of the patrician class and, as a result, the picture of Roman women we obtain from the evidence is not complete in depth or breadth. This material, nevertheless, will prove of some value to our study since it is possible that Priscilla (Acts 18) was a member of, or had close associations with, a patrician family.

In order to understand a Roman woman's position in a first-century Roman family, we must consider how the situation had changed since ancient times. In ancient Rome, the authority of the father was as great as or greater than that of a Jewish father in the context of rabbinic Judaism. A Roman father had the power of life and death over his children and wife, and his right to slay his child, particularly if it was a daughter, existed at least until the last century BC.[99] During the Republic, the power of a husband or father was evident from procedures involved in a marriage arrangement. The father 'sold' his daughter into the hand (*in manu*) of her husband by a form of marriage known as *coemptio*.[100] Livy remarks that during the Republic, 'Our ancestors permitted no woman to conduct even personal business without a guardian to intervene in her behalf; they wished them to be under the control (*in manu*) of fathers, brothers, husbands ...'[101]

The *coemptio* form of marriage began to be replaced even as early as 300 BC by a freer form of marriage. The woman remained primarily in the control of her father, and after age twenty-five was subject nominally to the supervision of her guardian or tutor. Legally, a woman could extricate herself from this looser form of marriage without grave difficulties. By the time of the Empire, the *coemptio* form of marriage was non-existent having been replaced by the *sine manu* variety; further, the role of the guardian had lost its importance. By Hadrian's time, the guardian was deemed to be totally unnecessary.[102] Both men and women were able to end a marriage on the flimsiest of excuses and life-long marriage became the exception rather than the rule among the aristocracy by the end of the Republic.[103]

In upper-class society marriage was an obligation for all women except the Vestal Virgins and women over fifty.[104] Marriages frequently were made and broken for financial or political reasons in the aristocracy.[105] Women were allowed to initiate marriages from late Republic days onward, but not to refuse a marriage unless they could prove their proposed husbands were morally unfit.[106] It is unlikely that girls twelve to fourteen, the normal age for marriage, could or would refuse a marriage in any case.[107]

We know that matrons were well educated by the standards of antiquity. Even among the poorer families both daughters and sons went to school, while in richer families both had tutors.[108] A girl's education ceased when she married; while a boy, who usually did not marry before seventeen or eighteen, went on to study with philosophers and rhetoricians outside the home for an additional three to four years. After this the boys were expected to find a mate. Unlike many other cultures in the Mediterranean, Romans saw the education of women not as an extravagance, but as a way to enhance a woman.[109] Despite their education, women were not allowed to vote or hold public office even in the age of the Empire, though often they were deeply involved and highly influential in affairs of state and matters of law. For instance, we know that Sempronia was involved with her husband, Cataline, in the conspiracy to overthrow the government in 63 BC.[110] There were two famous Fulvias, one of whom was involved in the Cataline conspiracy, while the other helped Mark Antony by being his agent in Italy and commanding one of his armies when Octavian besieged it.[111] Some matrons, such as Maesia, had special gifts for pleading a case and were acquitted on their own court testimony.[112]

Perhaps those matrons who had the greatest influence for good or ill in the political realm were the wives of the Emperors, such as Augustus' Livia and Claudius' Messalina. Livia was consulted often when Augustus needed good advice and he discussed many crucial subjects with her.[113] She was known to be an excellent administrator in her own right, managing a personal staff of over a thousand and property holdings in Asia Minor, Gaul, and Palestine.[114] She was the first to be named Augusta and the first priestess in her husband's cult when it began after his death.[115]

In the home as well matrons wielded great power and influence. They were not housewives in the ordinary sense; indeed, though they bore sole responsibility for the home, usually they assigned tasks to the servants. Meanwhile, they went to market, to recitals and festivals, to the games, or stayed home and supervised the children's education.[116] Though in the Republic it was usual for a woman to nurse her children, by the time of the Empire it was not uncommon for a matron to allow a female servant to nurse or raise the children.[117] Most matrons did spend the majority of their time in the home, however, and even in the Empire they were expected to cultivate the time-honored domestic practices of spinning and weaving. Augustus was fond of wearing wool items made by his wife and daughters as an advertisement for his plan of re-establishing 'old-fashioned' ideas.[118] Until the second century BC matrons were required to bake bread, but by the time of the Empire it was a poor house indeed where a wife had to perform the household chores she would be expected to do in Greece.[119] When we consider how seldom the husband might be home, especially if he was in the army, we can understand why matrons were often the family's *de facto* head and business manager.

In order to discuss a Roman woman's role in religion we must first consider the most well-known examples, the Vestal Virgins. Though they were dedicated for thirty years to virginity and tending the sacred flame (which represented the health and salvation of Rome), they were not under the power of any man, not bound by oaths other than their sacred one, and not subject to the limitations of the Voconian law of 169 BC which prevented women from testifying without swearing an oath.[120] Vestals were women of property. At the beginning of their service (six to ten years old), they were given a dowry twice that of a rich matron because they had 'married' the state for thirty years.[121] They were required to attend certain religious festivals and were allowed to go to lavish dinners and to visit matrons if they were not on their eight-hour duty period.[122] They had the power to remit the sentence of a prisoner if they happened to pass one on the street.[123] The Vestals were considered to be so trustworthy and sacrosanct that statesmen would leave important documents and wills with them to guard.[124] They were also emissaries of peace for the state or imperial family. After an evil hit Rome (a plague or fire), the Vestals were called upon to do propitiatory acts.[125] There were only six Vestals at any one time, however, and thus they were not representative of the relationship of the average matron or freed woman to Roman society or to Roman religion.

What then was the relation of an average Roman woman to Roman religion? There were basically two types of Roman religion – native cults supported by the state, such as that of Vesta, and imported oriental cults such as that of Isis or the Eleusinian mysteries.

The Romans, using their gifts for organization and categorization, had different native cults for different stages in a woman's life. Rome used these cults to promote socially desirable behavior. The goddess Fortuna Virginitis was patroness of young girls who, when they came of age, were expected to dedicate their togas to this deity.[126] Fortuna Primigenia was patroness of mothers and child-birth, as well as giver of virility and material success to men.[127] There was the cult of Fortunata Muliebris for women married only once; and the cult of Venus, Changer of Hearts, dedicated to encourage women to marital fidelity.[128] This latter cult began when several

matrons were discovered to be adulterous and their husbands wanted
to create a permanent warning against such infidelity.[129] In contrast,
Fortuna Virilis was a prostitutes' cult in which such women met in
the men's baths to worship a god of sexual relations.[130]

Obviously, in his social reforms Augustus promoted the cults
advocating chastity, childbirth, and strong familial bonds. Coupling
this with Augustus' effort to legally force widows and divorcees to
remarry, and the fine (*uxorium*) he placed on both males and females
for remaining single past acceptable ages, we can see how much
Augustus desired to eliminate public and private situations where
women were independent of men.[131] His attempts to recapture the
morality of 'idealized' ancient Rome by legislation and other sorts
of inducements appear to have failed on the whole;[132] however, his
efforts did affect women and their relationship to the cults.

Augustus could boast of having restored or built eighty-two
temples in an attempt to rectify the neglect of traditional religion in
Rome.[133] It is important to recognize that Augustus tried to assert
the older views about male dominance (evident in the marriage laws
discussed above) through this building campaign. For instance,
originally the shrine of Apollo stood in the shadow of the older shrine
of the Sybil of Cumae, and originally the god Apollo was brought
to the Roman scene as a deity connected with the prophetess and cult
of the Sybil.[134] Augustus, however, built a new shrine for Apollo on
the Palatine hill and transferred the books of Sybilline oracles to
Apollo's new temple, thus subordinating the Sybil's shrine to that of
Apollo. Even when Augustus did bring the temple of Vesta to the
Palatine hill, this was to inculcate traditional values, not to liberate
women.

Festivals and cults which formerly had been the exclusive domain
of women were integrated, while male-only public rituals, such as the
sacrifice to Mars for the well-being of the herds, were retained.[135]
Thus, women were not likely to find new roles in the traditional cults.
As early as the second century BC these cults had been dying, and
Augustus' attempts to revive them were too little, too late. It was the
influx of eastern religions as the traditional cults began to fade which
was to give women new religious roles as they worshipped Isis, Serapis,
Cybele, or Attis.[136]

Symbolic of how much the matrons welcomed these new cults is
the fact that when the cult of the Idean mother was introduced in 204
BC they went out of the city to welcome its arrival.[137] When the
Bacchanalia was introduced in 186 BC it was open to women only

and the matrons became its priestesses. The inclusion of men into the cult led to scandal and its suppression for a while, though it sprang up again in the later Republic.[138] Gradually, these foreign gods won most of the female population so that in the first century AD Petronius bemoans the fact that Roman matrons no longer worshipped the traditional gods at all.[139] Tacitus records legislation attempting to eliminate certain Egyptian and Jewish rites.[140] Juvenal lampoons the chorus of the frantic Bellonia, and the women who break the ice on the Tiber, plunge in, and then crawl across a field naked on bleeding knees for the sake of Isis.[141]

It was Isis above all the others which Roman men rightly feared. The reasons why this cult had such a powerful impact on Roman women are several. First, probably the only state cults allowing women even a limited role as priestesses were that of Vesta (six women) and that of Ceres, a goddess of fecundity, production, and procreation.[142] Second, the cult of Isis, unlike any of the previous cults, was not for the benefit of the state, but to meet the religious and emotional needs of individuals. Isis promised healing, blessing, understanding, and sympathy for her devotees' sorrow and pain, for she herself had lost a son. Thus, she was a goddess of loving mercy with whom women could identify and to whom men could become intimately attached as a compassionate mother figure.[143] She was all gods summed up into one personality and was said to have certain powers that usually only male deities possessed.[144] Finally, unlike other cults, the rituals of Isis were flexible and her temples were at once a haven for prostitutes and a sanctuary where women could spend their nights dedicated to chastity. Thus, the cult of Isis had tremendous appeal because it was open to all, it ignored class barriers, and both men and women could hold high office.

Naturally Isis most benefited the lower-class members for they held equal status with the upper-class members of the cult.[145] From the extant inscriptions we know that at least one-third of Isis' devotees were women but this figure probably underestimates the number of females since, instead of being categorized, women were treated as equals with men. We read of at least six women priestesses in this cult including one of senatorial rank and one freed woman in Italy.[146]

We should not think that this cult affected only a small minority just because the temples of Isis were not allowed within Rome's walls until AD 38.[147] On the contrary, there were a multitude of temples just outside the city wall long before the reign of Gaius Caligula. Five times during the Republic there were attempts to abolish this cult which honored only the individual and not the state. In 50 BC a consul thought it important enough to order a particular temple of Isis demolished. When no one would do the job he himself began to take an axe to it.[148] In 28 BC Octavius and later Tiberius attempted to abolish Isis' cult, all to no avail. It is certainly more than a coincidence that the rise of the cult of Isis in the later Republic period coincided with the increase in women's liberation in Rome. It is likely that these two trends fostered and furthered each other, and it was perhaps in reaction against this that Augustus undertook his ill-fated attempts at moral and religious reform.

Little is known about the status and roles of freed women and slaves in Rome apart from comments made by upper-class writers and politicians. What we know of customs and conditions in Rome does give us some additional indirect evidence. Most freed women were shopkeepers, artisans, or domestics; while some were known to be physicians, commercial entrepreneurs, brick-makers, and perhaps even owners of brick-making or ship-building operations.[149] Financially, some freed women were apparently secure for they could afford a respectable burial place;[150] others remained in the service of their mistresses rather than become one of the free poor. In some regards it was better to be a slave than a free-born poor woman, since slaves often were treated well, were secure, and were educated in the essentials so that they could read to their matrons and their matrons' children. Cato tells us that it was the responsibility of the female housekeeper to keep the hearth clean, to hang a garland on the hearth at the kalends, to keep a supply of cooked food on hand, and not to visit the neighbors too often.[151] Though the evidence is not vast, it is probably fair to say that freed women and female slaves in Rome were in a much better position than their counterparts in Greece, since Rome had the more liberal property laws and since a female slave of a Roman matron could acquire a rudimentary education and even money if she were a good worker.

Roman women had both more and less freedom than their counterparts in the Mediterranean world depending on which country and which aspect of a woman's life one uses as a basis for comparison. It is certainly true that Roman women had more political power than women in Greece or Palestine because, though they could not sit on the throne or hold elected office, they could be the power behind such positions. The fact, however, that women could not hold such offices in Rome makes clear that politically upper-class or imperial Macedonian women had more freedom since they often did sit on the throne in the Hellenistic and Roman periods. Roman women do not compare favorably in political rights with women in Asia Minor who often held public offices.

Until the advent of the foreign cults into Rome, women there had fewer opportunities to be priestesses than women in Greece. On the other hand, educated women were more plentiful in Rome than elsewhere in the Mediterranean. A Roman woman's right to property and freedom in marriage (with the rise of the *sine manu* marriage contract) rivaled or surpassed all other Mediterranean women except native Egyptians. It is fair to say that Roman matrons had the opportunities to perform more than the functions of mother and wife, and this cannot be said of Greek citizen-women. Even a Roman freed woman was in a better position than many citizen-women in Athens. It is certainly to the credit of the Romans that they at least raised the question of the place of women in society, unlike many other Mediterranean cultures.[152]

As elsewhere in the Empire, there is no denying that Roman society operated within a definite patriarchal framework. That many Roman women were able to lead full, informed, and satisfying lives perhaps testifies to the fact that patriarchy need not always lead to misogyny. Rome offered more to women than Greece or Palestine, but Roman women had more disadvantages than some of their counterparts in Asia Minor, Macedonia, and Egypt until the advent of various foreign cults and certain Hellenistic and Egyptian ideas into the Eternal City.[153]

2

WOMEN AND THE PHYSICAL FAMILY IN THE PAULINE EPISTLES

As we embark on a detailed discussion of texts in the Pauline epistles that reveal something about women and their roles, it is crucial to underline the fact that we are dealing with letters, not gospels or documents such as the Acts of the Apostles. Several facts must be borne in mind about the nature and purpose of letters before we proceed with our exegesis.

The letters of Paul are, for the most part, occasional in nature, written to meet certain needs or to answer certain questions. Second, we must recognize that since almost all these letters were written in response to a communication from those Paul is addressing (or from Paul's assistants), they represent only a portion of a larger dialogue, are not complete in themselves, and often require us to reconstruct the questions being raised or the pleas being urged that prompted his letters of reply. There are gains and losses in dealing with letters instead of other NT literature. On the one hand, Paul's letters reveal in a more direct manner the views of their author on certain subjects than do the Gospels or Acts. This means that we can concentrate on Paul's views of women and their roles to a degree that is not possible when dealing with the documents of the Gospel writers. On the other hand, in order to evaluate women and their roles in Paul's communities, we will need to read between the lines to a degree that is not necessary when, for instance, we study women and their roles in Acts (see chapter 4). Paul, unlike Luke, does not intend to give us a chronicle of life in the early Church, though within the framework of his intentions we do get many glimpses of the life of the primitive Christian Church.

Another consideration is that Paul wrote more than one type of letter. Broadly speaking, Paul's letters fall into four categories: (1) a letter of introduction commending his work and theology to a church he had neither founded nor visited (Romans); (2) letters responding to problems in churches he founded (1 and 2 Corinthians, Galatians); (3) a letter urging progress in the direction a church was already moving (Philippians); (4) a personal letter of advice to a worker in the ministry or a Christian friend (Philemon, the Pastorals).[1] The distinction between the second and third types is not rigid, since there is some commendation and exhortation to progress in certain letters that mainly combat problems, and there is some correction of difficulties in 'progress' letters.[2] Nonetheless, the general tone and character of a letter must be noted.

As we begin our discussion of Paul's views of women in relation to the physical family, we are thrust into the context of the letters that are of either a problem or progress nature. It should be recognized that what an individual says to correct an error cannot be taken as a full or definitive statement of his views on a particular subject. Such responses give an indication of a person's views but cannot be taken as a treatise. Further, Paul, as a task theologian, does not dichotomize between theology and its ethical implications, a trend we often find in modern biblical discussions. When Paul writes, he is attempting to further the cause of Jesus Christ and His gospel in whatever way the situation demands. Thus, in the heat of debate, Paul may use hyperbolic language to emphasize his point (cf. Gal 5.12). It also means that Paul often tries to be diplomatic in order to achieve his ends (cf. 1 Cor 6.12–13, 9.19–23). Further, one must not make too much of what Paul does *not* say, since to a large degree the agenda of his letters is set by the needs and problems of his audience. Finally, a context of controversy leads Paul to stress certain points not because they are of great importance, but because he must redress an imbalance in the thinking of his audience.

Problems have been caused in the study of Paul's view of women and their roles both by a failure to be sensitive to the above points, and by an overemphasis on one or a few texts at the expense of others. The corrective we will attempt to implement here in order to avoid imbalance and insensitivity to the character and nature of our material is both a close attention to the immediate context (literary, historical, theological) of a passage, and a careful comparison of the material that commands our immediate attention with the relevant material in the rest of the Pauline corpus (and possibly the rest of the NT). In this way we hope to go beyond the narrow classification of Paul as either chauvinist overly influenced by his Jewish past, or early feminist.[3]

A. 1 Corinthians 7

Paul's view of marriage and divorce is often debated. Was Paul an ascetic who merely tolerated marriage in the Christian community because of the weakness of the flesh? Was he a disillusioned bachelor or widower who begrudged others a happy marital experience? Could he be called a champion of normal family relationships? Was his attitude toward human sexuality healthy? The large differences of opinion on these questions reflect the difficulties inherent in assessing the material of 1 Corinthians 7 and Ephesians 5.[4] We will deal with each in turn as well as with related material in the Pauline corpus.

First, we must take note of the general structure and recurring patterns in 1 Corinthians 7. It is evident that Paul's main concern here is to answer questions raised by the Corinthians concerning marriage and related matters (which comprise only eight of the forty verses). The περὶ δὲ formula appears at 7.2, 25, and 8.1 to initiate a new section and possibly to indicate the topics that the Corinthians had written about specifically.[5] The discussion of circumcision and slavery (vv. 17–24) has puzzled commentators in terms of its placement in the middle of a chapter on marriage; however, it seems probable that S. Scott Bartchy has solved this dilemma.

Bartchy argues that while the Corinthians are the cause of Paul's discussion of male–female relations, once Paul begins his response his mind proceeds along a certain pattern found elsewhere in the Pauline corpus (cf. Gal 3.28, 1 Cor 12.13, Col 3.11). This pattern involves the three basic kinds of differences in first-century Corinthian society – sexual (male/female), social (master/slave), and ethnic (Jew/Greek). Thus, it is not incongruous that Paul digresses here to discuss the major social and ethnic differences in the Corinthian congregation. By structuring his response in this way, Paul emphasizes that God's call and demands have come to the Corinthians regardless of the category in which they find themselves, and that they are united into the one Body of Christ. Each one must evaluate these differences in the light of the transcendent unity in Christ and the priorities of the Christian faith. 'In 1 Cor. 7 Paul answers questions about marriage, virginity, and celibacy on the basis of his understanding of the meaning "no male and female in Christ".'[6]

Further proof that Paul's discussion in 1 Corinthians 7 is structured along the lines of his thinking about the unity and equality of male and female in Christ is to be found in the large amount of male/female parallelism in this chapter (vv. 2, 3, 4, 10–11, 12–13, 14–16, 28,

33–34). It is important to note the verses where Paul addresses the male and female together (vv. 5, 7, and possibly 8, 17, 28b, 32, 35).[7] As we shall see, at various points Paul differs from both Jewish and Greek ideas in assigning women equal rights and responsibilities with men in their relationships. Bartchy has also shown that there is a very deliberate and logical structure to Paul's arguments as he discusses various cases and possibilities in 1 Corinthians 7. The general pattern is that of laying down a general principle (or reacting to one), qualifying it by an exception, and then giving reasons for the principle or exceptions to it. Sometimes the reasons and exceptions exchange places in the order, or alternate if more than one reason or exception is given.[8] It is also true that in one or two cases the general principle is implied rather than stated. Still, the overall structure is evident and reflects an attempt to deal with the subjects at issue in a thorough and systematic fashion.

Finally, we shall point out certain repeated motifs in 1 Corinthians 7 before beginning our detailed exegesis. First, the principle stated in v. 17, which advises against changing one's status or situation unless it conflicts with being a good and faithful Christian or interferes with the peace to which God has called Christians (cf. v. 15b), is also present in vv. 8, 20, 24, 26, and 40. Closely related to this theme are the reasons given for this advice, reasons which seem to be interrelated and may have eschatological overtones (cf. vv. 26a, 29, 31b). Third, Paul stresses freedom of choice or freedom from any concern but pleasing the Lord (vv. 5, 7, 9, 15, 22, 32, 35, 36, 38, 39).[9] Finally, Paul expresses his wish that all were as he is, i.e., unmarried (vv. 7, 8, 37b, 38, 40). This wish distinguishes Paul from most of his contemporaries and sets him at odds particularly with his rabbinic background. Having taken into account the factors and structures mentioned above, we can now investigate the exegetical intricacies of 1 Corinthians 7.

1 Cor 7.1 immediately brings out the difficulty of discerning and distinguishing the positions of Paul and the Corinthians on the matters the apostle is discussing. What are we to make of Καλὸν ἀνθρώπῳ γυναικὸς μὴ ἅπτεσθαι? Is this Paul's view, the Corinthians' view, or both? Three possibilities emerge: (1) Paul is quoting a statement of the Corinthians without approval and intends to refute it; (2) Paul is quoting the Corinthians and/or his own previous teaching with full approval; (3) Paul is quoting the Corinthians and/or his own previous teaching with limited approval ('yes, but'), and intends to qualify the statement because of the misinterpretation of this earlier Pauline remark in Corinth.

Obviously there were contexts where Paul would agree that it was not good for a man to have intercourse with a woman (cf. 1 Cor 5.1, 6.13b–20).[10] Further, as Hans Conzelmann has pointed out, Paul uses καλόν elsewhere in this chapter in a similar sense (cf. vv. 8, 26).[11] It is clear from what follows in vv. 3–5 that Paul did not agree completely with such a statement if it was applied without qualifications to the married as well as the unmarried.[12] Thus, option (2) is ruled out. Elsewhere in 1 Corinthians it appears that Paul quotes a Corinthian slogan and, rather than rejecting the slogan outright (perhaps attempting to be diplomatic), he agrees with the remark within certain carefully defined limits (cf. 6.12). While the δέ in v. 2 is probably adversative,[13] it does not follow from this that Paul simply will refute v. 1 in what follows the δέ. Rather, it may be a strong qualification that follows ('yes, *but*').[14] Thus, all things considered, it seems that option (3) is the most likely, whether this phrase first originated with Paul or the Corinthians. There were contexts where Paul did agree with such views, but not as a regular practice between husband and wife. Paul's dilemma here is two-fold.

First, it is apparent from chapters 5–7 that there were both libertines and ascetics in Corinth.[15] If Paul agreed or disagreed with the statement in 1 Cor 7.1, then he would be siding with one or the other group, neither of which he agreed with in full. Second, Paul did wish to advocate the single life but without disparaging the married state. Thus, he must stand between the libertine and the ascetics in Corinth. This is perhaps why Paul is careful in this chapter to qualify his statements with exceptions and to give reasons for his views.

In v. 2 Paul gives one reason why the position stated in v. 1 cannot be accepted as applicable to all cases and people. It does not follow from this that the reason presented is Paul's only reason or even his best reason for advocating what he does. It is, however, the reason he thought most likely to fit the Corinthian situation – the most relevant and forceful reason he could give in the light of what was happening in Corinth (cf. 5.1–5, 6.15–20, and possibly 7.9) and in the light of what the ascetic mentality would fear the most – πορνεία.[16]

Because πορνεία is in the plural here, we should render v. 2: 'Because of cases of sexual sin (immorality), each (man) should have his own wife, and each (woman) should have her own husband.'[17] It is perhaps significant that Paul says ἕκαστος ... ἐχέτω ... ἑκάστη ... ἐχέτω which seems to imply that Paul thought marriage was and should be the normal state for both men and women in the Christian community.[18] Also worthy of mention is Paul's use of possessive adjectives here indicating that exclusive monogamy is required of Christians.[19] Paul sees marital intercourse as an obligation, not an option, for both partners,[20] and this fact militates against the view that Paul is advocating 'spiritual marriage' in vv. 36–38.

Both partners not only have obligations but also rights in sexual matters, for neither husband nor wife has authority over their own body – it is under the authority and power of their mate. This is, in part, what it means to belong to each other.[21] Therefore, Paul exhorts: μὴ ἀποστερεῖτε ἀλλήλους. This is not the advice an ascetic would give, and it was advice probably not accepted easily by the ascetics in Corinth. Paul allows for abstention within marriage only for a specific and limited period of time, and only for the sake of devoting oneself to prayer. It is to be noted that this abstention is to be undertaken by mutual consent of the partners (ἐκ συμφώνου). Paul knows that too long an abstention by a couple normally having regular marital relations may lead either or both of the partners into temptation and possible sin. Thus he says explicitly, καὶ πάλιν ἐπὶ τὸ αὐτὸ ἦτε.[22] Notable for its absence is any reference to intercourse being solely or even primarily for the sake of procreation. Rather, Paul implies that it is necessary as a part of the duty of self-giving each partner has to the other.

It is difficult to determine what the τοῦτο in v. 6 refers to in the preceding section. It seems unlikely that it refers to intercourse within marriage, since Paul not merely concedes this activity but stresses it as a duty of both partners. It may refer to all that Paul has said prior to v. 6 and thus be a reference to marriage and what it entails, or possibly to Paul's injunction to marry (v. 2). Verse 2 seems too far from the τοῦτο to be the logical antecedent, and it is illogical to argue that it refers to marriage since Paul does not think marriage is a necessary evil to be conceded in certain cases. Indeed, he goes on to say that marriage is no sin (vv. 28, 36) and he later says, ὁ γαμίζων τὴν ἑαυτοῦ παρθένον καλῶς ποιεῖ (v. 38).[23] Contextually, the most logical solution is that τοῦτο refers to something which Paul previously had allowed but not commanded or advised. The phrase εἰ μήτι introduces a clear concession in the verse immediately prior to the one containing the τοῦτο – the allowance of abstinence for prayer.

Paul emphasizes that abstinence (for prayer) is only a concession, not a command, thus forestalling the ascetics from using his words to order others to abstain.[24] Paul, in diplomatic fashion, strives in

v. 7 to identify with the ascetics in a limited way, perhaps in an attempt to exercise authority and to guide them. He says that he desires everyone to be as himself, by which he probably means unmarried (cf. v. 8, ὡς κἀγώ).[25] Paul realizes that to remain continent is a χάρισμα ἐκ θεοῦ, and that each has his own χάρισμα, and that not everyone's χάρισμα is to be continent. Thus, Paul cannot give a general command that all Christians be or become unmarried;[26] nevertheless, he expresses his desire and goes on to emphasize that because of certain factors he thinks it is preferable for a Christian to be unmarried (cf. vv. 8, 27, 38, 40).[27]

Paul now turns to address τοῖς ἀγάμοις καὶ ταῖς χήραις. If the καὶ in v. 8 is a real connective, then Paul is addressing two different but probably related groups. It is possible that the καὶ should be translated 'especially' in which case ἄγαμος is being used as a general term for the unmarried and Paul then singles out one group within that category that he wishes to speak to in particular – the widows.[28] Verse 9, however, would seem to support translating καὶ as 'and' since this verse speaks of control, a word of exhortation more appropriate for those who have been married (cf. v. 5, διὰ τὴν ἀκρασίαν ὑμῶν), but are now without a mate. Also in favor of this view is the fact that in Koine ἄγαμος can mean widower (or at least someone who has had a marital partner whether widowed, separated, or divorced).[29] Coupling this with the fact that Paul was probably a widower, makes his identification with these two groups quite natural. Further, Paul does not at this point go on to say anything in particular to widows, thus it seems unlikely that he is singling them out of a general group of the unmarried here.[30]

The alternative of self-control is marriage for these Christians (v. 9) – 'for it is better to marry than to burn'. How are we to understand πυροῦσθαι? Usually it is translated in a way that refers to human passions.[31] This seems likely in view of the reference to self-control. Further, 7.2a (διὰ δὲ τὰς πορνείας) and possibly the difficult ὑπέρακμος of 7.36 seem to support the traditional translation of this verse. M. L. Barre, however, has argued that πυρόομαι refers to the fires of judgment or Gehenna.[32] Elsewhere in the NT, πυρόομαι and its cognates are used in eschatological contexts.[33] In view of Paul's use of the term Satan in v. 5 and some of the reasons he gives for his advice later in this chapter (cf. vv. 26, 29, 31), a plausible case can be made for seeing here a reference to the eternal consequences of persisting in such sin to death. There is no warrant for translating ἐγκρατεύονται with 'cannot be continent' since a verb such as δύναμαι or ἰσχύω does not occur here and since the type of conditional clause found here (εἰ not ἐάν as in v. 8b) places emphasis on the reality of the assumption.[34] On Barre's view, Paul is not suggesting that marriage is a *remedium concupiscentiae* but that in the shadow of God's eschatological judgment one must be careful that misbehavior will not exclude one from the ranks of the saved. Paul is not adverse to giving such dramatic warnings when the problem is sexual sin or something equally serious (cf. 5.5, 13, 6.9–10, 14–20). On balance, the traditional reference to human passions is to be preferred; however, Barre's view cannot be ruled out.

In vv. 8, 10, and 12, Paul addresses three different groups of people. It is significant that he says παραγγέλλω only to the second group. This is the first explicit command of the chapter and it may result from the fact that Paul is drawing on some explicit teaching of ὁ κύριος. It appears from vv. 12–16 that Paul is directing his remarks in vv. 10–11 to married couples both of whom are Christians. The essential problem we face in vv. 10–11 is to determine the meaning of χωρισθῆναι and ἀφιέναι. Does Paul mean the same thing by both verbs? Does the former mean 'to separate', the latter 'to divorce', reflecting the differences between a man's and a woman's rights in regard to the termination of a marriage in Jewish and some Greek contexts? The problem is not made easier by the fact that there is no technical vocabulary of divorce in the MT, the LXX, or the NT.[35] If Paul does mean divorce by both terms, then he apparently knows a saying of Jesus similar to Mark 10.11–12. If by χωρισθῆναι Paul means separate, then he is closer to Matthew 5 and 19.

It is fairly certain that Paul means divorce by ἀφιέναι.[36] This means that in v. 13 Paul predicates divorce of a woman, a viable possibility in Corinth at that time.[37] What then of χωρισθῆναι? Perhaps a clue to its meaning is to be found in the fact that Paul does not see the marital bond dissolved as a result of the woman's action, for he then says, ἐὰν δὲ καὶ χωρισθῇ, μενέτω ἄγαμος ἢ τῷ ἀνδρὶ καταλλαγήτω. Another clue may be found in the fact that this conditional statement is predicated only of the woman, and in view of the way Paul has balanced male and female parallelism to this point, this departure may indicate that the activity of man and woman differs at this point.

That the woman is addressed first in vv. 3, 10, 11, 16, and 39 may be because women were leading the movement to break up existing marriages and to prevent new ones.[38] Favoring this idea is Conzelmann's view that the ἐάν clause refers to an existing situation:

'If she has separated herself …'[39] J.K. Elliott points out that the verb in question is often used in the NT to mean separate,[40] but these examples are not in the context of a discussion of marriage and there is evidence that this verb can mean divorce.[41] There does not seem to be any NT support for this translation, however, for in Mark 10.9 (Matt 19.6) it probably refers to the action of a third party. Even if the verb refers to the action of any human, it appears that the meaning is not divorce but put asunder, i.e., separate in an active sense of the word.[42]

We are now brought back to the context of 1 Corinthians 7. It seems more likely that Paul would be consistent in his use of terms in the space of only five verses, than that he would use words to mean different things without qualification. Thus, we conclude that Paul means divorce when he uses ἀφίημι in vv. 10 and 15.

In v. 12, Paul begins to give advice for which he has no precedent in the teaching of Jesus. Who are τοῖς λοιποῖς? They must be different from the group referred to in vv. 10–11 and, in view of what Paul says in vv. 12–16, they probably are to be distinguished from the group mentioned in vv. 8–9.[43] Since Paul has no desire to speak to those who have no connection to the Christian community (cf. 6.12), here he is addressing the situation of religiously mixed marriages (note ἄπιστος in vv. 12–15). Paul advises that as long as the unbeliever agrees to live together with the believer, they should not divorce. Far from the unbeliever contaminating the believer or making their progeny unclean, the believing partner has a sanctifying influence on the unbeliever and the children of such unions are holy or clean.[44]

In v. 15 Paul deals with a more difficult case, i.e., the unbeliever desires to separate though apparently the believer wishes to prevent this. Paul says that the believer is not enslaved.[45] Paul does not go on to say that these believers have the right to remarry, however, so it is doubtful that there is a 'Pauline privilege'. What Paul seems to mean is that the believer is not obligated to maintain the relationship against the will of the unbelieving partner. Rather, they should let the unbeliever leave since God has called believers to peace, not to the turmoil involved in trying to keep a marriage partner against his or her will.[46]

Is v. 16, then, to be taken as optimistic, pessimistic, or neutral? While J. Jeremias and C. Burchard have made a good case for taking this sentence in an optimistic sense, the parallels they produce are not identical to what we find in 1 Cor 7.16.[47] Our passage, unlike the parallels, has not one but two double questions with τί γὰρ οἶδας ... εἰ. The closest parallel is to be found in Ecc 3.21 (LXX, τίς οἶδεν ... εἰ ... εἰ) where the outcome of the questions is uncertain. As S. Kubo rightly argues, the sense is not determined by the structure but by the context in which these questions occur.[48] It is awkward to make a sharp break between 15ab and 15c.

If v. 16 implies optimism about the conversion of the unbeliever, then why has Paul just advised the believer to allow the partner to leave? To take v. 16 in an optimistic sense requires one to see the peace referred to in 15c as the peace (?) that occurs when the Christian tries to prevent the dissolution of the marriage. This is too difficult and it is more natural to see here a reference to the peace that results when the unbeliever leaves and the tension in this mixed marriage is no longer perpetuated.[49]

On the other hand, if v. 16 implies uncertainty, then v. 15c can be taken in its more natural sense. Jeremias' argument that 15c is a limitation of 15ab makes little sense since the believers addressed desire to maintain the relationship and Paul does not encourage this in 15ab. As Kubo says, 'Obviously, Paul would hardly use this missionary motivation for those who desire to maintain the marriage against the objection of the unbelieving partner who wishes to separate when Paul in such cases would counsel the believer to go.'[50] Thus, v. 16, if optimistic, can hardly refer to those in v. 15. Accordingly, C. K. Barrett, while accepting the optimistic understanding of v. 16, connects the verse with 12−14.[51] But the believers addressed in vv. 12−14 are concerned about the cleanness or legitimacy of their relationship, and Paul's words in v. 16 do not adequately answer their question; rather, v. 14 serves this purpose. It seems easier to see vv. 12−14 as a unit, with vv. 15−16 as another. In vv. 12−13 and 15ab, we have advice to the two respective groups. In vv. 14, 15−16, the reasons for the advice to each are given. Thus, only the uncertain rendering makes sense of this passage, and the *RSV* translation is to be preferred. The believer cannot be sure whether or not the unbeliever will be converted. The outcome is in doubt. Humanly speaking it seems unlikely that an unbeliever would be converted in a situation where force is used to maintain the relationship. Thus, Paul says let them separate.

Verses 17−24 do not concern us except that we should note the principle that Paul maintains in vv. 17, 20, 24, a principle Paul says is a rule − ἐν ταῖς ἐκκλησίαις πάσαις.[52] The εἰ μή in v. 17 would seem to favor the view of vv. 15−16[53] advocated above, in that here Paul goes on to reiterate that the Christian is not to attempt a change of status in the marriage. Rather, Christians are to remain in the situation or status in which they found themselves when God called them to be Christians.

Paul begins a new topic at v. 25 and immediately makes clear that as was the case with his advice to those involved in mixed marriages, he has no commands of the Lord to draw on in this new case.[54] Paul's advice to the παρθένοι is the same as his advice to the circumcised and the slaves in vv. 17–24: καλὸν ἀνθρώπῳ τὸ οὕτως εἶναι.[55] The reason he gives is, διὰ τὴν ἐνεστῶσαν ἀνάγκην. Is this a reference to a present or an imminent distress (or necessity)?

What sort of distress is Paul discussing? Because of the qualifying word (ἐνεστῶσαν), it cannot be a reference to the anxieties inherent to the married life (cf. vv. 32–35). Nor does it appear to be the sort of distress discussed in v. 37. Perhaps the phrase most likely to explain the meaning of ἐνεστῶσαν ἀνάγκην is found in v. 29 – ὁ καιρὸς συνεσταλμένος ἐστίν. Here there is also uncertainty about the translation of the key word συνεσταλμένος – 'short' or 'shortened'?

Are these references to some impending and crucial event in the eschatological timetable, or are they a reference to some sort of persecution that the Corinthians were facing because of their faith? Though Paul does not speak of θλῖψιν in v. 28, and elsewhere he does use this word in an eschatological sense of the tribulations that will befall Christians now that the end times have broken in (cf. 1 Thess 1.6, 3.3, passim); in v. 28, however, Paul is referring to the tribulations that affect married people specifically (τοιοῦτοι). It is more likely that the kind of distresses Paul refers to in vv. 32ff, not the Messianic woes, are referred to here.[56] The word συνεσταλμένος is not an adjective but a participle and should be translated shortened.[57] The word becomes not a reference to a future event but to some past happening which has dramatically changed the state of affairs. Something or someone has shortened the time. Because of this for the rest of the time (τὸ λοιπόν, v. 29),[58] Christians are to live in a characteristically different way from others. Their entire attitude toward all things that are part of this world – one's social position, race, marital status – must be different, παράγει γὰρ τὸ σχῆμα τοῦ κόσμου.[59] It is crucial to note the present tense of παράγει. Paul is not speaking of some future apocalyptic event but of an eschatological process already underway. As in Rom 13.11–14, Paul in v. 26 is talking about the present time and the things that are already happening, not some time that is about to break in or some impending distress. The distress is already upon these Christians though the day of salvation has not yet dawned. It is already true that ὥρα ἤδη ὑμᾶς ἐξ ὕπνου ἐγερθῆναι νῦν γὰρ ἐγγύτερον ἡμῶν ἡ σωτηρία ἢ ὅτε ἐπιστεύσαμεν (Rom 13.11).

Paul's imperatives in 1 Corinthians 7 are not grounded in what God had yet to do, but in the indicative of what God had already done and is doing in Christ.[60] It appears in this case that the possible imminence of Christ's return affects Paul's advice only in this regard – it gives it greater urgency and causes Christians to strive with greater intensity to reach the goal – for the time has been shortened. Christ *could* return soon.[61] It will be seen that if this is correct, then we have here an ethic grounded in the already of Christ's eschatological work which gains urgency and is given contingency because of what God is yet to do in Christ. It is an ethic affected by the possible shortness of time, but it is primarily determined by the eschatological events that have already transpired culminating in the death and resurrection of Jesus.

The decisive event in the eschatological timetable has taken place already. Human beings could no longer say that there was necessarily a long time before God would culminate His plan for history, since Jesus could return at any moment to bring history to a close (cf. 1 Thess 5.1ff.). Thus, the Christian must live realizing that all worldly things have been relativized by the ultimacy of the Christ-event and its implications for humanity. Worldly things pale in significance in comparison to the Christ-event. One can no longer place ultimate value or faith in the things of this world, for this world's form is already passing away. One can appreciate the things of this world, however, and use them as long as they are seen for what they are. These are the ideas that lie behind Paul's advice in vv. 25–40.[62]

Having stated his principle in v. 26 Paul then applies it in v. 27. It is difficult to determine whether δέω means 'to be bound in marriage' (as in v. 39 and Rom 7.2), or possibly 'engaged', 'bound in a promise of marriage'.[63] Note that Paul is addressing men exclusively in v. 29. It is reasonable, in view of Paul's advice in v. 11, that he thought the marital bond was not dissoluble by anything except death (cf. v. 20, Rom 7.2). This being so, it is not likely that in v. 28 Paul is addressing those who are divorced, whose former partners are still living. Thus, it does not appear that Paul means divorced by λύω in v. 27b. It is also significant that Paul does not say in v. 27b, 'Do not seek another woman.' Thus, it is possible that in vv. 27–28a Paul is addressing unmarried men, and in v. 28b unmarried women.[64] He is saying in v. 27, 'Are you bound in a promise to a woman? Do not seek to be free of that commitment. Are you free of such a commitment to a woman? Do not seek a woman.' In either case, Christians are not to change their status.

In vv. 29–31 Paul makes a statement about the Christian's basic orientation to the joys and sorrows, the things and institutions, of this world. The major point being made is that the Christian's existence is no longer to be determined by the 'form of this world'. Paul is not advocating withdrawal from or renunciation of the world, but that now the world is the sphere where the believer is called to obey God's will. The ὡς μή here does not reflect a tension between present and future but a dialectical relationship between a human being and the world. This is why we have present tenses in these verses. Bodily and worldly relationships have not become meaningless; rather, they are the very spheres where Christ's Lordship and demands are asserted (cf. 6.12, 7.28).[65]

'We have to do here neither with Stoic "indifference" nor with apocalyptic "renunciation" but rather with Paul's own understanding of Christian existence as a new creation.'[66] Paul does not say in v. 29 that those who are married are to abstain from marital relationships or the obligations of such relationships, indeed in vv. 2–5 he says quite the contrary. Nor does he say that Christians should not make use of the world, indeed in vv. 30b, 31 his advice is directed to those who are and will go on doing so (an action he does not forbid). Their attitude, however, is to change. Those buying things must not act as though they were possessing those things.[67] Those making use of this world must not act as though they were taking full advantage of the world.[68] Both the having and the not-having are to be taken with equal seriousness and are to be thought of within a Christian perspective.

'Striving after the goods of the world, however, no longer determines the existence of the Christian. Whoever buys should not think that what he buys can secure his future.'[69] Neither the world, nor human beings, nor Christ is to be regarded from a worldly or purely anthropocentric point of view (cf. 2 Cor 5.16). Paul in a sense agrees with some of the Corinthians in that things are not to be viewed according to the flesh but according to the Spirit. Paul, however, differs radically with the 'spiritualists' in Corinth over what this entails.

Paul's wish is that Christians be free from worldly anxieties that might distract them from the things of the Lord. The unmarried man has no such divided interests.[70] The married man, however, strives to please both his wife and the Lord. His interests are clearly divided. Likewise, the formerly married woman and the virgin are concerned with the things of the Lord.[71] The married woman, like the married man, has divided loyalties or at least divided concerns which can distract one from giving proper devotion to the Lord. Significantly, Paul severely qualifies these statements in v. 35. They are not binding commandments but what could be called good advice from Paul acting as a pastor.

Verses 36–38 represent a considerable challenge to the exegete, the main difficulty being to determine whom Paul is addressing – a man and his daughter, a man and his betrothed, or those engaged in a 'spiritual' marriage. We will consider the last possibility first.

The spiritual marriage view appears to have been in existence for only one hundred years,[72] but has found numerous followers. This view does not face insuperable grammatical difficulties, unlike the traditional (father–daughter) view. It does, however, face several historical, lexical, and contextual problems.

First, there is the historical point that there is no evidence for the existence of an institution that was similar to and possibly the fore-runner of the *virgines subintroductae* prior to the late second or possibly early third century AD.[73] Second, there is the difficulty already mentioned above that in 1 Cor 7.2–5 Paul insists that marriages be real marriages, i.e., fully consummated. Further, in v. 36 Paul indicates that at least one party wished to marry (ὃ θέλει ποιείτω … γαμείτωσαν) which would seem to imply that they are not yet truly married (at least in Paul's and possibly one partner's eyes). There is the further problem that there are no words in this context that indicate we are dealing with an exceptional case, such as the spiritual marriage. The word παρθένος does not seem to be used in an abnormal sense in vv. 25–35, and only the possessive adjective is used to qualify it in vv. 36–38 which is not enough to indicate we are dealing with a spiritual marriage.[74]

The traditional view that a man and his daughter is meant in vv. 36–38 does not do full justice to our text. Grammatically it is unsatisfactory because of the γαμείτωσαν in v. 36. On this view, Paul suddenly introduces a third party into the discussion (the daughter's husband-to-be), without any prior reference to him. A second problem arises over the word ὑπέρακμος. Even if it means 'past maturity' or even 'at the age of puberty', then it is difficult to see why the father's conduct should be described in terms of ἀσχημονεῖν, a word that elsewhere in Paul has a clear sexual connotation.[75]

Further, why would the father's will be out of control (cf. v. 37), and why would it ever be a necessity (ἀνάγκην) for him to give his daughter in marriage? Notice that Paul indicates that it is he who might have this necessity (not his daughter, for instance, because of misconduct), and yet manifestly the person he is addressing is in two minds. In what sense could the father commit a sin in any case? Why would Paul urge a scrupulous father to give his daughter in marriage because she is advancing in years? The argument that γαμίζω in v. 38 must mean 'give in marriage', and thus refer to the father is not very forceful in view of the fact that in Koine and in Paul there is evidence of the breaking down of the distinction between – έω and – ίζω verbs.[76] On the other hand, the argument that τὴν παρθένον cannot mean his daughter is incorrect, though it is not the usual meaning of παρθένος.[77] There is the historical point that by the first century AD, especially in Corinth where sexual conventions were not strictly followed, it is questionable that paternal authority (the *patria potestas*) would be a controlling factor in determining whether or not a daughter married. The effect of Hellenization was to allow the daughter and especially her husband to have more choice in the matter than in classical times.[78] Yet the discussion in 1 Cor 7.36–38, if it is addressed to the father, would seem to presuppose that the father alone would decide the question of marriage.

We are left with the view that a man and his wife-to-be are the subject of vv. 36–38.[79] This makes sense in the context of Corinthian Christianity. A young man is engaged to be married. He is full of strong passions for his wife-to-be,[80] but there are those in the Christian community at Corinth with ascetical tendencies advising him to refrain from marriage. He is thus of two minds. He knows what he wants (v. 36), and indeed he has strong feelings about his fiancée, but he does not know if his plans represent proper Christian behavior. In such cases Paul says that the marriage should go ahead – it is no sin – indeed, ὁ γαμίζων τὴν ἑαυτοῦ παρθένον καλῶς ποιεῖ (v. 38). This is especially so in the case of this young man, since he probably is behaving somewhat improperly[81] already towards his fiancée.[82] In such a case it is apparent that his feelings are preventing him from remaining steadfast or from having complete control over his actions. He ought to marry, says Paul.

Paul, however, wants to restate his preference that Christians remain unattached if they are not yet or no longer married. This is why he commends the behavior of the one who has decided not to marry but to keep his fiancée as she is.[83] In Paul's view, this person κρεῖσσον ποιήσει. Again, Paul gives his audience more than one option and does not command any particular behavior if there is no necessity to move in any one particular direction. The motivation for Paul appears to be based on his view that the unmarried person has more time for the things of the Lord.

The view advocated above does justice to the grammatical, lexical, and historical probabilities, and Paul's advice follows along the same lines as we find in vv. 2 and 9. The historical objection that it presupposes a formal engagement, like that found in first-century Judaism but not among Greek Gentiles, has little weight in view of the fact that Greece was adopting Roman customs. We know from Pliny the Younger that such engagements, involving mutual promises between the pair with consent from the father, existed in Paul's day.[84] We need not suppose that all the strict Jewish conventions about engagement are implied in this case in Corinth where there is no indication that a long engagement or other Jewish customs are involved. Nonetheless, it is noteworthy that Paul gives the couple only two options: to stay as they are or to marry. Perhaps this is because Paul, in light of his Jewish background, took engagement as a binding commitment (a view the Corinthians probably did not share), and since he ruled out divorce Paul does not here allow a total dissolution of the relationship.[85]

Paul concludes his discussion of marriage with a statement about the obligations of a married woman and the options of a widowed woman. A married woman is bound to her husband as long as he lives.[86] By this statement Paul rules out any possibility of a Christian woman initiating an end to her marriage. On the other hand, if the husband dies she is free to marry again. Paul makes one proviso – μόνον ἐν κυρίῳ – which probably means that she is not to marry someone who is not part of the Body of Christ.[87]

Paul does not think it wise for a Christian to become involved in a mixed marriage, and it is notable that only in the case of a mixed marriage does Paul say that the believer is not obligated to try and prevent the unbelieving partner from separating. It may be significant that Paul, in counseling widows, first says a widow is free to remarry before stating his preference for her to remain as she is (v. 40). Paul's parting remark on this subject may be his way of ironically saying to the spiritualists in Corinth that he too has the Spirit and thus his judgment is sound. Perhaps more likely it is his way of reassuring the Corinthians that the spiritualists are not the only ones with the Spirit and His enlightenment, and thus those Christians being advised by the spiritualists need not feel obligated to follow their counsel.

Our discussion of 1 Corinthians 7 leads us to draw the following conclusions. First, while it is certainly true that Paul expresses his preference for the Christian to remain single if that is his or her present condition, it would not be accurate to label Paul an ascetic. He does not belittle marriage or see it merely as a *remedium concupiscentiae*, though it does in some cases prevent illicit sexual activity. He says that those who marry do well, and he sees sexual intercourse as part of one's duty to the marriage partner. Paul does not give an unqualified 'yes' to what may have become a slogan of Corinthian ascetics (7.1). He appears to think that marriage is the normal state of affairs and that remaining single requires a special gift.

Paul does not think sexual relations or marriage are either evil or questionable. Both are seen as good within their proper perspective. Paul's advice to those unattached to remain unmarried is part of his more general advice to all Christians to remain in the situation or status to which they were called. His reasons for this advice are of a positive nature, and not due to negative feelings against marriage and its consummation. In fact, his reasons for preferring the single state are specifically Christian in nature.

It is because the decisive Christ-event has already taken place, relativizing the form of this world of contingencies and shortening the time this world has left, that the Christian is called to live unattached to the things of this world. It is this sort of detachment that gives freedom of choice – something Paul stresses in 1 Corinthians 7. It is this freedom that allows one to concentrate on things of ultimate importance – the things of the Lord and how to please Him. Since Christ can save regardless of one's sex, race, or social class, there is no need to change status in order to improve one's standing before the Lord. Indeed, to assert the necessity of a Christian changing his status is to imply the insufficiency of Christ for one's present situation and to intimate that Christ is less than Lord over all such worldly conditions and institutions.

Instead, Paul speaks of the Christian's *attitude* toward his status changing (vv. 29–30), and speaks of the ability of the Christian to transform his or her situation. The Christian has no need to draw back from or reject the world and its institutions, indeed he or she is called to be an obedient witness to and in the world. Far from the world controlling a Christian's life and freedom, the Christian influences a mixed marriage in a positive way (v. 14), and even a slave can be free in the Lord. The Christian, being under the dominion of the Lord (v. 22), is no longer under the dominion of the world with its institutions and priorities. It is only because the first priority of every Christian is the Lord that Paul allows a married Christian couple to abstain from intercourse for a time in order to commit themselves to prayer. Paul legitimizes no other reason for abstaining. He cannot be called an ascetic in any real sense. Indeed, 1 Corinthians 7 is both a criticism and a correction of various ascetical tendencies in Corinth! His view differs little from that expressed by Jesus in Matt 19.1–12.

Second, Paul actively stresses the equality of male and female. He discusses the rights, responsibilities, and options of both sexes in regard to the single and the married life. This sort of mutuality is not usually found or encouraged either in rabbinic Judaism or in non-Christian social codes. Both men and women are called to serve God in their own situation. That Paul rejects divorce outright, following Jesus' teaching, means greater security for Christian women married to the Lord. That Paul advocates the single state, perhaps also following Jesus, for both men and women, gives women a choice of roles they did not formerly have in this Greek setting. In either case, Paul argues that one must take seriously the obligations involved in one's situation, without allowing one's situation to control one's attitude toward life. The evidence in 1 Corinthians 7 shows Paul to be a pastor sensitive to the needs and wishes of both men and women (cf. θέλω, vv. 36, 39). He, in turn, expresses his own wishes, his strong advice, and his commands, taking care to allow Christians various options where a command is not required. There is no evidence here to substantiate a charge that Paul was a misogynist or a feminist (cf. vv. 3–4, 39).

Third, the structure of 1 Corinthians 7 is systematic, except perhaps in the case of vv. 39–40 which may be an afterthought. Consider the following:

(1) vv. 1–7, general discussion on marriage and conjugal rights;
(2) vv. 8–9, advice to widowers and widows;
(3) vv. 10–11, advice to Christian married couples about separation and divorce;
(4) vv. 12–16, advice to those involved in mixed marriages;
(5) vv. 17–24, illustration of how the principle 'remain as you are' applies not only to one's marital status, but also to one's ethnic or social status (conclusion: the principle applies to all Christians);
(6) vv. 25–38, advice to those considering engagement and to those engaged considering marriage (cf. vv. 27, 36–38);
(7) vv. 39–40, reiteration of advice and commandments given to women in vv. 8–11, with additional comment on a widow's freedom to remarry.

That women are addressed first in vv. 4, 10, 11, 16, and 39 may indicate that they in particular were considering divorce or separation. That the man is addressed in vv. 25–38 likely indicates the customs of the day whereby the man took the initiative in seeking engagement or, being already engaged, took the responsibility in deciding about the marriage. Paul's use of different verbs of the man and woman in regard to divorce (vv. 10–11) may indicate something about his source and its view that only a man can divorce, for Paul himself goes on to speak of a woman divorcing (v. 13), a custom known in Corinth at that time. The repeated themes of sexual passion or misconduct and, in response, Paul's stress on self-control (cf. vv. 2, 5, 9, 36, 37) probably tell us more about the problems in Corinth than about Paul's view of the purposes of marriage.

Paul shows no bitterness toward those married or contemplating marriage, but he does show concern about their having to face troubles, anxieties, distractions, etc., that might make difficult full devotion to the things of the Lord. Nevertheless, even if one does not accept Ephesians as Pauline, we have here enough evidence to show that Paul, far from being an ascetic, saw marriage as good, something that once undertaken should be fully consummated. As with all things, however, marriage for Paul must be seen within the perspective of the priorities of faith. The Christ-event conditions how one should live, whatever one's marital or social status. It calls for both a transformed attitude toward such worldly institutions as marriage, and an unqualified allegiance to Christ. This is why Paul can say on the one hand 'the one marrying his own virgin does well', and on the other hand, 'the one not marrying will do better'.

B. The Haustafel

One of the most fascinating areas of NT study is the examination of the 'household tables' (Col 3.18–4.1; Eph 5.22–6.9; 1 Tim 2.8–15, 6.1–2; Titus 2.1–10; 1 Pet 2.18–3.7). There are several prominent schools of thought about the origin, nature, and purpose of this material. On the one hand, it is claimed that here we have material primarily Hellenistic in origin, and parenetic (i.e., not situation specific) in nature which is attempting to come to terms with the world since the assumption of an imminent parousia was mistaken (cf. M. Dibelius, K. Weidinger).[88] On the other hand, it is contended that this material owes its origin and substance primarily to Hellenistic Judaism and/or the Old Testament (cf. E. Schweizer,

E. Lohse, J.E. Crouch, W. Lillie).[89] Yet a third opinion is that these tables are fundamentally Christian in origin (K. H. Rengstorf) and their ethical conceptions may go back to Jesus' teaching and example (D. Schroeder).[90] There is no consensus of opinion on these matters, nor is there likely to be in the near future. None of these views is utterly compelling or lacking in weaknesses.

Consider D. L. Balch's critique of the older view of Dibelius and Weidinger.[91] He makes an impressive case for seeing at least 1 Pet 2.18–3.7 as apologetic in function, not as an attempt by Christianity to settle down in the world in view of waning eschatological hopes. Further, M. Hengel has sufficiently demonstrated that neat divisions between Judaism and Hellenism in the NT era are no longer possible, and what may on the surface appear to be a 'Greek' element in a particular passage may, in fact, reflect an indebtedness to a Judaism that had been influenced earlier on by the spread of Hellenism.[92] Further, the nature of the Stoic ethical material was not essentially personal, nor in the form of personal addresses to various household members.[93] The older thesis of Dibelius, even with the modifications of Weidinger, becomes increasingly difficult to defend.

On the other hand, not only because of phrases such as ἐν κυρίῳ and 'as is fitting', but also because of the lack of material in the Decalogue that directly addresses the interrelationship between husband and wife with which the NT tables are so concerned, a purely OT origin for these tables seems implausible even if the OT is mediated through Philo or other Hellenistic Jewish sources.[94] Even Philo has no household tables though he does discuss in a general way the place of women in the home and in relationship to her husband. The evidence shows that there is a variety of influences that went into the formation of these tables. Even Rengstorf's view of a strictly Christian origin is too one-sided, for it fails to account for some interesting parallels between this material and the various proposed sources, both Jewish and pagan. Can we talk about a pre-NT household table that is the oral source or even the literary predecessor of the NT tables?

One of the more disturbing tendencies in this discussion is the continued assumption that there was a fixed household table (not merely ethical discussions about the household or duties) that the NT authors were drawing upon. This has yet to be demonstrated. It is also not impressive when it is asserted that there was a 'fixed' *topos* based on the evidence that the duties of masters, husbands, fathers, and their subordinates are discussed together in authors ranging from Aristotle to Hierocles. There is no question that the discussion of household management and duties was an important topic from the time of Aristotle onwards.[95] However, the repeated juxtaposition of husbands, masters, father and/or wives, slaves, children, coupled occasionally with a mention of their respective duties, is not impressive in view of the fact that these were the regular members of the family from well before the NT era until long after it. The fact that various authors over a wide period of time discuss precisely these three groups and usually manifest a patriarchal orientation does not demonstrate a chain of literary dependency. It does, however, reflect the fact that there was never a *fundamental* change in the dominant patriarchal orientation of the family from the time of Aristotle to St Paul, whether we are talking about pagan, Jewish, or Christian households.[96]

At this point we should review some of the relevant material Weidinger and others use to demonstrate the existence of a pre-New Testament household table that NT authors are supposed to have adopted and adapted for their own purposes. In Aristotle's *Politics* (c. 335 BC) we do find reference to a discussion of household members and management. However, notice the terms used: husband and wife are πόσις καὶ ἄλοχος,[97] and when he refers to authority and subordination it is τὸ ἄρχειν καὶ ἄρχεσθαι.[98] There is no table here, no series of imperatives directed to each or any household member, no use of key terms such as ὑποτάσσω and κεφαλή. Instead there is a general ethical discussion of the subject using different language. Yet, we are told by Balch that, 'This is the most important parallel to the N.T. codes. It demonstrates that the pattern of submissiveness ... was based on an earlier Aristotelian topos 'concerning household management'; the discussion of these three relationships in a household was not a Jewish or Christian innovation.'[99] We may well ask why the pattern of submissiveness in the NT codes could not have been picked up from the general cultural milieu, rather than from a direct or indirect dependency on Aristotle. This material shows that the discussion of social relationships was not a Jewish or Christian innovation, but it hardly demonstrates the reality or even the origin of a *Haustafel*.

When we turn to the 'clearest' Stoic duty list in Epictetus,[100] we find a phenomenon that repeats itself in other citations Weidinger and others used to prove the existence of a household table — a list of whom one has duties *to*, but we are not told what the duties *are*. Thus, for instance, we read of maintaining proper relations 'as a son, a brother, a father, a citizen'.[101] To this sort of shorthand we may compare Seneca, (*On Benefits*), Horace (*Art of Poetry*), Cicero (*De*

Officiis), and others.[102] In short, we are told that there are duties to
each individual or group mentioned, but we are not told what these
duties are. Even when there is an occasional reference to what a
particular duty amounts to, we do not have it in the form of a table,
nor is it imperatival, nor is it juxtaposed immediately with instructions
for another group or individual. Equally unsatisfactory is using texts
which only refer to the unwritten 'laws' of the ancients to demonstrate
the reality of a fixed or relatively fixed household table.[103] If these
are *unwritten* laws, then they may be widespread customs, but they
are not fixed or written household codes.

Sometimes there also arises a problem of dating. Thus, for instance, Epictetus (c. AD 55–135) did not begin writing until the last
two or three decades of the first century at the earliest. Seneca was
a writer in the first century AD as was Plutarch, but Hierocles was
not born until AD 117. The most one can derive from writers like
Seneca and Plutarch is that household duties were a topic of important
discussion in and before their day. They cannot be shown to be influences on NT documents that were written by their contemporaries.
They do, in some cases, bear witness to earlier material (though not
a fixed table), possibly shared in common with NT authors.

Due to the above considerations and to the careful work of Crouch
among others,[104] there has been a gradual turning *from* a view that
Greek (especially Stoic) authors were a major influence on NT
household codes and a turning *to* the suggestion that Hellenistic
Judaism and the OT may prove to be a more promising source.
Crouch demonstrated that there is no division of social duties in
reciprocal terms or in pairs, and the distinction between subordinate
and superior persons is absent in Stoic documents. Further, a concern
for household duties is foreign to the very nature of Stoicism. Let
us examine some of the parallels in Philo and Josephus.

The discussion of Philo has centered on such texts as the
Decalogue, *Special Laws*, and *Posterity and Exile of Cain*.[105] This
material does discuss an ordering of relationships in the household,
and *Special Laws* 2.225–227 talks in terms of superordinate and
subordinate groups of household members as does *Decalogue*
165–67. It is interesting, however, that as patriarchal as Philo is,
wishing women confined to the house, a woman is said to be a
governor of the household in charge of its management (cf. *Special
Laws* 3.169–171). In short, there is no mention of the husband being
the head of the household. Further, notice that in *Decalogue* 165–167
both parents are placed in the superior category, and wives are not

mentioned with children or slaves. This is because both here and in *Special Laws* 2.225–227 there are really only two categories of discussion – parents and children. With parents are associated seniors, rulers, benefactors, masters. With children are associated juniors, subjects, slaves, receivers of benefit. The husband/wife pair is not discussed as such in this material. At most we find a concern for obedience of subordinates, but wives and husbands are not separated into two separate categories.

More relevant is Philo's *Apology for the Jews* 7.3, 6[106] where we are told, 'wives must be in servitude to their husbands' (γυναῖκας ἀνδράσι δουλεύειν). A reciprocal duty for husbands similar to what we find in Colossians 3 or Ephesians 5 is not mentioned here. Note that ὑποτάσσω is not used, but rather a more severe or restrictive term. Once again, this is in the course of a general ethical discussion, not in the context of a household table. Of a similar nature is Josephus' famous dictum (*Against Apion* 2.199): 'Let her accordingly be submissive' (γυνὴ χείρων φησίν ἀνδρὸς εἰς ἅπαντα τοιγαροῦν ὑπακουέτω).[107] Again, we have no mention of ὑποτάσσω nor do we find in the NT any statement about the woman's inferiority to man. Instead of talking about authority, Ephesians 5 talks about love and headship, and Colossians 3 about love.

One other point is to be made about ὑποτάσσω. Even after extensive searching, Balch and others have gathered only two texts outside the NT which speak of wives submitting themselves to their husbands using the word ὑποτάσσω. One is from Plutarch, *Advice to Bride and Groom*, which is from the late first century AD, and could not have influenced Paul in Colossians or Ephesians (if they are Pauline).[108] A second text comes from Pseudo-Callisthenes where Alexander tells his mother she ought to be submissive to her husband (using ὑποτάσσω).[109] The problem here is that while some of this material may go back before the NT era as a popular romance, it is hard to say which portions are later additions and, in any case, the earliest manuscript of this document dates to AD 300. NT scholars ought to be very cautious about claiming that this particular material goes back before the NT era. What we may conclude from Josephus and some of the material in Philo and Plutarch is that the concept of the wife's submission was a topic discussed in the NT era usually with strong patriarchal overtones. We do not find, however, a duty table or any real discussion of reciprocal duties. More often we hear of the duties of the wife and the authority of the husband. Absent also are imperatives.

Though doubtless more texts could be reviewed, this short survey gives one a feel for the material.

I conclude that while discussion of household management was a standing topic in antiquity both before and during the NT era, I can find no direct evidence of a household table. Certainly, there is nothing similar to what we find in the NT with reciprocal pairs that are addressed directly with imperatives. I agree with Lillie when he concluded after his own survey, 'I find myself unconvinced, however, by the evidence presented by most writers on the subject that the early Church in any substantial way took over "the ancient housetable patterns" ... Yet when we examine the actual content of the [NT] house-tables, Jewish and Old Testament influences appear far more important.'[110] It is crucial that we distinguish between possible sources of ideas which influenced the NT authors and actual literary sources from which the household table pattern in the NT is derived. It is possible that the household pattern as we find it in the NT originated with Paul himself, though he would be drawing on a host of ethical material inherited both from his Jewish heritage and possibly from the wider pagan milieu. As C. F. D. Moule points out, it is certainly not the case that we have here a slightly Christianized Hellenistic or even Hellenistic Jewish duty code.[111] There are some similarities between Philo and the NT codes in that both side with the weak, the minor, and the slave, but this is part of the general OT heritage and may reflect a common dependence.[112] Schroeder has shown that there are substantial differences between the NT codes and both Stoic and Hellenistic Jewish materials.[113] While I hesitate to endorse Schroeder's whole thesis of the origin and form of this material in the teaching of Jesus, or Rengstorf's view that the early Christian interest in the οἶκος was the cause of this material, there is nothing improbable with supposing that some early Christians did give this material its basic form drawing primarily on Jewish and OT materials. Bearing all this in mind, let us now examine the material in Colossians 3 and Ephesians 5.

1. The Colossian *Haustafel* (3.18–4.1)

With good reason, various commentators have suggested that Col 3.18–4.1 is a pre-set piece inserted into its present context. First, 3.17 and 4.2 seem to go together naturally, both referring to prayer. Second, the sentences in the household code are terse and to the point, quite unlike the long periods we get in the first two chapters of

Colossians.[114] Further, while the similarities between Col 3.18ff. and Eph 5.22ff. may be a result of the sharing of a common author, or may be a case of literary dependency, it seems unlikely that the author of 1 Pet 2.18–3.7 knew of Colossians or Ephesians.[115] This being the case, it appears we have in Col 3.18ff. one form of an early Christian household table that we find in a different form in 1 Peter, but which existed in some form prior to the writing of either of these documents.[116] It is likely that Paul and others modified this household table to suit the particular needs of their respective audiences. Thus, for instance, the author of 1 Peter seems to have expanded both the slave and wife exhortations, and Paul appears to have expanded the slave section in Colossians 3 and the husband section in Ephesians 5.

In an attempt to find the connection between Col 3.18–4.1 and what precedes it, R. P. Martin[117] suggests that, as I Corinthians 14 shows, problems of order arose in the worship service that called for exhortations from the apostle. Here then we have such exhortations prompted by Paul's beginning to talk about worship activities in 3.16–17. This suggestion has plausibility, but one wonders whether all or even most of the exhortations in 3.18–4.1 are intended to regulate relationships specifically in worship. A more plausible explanation for the placement of 3.18–4.1 and its connection to what precedes lies in the fact that the early church met in homes and so there was an overlap between participants and behavior in the house and the house-church. Since the house was the context for both daily life and worship, it is natural to address proper household behavior *in general* in the context of discussing worship *in particular*. A household that was not unified in Christ and harmonious could not be a good context for orderly worship.

The material in Col 3.18–21 may be the most primitive form of the household table we have.[118] Several structural elements should be kept in mind: (1) the subordinate member of each pair is addressed first – wives, children, slaves; (2) each exhortation consists of an address, an admonition, and in some cases, a motive or reason, sometimes a specifically Christian one; (3) the groups are arranged from closest relationship (wives/husbands) to least close relationships (slaves/masters).[119] Another crucial structural point to remember is that the husband, father, and master all refer to the same person in the household, but the subordinate members of each pair refer to different household members. Obviously, the table is arranged to focus first and foremost on the roles of the subordinate household members to the head of the household. The duties of the head of the household are also addressed, but they are divided up according to the role he is assuming. G. E. Cannon suggests the following reasons why this material is included and arranged as it is.

> The facts are that inordinate freedom and enthusiasm were major problems in Paul's mission and ministry. The special focus which he gave on the inclusivism of the gospel would have made the slave and women issue a very real threat to the orderliness of the church both in worship and in social issues. Paul's insistence that Jewish Christians should not expect Gentile Christians to live Jewishly gave birth to an inclusivism that specially marked his development of the gospel in Romans and Galatians. The proclamation that in Christ there are no distinctions (Galatians 3:28; 1 Corinthians 12:12, 13; and Colossians 3:11) would understandably generate a longing for full acceptance in the church by slaves and women. The Colossians-type *Haustafel* was especially appropriate for dealing with that problem. Later, when the Jew—Gentile issue faded in the life of the church, the Colossians-type *Haustafel* was not as fitting and other forms of the *Haustafel* became more useful. In other words, a post-Pauline provenance for the Colossians-type *Haustafel* is less fitting than a Pauline provenance.[120]

If Cannon is right, then this household table was intended as a corrective for problems, perhaps created by a misunderstanding of the implications of Paul's teaching about freedom and oneness in Christ.[121] The code then would function to qualify certain misunderstandings, egalitarian in nature, that may have arisen as a result of Paul's own teaching. Let us now examine vv. 18–21 in detail.

Γυναῖκες are addressed first and in view of v. 19 this must surely refer to wives. This means that Paul does not say what the relationship of women to men is in general, or in worship in particular. He is not addressing single women, widows, or female minors here – only wives. Further, what is said of wives applies to their relationship to husbands. We are not told whether there is or should be any analogy between the relationship of wives to husbands, and the relationship of women (or wives) to male church leaders. Clearly, the focus is on family relationships, not on relationships with church authorities. The structure of the family had bearing on general church matters, and so it is included in a letter addressed to a church, but the focus is on the structure of the family. Here and elsewhere in the

Christian household tables, the subordinate members of the family (including slaves) are addressed as persons who are expected to be morally responsible for their behavior as their husbands, fathers, or masters are.[122] Further, Paul is only addressing a household in which all members are Christians and so all could be addressed in a letter to a church. He does not have in mind families where several religions are practiced.[123]

The verb ὑποτάσσω is a crucial one. Here it is in the present tense and in the middle voice. This suggests both that this is a continual activity expected of wives, and that it is something they must do themselves. Paul does not tell husbands to insist that their wives perform this duty. The verb ὑποτάσσω was by no means widely used in Greek literature dealing with marriage.[124] Nonetheless, the use of it in Plutarch shows it was sometimes used in non-Christian contexts in the first century.[125] The verb in some form appears twenty-three times in Paul, but most crucial is its use in the middle in the indicative, or as a participle or imperative. In these cases it is used to describe Christ's relationship to God, members of the congregation to one another, members of the household to its head, and even believers with prophetic gifts (cf. 1 Cor 15.28; Eph 5.21–22; 1 Cor 14.32). ὑποτάσσω in the middle or passive is also used of a child in relation to his parents (Luke 2.51), and of all believers in relation to secular authority (Rom 13.1; Titus 3.1; 1 Pet 2.13) or to church officials (1 Pet 5.5), or finally to God or Christ (Jas 4.7; 1 Pet 5.6). It has been suggested that the NT use of this word draws on the LXX usage where its usual meaning is 'subject or submit oneself' or in the passive, 'be subjected or subordinated'.[126]

That the verb is used of Christ likely indicates that it does not indirectly imply an idea of inferiority of the submitter to the one submitted to, so far as their personhood or worth is concerned. Rather, it appears to have more to do with following the example of Christ who willingly humbled himself or took a lower place in relationship to the Father. Thus, S. Delling may be right that the idea this verb conveys has to do with humility and servanthood as the believer models him or herself on the Christ.[127]

This verb does not make a statement about the (inferior) nature of Christ, or women, or all believers. Rather, ὑποτάσσω says something about the relationship *between* two people or groups of people.[128] Further, it is certainly not gender specific since it is applied to Christ himself as well as to male children and slaves. Indeed, as we shall see when we get to Eph 5.21–22, ὑποτάσσω can be predicated of all believers in their relationship with one another. What this verb seems to describe is the shape of Christian humility or service particularly appropriate for the Christian wife in relation to her husband. She is to submit or subordinate herself to him.[129] Unfortunately, we are not told what this submission amounts to in practice, nor how it works itself out in the day to day affairs of the household. Presumably, Paul's audience knew what was implied.

The phrase ὡς ἀνῆκεν has suggested to various commentators that Paul or his Christian predecessors who created this household table were in touch with Stoic or pagan ethical discussions and exhortations which dealt with what was fitting behavior.[130] Note that what we have here is not καθήκει (it is fitting) but the imperfect form ἀνῆκεν (cf. also Eph 5.4), which is not classical or Stoic usage.[131] The point seems to be that this action has been customary practice before and is still fitting now.

Lest it be thought that Paul intended this phrase to mean something like 'as is fitting' in our day, or in this culture, or in the light of human nature or customs, ἀνῆκεν is qualified by ἐν κυρίῳ. He sees this exhortation as behavior appropriate for Christians in particular, not society in general.[132] Unlike 1 Pet 3.1, the reason for this behavior being inculcated here is not missionary. In 1 Pet 3.1 submissive behavior is urged in order to win a husband to Christ. Here Paul is probably not addressing households where only some are Christians. Further, Paul is not urging conformity to society's norms or what is 'natural' (whether for apologetic reasons or otherwise) but conformity to Christ. His behavior was the ultimate norm and pattern for Christian behavior. Thus, Moule rightly indicates that this phrase should not be seen as a mere Christianizing of a Stoic ethic, but rather, '... it is incorporation in the Christian community which makes a new thing of conduct'.[133] Not only is there a new *raison d'être* given for this exhortation about submission, which in itself admittedly is not uniquely Christian,[134] but a new model may be implied by which to gauge one's conduct − the Lord. Elsewhere, Paul grounds similar advice in the creation order (1 Corinthians 11), but here the basis for such conduct is that one is 'in the Lord'.

Turning to the parallel exhortation to husbands, we find the verb ἀγαπάω coming to the fore. This verb or its noun form is not unknown in antiquity prior to its appearance in the NT, but it is not used in the discussion of household duties in Hellenistic literature.[135] It is not a uniquely Christian word or one that only Christians used to refer to the relationship of husbands and wives. It is interesting that wives are nowhere exhorted to love their husbands in the NT household tables. Perhaps this is because Christian husbands in particular needed this exhortation. F. F. Bruce points out that ἀγαπάω does not in itself imply a selfless or self-sacrificial love like Christ's, for there are various NT texts where it can refer to an unworthy or self-regarding love (cf. John 3.19; 2 Tim 4.10; 2 Pet 2.15; 1 John 2.15).[136] We will postpone our discussion of the Christian use of ἀγαπάω until the next section on Ephesians.

μὴ πικραίνεσθε πρὸς αὐτάς probably is meant to be a negative expression, a corollary of the positive injunction to love.[137] It appears that πρὸς has the force of 'against' and so we should translate 'be embittered against', a phrase also found in Plutarch with reference to women.[138] Both of these exhortations serve to make clear that the Christian husband is not free to do as he pleases with his wife. His actions and even his anger must be limited by love. What seems to be in view is an ongoing anger or deep-seated resentment toward one's wife.[139]

At v. 20, children (male and female) are addressed and told to obey. It is uncertain how much difference in meaning there is between ὑποτάσσω and ὑπακούω. It appears the former verb only sometimes connotes 'obey' whereas the latter always does.[140] Certainly, in 1 Pet 3.5–6 Sarah's obedience is taken to be an example of subordination or submission. Perhaps we may say that obedience is one form that submission takes. In Col 3.20, however, two things distinguish the exhortation to wives from that to children: (1) in the exhortation to children ὑπακούω is in the active imperative which suggests absolute and unquestioning obedience;[141] and (2) the command is made comprehensive by the inclusion of the phrase κατὰ πάντα. This imperative may have developed out of the OT injunction, also found in the teaching of Jesus, to honor one's parents (cf. Exod 20.12; Deut 5.16; Mark 10.19). It is also true that the non-Christian parallels demand honor, not obedience, of the children.[142] This suggests that the Christian household table injunction to children is not merely a reproduction of earlier injunctions, but also a further intensification of them.

The motivation for the children to give such unconditional obedience is, 'for this is pleasing in the Lord'. Elsewhere Paul uses the term εὐάρεστος to describe that which is pleasing or acceptable to God (cf. Rom 12.1–2, 14.18; 2 Cor 5.9; Eph 5.10; Phil 4.18). The term is also used in a variety of contexts outside the NT to designate that which was considered proper.[143] As Peter O'Brien points out, since Paul has the Christian family in view here, Paul can say κατὰ πάντα with the expectation that Christian parents would not demand their children to do something contrary to Christ's teaching.[144] Once again we find the phrase ἐν κυρίῳ while a few manuscripts have τῷ κυρίῳ.[145] Probably, this is an attempt to smooth out the awkward use of ἐν in v. 20. Here, as previously, the phrase probably means 'in the Christian community' and refers to the context where Christ's Lordship and grace is recognized and respected.[146]

Verse 21 begins with the words οἱ πατέρες which could mean simply 'parents' (cf. Heb 11.23 and the plural there), but more likely has fathers particularly in view.[147] If so, then we have a perfect parallelism between the subjects of the second member of each pair of exhortation – husbands, fathers, masters all refer to the same group. Children are called to obey both parents in all things (τοῖς γονεῦσιν, v. 20), but the father has a particular responsibility as head of the family not to provoke his children so as to break their spirits. While it is true in the case of the Roman *patria potestas* and apparently in some contexts in Hellenistic Judaism that the father had almost unlimited authority to do as he pleased with his children, here Paul is specifically limiting that authority and privilege.[148]

What conclusions may we draw from Col 3.18–21? First, we do not find here a total rejection of a patriarchal family structure, but we do find a modification and limitation of the husband/father authority structure and his rights as head of the household. Notably, the husband/father exhortations are not supported by specifically Christian motivational phrases such as ἐν κυρίῳ. Perhaps Paul felt that the church needed to know whether or not, in light of such pronouncements as Gal 3.28, subordination of wives and obedience of children was appropriate behavior in the Christian community. Paul affirms such behavior in a Christian context where Christ's Lordship is recognized and manifested. However, the exhortations to husbands/fathers serve to limit the exercise of authority and power of the head of the household and make clear that he too, equally with wives and children, has extensive obligations in his family. What we see is not a mere adoption, but a reformation of the general patriarchal structure of the family prevalent everywhere in that era. Further, in some cases we see an intensification of the demands placed on children and even on husbands/fathers in the OT and in Jewish contexts. In various ways, then, this Christian household table presents something somewhat different from what we find either in contemporary Judaism or in Hellenistic contexts. Being 'in Christ' requires a reforming of traditional social structures, not a mere reproduction or repudiation of them.[149]

2. The Ephesian *Haustafel* (5.21–33)

When we turn to Eph 5.21–33 we see similarities with and differences from Col 3.18ff.[150] First, the Ephesian *Haustafel* is much longer – some 324 words to only 117 in Colossians. They share some seventy words in common. Second, some 60% of the Ephesian *Haustafel* is devoted to the husband/wife tandem. Both Colossian and Ephesian household tables have the order of: address, wives, husbands, children, fathers, slaves, masters. Third, while both tables seem to be drawing on traditional material though giving it a Christian setting and orientation, this is even more evident in Ephesians.[151] In Ephesians, Christ is drawn upon as a paradigm for husbands (5.25, 29) and for masters (6.9), whereas this was at most implicit in the Colossians' usage of ἐν κυρίῳ. We find the use of the OT both explicitly and implicitly in Ephesians (cf. 5.28, 31 alluding to Lev 19.18, 34).[152] J. Paul Sampley also suggests we have several commonplace expressions such as 'no one hates his own flesh' (5.29).[153] Colossians, by contrast, seems to have only terse exhortations.

The use of traditional materials as well as contextualizing Christological phrases may suggest we are dealing with a pre-set piece of material. If so, then the material has been transformed significantly, for in various ways it manifests the same theme as the whole letter – the unity and union of all in Christ, as well as the union of Christ with His Church.[154] The absence of the verb from v. 22 might speak against this being a pre-set piece except that we have admitted already that there appears to have been some transformations and additions especially in vv. 26ff, and there is no reason why the author could not have exercised similar freedom in vv. 21–22.

Ephesians 5.21 has been seen as an introduction to and leitmotif for what follows in vv. 22–33.[155] Note also that v. 21 is transitional and the form of the verb ὑποτασσόμενοι links it with the participles and imperatives which precede it (λαλοῦντες, εὐχαριστοῦντες). Thus, if we have the insertion of traditional material beginning at v. 22, it has been carefully integrated into the letter as a whole.

At this point several preliminary remarks are in order to explain the limits of our discussion. First, in Eph 5.21–33 we have a comparison, not an identification, of two different kinds of relationships – husband and wife, and Christ and Church. Everything that is predicated of Christ and Church here, cannot also be predicated of husband and wife. There are, however, some points of similarity. That we are dealing with an analogy here is perhaps best shown from the fact that husband and wife are addressed as married persons, but Christ and the Church are described as bridegroom and bride, as betrothed ones preparing for the wedding and consecration of their relationship.[156] This means that it is unwise to press the analogy beyond clear points of contact – love of Christ and love of husband which entails self-giving and self-sacrifice; submission of wife and submission of Church; headship of husband and headship of Christ; provision and care for wife like Christ's provision and care for the Church. This means that the material in vv. 26a–27c, the description of Christ's sanctifying work for and effect on the Church, while very interesting, is not meant to be a description of the husband's role or effect on his spouse. The flow of thought is that while Paul starts with the husband–wife relationship, after the analogy is drawn he moves away from that relationship to reflect only on Christ and the Church, a major theme of Ephesians. This is especially the case in vv. 26a–27c, but we see it already in 23c. The husband is not called the savior of the wife; therefore, we will not deal with such verses as 23c and 26a–27c.

Third, the direction of influence between these two pairs, husband–wife and Christ–Church, is not one way. By this I mean that the language and imagery of betrothal in Paul's day affects how he describes the relationship between Christ and the Church. On the other hand, it is also true that Christ's action for the Church in history (cf. 25c) conditions how Paul describes the headship role, not only of Christ but also of the husband. Likewise, the submissive and reverential response of the Church to Christ conditions how Paul describes the wife's response to her husband. Paul is well aware of the grounding that human marriage has in the story of Adam and Eve (v. 31a), but he is more concerned here to model Christian marriage on the pattern of the relationship of Christ and the Church. This is Paul's deliberate attempt to reform the patriarchal structure of his day, a structure he inherited, adopted, and adapted. Para-doxically, however, the effect was also to ground that revised patriarchal structure involving the husband's headship in the eternal relationship between Christ and Church. This serves to give an ongoing and permanent theological rationale for the husband's head-ship and wife's submission. Yet, how Paul describes headship and the way he prefaces the whole section with remarks about mutual submission, so alters the usual thinking about husband–wife relationships as to make this a very new teaching indeed.

If, in Colossians, we saw the beginnings of an attempt to give a Christian definition of what the family structures ought to be in the Christian community, then here we see that attempt carried much further.[157] It is possible that J. M. Robinson is correct in saying there was a traditional association of ecstatic speech coupled with a call to women's submission.[158] However, this pattern is much more in evidence in 1 Corinthians 14 than here, and if the *Haustafel* begins at Eph 5.22, then this material was not originally joined with 5.18. In any case, 5.21 does not focus on women's submission and it, not 5.22, is the link with what precedes.

Eph 5.21 is an exhortation to 'submit to one another' addressed to all church members, male and female. ὑποτασσόμενοι is a participle used as an imperative, a practice which may go back to Jewish usage of the Hebrew participles in a context where positive and negatives rules were under discussion.[159] This verse, however, does not focus specifically on the relationship of husbands and wives, and so it would be wrong to say it calls for mutual submission of marital partners. Rather, it calls for mutual submission of all Christians to each other which includes marital partners. Ephesians 5.21 has been seen as a criticism of the traditional patriarchal household code.[160] There is some truth in this remark, but if 5.22ff. is an attempt to go on and explain in one crucial context (the physical family) how that mutual submission works itself out, then it must be noted that there is no abandoning of the language of headship in what follows, nor is there any attempt to deny a certain difference in the way submission and service are modeled and rendered by husband and wife. In short, Eph 5.21 does not lead the author to speak of interchangeable roles. There is a mutuality of submission, but this works itself out in different ways involving an ordering of relationships, and exhortations according to gender. Ephesians 5.22ff. *qualifies* and explains the transitional remark.

The phrase ἐν φόβῳ Χριστοῦ in 5.21 bears witness to what we have just concluded because it is applied specifically to the wife in the *Haustafel* itself at 5.22 – γυνὴ ἵνα φοβῆται τὸν ἄνδρα (cf. 6.5 of slaves). If 2 Cor 5.11 is compared to Eph 5.21, it suggests that what is meant is a 'fear of the Lord', in view of the fact that a Christian's present conduct will come under the review of Christ when He sits on the judgment seat.[161] Eschatological sanctions for particular ethical behavior are common in Paul (cf. 1 Corinthians 7) and here we may have another example of it. We must conclude, then, that 5.21 is a general remark which, perhaps because of the use of ὑποτάσσω, triggers in the author's mind a desire to present the *Haustafel* and so explain how mutual submission affects physical family relationships.

Ephesians 5.22a has no verb – it is assumed from 5.21. The ellipsis implies that whatever the verb meant in v.21, it means the same in v.22. As in Col 3.18ff., the subordinate member of the pair is addressed first and called upon to be subordinating herself (middle passive participle) to her own partner.[162] The ἰδίοις is important in three regards: (1) it indicates that husbands and wives are in view here, not merely men and women; (2) it indicates that the subject here is family behavior, not the submission of men and women in worship or women to male church leaders in general; (3) it implies an endorsement of monogamy, something which is explicit in 1 Corinthians 7 and will become more explicit in this text when Gen 2.24 is quoted (γυναῖκα αὐτοῦ).

ὡς τῷ κυρίῳ is different enough from the motivational phrase in Col 3.18 to suggest that we have a variation pointing to common authorship of Colossians and Ephesians, but not literary dependency.[163] The textual problem involves various attempts to insert the verb ὑποτάσσω into 5.22, attempts which are probably trying to avoid an incomplete sentence here.[164] How we should interpret ὡς τῷ κυρίῳ depends on whether this phrase is meant to be preparatory for what follows or simply goes with what precedes. If the latter is the case, then it might mean 'be subordinating yourself to your own husbands as to a lord.' 1 Peter 3.6 might seem to give some support to this interpretation. Against this, however, we would expect to find ὡς τοῖς κυρίοις if that was meant here.[165] Accordingly, the Lord Christ seems to be in view here. This, however, raises the question as to whether or not husbands are to be treated as the Lord is treated by the wife. This is unlikely not least because only Christ is said to be the savior, and all of this behavior is inculcated out of a 'reverence for Christ'. Probably what is meant is that the subordination of the wife to the husband is *like* that she offers to the Lord, though on a lesser and completely human plane. Verse 24b may make more explicit what is meant – the wife is to submit to her husband in all things (ἐν παντί), just as she submits to Christ in all things. Obviously, this unconditional submission hinges on there being a Christian context. Paul is not dealing here with couples of mixed religion, nor does he envision the possibility that even the Christian husband might ask something which would not be in accord with Christian love, faith, or ethics. Paul is dealing in general terms. Even though we get a clearer picture as to what submission amounts to and why it is enjoined, we are still not told what it entails on a day-to-day basis, nor is a specific division of labor explained. We must remember that the comparison of husbands to Christ, and wives to Church, is in terms of similarity in position (or role) and action, not similarity of nature. Notice that the point of comparison lies either in a role described by a noun used metaphorically (head), a role one can assume only in relation to others, or by an action (verb), loving or submitting. The comparison then is not ontological, but speaks of relationships and activities.

Before examining v. 23a, note that here, as in Col 3.18ff, both husbands and wives are addressed as persons responsible for their own conduct. E. Kähler has stressed rightly that Paul nowhere exhorts the husband to subject the wife or even order her to submit, nor is the wife told to urge her husband to be her head. Each party is addressed *directly*. This suggests that Paul expects compliance to be voluntary in the sense that the onus is on the wife to assume a subordinate position, just as the onus is on the husband to assume the role of headship. The duties are expected to be undertaken without compulsion, but this does not mean that our author thought them to be optional.[166]

The crucial term in v. 23a is κεφαλή, a term found in Eph 1.22–23, 4.15 predicated of Christ, and elsewhere in the Pauline corpus predicated of both Christ and the husband (or man?, cf. 1 Cor 11.3). There is evidence that the term can mean 'source', as in the source of a river, and this may well be its meaning in 1 Cor 11.3.[167] A river is not a person, however, and in both Ephesians 5 and 1 Corinthians 11 the subjects are persons. In both cases κεφαλή is a term used to speak of a relationship. Indeed, it can be argued that the term is the counterpoint to the use of ὑποτάσσω of wives and of the Church. The point of using κεφαλή at least in Ephesians 5 would seem to be one's role and or behavior in an ongoing relationship. The question of origins is not at issue here. There is also evidence that Aristotle spoke of the head of the household,[168] which seems closer to the usage in the household table in Ephesians 5. Apparently, there is no need to revise Dibelius' judgment that 'we cannot say from where the idea stems that the husband is the woman's head'.[169] However, there is room for two possible conjectures: (1) either Paul derived it from the broader use of the term to speak of the head of the household, or (2) the term is applied to the husband as a result of its use of Christ and the analogy between Christ and husband. This last conjecture may be supported by the fact that Paul never speaks of the husband's headship except in a context where he also mentions Christ's headship (cf. Eph 5.23ff.; 1 Cor 11.3ff.). If this second conjecture has some merit, then it may be worthwhile to add that κεφαλή in Eph 1.22–23 is headship *over* (ὑπέρ) all things, while at 4.15 it is part of the head/body metaphor. In Ephesians 5 the point seems to be Christ's headship over the Church, His Body, though ὑπέρ is not used.[170] Note that Christ's saving activity for the Church immediately follows the mention of His headship, and this is followed by a mention of the submission of the Church. This strongly suggests that 'head' in Christ's case speaks of authority and power over the Church to which the Church is to respond by submission. The ὡς in v. 23 suggests an analogous view of the husband's headship – the wife, like the Church,[171] is called to subordinate herself in all things (in v. 24b) to her head. When Paul wishes to talk about roles or functions, he speaks of headship and submission. When he wants to talk about spiritual union between Christ and Church, or husband and wife, he speaks of head and body (cf. 4.15).

The imagery itself does not indicate how this headship (and the authority it implies) is to be exercised. What we learn from the analogy beginning in v. 25 is that headship means, as Barth says, for the husband 'to go ahead' and take the initiative in active loving and self-sacrificial serving as Christ has done for the Church.[172] It would seem that head refers to head servant, and we are reminded of the definition of 'the one who would be greatest' in the Gospel tradition (Luke 22.25ff.).

We move now to vv. 28ff. Verse 28 is introduced by the comparative mechanism – οὕτως ὀφείλουσιν – which is followed in the best manuscripts by καί which probably means 'also'.[173] Thus, we translate, 'in the same manner also'.[174] This means that the οὕτως refers back to the example of Christ's love for the Church. The husband's duty to love his wife is compared with Christ's love for the Church, not his own natural love for his own body.[175] The wife is to be considered and loved as being his own σῶμα (though σάρξ is substituted at v. 29). At first it would appear that Paul has a rather degrading view of the wife – she is merely the husband's 'body'. However, as Sampley rightly points out, vv. 28–29 must be read in light of the quotation of Lev 2.24 in v. 31. Indeed, the change to σάρξ in v. 29 is likely under the influence of the quote in v. 31. The point is the 'organic' unity between husband and wife – they are σάρκα μίαν.[176] Further, as v. 33 makes clear, what Paul has in mind is loving the wife ὡς ἑαυτόν, not merely as a part of one's self (in particular, the physical part). Verses 28–30 are dealing with imagery reflecting the one-flesh union. They are not a comment on a woman's nature or purpose. The wife is to be loved and cherished as one's nearest neighbor, indeed as one's very self.[177] Verse 29 exhorts the husband to feed and care for his 'other self'.

There is no question but that Paul interpreted Gen 2.24 to refer to some sort of organic (or at least spiritual) union of husband and wife. Indeed, in 1 Cor 6.16 he is able to use the text to talk about the 'one-flesh union' created when one has intercourse with a prostitute. For Paul, sexual intercourse is no mere momentary physical pleasure but an act which creates a bond between two people. In fact, it appears that in the case of the Christian husband and wife we are talking about a bond indissoluble except by death (cf. Rom 7.1ff.; 1 Cor 7.10, 11).[178] Though we cannot be certain, it may be that Paul felt free to draw an analogy between husband and wife, and Christ and Church, precisely because he assumed that both relationships were intended to be irrevocable and indissoluble during this life. It may also be the case that Paul would only use the head and body language of those who have an 'organic' or spiritual bond binding them together as one. If so, then it may help explain some of the difficulties of 1 Cor 11.3ff.[179]

What mystery is Paul referring to in v. 32? Is it the hidden meaning of the text,[180] or the mystery of Christian marriage,[181] or the mystery of Christ's relationship with the Church,[182] or the mystery of the analogy between the relationships of Christ and Church and husband and wife?[183] Paul tells us that he is speaking about Christ and the Church.[184] Verse 33 serves as a return to the initial topic of discussion – husband and wife – by way of contrast with what has been said in v. 32. In any event, whether the reference is to Christ and the Church, or the mystery has to do with the text, Paul is probably not suggesting that marriage is a sacrament here. Indeed, it may be even more probable that the mystery he is awed by is the 'one-flesh union' which exists between husband and wife and, by analogy in a transferred sense, between Christ and His Church.[185] It is the latter union that Paul mainly wishes to speak to in this passage (and epistle). Nevertheless, in v. 33 he will return one final time to speak of human relationships. It is, after all, probably the real union between Christ and the Church, and between husband and wife, that leads to Paul's use of head and body language applied to the respective members of both pairs. Head and body is the language of 'organic unity'.[186]

This being so, the great mystery is likely to be the union which makes that unity possible, whether oneness of husband and wife, or Christ and Church.

πλήν in v. 33 should be seen as resumptive of the original topic after a digression, and so we translate: 'In any case[187] individually each one of you must love his wife as himself.' We have here a strong imperative – ἀγαπάτω.[188] Paul wishes to stress the husband's responsibility to love. That Paul can command love suggests that he is talking about loving actions, not feelings, and particularly self-sacrificial actions analogous to Christ's actions for the Church. Actions can be commanded; feelings cannot. By contrast, the wife is called upon ἵνα φοβῆται τὸν ἄνδρα. This is a less strong exhortation and probably means something like 'may she fear the husband'.[189] The point is not that the wife should cower, or be afraid of her husband, but that she should respect him. Kähler suggests that what is meant is that she should respect his God-given position as head. The respect given is due to his headship, not due to his performance or circumstances. It is not conditional, any more than her reverence for Christ depends on performance or circumstances.[190] Perhaps Barth best sums up the matter when he says,

> She can have many *good* reasons to fear her husband, and can fear him in a way that does not degrade her in her own or in his eyes ... Instead of shaping and changing him after her heart's desire, she will feel thoroughly changed by him. Instead of bringing him under control, she ... awaits her lover's coming and the ever-new experience of his love with fear and trembling. A woman moved by *this* 'fear' will by no means seek to make herself autonomous in relation to him who loves her and she will receive him as one who in his own imperfect way reminds her of the true head of all the world, the church, her lover and herself: Jesus Christ.[191]

C. Incidental Pauline references to women's roles in marriage and the family

When the subjects of Paul's views of marriage and a woman's roles in the family have arisen, discussion has rightly focused on such passages as 1 Corinthians 7 and Ephesians 5. There are, however, passages in the Pauline corpus (Rom 7.1–3; 1 Thess 4.3–8; 2 Cor 6.14–7.1; Eph 6.1–4 [Col 3.20–21]) where these matters are discussed incidentally or mentioned in the course of dealing with another subject.

1. Exclusive monogamy and the marital bond (Rom 7.1–3)

It is not Paul's purpose at this point to discourse on women or marriage. Nevertheless, Paul's argument in these verses would have no force if the illustration in vv. 2–3 was not presumed by the Apostle to represent something that was true about at least some married women in first-century settings.

Romans 7 begins a new paragraph in Paul's discussion, though it has connections with chapter 6.[192] Here, however, the focus is on a Christian's relationship to the law now that he or she is part of the body of Christ (cf. v. 4). To what law is Paul referring? Is γινώσκουσιν γὰρ νόμον λαλῶ to be taken seriously? When Paul says 'surely you know', he may mean no more than 'surely, you ought to know'.[193] This being so, it is not necessary to think that the law Paul is speaking of is Roman law. Were that the case, then the illustration in vv. 2–3 would be ill-chosen, for a wife was not irrevocably bound to her husband for a lifetime, according to Roman law in Paul's day.[194] If Paul's example in vv. 2–3 is drawn from Mosaic law,[195] and Paul goes on in v. 4 to argue that the Christian has died to this law, then the illustration could not be presumed to be an accurate description of the status of a Christian's wife. It certainly seems that Paul intends to draw on an example that he and his audience would both accept as true, and which would confirm Paul's argument about the law. Perhaps the simplest way out of this dilemma is to recognize that Paul is drawing on a legal principle which, while likely Mosaic in origin, was accepted as valid by the Christian community (or at least by the Apostle; cf. vv. 1–2 and 1 Cor 7.39).[196]

The second half of v. 1 states the principle, an aspect of which will be illustrated in vv. 2–3, and applied in v. 4 as Paul draws his conclusion from the principle. It is unlikely that Paul intends vv. 2–3 to be an allegory or parable in preparation for v. 4. The main reason this is sometimes suggested is because of the similarity between γένηται ἀνδρὶ ἑτέρῳ (and also γενομένην ἀνδρὶ ἑτέρῳ) in v. 3, and τὸ γενέσθαι ὑμᾶς ἑτέρῳ in v. 4.[197] W. G. Kümmel may be right, however, that γενέσθαι with the dative in v. 4 simply means 'belong to', and thus is not evidence of a marriage image here.[198] Further, in the illustration, the first husband is not, nor does he represent, the law, though the law gives him a right to his wife's fidelity while he and his wife live. It is he, not the law or his wife, who dies and the wife who is thereby freed. The wife is not the Christian, nor the soul. She does not die to the law, though by her husband's death she is no longer under its authority so far as the marriage law is concerned.[199] Even if we do have an example in v. 4 of Paul using the marriage imagery of Christ and the Church,[200] this is best explained not by seeing an allegory in vv. 2–3, but by suggesting that the marriage illustration in vv. 2–3 led Paul to speak of Christ and His Body using similar language.[201]

The principle stated in v.1b is that the law governs or has legal validity over a person only as long as he or she lives.[202] This is true not only of the one who has died, but also of the surviving partner if the law in view is dealing with a relationship between two parties. Paul states in v. 2 that a woman under the authority of a husband is bound by law to her *living* husband.[203] The word ὕπανδρος is found nowhere else in the NT. While it can simply mean 'married', it probably means 'under the authority of a husband' because Paul is presenting an example whereby a woman is under the authority of the law, and because it appears that Paul has Num 5.20–29 (LXX) in view here where the word is used and where the matter of a wife's faithfulness or her being labeled an adulteress also comes up.[204] If the husband dies, however, then she is no longer under, indeed she is released from, the law concerning the husband and his rights.[205] It becomes apparent from this that ὕπανδρος is used to describe the wife's legal position and does not refer to her voluntary yielding to her husband. Paul, for the sake of illustration, speaks only of the obligation of the wife (a factor which may favor seeing this as an illustration drawn from Mosaic law), but as can be seen in 1 Corinthians 7 (cf. Ephesians 5), this does not mean Paul thought the husband did not have the same obligation to be faithful. Still, we have here the expectation that the wife will be committed to exclusive monogamy. She will be bound to her living husband until death parts them. Implied also is that only death dissolves this marital bond, which comports with Paul's teaching in 1 Corinthians 7 and Jesus' teaching.[206]

Because what Paul has said in v. 2 is true, he can draw the consequences in v. 3 — 'so then if the wife consorts with another man while her husband is living, she shall be called an adulteress'.[207] It is possible that γένηται ἀνδρί has the sense 'becomes the wife of' or 'becomes the possession of',[208] but probably Paul is dealing with a case of adultery (not bigamy).[209] Paul proceeds in v. 3b to state the same thing he said in v. 2b — if the husband is dead, she is free from the law. Thus, she is not an adulteress, even if associating with or becoming the wife of another man.[210] Paul recognizes the widow's right to associate with and even marry another man (so 1 Cor 7.39), but the way he phrases this (τοῦ μὴ εἶναι αὐτὴν μοιχαλίδα γενομένην ἀνδρὶ ἑτέρῳ) may indicate that in his view this was allowed, though perhaps not encouraged or preferred. If this is the nuance of 3b, then we have similar views to those expressed by Paul in 1 Cor 7.39–40.[211]

Romans 7.1–3, while brief and complicated by several factors, gives us evidence about Paul's view of a woman's position in marriage. Legally, she is under her husband's authority and should submit to the legal principle that she is bound to her husband as long as he is living. Because the marital bond is only dissolved by the death of one or both partners, a woman who associates with another man while still having a living husband is an adulteress. She has violated the law, though her act has not dissolved the bond. Indeed, that she is an adulteress implies that the first relationship is ongoing. Once the first bond is dissolved by death, she is free not only from the obligation to be faithful to her former husband but also to associate with another man. Verse 3b thus states her rights, while v. 2 focuses on the husband's rights. Finally, Paul envisions marriage as an institution in this life (and by implication not afterwards). He envisions a permanent and ongoing union, as long as both partners live, which entails a wife being bound exclusively to her living husband, being under his authority legally, and having no extra-marital sexual relationships.

2. ἑαυτοῦ σκεῦος κτᾶσθαι (1 Thess 4.3–8)

In 1 Thess 4.3–8, Paul begins to address the Thessalonians on particular ethical issues. Paul's concern is that they conduct themselves in a sanctified manner in their personal relationships (v. 3).[212] The question is, what sort of relationships are we talking about — the relation of a man toward his own body or toward his neighbor's wife? It has been suggested that v. 6 refers to a man's business relations with his 'brother'.[213] We can reject this suggestion for the following reasons. First, while πρᾶγμα can refer to business matters when found in the plural, there is no evidence of this meaning in the singular.[214] We have here ἐν τῷ πράγματι ('in the matter presently under discussion'). We cannot translate here 'in any matter'.[215] Second, a discussion of business ethics breaks in abruptly when what precedes is manifestly about sexual conduct and what follows points in the same direction. In Paul, ἀκαθαρσίᾳ frequently refers to sexual impurity.[216] Third, τὸ μὴ in v. 6 need not indicate a new subject at this point. It is possible that τό is used here in the sense of ὥστε (cf. 3.3, Phil 4.10) to express result or consequence.[217] Thus, it is more probable that the subject of v. 6, like that of vv. 3–5 and 7–9, is sexual ethics.

Our second and more vexing problem involves determining the meaning of τὸ ἑαυτοῦ σκεῦος κτᾶσθαι for it is possible that v. 4 is referring not to the relationship of husband and wife, but to that of a man to his own body. Literally, the word σκεῦος means 'vessel' and can be used both literally of things and metaphorically of persons.[218] It is not what σκεῦος denotes according to its usual lexical meaning, but what it connotes in this context that is at issue. Commentators have been divided throughout church history as to whether σκεῦος here refers to the human body or to a man's wife.[219] In favor of the former view, the following points are advanced. (1) The ἕκαστον ὑμῶν in v. 4 refers to all those whom Paul is addressing, or at least all the men including the unmarried.[220] (2) Our passage has notable parallels of language and thought with 1 Cor 6.12–20 where the subject is clearly the believer's body.[221] (3) In 2 Cor 4.7, Paul clearly uses σκεῦος to mean body. (4) If Paul meant wife he would seem to have a low sensual view of the marriage relation and a low view of a woman's position in marriage.[222] (5) κτᾶσθαι need not mean 'acquire' for there is some evidence that it can have the force of κεκτῆσθαι and mean 'possess' or possibly 'gain (mastery over)'.[223] (6) While the Greeks might be accused of having a low view of the human body, Paul believed in honoring and caring for the body (cf. 1 Cor 6.12–20; Eph 5.29).

Before raising objections to these points, perhaps it would be best to summarize the arguments in favor of the 'wife' view. (1) In 1 Pet 3.7 σκεῦος is clearly used of the wife. This argument has even more force if it is true either that Silvanus is the amanuensis of both 1 Thessalonians (cf. 1.1) and 1 Peter (cf. 5.12), or that 1 Peter is in literary dependence on parts of the Pauline corpus and, in particular, this piece of parenthesis in 1 Thess 4.3–8. If there is a literary relationship between 1 Thess 4.3–8 and 1 Pet 3.1–7, then we have clear evidence that some early Christian(s) understood Paul to mean 'wife' by σκεῦος in 1 Thessalonians 4.[224] (2) The normal meaning of κτᾶσθαι is 'acquire' and if it means that here, then the interpretation of σκεῦος as 'body' becomes highly improbable if not impossible. (3) There are certain parallels between 1 Corinthians 7 and 1 Thess 4.3–8 which would lead one to suspect that, like 1 Corinthians 7, 1 Thess 4.3–8 is about those who are or ought to be married.[225] (4) κεκτῆσθαι is used of marrying a wife (LXX, cf. Ruth 4.10; Eccles 36.24).[226] (5) πλεονεκτεῖν could be alluding to a man defrauding his 'brother' by adultery, but if 'the matter' at hand is homosexual sin (i.e., how one behaves with one's body in relation to one's 'brother') then it is hard to see how the term applies. (6) There are rabbinic parallels to our passage where the wife is referred to as a husband's vessel.[227]

Against the arguments advanced in favor of the 'body' view the following may be said. Point (1) has no force in light of Paul's use of ἕκαστος in 1 Cor 7.2 (cf. Eph 5.33). In each of these three cases the context limits the meaning of ἕκαστος to the men in Paul's audience and in any case Paul's point in 1 Thess 4.4 may simply be that 'each of the men knew how to'[228] do as Paul advises (cf. v. 6b), even if for some the advice no longer or never will or does not yet apply. While there are similarities between 1 Cor 6.12–20 and our text, these are mainly a result of both texts dealing with sexual relationships, not necessarily that both are dealing with the same sexual problems. One can point out parallels between our text and the discussion of marriage in 1 Corinthians 7. In neither case do the parallels really settle the matter, and there remains the unexplained problem of why Paul uses σῶμα in 1 Corinthians 6 but not in 1 Thess 4.4 if both are dealing with exactly the same matter.[229] The issue in 2 Cor 4.7 is not sexual and the point is to show the frailty of humanity (in contrast to God's power). It is a text which has more in common with Rom 9.21–23 than with 1 Thess 3.8. σκεῦος, when used by Paul of both male and female human beings, is not degrading in Romans 9 (noting that he is not likely to be referring just to physical bodies in this text), and thus there is no reason to see it as degrading in 1 Thessalonians 4 if applied to wives. Those who argue that the reference to the wife as the 'weaker vessel' in 1 Peter 3 is degrading, usually overlook that by implication the husband is also referred to as a vessel. In any case, as Lightfoot points out, the fact that Paul goes on to say ἐν ἁγιασμῷ ... must surely correct, if not positively rule out, any possible negative connotation implied by σκεῦος.[230] Paul's desire is that this σκεῦος be honored, not dishonored and degraded.

In rebuttal to point (5), while it may be granted that κτᾶσθαι can sometimes have the force of the perfect ('possess'), I can find no other example where the translation 'gain mastery (or control) over' is suitable. Indeed, such a translation is not the same thing as gaining, keeping, or possessing. The idea of mastery or control must be introduced into the text to make sense of it.[231] As to point (6), while it is certainly true that Paul cannot be accused of having a low view of the human body (cf. 1 Corinthians 6 and 15), this does not prove that this is Paul's subject in 1 Thess 4.3–8. One might suggest that Paul would not use σκεῦος in the process of discussing the honoring of the human body, because to a predominantly Gentile audience this would conjure up the Greek notion of the body as the container or prison of the soul – a view not held by Paul.[232] If, however, Paul is using the term metaphorically of the wife in order perhaps to focus discreetly and somewhat euphemistically on her role in relation to her husband in marital intercourse, then there is no negative connotation implied.[233]

The objections which may be raised against seeing σκεῦος as alluding to the wife are far less formidable than those discussed above against σκεῦος being a reference to the human body. In content and context, 1 Pet 3.7 is close to our text, though not a perfect parallel. Further, it is a clear example where the term σκεῦος is used of a wife in the midst of a sentence encouraging husbands to honor (τιμήν) their wives.[234] If κτᾶσθαι means 'possess' or 'keep', having durative force, then this still fits with the 'wife = σκεῦος' view. Indeed, it is perhaps preferable for it goes more naturally with v. 5. Paul then would not be warning against marrying on the basis of the 'passion of desire' but against relating to one's wife in a lustful manner as if she could be treated merely as a sex object or a piece of property ('just as the pagans do who do not know God').[235] On the other hand, the LXX parallels favor the view that κτᾶσθαι means 'acquire' or 'marry'. Finally, the view that σκεῦος alludes to the wife makes the best sense in the context of the whole argument of vv. 3–8. Paul, after stating the general principle that ὁ ἁγιασμὸς ὑμῶν involves abstaining from sexual immorality (v. 3b), then proceeds to particularize how this is implemented in a positive way (vv. 4–5 – 'You know how to possess your own wife in a sanctified manner and in honor; not in the passion of desire') and then in a negative way ('so that you do not transgress against or defraud your brother in this matter'). He enforces this appeal with a reference to his own previous exhortations about the Lord as a punisher of sins (v. 6b); implies that sexual immorality can happen in marriage if one possesses his wife in the passion of lust; reminds them that God's call was not for impurity but for holiness (v. 7); and finally enforces this appeal by reference to God's Spirit which is holy and has been given to the Thessalonians (v. 8).

Living a sanctified life involves abstaining from any sort of sexual immorality,[236] whether this involves the mistreatment of a wife or the defrauding of a Christian brother through an adulterous relationship.[237] Paul warns the *men* in his audience that misconduct in marriage is just as much a sin as the offense of adultery. If v. 4 is referring to marrying, rather than misconduct in marriage, then Paul would be warning against taking a woman as one's wife on the basis of the wrong motives − satisfaction of lustful passions.[238] More likely it refers to one's behavior in marriage.

From what follows in v. 5 it is clear that by holiness and honor Paul means that the wife is to be treated as an end in herself, not as a means to satisfy lustful ends. If J. B. Lightfoot is right about the τὸ in v. 6a ('so that'), then Paul does see one purpose of marriage as being the prevention of adultery (cf. 1 Cor 7.2−5). It also indicates that Paul saw marital intercourse as the proper alternative to such sins, and thus v. 4 intimates that marital intercourse is not only a means of avoiding impurity (v. 7) but, more positively, something which can be done ἐν ἁγιασμῷ καὶ τιμῇ. Though not stated, it is implied that Paul saw marital relations as a positive good when performed in the context of honoring the marriage partner and relating to her in a sanctified manner.[239] Far from something which works against God's will, intercourse is seen as a means to that will and fully compatible with the process of sanctification.

Paul's stress on sexual matters is not a result of his own personal preoccupation, but a product of his knowledge of how acceptable all sorts of sexual aberrations were in the Gentile world.[240] His warning against adultery is understandable not only in light of the permissive Gentile environment, but also because Thessalonica was a port city like Corinth. Further, in a permissive society it is easy to see how the intimate fellowship of early Christians who met in the confines of homes, shared in the Lord's Supper, greeting each other with a holy kiss, and allowed men and women to participate in all these activities, *could* lead to an intimacy of the wrong sort between certain members of the Christian family.[241]

Paul's instructions amount to a severe curtailment of a man's sexual freedom and thus would likely serve to improve a woman's position and security in marriage. Her position is further aided by Paul's statement that a wife is to be possessed (or acquired) not as a tool of sexual self-gratification (v. 5), but in an honorable and sanctified manner. She is not to be treated as less than a person who deserves respect and morally correct treatment. It is just as wrong to abuse one's own wife in the passion of one's lustful desires as it is to abuse a brother's wife. On the other hand, sanctified behavior in one's marital relations is a proper way of avoiding the sin or temptation to commit adultery. When the τὸ ἑαυτοῦ of v. 4 is coupled with the advice in v. 6, it is clear that Paul is again advocating exclusive monogamy. Each should have his own wife and should not break into someone else's marriage. God has not called Christians for sexual impurity, but into sanctification.[242] Thus, in a sense Paul is advocating holy wedlock to the exclusion of all other forms of sexual relations.[243] Finally, we may note that this is probably the earliest evidence we have of Paul's views on marriage and sexual relations. That they are consistent with what we find in 1 Corinthians 7 (especially vv. 1–5) and other Pauline statements (cf. Rom 7.1–3, Eph 5.21–33) leads one to suspect that Paul had formed his views on this subject at an early date, not in reaction to any particular situation (such as that at Corinth) but as a result of his Christian principles – instructions he took to be God-given (1 Thess 4.8) and in some cases Christ-spoken (cf. 1 Cor 7.10).

3. Mixed marriages? (2 Cor 6.14–7.1)

We will only deal briefly with 2 Cor 6.14–7.1 as it may be a non-Pauline or even anti-Pauline interpolation,[244] and even if it is Pauline, it only confirms a principle we have already seen Paul draw in our discussion of 1 Corinthians 7. If our passage is dealing with only certain sorts of associations between believers and unbelievers, then it is reasonable to first ask whether or not marriage is one of these associations.

It cannot be assumed that marriage is necessarily in view in 2 Cor 6.14–7.1 since ἑτεροζυγοῦντες is used metaphorically like many other terms in this passage, and since it is possible that not Lev 19.19a, but Deut 22.10, is in the background.[245] Further, Paul clearly allows religiously mixed marriages (1 Corinthians 7), and far from seeing such an association as immoral or defiling, claims that the believing partner in some sense sanctifies the unbelieving partner. Since this is a theological principle, Paul is not basing his advice in 1 Cor

7.12–16 on purely pragmatic considerations, and thus it seems unlikely that Paul would later give contradictory advice to a congregation (part of which was already predisposed to separation from unbelieving partners), or change his mind on such an important subject. This means that either 2 Cor 6.14 probably does *not* refer to marriage relations at all (possibly only alluding to immoral or idolatrous associations),[246] or γίνεσθε is to be translated 'become' and refers only to entering into a new marriage with an unbeliever.[247] Paul believes that a Christian can only be equally yoked (cf. Phil 4.3 – σύζυγε)[248] with Christians; thus here he would be advising against becoming unequally yoked with an unbeliever in marriage, or possibly in some other form of association. Thus, if our text says anything about Paul's view of marriage between believer and unbeliever, then it is little different from the advice given in 1 Cor 7.39 where Paul advises Christian widows only to remarry in the Lord (ἐν κυρίῳ). It does bear witness, however, to the fact that Paul recognized, as did at least some of the Corinthians (cf. 1 Cor 7.12–16), that there was a certain tension or inequality that existed between the partners of a religiously mixed marriage. Despite that, Paul does not counsel the believer to separate or divorce the unbelieving partner, but he does allow believers to let the unbelieving partner do so. This latter part bears witness to Paul's recognition of the difference between Christian and mixed couples, and it is perhaps Paul's way of helping Christians out from under an unequal yoke without violating Christian principles.[249]

4. 'Honor your father and mother' (Eph 6.1–4, Col 3.20–21)

As we conclude our survey of texts that tell us about Paul's views on the role of women in the family, we turn briefly to the *Haustafel* instructions to parents and children. In both Eph 6.1 and Col 3.20 the subordinate member of the pair is addressed first (in this case, children; cf. Eph 5.22, Col 3.18), but Paul, unlike many non-biblical 'duty' lists, also goes on to address the superordinate member. One must say member, rather than members, because in both Eph 6.4 and Col 3.21 it is only the fathers who are addressed. This slight incongruity is not entirely surprising for it reflects Paul's view that the father alone is the head of the household and that he is especially or ultimately responsible for the children's discipline and instruction in the Lord.[250] At the same time, however, children are called to be equally obedient to both parents.[251] In Eph 6.2 we have a free quotation of the OT injunction to honor father and mother.[252] That Paul does not qualify this remark probably indicates that he, unlike some rabbis, thought that father and mother were to be honored equally by their children. Thus, we have an indication of what can also be noted in Eph 5.21–33 (Col 3.18–19) – Paul affirms the equality of husband and wife with each other and in relation to other members of the household. This does not, however, preclude or contradict Paul's principle of the husband's unique headship over the wife, or the fact that he has special responsibility for his children and slaves as head of his household. Equality of husband and wife, and a certain order in the family structure, are both affirmed in one and the same breath. It is significant that the power and authority of the father over his children is defined and delimited according to Christian principles (cf. Eph 6.4 – καὶ νουθεσία κυρίου), just as the children's obedience is so qualified (Eph 6.1, ἐν κυρίῳ;[253] Col 3.20, τοῦτο γὰρ εὐάρεστόν ἐστιν ἐν κυρίῳ).

5. Conclusions

If it is true that what someone says in passing is often as revealing of a person's true views as what he says explicitly, then there is much to be learned from the incidental passages we have just examined. In Rom 7.1–3 Paul is clearly addressing Christians, and it is a fair inference that he only has interrelationships between Christians in view, even though he may be drawing on a principle from Mosaic law. If this is so, then we may draw the following conclusions.

First, Paul sees marriage as a relationship that *only* exists while both Christian partners live, and *always* exists while they live. Second, apparently, he believes that nothing short of death dissolves the marital bond, for a person who engages in relationships with another or others is committing adultery if the partner still lives. While Paul only deals with married women in vv. 1–2, it is unlikely that Paul thought that these conditions did not also apply to men. Third, the word ὕπανδρος is used to describe the woman's legal position. It is probably pushing the term too far to try and deduce whether or not Paul's use of this term implies that he thought the Christian wife was subservient to the husband in marriage. Fourth, the way the end of v. 3 is phrased may imply that Paul allows remarriage but does not encourage or prefer it (cf. 1 Cor 7.39–40). There is nothing here that does not comport with Paul's teaching elsewhere on this subject.

If 1 Thess 4.3–8 is dealing with conduct toward a wife, or the ways and motives for gaining a wife, then it reveals several key insights into Paul's thoughts on women and their marital roles. Clearly, Paul believes in exclusive monogamy (v. 4). He also believes that the basis for marrying or relating to a marital partner should not be 'the passion of lust'. There is to be something distinctly different about Christian marriage; namely, it is to be holy. Partners are to be chosen or related to not merely as sex objects but as sexual persons. Paul is concerned to limit Christian men in their sexual activity to the context of marriage. A by-product of this teaching is a greater security for the woman in the marital relationship. Equally significant is the fact that Paul does not see marrying or marriage as incompatible with holiness or the process of sanctification. There is no evidence of the view that marriage is a necessary evil or merely a *remedium concupiscentiae* here. Marriage is a means of avoiding impurity, but it is also a means of holy relating which is a positive good. Paul makes clear that one's sexual and spiritual identities and orientations are not unrelated but impinge on each other. If Paul is referring to an existing marriage, it is important to note that he is counselling against sexual abuse of the wife.

If 2 Cor 6.14–7.1 is dealing with mixed marriages, then Paul's advice is *not* that Christians should never associate with non-Christians, but rather that it is ill-advised for Christians to enter into marriage with them. This advice varies little from what we find in 1 Cor 7.39. Ephesians 6.1–4 (Col 3.20–21), if it is Pauline, probably reflects Paul's patriarchal views about the structure of the family. Notably, however, the wife is to be honored by the children equally with her husband, and in view of the fact that Paul exhorts husbands in this passage, it appears he is going beyond some traditional household tables to stress the Christian responsibility *husbands* have for their children.

In the end, what we see is evidence that corroborates and expands upon some of the main points of Paul's teaching in 1 Corinthians 7 (cf. Ephesians 5). Paul appears to be adopting certain traditional norms and a traditional family structure, but adapting such institutions to suit the higher standards of Christian faithfulness, lifelong commitment, and sanctified interrelating he sees as mandatory for Christians. The net result would seem to have been more security for Christian women in marriage due to the restraint of male freedom in sexual relating, but also less freedom to change partners as was allowed in Jewish, Greek, and Roman contexts in the first century.

Paul's insistence on exclusive monogamy finds its authority and possibly its source in the teachings of Jesus (cf. Mark 10 and 12, and parallels).

D. Conclusions

Our study of Paul's views of a woman's status and roles in the physical family leads us to see that Paul does not fit neatly into either the category of male chauvinist or feminist. Nor may it be argued that he is some amalgam of the two extremes. Paul's views are at one and the same time egalitarian and, in a limited sense, patriarchal. His views are grounded in and grow out of his Christian principles. The cumulative effect of Paul's teaching on marriage was that women were given greater security in marriage and greater freedom to choose whether or not they would assume the roles of wife and mother. These effects result from Paul's views that the marital bond is not dissoluble by anything but death (Rom 7.1–3); that exclusive monogamy is the proper Christian practice (1 Cor 7.2; Eph 5.22, 24, 28, 29). His own personal preference for the single life and encouragement of other Christians to remain single (cf. 1 Cor 7.7–8, 40) would allow unmarried or formerly married women to devote themselves to the things of the Lord and His community (cf. 1 Cor 7.32–35).

Paul's teaching addressed to married women is striking in many regards. He treats wives equally with husbands as responsible human beings who deserve to be addressed, exhorted, and encouraged as full members of the Christian community. In both 1 Corinthians 7 and Ephesians 5 Paul stresses the reciprocal nature of the privileges and responsibilities of husband and wife. Though their roles or functions may sometimes differ, their commitment to each other 'in the Lord' is to be total. It is significant that Paul stresses that both husband and wife belong to each other bodily and have an obligation to meet each other's sexual needs, in view of the fact that some rabbis argued that only the wife had a right to sexual pleasure and only the husband had an obligation to procreate. Even more striking is the absence of any mention of an obligation to 'raise up a seed'. Thus, marital intercourse was not seen as merely a means of procreation, but also as a means of marital communion between husband and wife. Marriage, in Paul's view, was to involve a total sharing with one another. There were to be no spiritual marriages. All of this could only serve to improve a woman's status in marriage, for she could no longer be treated as simply a necessary means to the end of

continuing the family line. She was to be seen as an end in herself
– indeed, the husband's alter ego (cf. Eph 5.28).

Besides Paul's warnings against illicit sexual relationships of
various sorts, Paul's positive statement that the husband is to love
his wife as Christ loves the Church implies a standard of self-giving
and fidelity that precluded the husband from even contemplating any
other partner than his wife. Further, to love the wife in this way
implies not treating her as a mere sex object or appendage (cf. 1 Thess
4.4–5 and Eph 5.22–33). The husband is to honor and love his wife
because she is 'his own' body, 'his own' vessel. He is to treat her in
a sanctified manner. There could be no devaluation of her personhood, her value in the family, her importance to the husband's life
both physical and spiritual. If it is right to see Eph 5.21 as an
announcement of the theme of what follows in vv. 22–33, then we
can see that husband and wife are called to a mutual self-giving that
is to be total and rules out the idea that one member is superior to
the other. It does not preclude the husband's headship or the wife's
submission, but it does so define those roles that the husband becomes
the chief servant, like Christ, and the wife an example of one who
responds to her serving lover with loving submission as the Church
does in relation to Christ. This is what it means for a wife to 'fear'
her husband – she acts in a way that recognizes and respects the role
and responsibility given to her husband.

The one-flesh union that husband and wife share is a great mystery,
and it may be that this bond is what led Paul to apply the combined
metaphor of head and body to husband and wife, or perhaps it derives
from Paul's application of the former first to Christ and the Church.
Whether a Christian woman is married or single, she is ἐν κυρίῳ and
as such she is subject first and foremost to the call and service of
Christ. While Paul saw that in some respects it was easier for a single
person to heed this call, he also saw how the marriage relation could
be modeled on the relation of Christ and Church and thus likewise
become a truly Christian mode of being. It is a mode, however, that
exists in this life only (cf. Rom 7.1–3; 1 Cor 7.39) and thus does not
have the permanence that the relation of an individual to Christ has.
The Christ-event – past, present, and future – so rearranges the state
of affairs for man and woman that even marriage is relativized and
can no longer be seen as obligatory even for men (as it was in
Judaism). It is likely to be the Christ-event, more than any other
factor, which leads Paul to state a clear preference for the single
state.

Paul, therefore, presents his readers with two basic options, either marriage in the Lord (which he considers good), or remaining single (which he considers better). Because of Paul's views about the indissoluble one-flesh union, he does not counsel divorce or separation by the Christian if the partner is not Christian. He does recognize, however, that such a marriage involves a certain inequality and tension between the partners and thus he allows the Christian to be separated from his or her unbelieving partner if the latter initiates the break (cf. 2 Cor 6.14; 1 Cor 7.15–16).

In all the above, a Christian's freedom is defined and delimited according to Christian principles intended to thoroughly ground a person and his relationships and actions ἐν κυρίῳ. Thus, while a single Christian woman had the freedom, indeed was encouraged to remain single, her freedom was to be used for devotion and service to the Lord. As we shall see, this entails assuming roles in the Christian community which were not open to women in Judaism. Likewise, a Christian wife could be freed from many of the causes of her insecurity and devaluation in first-century society when Paul ruled out extra-marital sex, and argued that the marital bond could only be dissolved by death, and did not argue for the necessity for Christians to procreate. Again, however, it is a freedom that is to be used to better one's partner in a Christian manner. Paul's views on women and their roles in relation to the physical family are consistent throughout his letters and consistently aimed at liberating women from the non- or un-Christian aspects of their society, so that they would be free to live a fully Christian life as full members of the Christian community, whether as wife, mother, or single person.

3

WOMEN AND THE FAMILY OF FAITH IN THE PAULINE EPISTLES

Our discussion of the Pauline material thus far has been limited to family relationships, but it is now time to investigate Pauline texts dealing with women and their involvement in worship, evangelism, and other aspects of church life. True, the material studied in chapter 2 also dealt implicitly with these areas, for it was advice to the Christian family given in the context of a letter read in worship. Now, however, we will focus on texts that not only address but also deal with women in worship. This will mean giving 1 Corinthians 11 and 14 close attention to determine not only what roles women were assuming in worship, but also how Paul viewed these roles.

We will also look at Romans 16 (the name list), the tantalizing reference in Phil 4.2, and the much controverted Gal 3.28. At the end of this chapter we will examine some of the later Pauline epistles (the Pastorals) because, even if this material is written not by Paul but by a Paulinist, it is likely to reflect a line of thinking that developed from Pauline remarks or practices. The Pastorals, then, may give us a hint as to how Paul's thought was being applied in the last third of the first century, and provide us with a point of comparison when we discuss in chapters 4 and 5 some of the trajectories of thought in the redactional work of the Evangelists during that same period. We will begin our investigation by examining what is often taken to be Paul's most programmatic statement about male–female relationships in Christ – Gal 3.28.

A. Rite and rights for women (Gal 3.28)

Since I have already published a detailed, exegetical study of this passage,[1] I intend only to summarize some insights vital to our discussion of Paul's view of the family of faith. First, no discussion of this text is satisfactory which ignores the fact that the antithetical pairs format of this material is also found in 1 Cor 12.13 and Col 3.11.

This may suggest Paul is working with a pre-set piece here.[2] Paul could be adopting and adapting material formulated at an earlier time and by someone other than himself. In particular, the argument that this is part of an early baptismal liturgy is quite impressive. If so, then it makes sense that this text is a commentary on entrance requirements (or the lack thereof) and, more to the point, about the fact that neither social, sexual, nor ethnic differences should affect whether or not one can be or remain in Christ. While it is worthwhile to point out that the entrance ritual of Christian baptism is not gender-specific, it is probably wrong to make too much of this fact since proselyte baptism seems to have been widely practised by Jews in the first century.[3]

Galatians 3.28 also seems to imply that the differences mentioned above should not be used to divide the Body of Christ or to calculate one's position in the Body. All are one person in Him. This does not mean that the distinctions are obliterated by some sort of spiritual transformation, but that they no longer have any salvific significance. Paul states this polemically to combat suggestions (probably by Judaizers) that some are 'more equal' than others. It is perhaps likely that Paul is combatting the divisions the Judaizers were creating by insisting on things that promote social, ethnic, and sexual distinctions.

Second, whatever one makes of Gal 3.28, no interpretation of this verse is adequate which ignores the fact that Paul breaks the parallel structure by saying no male *and* female, probably alluding to Gen 1.27 and 2.18 ff., a combination of texts that probably lies behind some of Paul's argument in 1 Corinthians 11.[4] Since the duty to procreate was so widely held,[5] Paul had to clearly affirm his teaching that there was a place for the single person in Christ (cf. 1 Corinthians 7). Here then 'no male and female' may be a reminder of such teaching. Women and men do not necessarily have to be coupled in Christ, contrary to what Paul's opponents seem to have insisted.

Thus, this text definitely does have social implications for women in Christ. First, it implies they may remain single if they have the χάρισμα to do so. This in turn means they can be free to assume roles in the Christian community other than those of wife and mother. They can be free to concentrate wholly on 'the things of the Lord' (cf. 1 Cor 7.34). Second, it implies sexual, social, and ethnic distinctions cannot be used to determine whether or not one may be or remain in Christ. Third, it implies that such distinctions, while they still exist, should not be used to determine one's standing in Christ, much less to divide the Body of Christ. Baptism into Christ means that one should use one's social, sexual, or ethnic condition to glorify God and build up the Body of Christ. Accordingly, Paul combats a misuse of such distinctions. This does not lead to an agenda of obliterating or ignoring such distinctions and their relative advantages. Indeed, in the proper context, Paul is willing to argue that there are still advantages to being Jewish (cf. Rom 9.4ff.). It is just that these distinctions do not have the significance for one's spiritual status that Paul's opponents seem to be claiming.

B. An unveiled threat? (1 Cor 11.2–16)

No doubt various of Paul's pronouncements were taken to mean new freedom for women – but in what ways and to what extent? These questions would be likely to arise where there was an ongoing stress on spiritual gifts not bestowed on a gender-specific basis. In short, these sorts of questions would probably arise in Corinth.

There is good reason to believe that Paul spent perhaps 18 months from the Spring of AD 50 to the Fall of AD 51 in Corinth.[6] It is likely that the Corinthians had numerous occasions to hear Paul preach or teach on the new freedom in Christ. But freedom can be abused. Apparently, not all the implications of what this new freedom meant were clear, especially for women and particularly in the context of Christian worship. In 1 Cor 11.2–16 Paul seeks to clarify some of these implications.

The question has been raised as to whether or not 1 Cor 11.2–16 was penned by Paul himself. W. O. Walker, L. Cope and G. W. Trompf have all argued that this passage is an interpolation.[7] This conclusion is reached on the basis of form critical and contextual analysis as well as the examination of this passage's content. There are, however, serious problems with these arguments, and it appears that they may arise out of a desire to exonerate Paul of the charge of male chauvinism.

In so far as textual criticism is concerned, there is no evidence for the omission or displacement of this passage in the Greek manuscripts of the NT. It is precisely because there is such displacement in some manuscripts of 1 Cor 14.34–35 that the argument for interpolation there has some real merit. Such objective support is lacking in the case of 1 Cor 11.2–16. Second, the argument that 1 Cor 11.2–16 does not fit the context is singularly myopic. The argument about eating and drinking in a context other than Christian worship has come to a close in 10.31–11.1, and 11.2 should be seen as a transitional verse which also serves to introduce the new subject. Verses 2 and 16 form a sort of *inclusio* indicating that what Paul teaches on this subject is not original but part of a Church tradition observed in various places and passed down by Paul to the Corinthians. Further, 11.2ff. fits nicely with what follows in 11.27–14.40. All of this material covers a discussion about what is proper in the context of Christian worship. In fact, G. Bornkamm has argued that 10.14–14.40 is all part of one sequential argument dealing with the service of the word (10.14–22, 11.2–16), the service of the sacrament (11.23–34), and then a return to the service of the word (chapters 12–14).[8] Against this, however, the Lord's Supper is mentioned only at 10.16–21 as a point of comparison. The subject there is not the Eucharist but the eating of idol meat and the participation in idol worship. The discussion of Christian worship does not begin until chapter 11.

The case for interpolation based on vocabulary and syntax is weak, not least because the special vocabulary is subject-specific and Paul does not address this subject *per se* elsewhere in the Pauline corpus. Further, we do find various phrases and words that can be paralleled in the undisputed Paulines: (1) ἄγγελος appears more frequently in 1 Corinthians than anywhere else in the undisputed Paulines (cf. 4.8, 6.3, 13.1); (2) διὰ τοῦτο is characteristically Pauline (cf. Rom 4.16, 5.12, 13.6; 1 Cor 7.17; 2 Cor 4.1, 13.10) and in fact the use of διὰ τοῦτο followed by δἰα in 1 Cor 11.10 is closely paralleled in 1 Thess 3.7; (3) the ἐν κυρίῳ formula; (4) τὰ δὲ πάντα ἐκ τοῦ θεοῦ (cf. 2 Cor 5.18); (5) φύσις (cf. Romans 1–2, especially 2.14); (6) ἐξουσία is found nine times in 1 Corinthians alone and always refers to a power or authority held in one's own hand.[9] The elliptical nature of some of the material in 1 Cor 11.2–16 should not be used as evidence that this is non-Pauline since: (1) Paul's writings often involve anacoluthon, ellipsis, and various other forms of grammatical infelicities; (2) this material is written as part of an ongoing dialogue with the Corinthians and such phrases as διὰ τοὺς ἀγγέλους, which puzzle us so, probably alluded to previous discussions and would have been understandable to the Corinthians. Thus, unless the content of 1 Cor 11.2–16 is clearly un- or non-Pauline, the interpolation hypothesis must be seen to be less plausible than the traditional view.[10]

In the past decade a great deal of useful work has been done exploring the sociological context of Paul's letters. This work has been fruitful especially in regard to the social setting of the Corinthian church; thus, we now better understand the context and audience Paul was addressing there.[11] The city, having been re-formed as a Roman colony in 44 BC, had little continuity in its traditions though it may be that the wider Greek milieu had considerable influence on Corinthian citizens in terms of dress, gods worshipped, etc. G. Theissen cautions that the inscriptional evidence as well as the amphitheatre constructed in Corinth reveal a strong Latin influence.[12] This means that in our text it is important to know not only about Jewish customs, but also about Greek and Latin customs as well. Corinth was no backwater, but a major commercial center with a constant influx of people from all over the Mediterranean. The deleterious effect that being a seaport had on the moral climate of Corinth is too well-known to need rehearsing.[13]

The hints we have from Paul's letters suggest that the Christian congregation in Corinth, as was typical of first-century Christian congregations,[14] was composed of city dwellers who were a cross-section of the social and economic classes that existed in that city. There were a few relatively well-to-do people who could house the meetings (e.g., Stephanas, 1 Cor 16.15), a variety of artisans (Aquila and Priscilla), and the poor, both freedmen and slaves (1 Cor 11.22). There is no reason to dispute Paul's remarks that suggest there were 'not many wise ... not many influential ... not many of noble birth' (1 Cor 1.26). Now all of this is of real importance to our study for several reasons. First, customs in regard to headgear in rural areas or even small isolated villages (in Greece or elsewhere) will probably not be of much use to us in illuminating our text. Second, customs that could be practised (or afforded?) by the well-to-do are likely to be of little relevance for our discussion, for Paul specifically says he is addressing πᾶς ἀνὴρ and πᾶσα γυνή (1 Cor 11.4–5). Whether this means all men and women, or all husbands and wives, Paul clearly is not limiting his discussion to one class or socio-economic group. It may be that the well-to-do tended to take the positions of leadership in the early Church in Corinth and elsewhere. Corinth, however, was in the midst of an economic boom and this meant that more people had more time and money to invest in secular and religious groups.[15] Third, Christian meetings took place in people's *homes*. Thus, the question to be raised is, what did Paul see as appropriate 'in house' and, more specifically, in worship in the house? Apparel or behavior proper for a journey or the marketplace is irrelevant unless there was one general standard for dress and behavior in public (indoors or out). It appears that it is worship behavior, not home behavior, that Paul is concerned with in 1 Cor 11.2–26 (though how

much the two overlap is difficult to say). As we shall see, there appear
to be certain customs and apparel that are especially appropriate for
women in Corinth in ritual contexts (i.e., weddings, funerals, religious
processions, festivals, and worship).

The matter of the πνευματικοί must also be addressed before looking more closely at 1 Cor 11.2–16. There is no question that Paul
spends considerable time in this letter dealing with the problems
caused in Corinth by the πνευματικοί.

> The problem of the πνευματικοί of 12.1ff. is related to the
> background of the Corinthians in pagan ecstatic religion,
> 12.2, and Paul indicates that an outsider coming into their
> community would interpret what he saw and heard in those
> terms, 14.23. The evidence suggests that Paul saw the pro-
> blem in terms of the influence of the pagan mysteries on
> Corinthian Christianity.[16]

Chapter 11, like chapter 14, deals with those who prophesy and so
John Painter's comment above can be applied *mutatis mutandis* to
1 Cor 11.2–16 as well as to chapters 12–14. It is quite plausible that
various prophesying women were behaving in the same fashion in
which they had seen men and women behave in the mystery cults. The
inscriptional evidence suggests that it was possible for women to participate in the mystery processions and rites with a bare head.[17] The
specific evidence we have for Corinth, however, seems to indicate that
this was not the usual practice in most religious contexts. Thus for
instance, in a description of the Isis festival at Corinth, Apuleius says,
'The women had their hair anointed, and their heads covered with
light linen, but the men had their crowns shaven and shining
bright.'[18] In addition, C.M. Galt has collected a vast amount of
evidence, both pictorial and inscriptional, to show that the predomi-
nant custom for adult women in Greece during the Hellenistic age
and later in ritual contexts was to wear a head-covering.[19] She has
also shown that in Greek religious rites and dances adult women
commonly wore a head-covering and that this custom is evident particularly in Corinth.[20] To be sure, much of the evidence which Galt
presents dates from before the time of the Roman Empire, but she
substantiates the continuation of the custom during the Empire as
well (especially by the Romans).[21] Inasmuch as Corinth was a
Roman colony this evidence is especially important. Plutarch speaks
of the Roman custom of women going forth ἐγκεκαλύμ μέ ναις
while men go out ἀκαλύπτοις.[22] When Plutarch goes on to speak of

Roman customs at religious festivals (such as sacrifices), he states that head-coverings are worn except at the *honos* sacrifice.[23]

We should briefly mention Jewish practices in Judea and in Paul's home area of Tarsus. Fortunately, we have clear evidence from these areas. This material is relevant because there is good reason to think there were Jewish Christians in Corinth (cf. 1 Cor 9.20, 10.32; Acts 18.2ff). Paul does not wish to alienate or give any unnecessary offense to either Jewish or Gentile Christians in Corinth. It is unlikely that he or the Church would simply impose an alien custom on the Corinthians. It was difficult enough to bring about unity in Corinth without that. But we have seen that the custom of veiled women in ritual contexts (except perhaps in some of the mystery rites) is well documented for Greece in the Hellenistic age and later, for Corinth in particular, and for Romans during the Empire. Now we may add that the evidence suggests that in the city context in Judea (particularly Jerusalem) Jewish women were expected to wear head-coverings.[24] There is both literary and numismatic evidence for the use of head-coverings in Tarsus.[25] The former evidence is important because Jewish Christians in Corinth and elsewhere looked to the Jerusalem Church for guidance and precedents for such matters. Perhaps, more importantly, Paul got his theological training in Jerusalem. The Tarsus evidence suggests that Paul grew up with the custom of women wearing head-coverings in public, perhaps especially in worship.

How do we assess this evidence? It seems sufficient to show that the wearing of a head-covering by an adult woman in public (especially in a ritual context) was a traditional practice known to Jews, Greeks, and Romans. This may be contrasted with the evidence that girls, maidens, harlots, and immoral wives were expected to be bareheaded in various contexts.[26] The Roman and Corinthian evidence is important to show that Paul was not likely to impose any alien or uniquely Jewish customs on the ethnically mixed group in Corinth (cf. Gal 2.14). He may have endorsed a traditional Greek and Corinthian practice that he found theologically significant and useful, a practice some of the female πνευματικοί may have discarded perhaps under the influence of observed behavior at some of the mystery rites in or near Corinth. But what sort of head-covering is Paul arguing for in our text?

When one surveys the vocabulary Paul uses in 1 Cor 11.2–16, notable for its absence is the term for veil (κάλυμμα), a term introduced by various versions and patristic witnesses at 11.10 as a sort of explanatory note.[27] Instead, we have the term περιβόλαιον at 11.15. So far as I can see, there is no evidence, apart from 1 Cor 11.15, that this word is used to refer to a veil that would be drawn across the face. The root meaning of the word is that which is thrown around or thrown over, and it is used to refer to a cloak or mantle for the feet, a dressing gown, or even a bedcover.[28] In the descriptions of a Greek woman's attire, H. Licht points out that a veil was distinguished from a mantle.[29] Thus, Moulton and Milligan state that περιβόλαιον has a wider sense of clothing rather than a veil.[30] This is significant since, for instance, Paul is arguing that a woman's long hair has been given her in place of (ἀντί) a mantle or cloak (11.15).[31] Paul's analogy here is an apt one only if περιβόλαιον means cloak or mantle, not veil, for the latter comes across the face and covers it except for the eyes, whereas a woman's hair does not cover her face.[32] Paul must be talking about the natural purpose of a women's hair (notice the reference to φύσις in v. 14), i.e. protection and warmth. He is not speaking about its ritual function or use. Nature should tell a woman that her long hair is her glory given to her instead of a cloak or mantle.

As we shall see, the point is not to argue that long hair is the proper head-covering for women in worship. Rather, the point is that even nature suggests that a women should have a lengthy head-covering. This is simply a subsidiary argument meant to bolster the general contention – women ought to wear a head-covering in worship. Those who contend that hair is the head-covering Paul is advocating must explain why Paul calls the head-covering 'authority'. A woman's hair might be her δόξα, but it is very unlikely Paul would call it her ἐχουσία![33]

One further point must be mentioned before looking at the exegetical particulars. Notice that Paul says the head-covering he has in mind is something that comes down from the head (κατὰ κεφαλῆς ἔχων, v. 4). This does not suggest a small or transparent facial veil. As Galt makes clear, women did wear such facial veils 'which covered the face up to the eyes, and fell over the neck and back in folds'.[34] These veils were called κρήδεμνον, καλύπτρα, or κάλυμμα. Paul uses none of these terms in our passage and, if he did, he would be arguing at cross-purposes, permitting women to pray or prophesy but asking them to cover their mouths while doing so! I conclude that Paul is interested only in a head-covering, not a face-covering, hence not a veil *per se*. That a head-covering is the subject in view would fit well with the repeated reference to κεφαλή, both metaphorical and literal in our passage.

In terms of the flow of the argument in our passage we find that Paul appeals to tradition (vv. 2, 16), scripture (vv. 7–12), human judgment (v. 13), and nature (v. 14). In short, he pulls out all the stops to make his case. The bulk of the case is made on the basis of theological argumentation from Genesis 1–2, but Paul's last word is about Church tradition which he has passed on and which is the custom of the ἐκκλησίαι τοῦ θεοῦ. This may refer to Paul's other churches (cf. 2 Thess 1.4?), but may also include the Jerusalem churches, or even all other churches in view of the fact that he has begun this section by talking about traditions handed down to the Corinthians.[35] It has been shown that this παραδόσεις Paul received and passed on probably included a variety of theological and ethical traditions including credal statements, witness lists (cf. 1 Cor 15.3ff.), and ethical enjoinders (cf. Rom 6.17).[36] Paul has not created this teaching on the head-covering out of his fertile imagination, but I suggest that his way of arguing reflects his own thoughts on the matter.

After the *captatio benevolentiae* in v. 2, it appears that Paul gives us some sort of chain of being in v. 3, or some have seen it as a chain of command. How we view v. 3 will be determined largely by how we interpret the word κεφαλή. It is clear that the usage in v. 3 (unlike v. 4) is metaphorical. The word can be used to denote supreme or superior rank, but it can also be used to indicate the source of something (such as the head of the river). The former sense appears to be in evidence in the LXX (cf. Deut 28.13, 43f.), but the latter is well-known in the extra-biblical Greek literature.[37] In either case, Paul is probably not talking about a ruler–servant chain of command here. Note that there is no reference here to a κυρίος or to a σῶμα. Thus, the meaning of κεφαλή here probably is unlike what we find in Eph 5.22ff., for instance, where κεφαλή and σῶμα must be explained in light of each other. The point is not to discuss the role relationships of those who share a mysterious or even a one-flesh union.

S. Bedale has pointed out how well the meaning 'source' or 'origin' fits our text.[38] In the first place, Paul clearly goes on to talk about the source of man and woman in vv. 8–9. Second, the question may be raised: in what sense is God of superior rank to the exalted Christ? 1 Cor 15.28 seems to suggest that the exalted Lord will not be subordinated under the Father until some future time when the Kingdom comes. Phil 2.9–11 indicates that Christ already has the name above all names; even the OT name for God in the LXX, κυρίος, is applied now to Jesus. Further, P. B. Payne asks, in what sense is Christ now 'supreme' over all, many of whom do not yet recognize him and some of whom clearly reject His Lordship?[39] Would it not make more sense to talk about Christ as the source of all humans, by being the true agent of creation (an idea expressed in 1 Cor 8.6)? Further, there would seem to be little problem for Paul in talking about God being the origin or source of Christ whether this refers to God's sending of the Son at His human birth (Gal 4.4) or His pre-mundane origin as the wisdom of God (1 Cor 1.30, 2.7). I conclude that Paul is using κεφαλή here to mean source or origin. Verse 3 seems to indicate that this is a new teaching Paul is offering in addition to what they have known before (θέλω δὲ ὑμᾶς εἰδέναι).[40]

As the argument in the passage proceeds, the possibility that ἀνήρ first mentioned in v. 3 means husband, and γυνή means wife becomes increasingly difficult to maintain. But even in v. 3 it seems implausible. Why would Paul stress that Christ was the head of all husbands (Christian and non-Christian)? Why would it be that only husbands would dishonor their heads by praying or prophesying with a head-covering on? It thus appears that already in v. 3b when Paul says κεφαλῆς δὲ γυναικὸς ὁ ἀνήρ, the man he has in mind is Adam. He is the ultimate source of woman.

Paul's injunctions in vv. 4–5 should be read together for they are comprehensive, referring to all adult men and women in the Corinthian congregation. Taking vv. 4–5 together we notice that κατὰ κεφαλῆς ἔχων should be seen as the opposite of ἀκατακαλύπτῳ. The former refers to something down on the head; the latter simply means uncovered.[41] What is proper apparel for the man is the opposite of what is proper for the woman. Clearly, the reason for this is gender, but it also has to do with the source of each gender. Hair in itself cannot dishonor the male head (though long hair might, cf. v. 14), so it is unlikely that hair is in view in v. 5. A woman with unloosed hair falling down on her shoulders still has her head covered with hair (as v. 15 probably hints). Thus, Paul is not referring to a natural head-covering of hair in vv. 4–5.[42] It follows that v. 5b means the effect of the uncovered head is the same as if the woman were shaved, a clear sign of disgrace for a woman.[43] Paul is not suggesting that uncovering is identical with shaving in the case of the woman, only that she might as well be shaved since the disgracefulness of the deed is ἓν ... καὶ τὸ αὐτό. The two deeds are not identical but they have an equivalent effect.[44]

It ought to be noted that Paul may be using κεφαλή as a *double entendre* in v. 4b (his head = the man's physical head but also Christ),

but not in v. 5b (her head = her physical head).[45] Verses 6–7 favor
the view that 5b only refers to a woman's physical head since that
is Paul's focus in these two verses. In v. 6a Paul is arguing that if a
woman is going to be uncovered in worship, then let her also be close
cropped (she might as well go all the way with her disgraceful deed).
In v. 6b he takes it for granted that the Corinthians would see a short
hair-cut, or even a shaved or sheared head, as disgraceful. In short,
Paul is trying to link a deed that must have been seen by the Corinthians as disgraceful with the deed of going without a head-covering
in worship. If the linkage is accepted, then the conclusion must be –
κατακαλυπτέσθω.

Though it appears Paul's main concern is to correct the behavior
of the Corinthian women, it is striking how he alternates between
speaking about men and then women in vv. 7–10. This subsection
should be taken together. Notice how Paul begins by saying what men
ought (ὀφείλει) to do but concludes in v. 10 with what women ought
(ὀφείλει) to do. The use of the verb suggests a moral obligation, in
short, something the Corinthians should take it upon themselves to
do. Paul was hoping that an inner sense of obligation recognized
by the individuals in question could be or become the motivating
factor.[46] In v. 7 we are finally given a theological reason for a man
not wearing a head-covering – he is the image (εἰκὼν) and glory
(δόξα) of God from the beginning (ὑπάρχων). J. Jervell sees here
the beginning of a sort of Jewish midrash on Gen 1.27, 2.22. This
does not entail a clear citation of the texts, but an allusion to them
with a current application.[47] This, argues Jervell, probably indicates
an audience in Corinth that would include enough Jewish Christians
familiar with Jewish speculation on Genesis 1 and 2 to correctly
interpret Paul's meaning.[48] The word ὑπάρχων suggests that ἀνήρ
is used in a generic sense in v. 7, i.e., humanity in general. There is
presumed to be a clear and historical connection between the first
man, Adam, and all ensuing men who are likewise the image and glory
of God. We might paraphrase here: 'man ought not to cover his head
because he has always been (from the beginning of the race) the image
and glory of God.'[49] Notice Paul does not say man is *in* the image,
but that he *is* the image (the verb 'to be' must be inserted in v. 7b).

As Barrett points out, the focus here is on δόξα, not εἰκών. Notice
the close connection of image and glory in reference to Christ in 2 Cor
4.4–6. Verse 6 suggests that 'image' is similar to 'likeness' for Paul.
The glory of Christ is, in fact, the glory of God which can be seen
in the face of Christ. This may suggest that image has to do with face.

Glory can be seen in the image, but the two are not identical. Clearly, for Paul δόξα has its basic meaning of brightness or splendor (2 Cor 4.4; notice the repeated reference to φωτισμὸν in vv. 4–6). This may also be the meaning in 1 Cor 11.7ff.[50]

Verse 7c indicates that by contrast (δὲ) the woman is the δόξα of man. It cannot be emphasized too strongly that Paul does not suggest that women are not in the image of God; everything else about this passage suggests Paul thinks they are. Not only does he address them in the same breath and on the same terms as men, but he expects them to relate to God in worship as men do.[51]

Woman is the glory of man because woman came forth from man (ἐξ, clearly a reference to Genesis 2), while man did not originally come from (ἐκ) woman.[52] The origin of man and woman differ, but now in v. 9 we will be told they differ somewhat in their purpose. With the accusative, διά should be translated "for the sake of".[53] Man was not created for the sake of woman (being made before her according to Genesis 2), but woman for the sake of man.[54]

When we get to v. 10, the question becomes: does διὰ τοῦτο have a backward or forward reference? In the majority of cases in the un-disputed Paulines, this phrase points forward (cf. Rom 4.16, 5.12, 13.6; 1 Cor 4.17; 2 Cor 4.1, 13.10; Phlm 15; and especially 1 Thess 3.5, 7).[55] The advantage of seeing διὰ τοῦτο as pointing forward is that διὰ τοὺς ἀγγέλους ceases to be a dangling appendage. But the point of this whole argument is to explain why a woman ought to have a head-covering. Thus, as Barrett argues, διὰ τοῦτο in this case is most naturally taken as referring backward – because of the origin and purpose of a woman's creation, she ought to wear a head-covering.

The phrase ἐξουσίαν ἔχειν ἐπὶ κεφαλῆς is a notorious crux, so much so that various manuscripts altered ἐξουσίαν to κάλυμμα. The more difficult reading, ἐξουσίαν, should be accepted. This word can mean 'power' or 'authority' but there is no evidence that it means power or authority exercised by someone *else* over the person in question. Indeed, the idea that Paul has in view an authority to which a woman is subject was long ago said to be 'a preposterous idea which a Greek scholar could laugh at anywhere except in the N.T.'[56] More recently, M. D. Hooker demonstrated that most of the usual interpre-tations of this word, including the subordinationist one, are unlikely if not impossible.[57] We are talking, then, about an authority or power which the woman has. It is best to translate ἐξουσία as authority, not power, for it is evident from 1 Corinthians 12–14 that Paul thought the power to prophesy came not from a magical head-covering but from the Spirit.[58] Some have seen here an argument by Paul that women ought to control their own heads.[59] This is unlikely on two counts. First, Paul says women ought to have authority on or over (ἐπί) their heads. He is not talking about exercising control, but having authority. Women had to have authority to do what they were doing in worship — praying and prophesying. Paul insists that women ought to have this authority, but he is not suggesting that they did not already have control over their own head. Second, as Hooker says, 'This picture of woman having to control her rebellious head by covering it is to say the least a quaint one; it is especially difficult in a context where Paul had been playing on the meaning of the word head, for we may be sure that he does not mean to suggest that woman ought to exercise control over man!'[60] The authority on or over the woman's head must be seen as an authorization to do something which she would otherwise not be able to do. It is also likely that Paul is implying that this is a new authority, for there is evidence women were expected to be silent in the synagogue.[61] As one proceeds through this difficult argument it becomes clear that Paul would not have gone to all this trouble to explain how these things are to be done if he had not first accepted and affirmed a woman's authority to pray and prophesy in Christian worship.[62]

Because of the order and nature of human creation as male and female, a woman ought to wear a head-covering in worship. Paul adds a subsidiary reason — διὰ τοὺς ἀγγέλους. This puzzling reference has been explained in light of the Qumran material.[63] The older idea that evil angels are in view, and that a woman needed protection from their lustful looks,[64] founders because: (1) Paul says nothing about evil angels, or angels of Satan, here; and (2) how would a head-covering protect or hide a woman from the gaze of a supernatural being in any case? Now, it is clear that Paul thought of angels as observers of the created order (1 Cor 4.9). At 1 Tim 5.21 we seem to have the idea of angels as watchers of believers, and at Rev 1.20 we find that churches have angels. G. B. Caird and Hooker have argued that Paul associates angels with the principalities and powers that govern the world.[65] The Qumran evidence suggests their presence at worship, but this idea seems already present in the OT (Ps 138.1).

Not all of this evidence is of equal value for interpreting our text, but it allows a plausible conjecture. Paul says angels are guardians of the created order, and perhaps also are guardians of the proper order in worship.[66] Why then mention this at this point? As Hooker argues, only God's glory must be in evidence in Christian worship.

If a woman is man's glory, and a woman's hair is her own glory, then there is good reason why a woman's head should be covered. Neither a man's nor a woman's glory should be in evidence in the midst of Christian worship, but only God's glory symbolized by the uncovered head of the man.[67] The wearing of a head-covering by the woman has a dual function: (1) it preserves the proper order in worship (only God's glory is revealed there); and (2) it authorizes women to pray and prophesy without denying the creation order distinctions. Paul considers it important to recognize and symbolize the creation order distinctions in Christian worship. New creation for Paul does not obliterate the original creation order distinctions. What the new creation does accomplish, however, is to grant women new freedom, roles, and responsibilities in the community of faith. Paul endorses the new freedom of women but still maintains the old creation order distinctions in a transferred and transformed sense.

Verse 11 begins with πλήν, which breaks off the preceding discussion and offers a qualification.[68] Some may conclude that Paul was simply reasserting the old patriarchal order with a stress on the superiority of the male and the inferiority of the female. This is not the case. Paul does allow praying and prophesying for both men and women, and shows that in the Lord there is neither man without woman, nor woman without man. The point is that it is not merely a matter of women being dependent upon men, but rather a mutual dependency of each upon the other. Though woman originally came from man, now all men come into the world through women, and all things ultimately come from God.[69] ἐν κυρίῳ here probably means 'in the Church' or 'in the Body of Christ'.[70] Men and women stand together, mutually dependent upon each other, not only in creation but also ἐν κυρίῳ. This means that both men and women are equally necessary and important to each other for their ongoing existence.[71] Thus, vv. 11–12 make clear that Paul does not wish to imply the inferiority of women in comparison to men.

The arguments in vv. 13–15 must be seen as subsidiary and corroborative. It is worth noting that v. 14 indicates Paul saw certain signs of gender distinction as natural and even indicated by nature. These distinctions are not obliterated, but reoriented ἐν κυρίῳ.

Finally, at v. 16 we have a reiteration of the appeal to what is customary in all the other churches. Too many translators have misrendered τοιαύτην.[72] Paul is saying, 'we have no custom such as this nor do the churches of God'. I do not consider 'being contentious' a custom (συνήθειαν).[73] Perhaps Paul is referring to the custom of women wearing long hair instead of a cloak. This is the nearest antecedent. If the Corinthian women had been arguing that their hair was a sufficient head-covering, Paul's response could easily have been, 'we have no such custom of women using only hair as a head-covering in worship'. Possibly, v. 15b, which begins awkwardly, is a quote from the Corinthians themselves. In any case, the view that Paul is saying 'we have no such custom as women wearing *additional* head-coverings beyond the hair' requires reading something into the text and historically is an unlikely remark. It would be surprising if Jewish Christian women did not have the custom of wearing a head-covering. Thus, Barrett rightly concludes, 'By custom Paul means praying and prophesying by unveiled women'[74] (or, as we would prefer to say, uncovered women).

We have not tried to answer the question of what Paul meant by praying and prophesying in 1 Cor 11.4ff. because that will be covered in the next section of this chapter. Paul implies that both men and women have the ability and permission to do some sort of speaking in worship. It would be natural to see praying as speaking to God, and prophesying as speaking to fellow believers. If so, then it is significant as a departure from Paul's Jewish heritage, especially in regard to women addressing men in worship.[75] We hear in this passage both the old (a creation order reaffirmed) and the new (women praying and prophesying in worship). Paul is delivering a received Church custom or tradition; however, he does not wish it to be interpreted in such a way that women are silenced in Corinthian worship. This raises the question, what do we make of 1 Cor 14.33bff.? We will turn to this question after one parting remark.

There is nothing un-Pauline about the content or form of argumentation in 1 Cor 11.2–16. Perhaps we have shown that Paul can be exonerated of 'male chauvinism' in this passage without the radical surgery suggested by those favoring some form of an interpolation theory.

C. Silence in all the churches? (1 Cor 14:33b–36)

1 Corinthians 14.33b–36 (or 34–36) has been taken by an increasing number of scholars to be a clear case of interpolation of non-Pauline material into this Pauline letter.[76] This is argued on several bases: (1) the textual difficulties; (2) the fact that these verses interrupt the flow of the argument and that v. 37 follows nicely with 33a; (3) the

fact that these verses blatantly contradict the clear implications of 1 Cor 11.5; (4) peculiarities of linguistic usage. Taken together, these arguments appear formidable, and a reasonable case can be made that these verses are derived from 1 Tim 2.8ff. Each argument deserves individual scrutiny.

The textual problem involves a case of transposition of vv. 34–35 from their generally recognized place to a position after v. 40. The witnesses for this transposition are generally late and chiefly Western (D, F, G, 88*, it[a,g], Ambrosiaster, Sedulius-Scotus).[77] W. Grudem points out that the earliest of these manuscripts is Ambrosiaster (c. AD 375).[78] More important is the fact that there is no manuscript evidence for the omission of these verses. Thus, even Conzelmann (who backs the interpolation theory) admits, 'The transposition of vv. 34f. to follow v. 40 in D G is, of course, no argument for the assumption of an interpolation; it is a secondary simplification. Its compass does not coincide with that of the interpolation which is to be assumed.'[79]

The argument that vv. 33b–36 or 34–35 interrupt the flow of the argument depends on an assumption that they do not fit with what precedes and follows, but address a different subject. Sometimes the fact of transposition is pointed to as evidence that it was perceived early on that these verses do not fit in their present location. Several factors count against this. First is the rather large amount of significant vocabulary that our few verses have in common with what precedes and follows (ὑποτάσσω, vv. 32 and 34; λαλέω, vv. 14, 23 and numerous times before 33b; v. 34; v. 39; σιγάω, vv. 28, 30, 34; ἐν ἐκκλησίᾳ, vv. 28, 35). Second, E. E. Ellis has argued for a catchword connection with σιγάω binding vv. 33bff. to what precedes.[80] Third, in a slightly different vein, Robinson has found a pattern of exhortations about inspired speech (prophecy, tongues, spiritual songs) that is regularly followed by a command to women involving ὑποτάσσω (cf. Col 3.18ff.; Eph 5.19ff.; 1 Cor 14.27ff.). This could argue that Paul is following a set pattern of ethical exhortation here in which case the connection between vv. 33b–36 and what precedes would not be by continuous flow of argument but by 'Die Verbindung ... durch das Stichwort ὑποτάσσεσθαι'.[81] Fourth, S. Aalen has pointed out that often the verb 'permit' is used in the context of a citation or allusion to a text in the OT involving a prohibition (particularly in the Pentateuch) and it is usual that such is followed by a reference to a command(ment).[82] On this basis he has linked v. 37 closely with v. 34 (ἐπιτρέπεται ... ὁ νόμος λέγει) seeing a rabbinic formula and procedure in the background here.[83]

The argument that 1 Cor 14.33bff. clearly contradicts 1 Cor 11.5 depends on how one understands 1 Cor 14.33bff. We will not be able to assess this claim until we exegete the text, but it may be asked, if the contradiction is so obvious, why didn't the interpolator notice it? In textual criticism the more difficult reading is usually assumed to be the original. One wonders why this principle should not apply in the case of some difficult texts as a whole. Further, if the contradiction is so clear, why is there no evidence for omission of this text by later copyists?

Finally, there are few linguistic peculiarities. Conzelmann points to the use of ἐπιτρέπω, but if Aalen's explanation is correct, then it is understandable why Paul uses this term.[84] The reference to ὁ νόμος is surprising but not inexplicable if Aalen is correct, but we will deal with that when we do the detailed exegesis. At this point our working hypothesis will be that this material is Pauline and can be explained in terms of its immediate context – the discussion of prophecy and the judging of the prophecies in chapter 14 – and the larger context – the discussion of abuses in Corinthian worship caused by the πνευματικοί in chapters 11–14. Some of these πνευματικοί were women prophetesses[85] that seem to have been imitating some of the practices of women involved in the mysteries. The result was significant disorder in the Corinthian worship.[86] Now let us consider Paul's views on prophecy.

The study of prophecy in the Pauline epistles has been undertaken by numerous scholars.[87] It is clear that Paul thought of prophecy as an important gift for building up the Christian community (Rom 12.6; 1 Cor 12.10, 13.2, 14.6; 1 Thess 5.20). It is not by accident that Paul lists this gift ahead of glossolalia in Rom 12.6 and 1 Cor 12.10, and in 1 Cor 12.29 (cf. Rom 12.1–7) prophets rank immediately after apostles but before teachers. Indeed, J. D. G. Dunn points out that if one looks at all such lists in the Pauline corpus, the only constant member is prophecy or prophet (Rom 12.6–8; 1 Cor 12.8–10, 28ff., 13.1–3, 8ff., 14.1–5, 6ff., 26–32; Eph 4.11; 1 Thess 5.11–22).[88]

Paul indicates that prophecy is not only a desirable gift but also one which the Corinthians should seek (14.1). 1 Corinthians 14.30 makes clear that prophecy is not a learned art, but depends on the receiving of revelation from God which must then be delivered. Prophecy is not equivalent to revelation, but is dependent upon receiving revelation.[89] 1 Corinthians 14.19 suggests a contrast between speaking with the mind and speaking in a tongue (glossolalia). This means that prophecy is an intelligible communication that even non-believers can hear and be convicted by (1 Cor 14.24−25). This contrast with glossolalia is important and supports the idea that Paul does not view prophecy in the same way as the oracles of the pythia at Delphi. The pythia spoke in a state of trance or 'possession' by the god which induced an ecstasy. This led to utterances including moans, cries, and phrases to be interpreted later by a prophet.[90] Christian prophecy does not need such interpretation, but it may need 'weighing'. In short, if anything was like pagan utterances it was glossolalia which led outsiders to the conclusion that the speaker was mad (1 Cor 14.23). Perhaps a large part of the problem at Corinth was that the Corinthians viewed prophecy on the 'mantic' model, while Paul viewed it more along the line of certain OT models.[91] Paul indicates clearly that the prophet had enough conscious control over his utterance that he could wait until another finished before standing and delivering the prophecy (1 Cor 14.29−32). Apparently, the Corinthians thought that they just could not wait and so several were blurting out a prophecy at one time with the result being chaos and confusion.

There is little doubt that Paul views prophecy, like glossolalia, as inspired speech. The latter, however, appears to be a sort of prayer language, perhaps even an angelic language (1 Cor 13.1), that is directed toward God and can edify only the individual speaking it unless interpreted. The interpretation makes it profitable for others, but there is no clear basis for concluding that glossolalia plus interpretation is equivalent to prophecy. The latter serves a different function from the outset, namely, the upbuilding of a congregation (1 Cor 14.4), rather than the uplifting of the individual.[92] Prophecy is to be distinguished from preaching and teaching not in its purpose so much (for surely preaching and teaching also serve the functions of upbuilding, encouraging, consoling, etc.), but in its source. 1 Corinthians 14.30 states that prophecy is the utterance of a revelation that comes to a person spontaneously. Teaching is also a charismatic activity (Rom 12.7) but it is likely to entail giving new or pertinent insights into an old word of God, tradition, or practice of the Church. In short, it was something that drew on the speaker's prior knowledge of God's word and the Church traditions and preaching. 'Recent scholarship is correct in claiming that the characteristic feature of the teacher's work is to be found in his relation to tradition.'[93] Nonetheless, it is clear Paul believed that what he taught came to him from God through Jesus Christ (Rom 15.30; 2 Cor 4.5; Gal 1.1; 1 Thess 4.2). Thus, there may be some overlap between teaching and prophecy, but a distinction is still possible. Teaching might involve a new and inspired exegesis of older texts and material (Rom 11.25ff.; 1 Cor 9.8ff.; Gal 3.8),[94] while its function is to instruct. One gets the feeling both from the effect prophecy is said to have on non-believers, as well as from the terms used to describe its functions, that Paul sees prophecy as a form of moral or ethical exhortation or encouragement. Thus, Barrett calls it, 'The moral truth of Christianity proclaimed in inspired speech ...'[95]

As Dunn cautions, however, we should not view prophecy as simply forth-telling, for there is no reason why it could not also involve fore-telling to warn, exhort, comfort, or build up the congregation.[96] Prophecy might even reveal a mystery of the faith (1 Cor 15.51; Rom 11.25).[97] But again, a revelation of a mystery would be the sharing of a new truth, not merely the explanation of an old one.

The relationship of prophecy to preaching is not unlike that of prophecy to teaching. There is overlap, but the two are not identical. Prophecy, as described in 1 Corinthians 12–14, is directed to the community (though it may affect a visiting outsider), and does not involve preaching the kerygma. It appears G. Friedrich is close to the truth when he says, 'The prophet is the Spirit-endowed counselor of the community who tells it what to do in specific situations, who blames and praises, whose preaching contains admonition and comfort, the call for repentance and promise.'[98] D. H. Hill calls prophecy 'pastoral preaching'.[99] Preaching is also an inspired gift, but it is not by accident that prophecy is grouped next to miracles, distinguishing between spirits, and tongues (1 Cor 12.20), rather than with the utterance of wisdom or knowledge. In Rom 12.6 Paul speaks about 'gifts that differ' and lists the one who prophesies separately from ὁ διδάσκων and ὁ παρακαλῶν. 1 Corinthians 12.24 distinguishes between apostles, prophets, and teachers (are the apostles the preachers in this list?). Prophecy brings a new revelation from God given at the point of need; it is not merely the proclaiming of the older Gospel traditions.

Two other matters should be discussed before turning to 1 Cor 14.33bff. First, Grudem is probably correct in pointing out that some regularly prophesied and some only occasionally prophesied, but 1 Cor 12.29 makes clear that not all were prophets.[100] 1 Corinthians 14.37 suggests we should not talk about an appointed office of prophet, but rather of an individual who perceived him or herself as a prophet, i.e., a person who, inspired by the Spirit, would stand up and give a word to the congregation. Probably, Paul uses the term prophet to describe what a person did, not to indicate a church office.

Second, how do we interpret Rom 12.6b (κατὰ τὴν ἀναλογίαν τῆς πίστεως) and 1 Cor 12.10 (διακρίσεις πνευμάτων)? The former appears to mean 'according to the measure or proportion of one's faith'. Dunn says faith here means the degree of 'a believer's confidence that God's Spirit is speaking in the very words he is then uttering'.[101] This means that the prophecy given could be an admixture of God's word and human words. In short, the greater one's faith and openness to the source of revelation, the more nearly the utterance could be completely a word of God. If so, then this suggests why the prophecy spoken of in 1 Corinthians 12–14 had to be weighed – because its content might be three parts inspiration and one part imagination. The ability to weigh the prophecy was also a gift, but the οἱ ἄλλοι of 1 Cor 14.29 may be the other prophets, not the whole congregation, though the latter view cannot be ruled out.[102] 1 Corinthians 12.10 can be interpreted then to mean 'an evaluation, an investigation, a testing, a weighing of the prophetic utterance'[103] or weighing as to whether a particular utterance came from the Holy Spirit or from a human (or evil?) spirit. This gift is intended to check the abuse of the gift of prophecy. One may conclude that prophecy in Corinth did not have the same absolute status, the same given 'thus saith the Lord' quality, of OT prophecy which did not need to be weighed but only received and applied. Thus, Grudem concludes that Corinthian prophecy had an inspiration of general content, but the particular words had to be weighed carefully as truth could be mixed with error.[104]

The implication of all this for our study of women is important. First, it suggests that women were allowed to engage not only in prophecy but also in the weighing of prophecy even if the latter was a separate gift also exercised by prophets. Second, prophecy which women in Corinth offered (1 Cor 11.5) was only authoritative to the degree it was inspired. In short, it is unlikely that we are talking about an office that bestowed authority on the individual prophesier. Third, this feature of prophecy may be distinguished from teaching and preaching, though there may be some overlap in the audience, in the function of these gifts, in the fact that all are gifts of the word, and all are gifts of the Spirit.

Prophecy is addressed to the whole congregation – including the men. Since prophecy involved authoritative exhortation or a new word of God, then it had a didactic purpose. Prophecy is not merely a personal testimony. There is nothing in 1 Corinthians 12–14 to suggest that prophecy (or preaching or teaching) were gender-specific gifts. How then do we interpret the silencing of women in 1 Cor 14.33b–36?

It is evident from what precedes and follows 1 Cor 14.33b–36 that Paul is concerned with proper order in the Christian worship. If this passage does belong between vv. 33a and 37, then it is reasonable to expect Paul is dealing with some sort of disorderliness here. To re-establish the proper order of things, Paul begins by citing the proper rule of order followed in all the churches (or all his churches?). Should the phrase ἐν πάσαις ταῖς ἐκκλησίαις go with what follows or what precedes v. 33b? Barrett suggests that v. 34 is the beginning of a new idea or section because he feels ἐν πάσαις ταῖς ἐκκλησίαις and ἐν ταῖς ἐκκλησίαις would be awkwardly juxtaposed if v. 33b went with v. 34 (cf. *NEB*, *KJV*, Phillips). There are some strong reasons for rejecting this opinion. First, Paul is referring to two separate things by these two phrases, so they are not a repetition. In ἐν πάσαις ταῖς ἐκκλησίαις Paul is referring to the Church universal (or at least all the churches resulting from his missionary work), whereas ἐν ταῖς ἐκκλησίαις in v. 34 refers to 'all the meetings of the church of Corinth'.[105] We might have expected ἐν πάσαις, not 'Ως ἐν πάσαις, if the text went with what precedes. It is also questionable whether or not the phrase 'Ως ἐν πάσαις ταῖς ἐκκλησίαις can stand the further qualification necessary to place it with v. 33a.[106] When Paul uses this phrase or a similar one in other parts of this letter (1 Cor 4.17, 7.17, 11.16), he is not referring to the behavior of God in all the churches, but trying to set forth a rule of behavior, his rule, or the rule of all the Christian churches. Paul is not focusing on how God acts in all the churches in 14.33, but rather on how the Corinthians conform to the practice elsewhere in the Body of Christ.[107]

The above is reinforced when one studies the word ἐκκλησία. It is easy for Paul to pass from the singular to the plural and let it be anarthrous or have the article, because ἐκκλησία is almost a proper name. Paul's concept of Church is such that:

> The sum of the individual congregations does not produce the total community or the Church. Each community, however small, represents the total community the church ... [It] is not 'the Corinthian congregation' which would stand side by side with the Roman, etc., but the congregation, church, assembly as it is in Corinth. If anyone is despised

in such a gathering (1 Cor. 6.4), if people come together in it (1 Cor. 11.18, cf. 14.23, Ac. 14.27), if women are to keep silent in it (1 Cor. 14.34), ... these things apply to the church as a whole and not merely to a local congregation.[108]

Amidst the myriad of pagan temples and beliefs, the Corinthian Christians were not to be conformed to the immoral and libertine Corinthian attitudes, but were to be God's transformed option in Corinth – the Church.

It is difficult to assess whether αἱ γυναῖκες ἐν ταῖς ἐκκλησίαις σιγάτωσαν is normal or novel advice from Paul. We know from Pausanias, Strabo, and archaeological digs that among the many temples in Corinth there were some (Dionysius, Isis, Serapis) in which women could take important roles in the services and speak. Oepke remarks:

> Throughout antiquity the participation of women is customary not merely in the family cultus, but also in the public cultus and the celebration of Mysteries ... In the Dionysian cult women played a very prominent part as maenads and thyads. Priestesses were very common both in the public cults and in those of the Mysteries (the Hierophants in Eleusis, and the priestesses of Isis, etc.). Their ministry is not in the least restricted to men. Outstanding ecstatic endowment assures women a prophetic rank as sybils ...[109]

From this we may deduce that the Corinthians were surprised at Paul's silencing of women and that Paul is not drawing on conventional Corinthian or Greek views of a woman's role in worship. Nor is he merely drawing on his own Jewish background, for why would he allow women to pray and prophecy (1 Cor 11.5)? More likely, in 1 Cor 14.33bff. Paul is dealing with a specific problem in the Corinthian worship service which led him to counsel women to silence.

Even if it is only a particular thing the Corinthian women are not supposed to say or do, this does not mean they are violating only a minor church rule. They could be violating a basic Christian principle or a standard church practice. If it is a principle, then this might explain why Paul's prohibition is so absolute, and why his rhetorical questions in v.36 are so strong (cf. 1 Cor 11.16). It would seem by Paul's reaction that more than just a minor practice is at stake here. Indeed, he musters five authorities to get Corinthian women to adhere to this ruling: (1) general church practice (v. 36b); (2) the law (v. 34);

(3) common conventions of what is proper or disgraceful (v. 35); (4) the word of God (v. 36); and (5) his apostolic authority (if we apply vv. 37–40 to what immediately precedes it, as well as to 14.1–33a). This piling up of authorities, coupled with an appeal to what is honorable or disgraceful, is a common Pauline practice when something important is at stake (1 Cor 11.2–16), and strongly suggests 1 Cor 14.33b–36 is authentic Pauline material.

From the immediate context we may discern two more general problems at work here. It appears the Corinthians are trying to make up their own rules, perhaps thinking their own word is sufficient or authoritative or even the word of God for themselves (cf. v. 36).[110] We also know from vv. 33a, 40 that things were not being done decently when the spiritual gifts were used in the worship service.

Perhaps here is the place to discuss the interesting conjecture of D. W. Odell-Scott that Paul is quoting a ruling that at least some of the Corinthians were arguing for (vv. 34–35), and the forceful rhetorical questions in v. 36, introduced by ἤ, indicate that Paul's position stands in contrast to such a view. Odell-Scott adds the conjecture that the masculine μόνους in v. 36 indicates that Paul is criticizing the males in Corinth who apparently came up with this ruling.[111] This view has two strengths. First, Odell-Scott is able to show that ἤ serves to establish a disjunction between separate ideas or convictions, and that it displays its sharpest disjunctive characteristics in interrogative sentences often introducing an argument *ex contrario*.[112] Second, there are cases in 1 Corinthians where Paul is quoting the opposition and then qualifying their dictums.[113] There are some problems with Odell-Scott's arguments. First, our whole passage is in the masculine gender (cf. οἱ ἄλλοι in v. 29; εἷς in v. 27, etc.). There is, therefore, nothing unique or surprising about the μόνους at v. 36 – it is simply the gender-inclusive masculine as elsewhere in this chapter. Second, Paul's argument is introduced by 'as in all the churches', and even if this is not part of the quote, ἐν ταῖς ἐκκλησίαις in v. 34 is. Is it plausible that the Corinthians were arguing that *their* view was the same as in all the churches (or at least in the vicinity of Corinth), and that Paul turned around and accused them of thinking that the word of God originated with them (v. 36a)? The rhetorical question makes sense if the Corinthians were appealing to their own inspired utterances alone, but not if they were appealing to: (a) conventional church practice; (b) the law; and (c) what was shameful.

Thus, v. 36 should be seen as a typical Pauline outburst that had been building up for a while in reaction to all the abuses he had been dealing with in 1 Corinthians 11–14. They were pursuing an autonomous route; thus, the re-emphasis by Paul on common church tradition. 1 Corinthians 14.36–40 is the conclusion to the whole section (chapters 11–14), and reveals Paul's frustrations with the whole mess he had been dealing with since 11.2. Further, in earlier cases where Paul was quoting the Corinthians, he then went on to qualify or rebut their views (cf. 7.1, 2, δέ followed by an argument), not engage in mere rhetoric or sarcasm, and ἤ is not always a disjunctive particle – it can be conjunctive. I conclude that the cases of Odell-Scott and of Flanagan and Snyder before him, are possibilities but they raise more questions than they answer. In all probability, Paul is anticipating the response he expected to get (v. 36) when the Corinthians read his argument (vv. 34–35).

When Paul says women are not permitted or allowed to speak (v. 34), using the verb ἐπιτρέπω in a passive form, it appears that 'the passive points back to an already valid regulation'.[114] ἐπιτρέπω deals with someone not being permitted something.[115] Thus, 'no permission' (*JB*) is most appropriate. Why would women have no permission to speak, and where did the rule banning their speaking in Christian worship originate? These questions can be answered later. It would seem that if the problem was simply a matter of decorum, decency, or order (as with 14.1–33a),[116] then Paul would not have banned women from speaking but reinstructed them to do it properly and in order. But perhaps he *has* reinstructed them, telling women to ask at home.

Why is the women's speaking contrasted with ὑποτάσσω (by ἀλλά), and why are silence and subordination associated? In what way was the women's speech insubordinate? Is it (1) the bare fact of speaking in church, in which case v. 34 is an absolute prohibition against women speaking in church, or (2) what they said, or (3) the way they went about saying it, or (4) the sort of speech involved (questions?)? In regard to the third possibility, Moffatt and others have suggested that λαλέω means chatter – the problem being women gossiping during the service and disrupting it.[117] λαλέω can be used in this way in classical Greek, but it seems doubtful that this is the case here. Barrett correctly points out that the word does not normally have this meaning when Paul uses it. Throughout chapter 14 it is used in the sense of 'inspired speech'.[118]

F. W. Grosheide and others have suggested that the way to understand λαλέω here, in contrast to 11.5, is as a reference to speaking in public worship, whereas in chapter 11 Paul was referring to speaking at home or in a small prayer group.[119] This distinction, however, cannot be made. Whiteley is right in saying that in 1 Cor 11.4 Paul is referring to men praying and prophesying in church services, and he uses the same participial construction in the next verse to refer to women doing the same thing. Thus, it is unlikely that Paul could be referring to their praying and prophesying anywhere else.[120] Nor is it helpful to argue that Paul only grudgingly allows women permission to speak in 11.5, but gives his real opinion here in 14.33bff. There is no indication of any such reluctance in chapter 11.[121]

If we are to find a solution to the apparent contradiction between 11.5 and 14.34, then we must look elsewhere. Our understanding of this passage hinges on the interrelationships of σιγάω, λαλέω, and ὑποτάσσω.

There are three options for the referent of λαλέω: (1) 'inspired speech' (with Barrett); (2) uninspired speech — questions perhaps, but not chatter (with J. Héring); or (3) an authoritative word of wisdom (1 Cor 2.6–7).[122] Which option is most appropriate depends on the nature of the silence that Paul is imposing. Accordingly, we now look at the interrelationship between σιγάω and ὑποτάσσω.

It appears that the word σιγάτωσαν (v. 34) is qualified or governed by the word ὑποτασσέσθωσαν which immediately follows in v. 34b. Paul is contrasting σιγάτωσαν with λαλεῖν. The silence he enjoins is due to the fact that γυναῖκες were speaking in some sense in the church. They are to be silent because (causal γάρ)[123] it is not permitted them to speak. Paul carries his explanation further by adding 'but they are to be ὑποτασσέσθωσαν'. We have here a characteristic method of contrast: not this (οὐ), but this (ἀλλά). Thus, it is likely that the word σιγάτωσαν, since it too is contrasted to λαλεῖν must have some correlation to ὑποτασσέσθωσαν. The latter governs the former.

The word ὑποτάσσω is important not only because of its close relationship to σιγάω, but also because it provides the main rationale for women to be silent. It is the reason which Paul intimates is backed up by some principle or part of scripture (ὁ νόμος). Parenthetically, we should say that Paul also appeals to the αἰσχρός (shame/disgrace) in their speaking. As in 1 Cor 11.4–5, the shame or disgrace is a secondary argument meant to help correct the problem. In both 1 Cor 11.2ff. and 14.33bff., Paul first plays his theological trump card (11.7ff., 14.34) and then backs it up by arguing by what was considered at that time natural, normal, or honorable for Christian women (11.13ff., 14.35).

The word ὑποτάσσω (in the passive) draws on the LXX usage or its more prominent meaning, and is translated 'subject oneself', or 'be subjected', or 'be subordinated'.[124] It is used to describe: (1) the position of the wife in relation to the husband (Eph 5.22; Col 3.18; Titus 2.5); (2) the child in relation to the parents (Luke 2.51); (3) slaves in relation to their masters (Titus 2.9; 1 Pet 2.18); (4) all men in relation to secular authority (Rom 13.1; Titus 3.1; 1 Pet 2.13); (5) Christians in relation to church officials (1 Pet 5.5); (6) all in relation to God (Jas 4.7; 1 Pet 5.5); (7) believers in relation to Christ (Eph 5.22). In our context Paul does not say to whom women should be subordinate; nonetheless, it is obvious that numbers (2) and (3) do not apply. Number (4) does not apply since the context is specifically Christian worship. There is also no indication here that Paul was telling women to be subordinate to church officials since he never mentions them in this context.[125] As for number (6), can we really believe that Corinthian women thought they did not have to be subject to God especially in a worship service? Finally, it is also unlikely that Paul is referring to a general category of obedience to Christ by all believers since only women are singled out here.

This leaves us with the first possibility given above. Perhaps Paul is telling the women to be subordinate to their own ἀνήρ. The reference in v. 35b to τοὺς ἰδίους ἄνδρας might favor such a view. But why would such an exhortation be needed at this point?

Hurley has suggested that women were asking questions in such a manner as to stand in judgment over prophets or, even more likely, they thought themselves to be prophetesses or spiritual (v. 37) with the gift of interpretation or weighing of prophecy (v. 29).[126] The problem then would be as follows: (1) some Corinthian wives were prophetesses who thought they had the gift of judging the prophecies of others in the Christian worship; (2) the others just happened to be either their own husbands or other male prophets in the congregation; (3) Paul had apparently said before and is reiterating now, καὶ πνεύματα προφητῶν προφήταις ὑποτάσσεται (v. 32); (4) these wives were asking leading questions presuming to speak in an authoritative way over their own or another's husband; (5) the result was that these wives, in trying to subject the men's prophecies to their judgment, were not being subordinate to their own husbands or other men by so doing. Most likely, it was the insubordinate manner in which the wives were judging prophecy, not the mere fact of their weighing prophecy, that is the problem here.

The merits of such an interpretation are several. First, it in no way negates a woman's right to pray or prophesy in church, but only restricts her from judging prophecy in some manner so as to lord it over either her husband or men in general. It fits well with what precedes and follows our passage contextually. If Paul is speaking of the judgment of prophecy in 14.33b–36, then this would be a natural outflow of 14.29–30. Paul would be turning from a more general exhortation to orderly procedure in regard to weighing prophecy (vv. 32–33), to the more specific case of women weighing or questioning prophecy. This would also explain why Paul says in v. 37, 'if anyone thinks they are prophets or spiritual' (i.e., whether prophets as in 14.30–33a, or prophetesses as in 33b–36). It would also explain why Paul uses the word ὑποτάσσω twice in such close proximity. If women were 'laying down the law' or judging their husband's prophecy by leading questions and, by implication, questioning the veracity of their husbands or other men in regard to prophecy, then they were creating a situation where the Corinthian worship might become a family feud. A natural way for Paul to deal with this problem would be to reassert that women or wives, rather than being dominant over men or their husbands, were to be subordinate and to show their subordination by asking their husbands their questions at home.

If ὑποτάσσω in this context refers to the subordination of wives to their husbands, then we need to see how this qualifies or clarifies why Paul tells women to keep silent in the worship service. A survey of various uses of the Hebrew words for silence reveals that the only time silence is associated with submission in the OT is out of respect for God (Hab 2.20; cf. Isa 46.1; Zech 2.13), or one in position of authority (Jdgs 3.19), or wise men noted for their knowledge and counsel (Job 29.21), or it is a silence imposed by God on someone who speaks insolently to a righteous person (Ps 31.17). There are no NT parallels using either σιγάω or ἡσυχία except for 1 Tim 2.8ff. Of the OT passages cited, Job 29.21 has the closest connection with our passage. It involves the silence of respect for a teacher, the silence of someone who is a learner.

This discussion of the OT reference that Paul had in mind when he says, 'as even the law says', raises the possibility of a slightly different view from that of Hurley. If the reason for the counsel to silence and submission is caused by disorder in the worship service, not disorder in family relations, then this explains why ὑποτάσσω is used here in the *absolute form*.[127] Women are not being commanded to submit to their husbands, but to the principle of order in the worship service, the principle of silence and respect shown when another is speaking. The Corinthians should know that the OT speaks about a respectful silence when a word of counsel is spoken (Job 29.21).

Thus, the scenario we envision is as follows. During the time of the weighing of the prophet's utterances, some of the wives, who themselves may have been prophetesses and entitled to weigh verbally what was said, were asking questions that were disrupting the worship service. The questions themselves may have been disrespectful or they may have been asked in a disrespectful manner. The result was chaos. Paul's ruling is that questions should not be asked in worship. The wives should ask their husbands at home. Worship was not to be turned into a question-and-answer session.

This solution has the merits of fitting the context just as well as Hurley's, but takes seriously that ὑποτάσσω has no personal object here. At this point we are able to conclude that vv. 34–35 cannot be taken as a prohibition of women praying or prophesying, or teaching or preaching, in a worship setting. λαλέω, then, refers to uninspired speech, i.e., questions. The alternative Paul gives these women is simply to ask in another setting. Paul rules out an *abuse* of proper speech in worship; the dictum 'abusus non tollit usum' is applicable.

It should not be argued that λαλέω in vv. 34–35 could not be limited in this fashion by Paul without further clarification. This clarification is given when Paul mentions asking at home, which gives a clear hint as to what the content of the λαλέω by women was. Further, as Grudem points out, Paul had already placed a restriction of time or place on λαλέω earlier in v. 28. Those speaking in tongues are to be silent in church (σιγάτω ἐν ἐκκλησίᾳ) if there is no interpreter. The silence has to do not with all speech, but with a specific kind of speech indicated by the context. Or again, in v. 30, there is a command for a prophet to be silent (ὁ πρῶτος σιγάτω) if another begins to speak. Once again, the context indicates that this is not a total ban on the person in question speaking. The object of this command to silence is order, but also so all may learn (μανθάνωσιν, v. 31) which was precisely what the women were seeking to do (δέ τι μαθεῖν θέλουσιν, v. 35). Thus, vv. 34–35 fit in well in their present context. The problem dealt with in these verses is an example of what is spoken of in v. 29b – a problem arising during the weighing of the prophecies. Verse 29a is spoken about further in vv. 30–33a; v. 29b is spoken about further in vv. 33b–36.[128]

As a final point, one may ask, why then are women singled out in vv. 34–55? The answer is that they were the cause of the problem, the ones needing correction (see also 1 Cor 11.2ff.). But Paul includes that correction in a letter to all the Corinthians and addresses them all both before our passage and in vv. 36ff. so they too may avoid this abuse.

I conclude that a creation order or family order problem was not at issue in this passage but rather a church order problem caused by some women in the congregation. Paul corrects the abuse not by banning women from ever speaking in worship, but by silencing their particular abuse of speech and redirecting their questions to another time and place. Paul does wish the women to learn the answers to their questions. This passage in no way contradicts 1 Cor 11.5, nor any other passage which suggests that women can teach, preach, pray, or prophesy in or outside the churches. Thus, while the argument for interpolation certainly cannot be ruled out, the discussion above suggests that there is another more plausible explanation of the data.

D. Paul and his co-workers (Phil 4.2–3; Rom 16.1–6)

Without question Paul relied on many Christians all over the Mediterranean to help him carry out the ministry to the Gentiles. What was the relationship between Paul and his co-workers? How did they function? Were they also itinerant missionaries, or was their sphere of influence primarily local? What was the relationship between Paul's co-workers and the local church leaders? To ask these questions is also a way of asking: what was Paul's vision of the Christian community and its structure, and what roles could women play in that community? If we are to assess texts such as Phil 4.2–3 and Rom 16.1–16, which speak of women who were Paul's συνεργοί, we must first understand how the Pauline communities were structured and what roles various parties assumed.

Traditionally, ἐκκλησία has been translated as 'church' or 'churches' but this is debatable. The most likely OT word in the background is *qahal* (assembly), used of either the assembling or the assembly of God's people. This is also the meaning in Philo and Josephus. When we turn to Paul, R. Banks maintains that any passage can be translated by 'assembly', but some passages in Romans cannot be translated 'gathering' because apparently there was no single gathering of all Christians in Rome.[129] Paul is flexible in his usage and can speak of the church/assembly of God by which he means the whole Church (Gal 1.13), the church/assembly in a particular locality (Thessalonica), the church/assembly in a particular household (1 Cor 16.19, Col 4.15), and he can talk about the churches plural in Galatia, or various other regions and locations, or the church singular in a particular location (1 Cor 15.9).

For Paul, then, ἐκκλησία in the singular can refer to an individual unit of believers meeting in a household (the church), a particular local or regional church, or the Church corporately worldwide. In the plural it can refer to the latter two usages. Doubtless, this reflects Paul's view of the nature of the church/assembly. 'One peculiar thing about early Christianity was the way in which the intimate close-knit life of the local groups was seen to be simultaneously part of a much larger, indeed ultimately worldwide, movement or entity.'[130] The basic unit of Christianity, the individual house church/assembly, overlapped with what was seen as the basic unit of society, the household and the family (usually extended) that dwelt in it. W. A. Meeks rightly stresses that '... the household was much broader than the family in modern Western societies, including not only immediate relatives but also slaves, freedmen, hired workers, and sometimes tenants and partners in trade or craft. However, the *kat'oikon ekklesia* was not simply the household gathered for prayer; it was not coterminous with the household.'[131]

There is plenty of evidence in Paul and in Acts that one of the main ways the Church grew was by the principle of household inclusion/ conversion into the faith (cf. 1 Cor 16.15; Rom 16.10b, 11; Acts 16.31ff.). Perhaps because of its meeting in households and because of the overlap with the household structure, the Church early on was called the household of God, and Christians were seen as a family, brothers and sisters in the Lord. These factors also explain in part the use of household codes (Col 3.18–4.1; Eph 5.21–6.9) for ordering the Christian household, and to some extent the Christian Church.

One might conclude that the Church adopted the hierarchical structure of the family, but there is more to it than this. Spiritual gifts, social/intellectual status, and a host of other factors affected how the Church was structured. Further, the hierarchical schema was significantly modified ἐν Χριστῷ. Thus, Theissen's description of the Pauline model of community as involving a sort of love-patriarchalism[132] is not fully satisfactory. Meeks, however, is nearer to the mark when he says,

> The adaptation of the Christian groups to the household had certain implications both for the internal structure of the

groups and for their relationship to the larger society. The new group was thus inserted into or superimposed upon an existing network of relationships, both internal – kinship, *clientela*, and subordination – and external – ties of friendship and perhaps of occupation ... The head of the household, by normal expectations of the society, would exercise some authority over the group and would have some legal responsibility for it. The structure of the *oikos* was hierarchical, and contemporary political and moral thought regarded the structure of superior and inferior roles as basic to the well-being of the whole society. Yet, as we shall see, there were certain countervailing modes and centers of authority in the Christian movement that ran contrary to the power of the paterfamilias, and certain egalitarian beliefs and attitudes that conflicted with the hierarchical structure.[133]

Banks argues that the household or family is Paul's dominant metaphor for the Church (though mainly in Galatians and Ephesians).[134] Now it was not at all common in Judaism to call one's fellow believers brothers or sisters, nor was this the practice even in pagan groups such as the Dionysians.[135] But this practice was fundamental to the early Christian churches, and there was a real feeling that Christians were the family of faith. It is notable that Paul often uses family language especially when he is trying to create or heal the unity between believers. The kiss of peace arose out of household customs, a common familial form of affection, though now it is a peace ritual, a sign of reconciliation and unity having no parallel outside the NT.

When Paul calls himself the father (1 Cor 4.15) or mother (1 Thess 2.7, 11) of certain Christians, and calls them his children (1 Cor 4.14), he seems to imply both a certain family relationship in the Lord, and also a certain authority structure and responsibility he has over those who came to know Christ through him. Barrett points out that Paul does not use the term father of the minister or local church leader, but of the evangelist or apostle through whom one is converted.[136] Did Paul see himself as the absolute head of various Christian churches/assemblies/families to which he wrote as father giving advice? Notice how Paul talks about converts as infants (1 Cor 3.1), and sees them as his children (4.14). Yet he also calls them brothers (2.1, 3.1) implying a certain equality. What patterns of leadership or community development are implied? Could Paul really not have provided for the local leadership of his churches after his death?

This is unlikely, and it is not surprising that it is almost exclusively in Paul's later letters (Phil 1.1; 1 Tim 3.1ff., if it is by Paul) that we get any mention of what may be called church officers (cf. Rom 16.1).

It appears that the structures and functions of Paul's community were complex and grew gradually, but there is no indication that Paul ever envisioned a time when his communities would be so mature that leadership would prove unnecessary. It is clear, however, that Paul does not envision some sort of radical clergy/laity distinction. There are several reasons for this. First, Paul makes clear that all members of the Body are given manifestations of the Spirit for the common good (1 Cor 12.7), i.e., he intends that all members of the Body use their gifts to minister one to another. Second, when Paul discusses gifts and functions in the Church (Rom 12.3ff) he is addressing the whole Church, not just some ministerial class. Here we also see a parallel between the grace given to Paul (v.3) and the grace given to us (v.6). Thus, how (not whether) a person ministers in the community is determined in part by what gifts and graces the Spirit has imparted. In a sense, it is the Spirit that determines who does what in Paul's communities. Barrett suggests that the reason Paul says so little about the local ministers (cf. Acts 14.23) is because all are called to be ministers. In the Romans 12 list the progression is from gifts to persons; in 1 Corinthians 12 it is the converse. Both persons and gifts affect the church structure. It is also clear from 1 Cor 12.28 that there are authority figures in and for the community. Paul seems to rank them (in order of authority?) as follows: (1) apostle, (2) prophet, (3) teacher, (4) miracle workers and others.[137]

A structure is also implied at Gal 6.6 which speaks of local instructors (κατηχούμενος τὸν λόγον) whom the local church is not only to heed but support. In 1 Thess 5.11–15 the job of exhortation and building up the Body is for everyone, but there are some that have specific leadership tasks as overseers of the church. Allan Chapple has argued:

> Their ministry is firmly set, both in a literary and in a theological sense, within the context of the mutual ministry of all the believers – they do in a special way (or a pre-eminent degree) what all do in a quite reciprocal way (namely, to admonish ... – vv. 12, 14). The responsibility of each believer is for his brother; the responsibility of the leaders is for the church. This responsibility is demonstrated

and discharged in the exercise of recognizable Christian ministries aimed at the growth and up-building of the church.[138]

If the 'overseer's' concern is for the church as a whole then this implies a role not assumed by those who are not 'overseers'. Notice how in Rom 12.8 leadership is mentioned separately (ὁ προϊστάμενος) though again we are not told specifically what this entails. Were they simply administrators (cf. 1 Cor 12.28 – the seventh person listed?). Yet 1 Cor 16.15 implies that Stephanas' task is to steer or preside. Notice how they 'devoted themselves' to this task, i.e., Paul did not pick or ordain them (perhaps the Spirit prompted them?). They are the sort that the whole church is to submit to.

At this early stage in Paul's ministry there does not seem to be any systematically ordered ministry or process of ordination. Some people single themselves out and devote themselves to the leadership work. In addition, numerous functions such as church discipline, service, and exhortation are to be exercised when the whole church meets (1 Cor 5.4–5). From 1 Corinthians 12–14 it is clear that prophecy was a gift of the Spirit that empowered various people to assume a crucial ministry of the word, and 1 Cor 11.5 implies that women were involved in this ministry.

As for the διάκονοι (Phil 1.1), if they were not the church's financial officers/treasurers, then it appears their task of service was to see to the physical needs of the community. Providing a place to meet, however, seems to have been the function of a well-to-do member or patron/ess (cf. Lydia in Acts 16.13ff.).[139]

Because of the elusiveness of this evidence, Meeks has attempted to see if any light comes from exploring contemporary parallels, i.e., Jewish or pagan organization of the day. The evidence is largely negative,[140] but in this connection we note that συνεργός commonly meant fellow-worker in a common trade.[141] Meeks says,

> ... the Christian groups were exclusive and totalistic in a way that no club nor even any pagan cultic association was. ... the boundaries of the Pauline groups were somewhat more open than those of some other early Christian circles, to be 'baptized into Christ Jesus' nevertheless signaled for Pauline converts an extraordinarily thorough going resocialization, in which the sect was intended to become virtually the primary group for its members, supplanting all other loyalties. The

only convincing parallel in antiquity was conversion to Judaism, although adherence to the sects of the Pythagoreans or the Epicureans may in some cases have come close.[142]

Meeks concludes that the church did not model itself on the pattern of clubs and their structure, and there is only a minimal amount of shared terminology. Such clubs did have διάκονοι which seems to refer to those who waited on tables at feasts. Paul also uses the term ἐπίσκοποι (Phil 1.1; 'overseer') in a similar way. At Rom 16.2, *prostatis* probably does not designate an office, and in the contemporary clubs it was a functional designation for a patron or presiding officer (1 Thess 5.12).

A more promising candidate for comparison might be the synagogue. Besides the obvious elements of theological continuity, Diaspora Jews, like Paul's Christians, saw themselves not only as members of a local group but also as part of the larger people of God. However, we should note that while some Diaspora Jews met in households, it appears it was common practice to have a special meeting house outside the home, the synagogue itself.[143] It appears Christianity also differed from Judaism in its life in the Spirit, in its expression of spiritual gifts, and in its rituals – baptism and the Lord's Supper (though there are comparisons to proselyte baptism and the Passover). While Paul's churches did adopt and adapt many OT principles, beliefs, and traditions, notably they did not take over much of the structure or terminology of the synagogue.[144] The uniqueness of the Pauline groups came primarily from the work and life in the Spirit.

The pattern that emerges seems to be the following: (1) apostles; (2) Paul's travelling fellow-workers who were over or involved in several congregations (Priscilla, Aquila, Timothy, etc.); (3) local leaders. Presumably other apostles may have also had co-workers. The old distinction made between local church officials and apostles, prophets, teachers, as those who function throughout the Church will not stand up to close scrutiny. It is obvious that prophets and teachers could be local, but also it is obvious that Paul's co-workers could be peripatetic. What supra-church authority they had depended in part on their closeness to Paul and their willingness to follow his authoritative word closely.

From even a brief survey of Paul's letters it appears his co-workers had a wide range of functions from assisting in writing letters (1 Thessalonians), to checking-up on and encouraging fledgling

Christian communities (1 Thess 3.2, 6), to carrying apostolic messages to a church (1 Cor 4.17, 16.10), to providing a location and oversight of a local house church, to instructing and evangelizing (cf. Acts 18 to Romans 16; 1 Corinthians 16 on Aquila and Priscilla). We must avoid thinking that the churches all developed at the same rate or with the exact same structures. Nor can we make a hard and fast distinction between the itinerants and the local leaders, for some, like Epaphras of Colossae, apparently were missionary church planters as well (Col 1.7ff., 4.12ff.), and itinerants could on occasion establish themselves at one location (Phil 2.25–29, 4.18). There is an apparent flexibility in these matters.[145]

We must still look at local church leaders and their range of functions. Possibly, late in Paul's life he found it necessary to establish certain officers in the local churches (if the Pastorals are Pauline). 1 Thessalonians 5.12 tells us about local church functions – laboring, administering, verbal discipline, acting as a patron or protector. The latter was handled by those at the higher end of the socio-economic scale who could confer certain benefits on the congregation – place of meeting, financial support, protection, lodging. This naturally developed into a form of church leadership or prominence (1 Cor 16.19). The cases of Priscilla and Aquila, Philemon, the household of Stephanas (1 Cor 16.15) make this clear. In short, we see certain practical and sociological factors affecting church leadership. Thiessen demonstrated that for Rome and Corinth well-to-do people (Erastus?) played prominent roles because of their abilities to host and support the church and its leaders.[146] These functions seem to be mainly practical, but they also appear to be partly pastoral (cf. 1 Cor 16.15; 1 Thess 5.12c). This is interesting because Paul, while not abolishing all social or natural distinctions (ethnic, sexual), does *use* them in the service of the Church. Previously, sexual distinctions were used to create religious barriers. Paul tries to use such distinctions to build up and knit together the Church. Thus, Paul turns the normal use of social distinctions on its head. Instead of being self-serving, they are to serve others, i.e., the Church. Robin Scroggs has rightly argued that 'Paul wanted to eliminate the *inequality* between the sexes, while the gnostics wanted to eliminate the *distinctions* between the sexes.'[147] I agree, but the elimination of social inequalities is not Paul's main agenda. It was something that Paul assisted in bringing about in the course of preaching the Gospel of Jesus Christ and working out its implications.

For Paul, pragmatic considerations (such as who was converted first in a certain area) no doubt affected how he proceeded to choose leaders, but Paul's over-arching criterion for assessing a leader was, does he (or she?) build up the Church? Does he or she serve or sever the Body of Christ? For Paul, diakonia or service was the key. Paul requires one to ask, does this or that activity, behavior, lifestyle, use of money, build up or tear down the community of faith? Thus, the community is not purely structured by the Spirit and His gifts. It is also structured by whom Paul or his co-workers appoint, and who is best able to host the church. One's authority then could come from revelation, from a spiritual gift, from being appointed, from one's closeness to Paul, from one's knowledge and use of scripture and authoritative traditions, or presumably from one's experience as one who had followed the earthly Jesus. In some cases, who housed the church was determined by who was financially able, and who first led a house church was determined in part by who was first converted. In the end, however, all offices/functions/leadership roles functioned in the context of the ministry expected of all Christians everywhere. For our purpose, what is most significant is that women were a part of the specific ongoing ministry involved in being συνεργοί of Paul.

1. Trouble in Paradise? (Phil 4.2–3)

As Ellis has observed, Paul's most used description for those who aided him in his ministry is not ἀδελφός, διάκονος, or ἀπόστολος, but συνεργός. Of thirteen uses of this term in the NT, all but one (3 John 8) are in the Pauline corpus. It is a term not used of believers in general (cf. 1 Cor 3.9; 1 Thess 3.2; Rom 16.3, 9; 1 Thess 3.2; Rom 16.21; Phil 2.25; Phlm 24; 2 Cor 8.23, 1.24).[148] Notice how at 1 Cor 16.16, 18 the Corinthians are urged to be subject (ὑποτάσσησθε) to all those who are συνεργοῦντι καὶ κοπιῶντι. Clearly, it is implied they have some leadership role in the Corinthian community. Ellis notes that συνεργός and κοπός are probably equivalent terms[149] for a particular group of Christian workers. If κοπός is simply a variant term for a συνεργός, then 1 Thess 5.12 becomes particularly important for it speaks of workers who are προϊσταμένους ὑμῶν ἐν κυρίῳ καὶ νουθετοῦντας ὑμᾶς. This implies a leadership function involving some form of authoritative speech. It is hard to say whether this means teaching, preaching, or both, but it appears likely it involved at least one of these, and unlikely that Paul has prophecy or its weighing in view since he uses none of that sort of language to describe what these laborers did.

In light of this evidence, Phil 4.2−3 becomes illuminating. First, Paul is dealing with two women in this passage. As Lightfoot pointed out, 'No instance ... of either "Euodias" or "Syntyches" has been found in the inscriptions.'[150] Further, αὐταῖς in v.3 removes all possible doubt on this score. Second, that these verses surfaced in a letter to the whole church suggests that these women were significant enough to cause problems for the church if they were not reconciled.[151] Third, ἐν κυρίῳ may mean 'in the Christian community' (cf. v.2 and 1 Cor 11.11), in which case we are dealing with a personal problem affecting the community. It required the church leaders to intercede for reconciliation and unity to be brought about ἐν κυρίῳ.[152] We simply do not know who Paul's yoke-fellow was (although γνήσιε must surely argue that it was a man).[153] Paul is apparently calling upon someone he felt had authority, was trustworthy, and could help reconcile these two women.

Most importantly, Paul says of these two women: 'they struggled together with me in the gospel' (ἐν τῷ εὐαγγελίῳ, v.3) 'along with Clement also and the rest of my co-workers' (τῶν λοιπῶν συνεργῶν μου). Notice that these women are ranked alongside Clement (a man) in their work, and alongside Paul's other co-workers. The λοιπός, coupled with the two uses of καί, suggests that Paul saw these women as his co-workers. Notice also the parallel between συνήθλησαν μοι and συνεργῶν μου. The verb συναθλέω is drawn from athletic terminology used of the pagan games or gladiatorial matches, and could easily be translated 'fought together side by side with'.[154] This hardly suggests a passive or quiet role in the spreading of the Gospel, but rather one that involved real activity, difficult struggles, and maybe noteworthy sacrifices (Phil 1.27). In light of what we have learned about Paul's συνεργοί, this text strongly suggests that the two women engaged in the spreading of the Gospel with Paul. An εὐαγγελιστής was one who preached the Good News. Paul's readers were unlikely to exclude these women from such a task when Paul called Euodia and Syntche his co-workers 'fighting with me in the spread of the Gospel'.[155]

Now this should not surprise us since we have already noted the somewhat liberated status of Macedonian women even before Paul's day.[156] In our investigation of Acts we will note that the Macedonian church was founded by a converted woman.[157] The conjecture that Lydia of Acts 16 was actually one of the two women of Phil 4.2−3 depends on a questionable assumption that Lydia was not a personal name but rather an adjective meaning 'the Lydian'.[158] In any event,

Philippians was written at least a decade after the encounter in Acts 16, and if Lydia was a merchant she might well have been elsewhere when Paul wrote. In any case, both Philippians and Acts suggest that women took leading roles in the Philippian congregation. But what of women's roles in other congregations that Paul addressed? Let us now look at the famous list in Romans 16.

2. Ancient greeting card? (Rom 16.1−16)

The controversy over whether Romans 16 was an original part of Paul's letter to the Romans,[159] or a letter of recommendation and greeting later appended,[160] and the controversy over whether those addressed in this letter were in Rome or in Ephesus,[161] is an ongoing one in the scholarly community. For our purposes, it is not necessary to settle these complex issues since none of the favored conclusions cast doubts on the Pauline authorship of Rom 16.1−16. As E. Käsemann says about Romans 16, 'Apart from the conclusion, its Pauline authenticity is not in doubt.'[162] From our perspective, two conjectures commend themselves: (1) this was originally a letter of commendation for Phoebe which required the mention of Paul's contacts in Rome (or Ephesus?), so that Phoebe would be well received by the Roman house churches, or (2) while vv. 1−2 are a commendation for Phoebe, the major purpose of vv. 1−16 is to establish contacts and a favorable reception for both Paul's letter and later Paul himself in a community he had not founded but felt responsible for as the Apostle to the Gentiles. The conjecture that this was written after the demise of Claudius in the mid 50s when (Jewish?) Christians had returned to Rome seems quite probable.[163]

Phoebe, for whom this section of Romans may have been written, is not only commended, but also called διάκονος and a προστάτις. She was the former in the church at Cenchreae, the eastern point of Corinth, and the latter for many including Paul himself. Rom 16.1 and possibly 1 Tim 3.11 are the only two places where women are given the title διάκονος in the NT. It may be possible to trace the development of this church function (or office?) from some of the passages in Acts,[164] Rom 16.1, Phil 1.1, and finally 1 Tim 3.8ff. It seems clear that this term was used for those devoted to 'the practical service of the needy'.[165] C.E.B. Cranfield points out that Paul's formulation here, διάκονον τῆς ἐκκλησίας, suggests we may already be at the stage where deacon(ess) was a definite church office or recognized ongoing function.[166] This fits well with the description of

Phoebe as a προστάτις. It is unlikely that this term is used here in its legal sense of a representative (often for a foreigner),[167] nor does it seem likely that Paul means Phoebe was his patroness.[168] There is inscriptional evidence that the term can mean an office-bearer in a pagan religious association,[169] but again this hardly suits our text where Paul is talking about something Phoebe did to help him. If one examines Rom 12.8 and the use of ὁ προϊστάμενος, it appears probable that we are talking about a person in charge of the charitable work of the church. It would be suitable if this task was assigned to a person who did not need such assistance.[170] Thus, προστάτις probably means something like helper or protector. It connotes the personal care or hospitality Phoebe had provided for Paul and others.[171] The sense of protectress would not be too strong if Paul implies that he had received assistance from a woman when he was in a dangerous situation, perhaps when he needed seclusion in a private home.

Later we will discuss in detail Aquila and Priscilla, a husband and wife team ministry and Paul's co-workers (συνεργοί).[172] Here in Romans 16 we are told they 'risked their necks' for Paul. Verse 4 suggests strongly what a large impact they had on the Gentile church as a whole. Between Acts and Paul's letters we hear of them playing important roles in Ephesus, Corinth, and Rome. One gets the impression they were two of Paul's closest and most reliable workers, and it is likely they were involved in a wide range of activities from providing hospitality for Paul, to church planting, to teaching and preaching (Rom 16.5; 1 Cor 16.19; Acts 18.1–3, 26–28). Clearly, they were a major factor in the Gentile mission (καὶ πᾶσαι αἱ ἐκκλησίαι τῶν ἐθνῶν).

In vv. 6–7 we hear of a Mary who has been a hard worker for Paul's audience. The name may be a Jewish one, but note how the rest of the names in this chapter are either Latin or Greek. Except where we have names derived from pagan mythological figures (Hermes, etc.), it is possible that not only Aquila, Priscilla, and Mary, but also various others named here were Jewish Christians.[173] This is significant because Jewish women would have seen the new religious roles allowed them in Christianity as being in stark contrast to what had been the case in the Jewish synagogue or home.[174] If Ellis is right that κόπας and συνεργός have virtually identical meanings,[175] Mary's work cannot necessarily be limited to hospitality or charitable work (cf. 1 Thess 5.12).

What then do we make of 'Ανδρόνικον καὶ 'Ιουνιᾶν? Are these two men or a man and a woman (probably husband and wife)? While it is possible that 'Ιουνιᾶν is a shortened form of Junianus, it is more probable that we should accentuate this word 'Ιουνίαν, a common Roman female name, Junia.[176] There is no evidence for the male name 'Ιουνιᾶς in this form, and the patristic evidence (particularly John Chrysostom) supports the view that a woman named Junia is meant here.[177] We must reckon with the possibility that another Christian husband and wife team ministry is in view here. Paul calls this pair his 'kinsmen' which probably means they are fellow Jews who converted to Christianity.[178] They too, perhaps with Paul, had been imprisoned (possibly for the faith).[179] In one of the more significant and vexing sentences in this chapter we are told that Andronicus and Junia were ἐπίσημοι ἐν τοῖς ἀποστόλοις, οἳ καὶ πρὸ ἐμοῦ γέγοναν.[180] ἐπίσημος can mean 'splendid', 'prominent', or 'outstanding'[181] when used in a positive context, as we certainly have here, and only in the NT is it found in a metaphorical sense.[182] Literally, it means something like 'stamped', 'marked' (cf. coins, shields, flags) hence 'notable' in a derived sense. The question becomes: how do we understand ἐν plus the dative case of ἀπόστολος? It could mean 'in (the eyes) of the apostles'[183] but it probably means 'among the apostles'.[184] If so, then we have reference to a woman apostle. The question then becomes, what did ἀπόστολος mean for Paul?

From the studies of Barrett and R. Schnackenburg, it appears there are four ways the term apostle was used in the NT.[185] (1) It could refer to the original twelve, the Twelve Apostles, but apostle in this case was not a technical term for a member of the Twelve. It required the modifier 'twelve' to delimit the term (cf. Matt 10.2). (2) It could refer to a person who had seen the risen Lord and was commissioned by Him for some special ministry — Paul himself, for instance. It appears Paul identifies apostles of this sort by the phrase 'apostle of Jesus Christ' (1 Cor 1.1; 2 Cor 1.1; Col 1.1). (3) It could refer to an emissary (*shaliah*?) or missionary sent out by a particular church to perform particular tasks (1 Cor 8.23; Phil 2.25). (4) It could be a term meaning missionary (Acts 14.4, 14 of Barnabas). Schnackenburg argues that at Rom 16.7 'emissary of the church' is unlikely to be the meaning and thus the background of the Jewish *shaliah* is not relevant.[186] Most likely, Paul means itinerant missionary.[187] This is important because Paul says God appointed them first for the Church (1 Cor 12.28; cf. Eph 4.11). He distinguishes them from prophets and elders though no doubt their functions overlap somewhat. At the least it would appear that Paul means Andronicus and Junia were engaged in evangelism and church planting, and that they were itinerants. That Paul says they are notable or outstanding probably implies that their work was noteworthy and had borne much fruit. Paul adds that they were converted before he was which suggests they were some of the earliest converts in the church. By the time Romans was written they could have had a decade or more of ministry behind them. Jeremias points out that Christian missionary couples are a variant on the Jewish practice of sending forth two yoke-fellows (1 Cor 9.5), a practice Jesus may have used (Luke 10.1).[188] Käsemann notes that this practice allowed the women to reach fellow-women and children which would have been difficult for men to do in typical first-century Jewish settings.[189] Paul, however, says nothing here about a gender-specific ministry.

Romans 16.12, 15 also call for a brief remark. Tryphena and Tryphosa, who may have been sisters,[190] are called 'workers in the Lord'. Persis, which may mean the Persian woman,[191] is called 'beloved' and said to have 'labored hard in the Lord' (another example where ἐν κυρίῳ = ἐν ἐκκλησίᾳ?). Finally, at v. 15 we have greetings for what may be another Christian couple – Φιλόλογον καὶ Ἰουλίαν – depending on how we punctuate the sentence.

The overall impression one gets from Romans 16 is that not only were a wide variety of women involved in the work of the church, but also that they were doing a wide variety of things including missionary work, carrying letters, serving in charitable tasks as deaconesses, providing aid or shelter for traveling apostles, etc. If Romans 16 was originally sent with Phoebe to the capital of the Empire, then we see here a picture of a vibrant, multi-faceted Church using the gifts and graces of both men and women to spread the Gospel. We noted earlier that in traditional Roman religions women did not have such a variety of roles,[192] and it is not surprising that Christianity would be viewed by pagan Romans as another Eastern cult like any one of the mysteries that was affecting large numbers of Roman women by giving them active roles to play. Rome's cosmopolitan nature was such that a wide variety of people could and did come there to settle, or stay awhile on business, and this led to a variety of contacts and converts for Christianity at the hub of the Empire. First-century people were more mobile than we might expect, and there is no reason why an Aquila and Priscilla could not have returned to Rome after Claudius' edict fell into abeyance. In any event, Paul realized his deep indebtedness to both men and women in his ministry. It is more than a little significant that he felt obliged to address both men and women before he came to Rome. This witnesses to the crucial roles women played in the Roman house churches.

Finally, in the undisputed Paulines we have seen evidence of husband and wife team ministries such as Aquila and Priscilla, or possibly Andronicus and Junia. Did Paul make any distinctions between the roles wives, as opposed to single women, could play in the ministry of Christ? In the later Paulines we will see widows playing specific roles. But there is no evidence in the undisputed Paulines that women had to be married to play significant roles in a house church. The conjecture that wives, under the authority of their husbands, might be allowed to do more for the Lord than single women has no basis in the material we have examined. Indeed, if anything Paul suggests that being single was preferable for Christian women (1 Cor 7.34a). We will now turn to the Pastoral epistles to see how Paul's teaching in regard to women developed with time.

E. The Pastoral epistles: proto-gnostic problems

Whether the Pastoral epistles were written by Paul,[193] or by a later Paulinist,[194] they still represent a development of Pauline thought and practice. Are the Pastorals a legitimate development of or away from the Pauline preaching and practice? This question becomes acute when we examine 1 Timothy 2 which on the one hand appears to be a development of 1 Cor 14.33b, but on the other hand seems to go against or beyond Paul's teaching in 1 Corinthians 14.

A linguistic comparison of 1 Tim 2.8−15 and 1 Cor 14.33b−34 shows striking parallels.

(1) ἐν πάσαις ταῖς ἐκκλησίαις	1 Cor 14.33b, cf. 34
ἐν παντὶ τόπῳ	1 Tim 2.8
(2) γυνή	1 Cor 14.34, 1 Tim 2.9
(3) σιγάω	1 Cor 14.34
ἡσυχία	1 Tim 2.11
(4) μανθάνω	1 Cor 14.35; 1 Tim 2.11
(5) ἐπιτρέπω	1 Cor 14.34; 1 Tim 2.12
(6) ὑποτάσσω	1 Cor 14.34
ὑποταγῇ	1 Tim 2.11
(7) ἀνήρ	1 Cor 14.35; 1 Tim 2.12

The above denotes a clear relationship between these texts, and we may conjecture that 1 Tim 2.8−15 is a modification of the same type of argument we find in 1 Cor 14.33bff. to meet a later and different situation. It is important to recognize that what we have here is not so much a fragment of a household code (but cf. 1 Pet 3.1–6), as a part of a *Gemeindeordnung*.[195] In both texts we are talking about behavior in worship, not behavior in general, though J. Murphy-O'Connor sees here a sketch of how a Christian community ought to live in a minority situation.[196]

Certainly a concern to portray oneself well in the world affects some of this advice, but it is also certain that the author is dealing with specific problems affecting worship. Thus, we hear at 2.8 about contention and grumbling among the men, and in 1 Tim 5.14–15 about backsliding or apostasy among the women. The problems addressed may be traced to the influence of false teachers who seem to espouse a proto-gnostic form of Jewish Christianity.[197] Their teaching involves some form of dualism that saw the physical side of human existence as having little or no soteriological significance. Thus, it was argued that one could either refrain from or indulge in sexual activity without it affecting one's status before God in any negative way.

This would account for both the libertine and ascetic qualities that we seem to detect in the problems with which the Pastorals dealt. If 1 and 2 Timothy are concerned with Christians in a cosmopolitan city like Ephesus,[198] where there was a wide variety of religious influences and forms of syncretism, then it is not surprising that from a pragmatic point of view a clear and conservative policy about theological and ethical matters was necessary. Christianity wanted to be a good witness to those who might be drawn to the faith, but at the same time wanted to protect the new Church from slipping into familiar pagan ways or a syncretistic compromise of the faith. This meant (1) being morally exemplary citizens, and (2) attacking any heresy or immorality that might compromise the witness to the city as well as the harmony of the community.

About the problems involving women we have the following hints. First, there were problems of a sexual nature involving young women, particularly young widows (1 Tim 5.11–16). Second, there were women weak in the faith, guilty of sin, and perhaps looking for an easy theological out (2 Tim 3.6–7). Third, it is possible that the τισίν in 1 Tim 1.3 means women were involved in (if not teaching) myths and endless genealogies and speculation involving the law.[199] With this background let us look at 1 Tim 2.8–15 more closely.

The tone of this section is indicated clearly by verbs such as βούλομαι (v. 8) and ἐπιτρέπω (v. 12). The author has the authority to command, but the tone is somewhat milder than this, perhaps because the letter is directed to a faithful colleague. From the outset, it appears the author is talking about men and women as groups, not husbands and wives. This is so not only because it is unlikely he would wish only husbands in every place to pray, but also because at vv. 9–12 we have the word women without the definite article.[200] Even at v. 14 where we have ἡ γυνή the reference seems generic.

ἐν παντὶ τόπῳ seems to parallel 1 Cor 14.33b, and while it may recall Mal 1.11,[201] it probably means 'in every (meeting) place', i.e., in all the house churches.[202] The key phrase is χωρὶς ὀργῆς καὶ διαλογισμοῦ. Apparently, there were some tensions between the men in this or in several of the Ephesian house churches. We do not know whether the disputes were over who should lift up 'holy hands' in prayer, or were related more generally to the problems in evidence elsewhere in 1 Timothy. The important thing to realize is that the author is dealing with abuses in worship. Verses 9–10 are elliptical and are most naturally taken to imply that the author is now giving the same injunction to the women as he gave to the men, as ὡσαύτως (likewise) suggests.[203] This is important on two counts. First, it suggests the author was not imposing absolute silence on the women here, but correcting an abuse. Second, it has important implications for our discussion of 3.11 where once again we have γυναῖκας ὡσαύτως. The author is calling for women to come to worship with modest apparel, but also without extravagant hair styles. There is abundant secular literature to illustrate what the author is criticizing. J.B. Hurley says:

> He refers ... to the elaborate hair-styles which were fashionable among the wealthy and also to the styles worn by courtesans. The sculpture and literature of the period make it clear that women often wore their hair in enormously elaborate arrangements with braids and curls interwoven or piled high like towers and decorated with gems and/or gold and/or pearls. The courtesans wore their hair in numerous small pendant braids with gold droplets or pearls or gems every inch or so, making a shimmery screen of their locks.[204]

Hurley concludes that when the author wrote 'braided hair and gold or pearls' he probably meant their braided hair was decorated with gold or pearls.[205] Thus, the author is arguing not only for modesty and frugality in dress and worship, but also against the wearing of ostentatious or suggestive apparel or hairstyles that could attract the wrong sort of attention and compromise the moral witness of the church. Women who profess religion should instead be clothed with good deeds.

In vv. 11 12 women are exhorted to be ἐν ἡσυχίᾳ. This is not quite the same word as we find in 1 Cor 14.34 – σιγάω. At 1 Tim 2.2 it means 'quiet', for the author surely is not exhorting Christians to a silent life. In all probability this is what is meant at 1 Tim 2.11–12 as well.[206] Paul is suggesting correct behavior for one who is learning; it is not a prohibition of speaking. The focus is on how one should listen and learn, not on whether or not one may speak at all in worship.

Verse 11 involves an imperative – μανθανέτω – which indicates that the author saw it as important for women to learn.[207] Besides learning quietly, women are also to learn ἐν πάσῃ ὑποταγῇ. This parallels ἐν ἡσυχίᾳ explaining *how* women should learn, and should be contrasted with the διδάσκειν ... αὐθεντεῖν ἀνδρός in v. 12 as the reiteration of ἐν ἡσυχίᾳ at the end of v. 12 makes apparent. This means that ἐν πάσῃ ὑποταγῇ[208] describes the proper attitude of receptivity to the teaching. Women are being ordered to observe the proper attitude in which one may learn. This is not an attempt to comment on the relationship of husbands and wives. It is, however, being contrasted with an attempt to teach and domineer the men present in the worship, as we shall see.

Verse 12 begins with δέ indicating the contrast with v. 11. The women are to learn in quietness and all submission, but not to teach. The verb ἐπιτρέπω (present active indicative first person singular) should be translated 'I am not permitting'.[209] This is to be distinguished from the possible use of a rabbinic formula at 1 Cor 14.34 where we have the third person singular, 'it is not permitted', with a possible reference to the νόμος (v. 34b) as the subject.[210] Here the author himself is denying permission; he is not relying on previous biblical sanctions or church rulings. As Payne points out, the author does not use the future here ('I will not permit'). He adds that there are no examples in the LXX or NT where ἐπιτρέπω in the present active indicative first person singular implies a perpetual ordinance; rather, a timely and specific prohibition is involved.[211] Of course, only the context can ultimately determine such a matter. We have seen at vv. 8ff. that the author is dealing with specific problems in worship, and there is no reason to doubt he is continuing to do so here. Whatever v. 12 means, it would not seem to rule out (1) women speaking in worship (v. 9 – ὡσαύτως); (2) women speaking in the course of their duties as deaconesses (cf. below on 3.11; cf. 3.8 – 'double tongued'); (3) possibly women teaching their children (including males) or other women in the faith (cf. 1 Tim 5.3ff.; 2 Tim 1.5–6). In short, there appear to be some hints in 1 and 2 Timothy of how οὐκ ἐπιτρέπω is to be qualified.

That v. 12, like v. 11, is addressed to women in general, not just the wives, suggests the author felt there was a sufficient problem in the congregation to impose a general, though possibly temporary, ban. The verb διδάσκω is simply a general one for teaching and does not suggest in itself a limitation to a particular kind of teaching, such as 'authoritative' preaching or teaching.[212] The only apparent limitation from the context is that the author is talking about what all women should and should not do in worship.

The real crux of the matter, however, hinges on how one interprets αὐθεντεῖν, a hapax legomenon in the NT. It seems clear, if one surveys all the extra-biblical and patristic evidence, that the verb αὐθεντέω is a strong verb and may be similar to αὐτοδικεῖν, a Koine verb meaning 'to be independent'. It has been suggested that αὐθεντέω 'originated in popular Greek vocabulary as a synonym of κρατεῖν τινος "to dominate someone"'.[213] G. W. Knight's survey of extra-biblical usage does show that the verb can be used in a positive or neutral sense 'to exercise authority'.[214] However, he is wrong that the verb cannot have the negative connotation 'to domineer' or 'to abuse power and authority'. Thus, for instance, the translation of αὐθεντηκότος in the letter from Tryphon (27–26 BC) that he urges is doubtful at best. Surely, what is being implied there is not merely 'I exercised authority over him and he consented' but 'I leaned on him and he consented' (i.e., a heavy handed or questionable use of one's authority).[215] Perhaps more important, however, is the patristic evidence. In Chrysostom we have the advice to the husband, μὴ ... ἐπειδὴ ὑποτέτακται ἡ γυνή αὐθεντεῖ which is rightly translated 'do not play (or act) the despot', or 'do not act arbitrarily'.[216] Now this sort of use of the verb should not surprise us. The noun form in secular literature can mean 'perpetrator', or 'master', and the inscriptional evidence suggests a meaning 'have absolute sway over' (αὐθεντία).[217] Moulton and Milligan conclude, 'The use in 1 Tim 2.12 comes quite naturally out of the word "master", "autocrat".'[218] The context of 1 Tim 2.12 here suggests a correction of abuses by both men and women in worship.

I conclude that the author means that women are not permitted to 'rule over', 'master', or 'play the despot' over men. If 1 Tim 1.3ff.

does include a warning about some women (and men) trying to teach different doctrines, desiring to lay down the (Mosaic) law (1 Tim 1.7) in the house church(es) in Ephesus, then this correction of the problem in 1 Tim 2.12 is quite understandable. It is advice given to correct a problem, and also suggests the author did not favor a woman domineering a man. Once again, however, the dictum *abusus non tollit usum* applies. One cannot assume that the prohibition would extend beyond the period of the abuse, or beyond cases where a similar abuse might arise elsewhere. There is no universal and unqualified prohibition of women teaching and preaching in this text. Further, it is inappropriate to try and read some sort of pronouncement about ordination of any kind into the text.[219]

In vv. 13–15, the author backs up his prohibition with an appeal to scripture. Does the γάρ introduce an appropriate example (explanatory γάρ) or is it an illative γάρ giving the reason for the prohibition?[220] If it is the latter, then it might imply some sort of broad anthropological judgment about women's susceptibility to deception, i.e., women should not teach because they are more susceptible to deception as Eve was. Not all women, but only weak and guilty women, are said to be susceptible to being led astray (2 Tim 3.6–7). It is only some younger widows who are saying what they should not (1 Tim 5.13–15). The author's solution for these young widows is that they remarry, have children, and rule the house (οἰκοδεσποτεῖν, v. 14). This is important for two reasons. First, it indicates the author was not opposed to women exercising authority in the home, even if males were involved. Second, this advice sounds very much like what we hear at 1 Tim 2.15. It is unlikely that our author is trying to pass some universal judgment on women's susceptibility to temptation and deception. Only some women in Ephesus were having that problem. Others were believing and trustworthy women who could be assigned tasks (1 Tim 5.16, cf. 2 Tim 1.5–6). This suggests that if γάρ (1 Tim 2.13) should be translated at all (and is not simply a connecting conjunction as so often it is in the NT), then we have here a γάρ which introduces an example ('for example'), not an explanation or statement of causation ('because'). What follows, then, is intended to be an historical example or precedent that explains the consequences of a woman being deceived and attempting to assume or assert an authority not given to her. The point of the example is to teach women not to emulate Eve, but rather to emulate the behavior outlined in v. 15.[221]

When examining vv. 13–14, remember that it is a short form of exposition on Gen 2.7ff. and 3.1ff. which alludes to more than it expresses, and assumes the audience knows the text in question. Whether or not this exposition is haggada, the use of these texts to teach women a lesson was common among Jewish expositors.[222] The curse on Eve was not childbearing but pain in childbearing, and the husband 'lording it over the wife'.[223] Genesis 3.15 suggests that bearing children will be a blessing in that it provides a 'seed' who will combat and overcome the tempter (the serpent). Genesis 3.20 indicates Eve would be called 'mother of all living' and 4.1ff. indicates Eve saw that God helped her to have a child. In short, being a mother is not a curse, but a blessing from God which will provide a means of combatting the source of temptation and evil. The author of 1 Timothy assumes his audience will understand the creation and fall stories.

Verse 13 speaks of the order of creation; verse 14 of the order in the fall. What is interesting about v. 13 is the suggestion that Eve was *made*, as was Adam, only second. Now this suggests not only an order in creation, but an identity in it. Adam and Eve were *made* in like manner.[224] The author makes no capital out of this assertion, however, as we saw Paul do at 1 Cor 11.8ff., but presses on to the real nub of the issue – Eve was first in the Fall being deceived γέγονεν ἐν παραβάσει.[225] There is nothing in this exposition or in the word παραβάσει which implies Eve's sin was sexual. Our author is more constrained in his assertions than some of his rabbinic counterparts.[226]

Verse 15 indicates that Eve's transgression was not without a remedy. This verse is difficult because of the shifting back and forth from singular to plural, but the point is relatively clear. Women in Ephesus are not to emulate Eve in being deceived and transgressing (listening to false teachers) but rather are to work out their salvation not by attempting to rule over men or engage in harmful teaching, but by being married, having children, and helping them continue in faith, love, and holiness. The subject of σωθήσεται in v. 15 must be ἡ γυνή from v. 15, but with a shift in meaning. In v. 15 γυνή means 'women' (generic), not the woman Eve in particular.[227] The phrase διὰ τῆς τεκνογονίας could be a reference to 'the childbearing', i.e., the birth of the Savior.[228] The solution to a woman's problems created by Eve came about through another woman, Mary. Despite the attractiveness of the solution and its endorsement by many Church Fathers,[229] an easier solution is ready at hand (and it is not Moffatt's innovative translation 'be kept safe through childbearing').[230]

Throughout this passage the author has been addressing *Christian* men and women. Notice in 1 Tim 4.14–16 the use of σώσεις of someone who is already a Christian.[231] We are familiar with the Pauline dictum at Phil 2.12 – 'work out your salvation with fear and trembling'. I thus conclude that exegetical gymnastics are unnecessary, for our author is not telling women how they may be saved, but how they may work out their salvation, how they may remain in faith, love, and holiness. As a second alternative σωθήσεται may mean saved from the problems enumerated earlier in the passage.[232]

If τεκνογονίας does not refer to the birth of Christ, then μείνωσιν in v. 15 in the plural may refer to the children born (the nearest antecedent), or the women and their children,[233] or (least likely) husband and wife. In either of the first two cases, it is implied that women have a responsibility to see that their children remain ἐν πίστει which may well suggest Christian instruction in the home.

Our author proposes an old remedy for a new problem. The problem involves women abusing the freedom they have in Christ, perhaps because they were used to even more freedom if they had participated in the rites at the temple of Artemis.[234] The solution here, as in 1 Tim 5.11ff., is a reaffirmation of women's traditional roles. Does this mean women were banned from meaningful work in the Christian community? A quick glance at 3.11 suggests the answer is no. Though the γυναῖκας of 3.11 could be a reference to deacons' wives, or even to single women (whether widows or unmarried women),[235] it is more probable that here we see the development of what we found at Rom 16.1 – a female diaconate. As R. M. Lewis points out, we would expect γυναῖκας ὑμῶν and possibly a καί instead of a ὡσαύτως if deacons' wives were meant at 3.11.[236] Unfortunately, it is not made clear what a deacon or deaconess did, only what character they must have. Whatever the tasks were, they may have involved practical service and charitable works such as those mentioned at 1 Tim 5.10, 16. It is difficult to say whether or not 1 Tim 5.9ff. indicates there was already an order of widows when the author wrote. The enrolment at 5.9 was presumably so they might be supported, not so they might serve. In any event, 1 Timothy 5 makes clear women could serve active and useful roles in the church community beyond the raising of a family. It is worth noting that at 2 Tim 4.19 Priscilla and Aquila are mentioned. If this is a genuine greeting and this ministering couple was in Ephesus, then we know at least that there was one woman who taught. This makes it all the more likely that 1 Tim 2.9ff. is advice specific to the situation.

F. Conclusions

We are now at the point of drawing conclusions from the detailed study of women's involvement in the family of faith in the Pauline corpus. Galatians 3.28 was probably a dictum serving the same function for women in Paul's audience as Matt. 19.10−12 did for Jesus, i.e., allowing women to remain single for the Lord, a condition Paul clearly prefers (1 Corinthians 7). As such it opened the possibility of women being involved in roles other than the traditional ones of wife and mother.

In 1 Cor 11.2ff. we discovered that Paul allows women to pray and prophesy. The latter was seen as crucial by Paul, a word of God for a specific situation whether as a proclamation, a teaching, or an exhortation. Prophecy, in its origin solely in the Spirit's prompting, could be distinguished from teaching and preaching. Perhaps in its content, prophecy also served the purpose of edification. In 1 Cor 11.2ff. we also hear Paul affirm the distinction of the sexes in the context of Christian worship, reaffirming the creation order in the Christian community. New creation had not obliterated the distinctions that came by way of creation, so that as long as creation order is recognized and affirmed Paul does not prohibit women from speaking in the congregation.

1 Corinthians 14.33bff. is to be seen as an attempt to correct a problem caused by women judging the prophets. Instead of disrupting the service, they should ask their husbands at home. As seen in 1 Cor 14.34 and perhaps also 1 Tim 2.11, ὑποτάσσω refers to submission, not to husbands, but to church principles of order and decorum in worship (assuming the proper attitude of one who is learning).

Romans 16.1−16 indicates an abundance of women were involved in some form of ministry, and Phil 4.2−3 intimates the same, though we cannot know the full extent of the service these various women rendered. The use of the terms συνεργός, διάκονος, and ἀπόστολος indicates that Paul was receiving assistance from women in ministry not only in practical ways but also in the ministry of the word. There is certainly nothing in the undisputed Paulines that would rule out a woman from teaching or preaching. Paul, however, did apply restrictions when new roles in the Christian community were taken to imply a repudiation of women's traditional roles and the importance of maintaining sexual distinctions. Certainly Paul does not warrant the title of chauvinist, but also he was no radical feminist. Rather, as was the case with our investigation of Jesus, what we see in Paul is:

(1) an affirmation of new religious roles for women, and (2) a reaffirmation with some Christian modifications of the traditional roles women had been assuming in the family. In some contexts, particularly among Jews and Jewish Christians, both (1) and (2) would have made Paul appear to be a radical. In other contexts, among some Gentiles, Paul's moral conservatism and reaffirmation of traditional roles for women would have appeared too confining (this appears to have been the case in Corinth). 1 Corinthians 11 and 14 seem to be Paul's reaction to those whom he perceived to be overly liberated women.

It would be untrue and unfair to say that Paul simply endorses the status quo so far as the physical family is concerned. Even in the *Haustafel* at Eph 5.21ff. Paul engages in transforming the perception of traditional husband and wife roles in the church, always in light of the salvific relationship between Christ and Church. The family of faith is central for Paul, as it was for Jesus, and this means the structure and roles of the physical family would be affected, and in some ways transformed, by the transcending practices of the family of faith. Paul walked a difficult line between reaffirmation and reformation of the good that was part of the creation order, and the affirmation of new possibilities in Christ. It is the same tension we see in Paul in other ways as well — between freedom and tradition — or, as Barrett says "freedom and obligation".[237]

In our study of 1 Tim 2.8–15 (with a brief look at 1 Tim 3.11), we find no universal prohibition of women speaking in church, but a dealing with some serious problems that caused the author to ban women from teaching and domineering men in Ephesus. We conjecture that this was a response to women being involved in false teaching and being led astray into apostasy. The remedy offered is a reaffirmation of women's traditional roles in the family. There is nothing in this material that suggests a permanent ban on women engaging in the ministry of the word — *abusus non tollit usum*. However, when certain isolated verses are taken out of context, such as 1 Tim 2.11–12, it is understandable how such a ban could arise. It must be admitted that the material in the Pastorals is much more tradition-oriented, and thus we see a more conservative position than in earlier Paulines. Perhaps this is only a development of one side of the tension that Paul maintains between freedom and tradition, due to the problems that excessive freedom caused. There is nothing in the Pastorals that repudiates or contradicts Paul's earlier affirmation of both sides of the tension, but there is more emphasis placed on the traditional side.[238]

In our next two chapters we will examine how the tension between new freedom for women and traditional roles is presented in some of the material from the Gospels and Acts. This advances our chronological study into the last quarter of the first century.

4

WOMEN AND THE THIRD EVANGELIST

A. Women in the ministry of Jesus

Of all the insights stressed by Lukan scholars in the past several decades, perhaps none has been more emphasized than the paradigmatic nature of the Nazareth speech of Jesus (Luke 4.16–30). Our purpose is not to answer the difficult historical questions raised by such texts as Luke 4.16–30, but to ask how the Evangelists as editors in the last third of the first century presented women first mentioned in their sources. Luke (4.16–30) indicates that the liberation of the oppressed and poor is an essential part of any ministry modeled on that of Jesus. For our purposes, we should note that Luke will stress again and again that women are among the oppressed that Jesus came to liberate. This is already evident at 4.26 where Elijah's action for a widow is cited as an example, but Luke does not content himself with citing examples.

Luke structures some of his Gospel material to illustrate the fulfilment of Isa 61.1–2 in the ministry of Jesus. Table 1 illustrates this idea.

Table 1

Luke 4.18–19 (Isa 61.1–2)	Luke 4.38–44	Luke 8.1–3
18 preach Good News to poor ⟵——————————⟶		1 preach and proclaim Good News
recovery of sight ⟷ to blind ⟵ ⟶	38 Jesus heals Simon's ⟷ mother-in-law 40 Jesus heals sick with various diseases	2 heals evil spirits and illnesses in women
set at liberty ⟵——⟶ the oppressed	41 demons cast out ⟷	2–3 examples of captives released, i.e., women
19 proclaim 'acceptable ⟷ year of the Lord'	43 preach Good News ⟷ to other cities (cf. v. 44)	cf. 8.4–15

Another structural element in Luke–Acts, even more noticeable than the one just mentioned, is Luke's penchant for male–female parallelism. This is evident not only in Luke's noted pairing of parables, but also in special Lukan material, as table 2 indicates.[1]

Table 2

Zacharias and Mary:	
the angelic annunciation	Luke 1.10–20, 26–38
glory to God	Luke 1.46–55, 67–79
Simeon and Hannah	Luke 2.25–38
widow of Sarepta and Naaman	Luke 4.25–38
healing of Peter's mother-in-law and demoniac	Luke 4.31, cf.
	Mark 1.21–31
centurion of Capernaum and widow of Nain	Luke 7.1–17
Simon the Pharisee and the sinner woman	Luke 7.36–50
man with the mustard seed and woman with the leaven	Luke 13.18–21
good Samaritan, and Mary/Martha	Luke 10,29–42
man with one hundred sheep and woman with ten pieces of silver	Luke 15.4–10
importunate widow and the publican	Luke 18.1–14
women at the tomb and Emmaus disciples	Luke 23.55–24.35
sleeping man and woman at the mill in Last Judgment	Luke 17.34–35, cf.
	Matt 24.40–41
Ananias and Sapphira	Acts 5.1–11
Aeneas and Tabitha	Acts 9.32–42
Lydia and the Philippian jailor	Acts 16.13–34
Dionysius and Damaris	Acts 27.34

As H. Flender rightly concludes, 'Luke expresses by this arrangement that man and woman stand together and side by side before God. They are equal in honor and grace; they are endowed with the same gifts and have the same responsibilities ...'[2]

A good deal can be learned about Luke's interests from the way he edits his Markan and Q source material, for here we are able to compare the source material and its redaction. For instance, at Luke 18.29 (Mark 10.28–30) Luke adds ἢ γυναῖκα, thus intensifying the cost of discipleship. This also reflects Luke's interest in and concern for women. This concern for a woman's condition is also evident in what he adds to the Markan story of the widow and her two coins (Luke 21.1–4 = Mark 12.41–44). Only Luke says she was πενιχράν. Further, Luke is sparing in his retention of 'truly' to introduce a saying of Jesus (only as 9.27, 12.41), but here he does so to stress this woman's good example.[3] More than any other Evangelist, Luke stresses Jesus' concern for widows, a particularly disadvantaged group of women (cf. Luke 2.36−38, 4.26, 7.11−17, 18.1−8, 20.47, 21.1−4).

Luke 11.27−28, unique to the Lukan account, implies that a person's chief blessedness is in one's response to God's word. This implies a criticism of any attempt to see a woman's chief blessedness in her traditional gender-specific roles. Luke 10.38−42, also unique, implies a similar criticism of any attempt to suggest a woman's traditional roles were more important than hearing and heeding the word of Jesus. The 'one thing needful' for women as well as men is a response to the Word, the 'best portion' of which they should not be prevented from partaking.[4]

Omissions from the Marcan source also give us clues to Luke's interest, as is shown in the way he handles the difficult material in Mark 3.21, 31−35 (Luke 8.19−21). Luke not only deletes Mark 3.21 (which implies a serious misunderstanding by Mary of Jesus), but also softens the contrast between Jesus' physical family and the family of faith. Another interesting example arises in the Q material at Luke 11.31 (Matt 12.42). Here Luke has τῶν ἀνδρῶν which may be an attempt to feature prominent women at the expense of certain men.[5] This may reflect Luke's tendency to stress male−female reversal, the praise of a woman (even a foreign woman) at the expense of certain men who ought to be setting good examples. This same motif is evident at Luke 7.36−50 and 13.10−17, both uniquely Lukan. Examples of this sort could be multiplied but have been covered in detail in my earlier monograph.[6] All of this demonstrates a redactional tendency by the Third Evangelist reflecting his interest in women and their roles.

B. Women in the resurrection narratives

Though there is no great stress on women or their roles in the Lukan resurrection narrative, much of which is unique, there does appear to be a notable structural example of male−female reversal and a stress on the validity of a woman's word of witness about the resurrection events. When the women visit the tomb on Easter morning, Luke highlights the angel's words to the women to remember what Jesus said to them while He was in Galilee (24.5−7). By this means, Luke implies the women were with Jesus in Galilee and were taught these prophecies, for they were among His disciples.[7] The μνήσθητε of v. 6 and the ἐμνήσθησαν of v. 8 perhaps are to be taken in the technical sense of calling to mind the word of Jesus and realizing the implications of their present fulfilment (cf. Acts 11.15; John 2.22, 12.16).[8] In this 'call to remember', the women are being summoned to be true disciples. There is no future element in the angel's words or any commissioning of the women to go tell the disciples (though Luke says they do so).[9] Thus, the women are treated not as emissaries to the disciples, but as true disciples in their own right, worthy of receiving special revelation about Jesus.

Luke adds an account of how the women's words were received. They abandon the tomb and announce all these things (ταῦτα πάντα) to the Eleven and all the rest (τοῖς ἕνδεκα καὶ πᾶσιν τοῖς λοιποῖς).[10] Only now, after recording the full scope of the women's roles in the death, burial, and resurrection of Jesus, does Luke give the reader a list of those involved in these events. This placing of a list *after* certain crucial events is similar to Luke's procedure in Acts 1.13–14.[11] The placement of presumably known names at a climactic point may be Luke's way of validating what he previously recorded. The Evangelist may be claiming that these specific people are witnesses and guarantors of these events. If so, then again we see Luke emphasizing the equality of women and their worth as valid witnesses to all three events. Perhaps Luke's mention of Joanna (instead of Mark's Salome) is an attempt to present a well-to-do witness, one who could relate to a similar audience.

Placing the list after the death–burial–empty-tomb sequence is appropriate because at this point the women are no longer the sole witnesses to what transpired, and Luke goes on to stress that the Eleven are the primary recipients of the most crucial appearance of Jesus. In Luke, the Apostles are designated witnesses and guarantors of the fact that the risen Jesus appeared (cf. 24.36–49; Acts 1.21–22).[12] Luke stresses that the women's witness is crucial for what takes place up to that point; in fact, even the Apostles can only validate their words (v. 12) and others among the disciples can only talk about them (vv. 22–24). Consider also the contrast between Luke 24.9 and 10. In the latter verse, it is the named women καὶ αἱ λοιπαὶ σὺν αὐταῖς who have to bear witness to the Apostles. In the former verse we are told that it is the Eleven καὶ πᾶσιν τοῖς λοιποῖς who receive this report. Thus, we note another example of role reversal – certain leading women and others with them instruct or announce the Good News to the men and even to the Apostles whose future it would soon be to make such proclamations.[13] Grammatically, v. 10 is difficult, and it must be admitted that Luke leaves the impression that the other women were the primary ones who spoke to the Apostles about these things.[14] Perhaps the difficulties have been created by Luke's insertion of a mainly traditional list of female witnesses (v. 10a).[15]

Luke appears to make a deliberate contrast between the women witnesses and the men who receive the witness. He says that their words seemed to be nonsense to the Apostles who refused to believe their report (ἠπίστουν αὐταῖς).[16] This reaction is typical of the common Jewish male prejudice against a woman's testimony;[17] however, Peter is portrayed as taking the women seriously enough to go and inspect the tomb.

Many scholars consider Luke 24.12 an insertion based on John 20.3–10.[18] Textually, however, there is no more reason to omit this verse than τοῦ κυρίου Ἰησοῦ in v. 3, or οὐκ ἔστιν ὧδε ἀλλὰ ἠγέρθη in v. 6, and there are good contextual reasons for including it.[19] For instance, Luke 24.24 seems to presuppose 24.12 and there is no textual question as to the originality of v. 24. Further, the style of v. 12 is Lukan.[20] It has been suggested that v. 12 is Luke's apology to his female readers for the Apostles' refusal to believe the women's witness about the empty tomb.[21] The content of v. 12 does not duplicate the story of the women's visit. No angels appear to Peter, nor is there any divine message given to him – these are the two primary features of the women's visit. The fact that Peter does not enter the tomb but sees the strips of linen lying by themselves also distinguishes this account from the narrative of the women's visit.[22] Only the fact of the visit and Peter's wondering (θαυμάζων, contrast ἀπορεῖσθαι, v. 4) is reminiscent of the women's visit. The parallels perhaps are Luke's way of informing us that the initial reaction of both women and men to an uninterpreted empty tomb is not faith but doubt and uncertainty.

Unlike the First and Fourth Evangelists, Luke does not recount a resurrection appearance to one or more of the women.[23] However, in Luke's main appearance story, the encounter on Emmaus road, there is evidence of male–female contrast even though the story does not feature women. In the midst of the carefully constructed dialogue (24.17–27), we note the following points of comparison and contrast.[24]

(1) καὶ γυναῖκές τινες ἐξ ἡμῶν (v. 22) } who
    καὶ ... τινες τῶν σὺν ἡμῖν (v. 24)

(2) ἐπὶ τὸ μνημεῖον (v. 22) } where
    ἐπὶ τὸ μνημεῖον (v. 24)

(3) καὶ μὴ εὑροῦσαι τὸ σῶμα αὐτοῦ   (v. 23) } *what*
    καὶ εὗρον οὕτως καθὼς καὶ αἱ γυναῖκες εἶπον (v. 24) } *was found*

(4) ἦλθον λέγουσαι καὶ ὀπτασίαν ἀγγέλων   (v. 23) } *what*
    ἑωρακέναι οἳ λέγουσιν αὐτὸν ζῆν   } *was*
    αὐτὸν δὲ οὐκ εἶδον   (v. 24) } *seen*

Though the structure is not perfectly parallel, we can see how a certain parallelism is maintained throughout. In (1) we have two parties who make a journey, the former exclusively female, the latter apparently male (in light of Luke 24.12 and the fact that Cleopas is speaking and seems to identify with the latter group). In (2) we see that the destination of the two parties is identical. In (3) we see reversal whereby the supposed idle tale of the women is confirmed by some of the men. Point (4) brings out male–female contrast; i.e., the women faithfully reported that the angels said Jesus was alive, while the men insisted they would have to see to believe.[25] In the phrase αὐτὸν δὲ οὐκ εἶδον, the word αὐτόν is in an emphatic position indicating the chief complaint of the men. The irony reaches its peak here since it is Jesus who is being told all this, and thus the men are made to look very foolish indeed. In conclusion, we see in Luke's main appearance narrative a vindication of Jesus' female followers at the expense of some of His male followers.[26] The women had seen the angels and reported accurately the empty tomb and Easter message. The men could only confirm the report of the empty tomb and did not see Jesus or anyone else.

In chapter 24, Luke masterfully re-emphasizes some of his key ideas about male–female relationships which he developed during the first twenty-four chapters of his Gospel. In 24.1–11 we see the new prominence of women as valid witnesses, worthy of being named as such in the Gospel story. We also noted evidence of male–female contrast and role reversal, for it is the women, not the men, who receive the more complete revelation and have the less inadequate understanding of the significance of the Easter events (cf. 24.1–11 to 24.12; 24.22–23 to 24.24 where the women remembered and Peter wondered). In Luke 24.33–53 and 24.24 in particular we may also see Luke's reassertion of the primacy of the community's male leadership. Remember that Luke, if he knew of such traditions, does not include any account of an appearance of Jesus to a woman or group of women. In a sense, Luke 24 presents a microcosm of his views on these matters and prepares us for the equality of relationship of male and female, the new prominence of women, and the reassertion of male leadership which we find in Acts as accomplished and accepted facts.

As we bring this brief look at Luke's editorial tendencies in the Third Gospel to a close, perhaps it would now be appropriate to focus on that section of the Gospel where most scholars think Luke's theological tendencies are most evident — the birth narratives. About one-third of the uniquely Lukan Gospel material involves and highlights women and their roles. Nowhere is this more in evidence than in Luke 1–2.

C. Women in the birth narratives

It is Elizabeth and Mary, not Zechariah and Joseph, who are first to receive the message of Christ's coming, who are praised and blessed by God's angels, and who are first to sing and prophesy about the Christ child. Luke presents these women not only as witnesses to the events surrounding the births of John and Jesus, but also as active participants in God's Messianic purposes. Perhaps they are also the first examples of the lowly being exalted as part of God's plan of eschatological reversal that breaks into history with, in, and through the person of Jesus.

The first mention of Mary in Luke's Gospel is found at 1.27 where she is introduced as a παρθένος engaged to Joseph of the house of David.[27] At 1.28 we find the significant greeting, χαῖρε, of the angel to Mary. This may be a normal Greek greeting; however, in light of (1) the parallels between Luke 1.28–38 and Zeph 3.14–20 (LXX), (2) the fact that normally a biblical 'call' narrative does not include such a greeting,[28] and (3) considering the way Luke depicts Mary's response to the greeting,[29] it seems more probable F. Danker is right in saying,

> Gabriel's greeting is unusual, for women were ordinarily not addressed in this way ... That Gabriel, one of the highest members of the heavenly council, should come to the insignificant village of Nazareth and present himself before this girl – this is a miracle of the New Age and presages the announcement of the Magnificat, that the mighty are brought low and the humble exalted (vs. 52).[30]

The connection between χαῖρε, κεχαριτωμένη, and χάριν (vv. 28–30) should be noted. Mary should rejoice because she is highly favored by God – she is to be graced with the privilege of giving birth to the Messiah.[31] Furthermore, Mary is even to be the first person to call His name. Luke appears to give Mary the same status as the First Evangelist gave Joseph (Matt 1.21).[32]

The crux of the annunciation story is to be found in Mary's response in v. 34: πῶς ἔσται τοῦτο, ἐπεὶ ἄνδρα οὐ γινώσκω. It is unlikely this is meant to be understood as a vow to virginity since elsewhere Luke portrays Mary as reflecting the normal Jewish mindset concerning marriage and children (1.48), and since Luke's audience could not have deduced such a vow from the text as it now stands.[33] Mary, unlike Zechariah who questioned the 'whether', is asking 'how', considering her state of betrothal and her abstinence from intercourse during that period, this conception and birth can take place now or in the near future.[34] She is seeking clarification, not proof (for which Zechariah was punished). The angel's response can be seen as a further explanation of how Mary will conceive prior to marital consummation. Thus, γινώσκω means not only that Mary has had no intercourse previously, but also that there is no prospect of it now or in the near future (an obvious necessity for normal conception).[35] This is why the angel must inform her that she will conceive (future) by the Holy Spirit.

The response of the angel (v. 35) is of particular interest because of the use of the verbs ἐπέρχομαι and ἐπισκιάζω. The former verb is peculiar to Luke with two exceptions (Eph 2.7 and Jas 5.1). The phrase πνεῦμα ἅγιον ἐπελεύσεται ἐπὶ σέ (1.35) should be compared to ἐπελθόντος τοῦ ἁγίου πνεύματος (Acts 1.8). Mary is present both here at the birth of Jesus and at the birth of the Church (Acts 1.14). In both cases, there is a promise that 'the Spirit will come upon you'. Luke may be intending for us to see Mary as a key link between the life of Jesus and the life of the Church.[36] The second verb, ἐπισκιάζω, is also of importance and here seems to mean 'to overshadow' in the sense of protection, and may allude to the idea of the Shekinah glory cloud of God's divine presence (cf. Luke 9.34).[37] Thus, it is not so much a reference to a miraculous impregnation (as ἐπέρχομαι is likely to be) as an assurance that Mary will have divine protection during the encounter with the Spirit and the resulting conception.[38] If so, then it is conceivable that Luke intends for us to see here the beginning of the eschatological reversal of the curse on Eve (Gen 3.16). In any case, one or both of these verbs is an explicit reference to a virginal conception.

The reaction in v. 38 to the angelic explanation is the classic expression of submission to God's word and will − 'Ιδού ἡ δούλη κυρίου γένοιτό μοι κατὰ τὸ ῥῆμά σου. Luke may have written 1.38 on the basis of vv. 47−49, in which case he is presenting Mary as a model disciple responding as she ought to God's call.[39] The first phrase of 1.38 is toned down by the translation 'handmaiden', for the actual meaning is 'Behold the slave of the Lord.' Thus, Luke portrays Mary as binding herself totally to God's will, giving up her plans and desires for the future.[40] Her response was one of submission in full recognition of what effect this act of God could have for her social position and relation to Joseph. We see the Evangelist presenting Mary as one who is willing to give up betrothal and reputation for God's purposes, the sort of self-sacrifice which, in Luke's Gospel, is the mark of a disciple.[41] 'Mary is thus a model of what Israel ought to be, and her self-description is a mark of identity for the new community ...'[42]

Mary is also important because Luke presents her as the connecting link between the various segments of his infancy narrative.[43] Thus, save for Jesus, she is presented as its central figure.

Mary goes to visit her kinswoman, Elizabeth, and receives from her a two-fold blessing. In vv. 42–43 we learn that Mary is blessed among women because she is the μήτηρ τοῦ κυρίου μου; i.e., because the fruit of her womb is blessed. This is a derived honor, for it is the fact that she bears Jesus that makes her favored. Interestingly, it is for God's work in the pregnancy that Mary is called blessed by all generations (1.48). The implication seems to be that motherhood and the blessedness it involves are affirmed and hallowed, for God has chosen this means to bring His Son into the world. Mary's blessedness in her role of mother is what Elizabeth first remarks upon, and yet Mary could not have been the mother of God's Son had she not first believed and submitted to God's word.

Elizabeth's second blessing relates specifically to μακαρία ἡ πιστεύσασα.[44] The word for blessing used in 1.42 is not used here. In v. 45 we have μακαρία which means 'fortunate' and it does not so much convey a blessing as recognize an existing state of blessedness or happiness.[45] In v. 42 we have Εὐλογημένη which recognizes that God has conferred a blessing on Mary.[46] In a sense, Luke intimates the resolution of the tension between physical and spiritual blessedness by presenting Elizabeth's pronouncement of both blessings – it is the blessedness of believing in God's promise that leads to the physical blessings (cf. 1.42, 45). Luke, however, indicates that Mary must yet wrestle to obtain a proper perspective on both (cf. 2.50). Her difficulty will be in learning and understanding not only her own priorities but also her Son's priorities which must first be with His spiritual Father and family, and secondly with His physical family (cf. Luke 2.49–51,

8.21). In the Lukan narrative, Mary has declared herself the Lord's slave, but she has still to learn that this entails her being Jesus' disciple first and His mother second.

What is the nature of the Magnificat? There is some internal evidence that favors the view that Luke meant this to be seen as an oracle of Elizabeth; for instance, (1) Elizabeth, as an older, childless woman is better described as having received mercy from Yahweh who was mindful of her lowly estate; (2) this song has affinities with the Song of Hannah (1 Sam. 2.1–10) whose old, barren condition is more like Elizabeth's state than Mary's; (3) the words of v. 56 support the idea that Elizabeth is the last speaker; (4) Luke 1.41 says that Elizabeth is filled with the Holy Spirit which is common before prophecy, but there is no mention of Mary being so filled.[47] Luke, however, wants to make clear that Mary and Jesus are more important than Elizabeth and John. Luke uses the concluding part of his narrative to underline the point he made in vv. 27–33 about Mary and Jesus. It is unlikely that Luke would have Elizabeth sing her own praises at this point.[48]

In its present context, since Luke has joined vv. 47–49 to what follows, the Magnificat has become a song of promise, prophetic protest, and powerful deliverance by the Lord of the poor and oppressed.[49] It is Jewish in nature and similar to the Psalms and the Song of Hannah, but it is also on the border between OT and NT literature, rooted in the OT past while shedding light on the NT present and future as God begins to do new things.[50] Mary is thus portrayed by Luke as a type of OT prophetess who proclaims OT hopes as the salvation of God breaks in; however, she differs from the OT prophetesses in that she herself helps bring in salvation. She represents Israel who obeyed God's commands, one of the lowly and poor upon whom God has bestowed unmerited favor. She is not merely a representative symbol of Israel's collective need and response, for the song in its introduction is about her individuality. She as an individual fulfils her people's hopes by being the vehicle through which God's salvation and Messiah comes. But it is wrong to suggest that Luke casts Mary in the role of a venerated saint. Rather, Mary recognizes (v. 48) that she is insignificant and of lowly estate. Her blessedness is in what God has done for her (v. 49), and thus it is God, not Mary, who receives praises in this song.[51] It is precisely because Mary is not portrayed as a sinless and angelic figure that she can be a model and a sign of hope for other believers.

The theme of Mary as ἡ δούλη κυρίου assumes greater proportions and importance[52] when we note the significance of Mary's role in *Heilsgeschichte*, summed up aptly by W. Grundmann: 'The fact that God has regard to the lowly estate of his handmaiden gives rise to the hope that His eschatological action ... is now beginning ...'[53] Mary is seen as a forerunner of a Christian disciple, one who reveals what God will do for those who accept God's will in regard to the new thing He is bringing about.[54]

In order to obtain a more holistic perspective on Mary's role in Luke's infancy narratives, we must examine her role in light of that which Elizabeth plays in Luke 1–2. Luke presents a somewhat developed picture of Elizabeth, but he takes pains to cast her in the shadow of Mary (just as Elizabeth's son is cast in the shadow of Mary's son).[55] The stories about Elizabeth and Zechariah are uniquely Lukan, though he may have found these narratives in his source and shaped them to show that both men and women are objects of God's salvation and subjects who convey His revelation.[56] Let us see how Luke works out this schema.

After the prologue, Luke's Gospel begins in similar fashion to the First Evangelist – an angel appears to a man and speaks of a miraculous birth. In Luke, the angel tells Zechariah of the birth of John; Zechariah expresses doubt; and Elizabeth expresses faith. She says, 'The Lord has done this for me ... In these days He has shown His favor and taken away my disgrace among men' (Luke 1.25). She speaks both as a typical Jewish woman and as one who has been liberated by grace to sing God's praises. Her response anticipates Mary's, 'I am the Lord's servant ... may it be to me as you have said' (Luke 1.38), and her '... for He has been mindful of the humble state of His servant' (Luke 1.48). Elizabeth perhaps is portrayed as the forerunner of Mary. As Luke presents things, Elizabeth's miraculous conception serves as a reassurance to Mary that the angel's word is true (1.36).

Elizabeth, in her relation to Mary, reminds us of her son John's role in the Gospels in relation to Jesus. When Elizabeth is visited by Mary she says, 'Blessed are you among women and blessed is the child you will bear! But why am I so favored, that the mother of my Lord should come to me?' (Luke 1.42–43). Compare this to the Lukan form of John the Baptist's words: 'He who is mightier than I is coming, the thong of whose sandal I am not worthy to untie' (Luke 3.16, cf. Mark 1.7). Both texts convey the sense of unworthiness and the clear distinction between the lesser and greater person.

Luke certainly portrays Elizabeth, not Zechariah, as a person of faith. To the surprise of all the relatives and neighbors, Elizabeth gives to their son the name John, as the angel told her (Luke 1.60).[57] It is only when Zechariah concurs with Elizabeth's words that he is freed from his dumbness and is able to praise God (1.64). Even when he does speak, his song in many ways is an echo of Mary's (cf. 1.54 and 1.68; 1.55 and 1.72−73; 1.52 and 1.71).[58]

Just as Elizabeth is given more prominence than Zechariah, and is cast in a more favorable light as a model of faith, so too is Mary in relation to Joseph. There is little mention of Joseph (cf. 1.27) until after the major prophecies and songs have been given concerning Jesus. It is Joseph, like Zechariah, who is silent in Luke's Gospel in contrast to Mary's silence in Matthew 1−2. In his way, perhaps Luke gives notice of the new freedom, equality, and importance of women in God's plan, in contrast to the prejudices and limitations they often faced in Judaism. Luke does indicate, however, that it is Joseph who leads and guides the family on a journey, and it is to the town of his family line that they go to register (Luke 2.4−5, cf. Matt. 2.13−23).[59] While Luke's vision of the new age does include the idea of equality for women in service and importance to the Lord, there is no indication that he is rejecting patriarchy outright in his infancy narrative.

To this point we have seen that through the prominence of Elizabeth as Mary's forerunner and by the absence of Joseph, Mary is cast in a central role in this infancy narrative. This becomes more apparent when we examine Mary's relationship to Anna and Simeon in the Temple.

Anna and Simeon in Luke 2 are representatives of the old order of Jewish piety and of the longings of their people for the Messiah. Simeon is described as one who has been looking for the 'consolation of Israel', a term for the salvation that would come to Israel in the Messianic era.[60]

Luke has Simeon bless both Joseph and Mary to indicate God's endorsement of them in their roles as mother and father. Luke 2.33 indicates that Luke, like the First Evangelist, recognizes Joseph as Jesus' legal parent.[61]

Luke 2.35a has been seen as a reference either to Mary's doubts about Jesus at the cross, or to her co-suffering with Jesus beneath the cross, or to the word of God as a sword piercing Mary.[62] Luke, however, makes no mention of Mary at the cross; therefore, views involving the cross are probably inconsistent with the Evangelist's purpose. The sword (ῥομφαία) is symbolic of the cause of Mary's anguish, i.e., seeing her son spoken against and rejected by her own people. She is part of true Israel, yet she is being divided between Israel and her son.[63] If the sword represents this general rejection which causes anguish, then we can see that the clause which follows refers to this rejection which reveals Israel's true nature.[64] It is possible that Luke means to imply that Mary's sword of rejection also entails Jesus' apparent turning away from her (cf. Luke 8.19–21), even as early as the next scene in Luke's account (2.41–52).

Luke frames the infancy narrative in general with a man and a woman who are connected closely with the Temple (cf. 1.5–25, 2.22–40).[65] The woman who completes the two halves of the parallel structure is Anna. She, like Simeon, is old and devout (2.37). It is possible, though not probable, that Luke intends us to see Anna as a part of an order of widows with specifically religious functions in the Temple (hence her constant presence there).[66] In view of other parallels noted between Luke 1–2 and Acts 1–2, it is possible that Luke intends that we should see in Anna a foreshadowing of the pouring out of the Spirit of prophecy on men and women (Acts 2.17).[67] In fact, she is the only woman in the NT of whom the word προφῆτις is used. She stands in the line of such OT figures as Deborah and Huldah, and Luke's shaping of the material may be the cause of her resemblance to Judith, a heroine in inter-testamental Jewish literature.[68] Possibly, Luke mentions her because she is the second and validating witness to testify of Jesus' significance (Deut. 19.15).[69] If so, then Luke is deliberately placing a high value on the witness of a woman. Once Anna arrives and sees Jesus she goes forth to witness to the rest of the righteous remnant who longed for the Messiah (2.38). She is presented as both a prophetess and a proselytizer for the Messiah. Alfred Plummer has made an interesting comparison of Anna and Simeon.[70] Simeon comes to the Temple under the influence of the Spirit, while Anna is always there. The sight of the Messiah makes Simeon happy to encounter death, while Anna goes forth to proclaim what she has discovered. Do these two represent in Luke's schema respectively the OT prophetic order satisfied to see the Messiah and die out, and the NT proselytizing plan that goes forth proclaiming the new thing God is doing? If there is anything to this, then it probably reveals how Luke has carefully cast his material in such a way to bring out the theological themes he desires to present.

Luke does wish to show that true Israel (Zechariah, Elizabeth, Simeon, Anna) recognizes the Savior, even when Jesus' own parents do not understand fully. Mary in a sense is put in perspective as one potential disciple (among many) who does not always have the clearest insight among those who are 'true Israel'.[71] This lack of complete understanding on Mary's part comes out at several points in the narrative. Luke 1.29, 34, and 2.33 all point in this direction and all these verses were probably composed by Luke. In 2.41–52 it is said explicitly of Mary and Joseph – καὶ αὐτοὶ οὐ συνῆκαν τὸ ῥῆμα ὃ ἐλάλησεν (2.50). Luke's inclusion of this phrase says something about his own views on the matter of Mary's understanding. Luke does not paint an idealized portrait of Mary, but is willing to reveal both her insight and her lack of understanding. Along with the statements or implications of Mary's lack of full understanding, we have affirmations by Luke that Mary πάντα συνετήρει τὰ ῥήματα ταῦτα συμβάλλουσα ἐν τῇ καρδίᾳ αὐτῆς (2.19, cf. 2.51). Thus, we see that Luke is presenting Mary as an example of a person growing toward full understanding. The point is that it will take time for Mary to understand all that happens in the course of Jesus' earthly life.[72] Raymond Brown says,

> ... Luke's idea is that complete acceptance of the word of God, complete understanding of who Jesus is, and complete discipleship is not yet possible. This will come through the ministry of Jesus and particularly through the cross and resurrection. It is no accident that the final reaction of the parents of Jesus in the infancy narrative is very much like that of the disciples of Jesus after the third passion prediction: 'They did not understand any of these things, and this word (rēma) was hidden from them' (18:34). But Luke does not leave Mary on the negative note of misunderstanding. Rather, in 2.51 he stresses her retention of what she has not yet understood and (implicitly – see 1:19) her continuing search to understand.[73]

In Luke 2.41–52 the tension between the claims of the physical and spiritual family on Jesus are made evident when Mary[74] speaks of His father (Joseph) and Jesus replies in terms of His real Father (God).[75] In the conclusion of the pericope the Evangelist deliberately draws on a certain parallel between Mary and Jesus. He states that Jesus grew in wisdom and stature, and also that Mary stored up information and gave it careful consideration so that she could understand her son. Thoughtful learning is a characteristic mark of the growing disciple (Luke 8.15, 18–21, 10.39).[76] It may be that Luke wishes to make clear that while Mary recognizes Jesus' miraculous birth, she does not understand what this may imply in regard to His life work and mission. In this she would be like other disciples who do not understand fully until after the resurrection (Luke 24.45–47). Mary is thus a very approachable model of faith with its struggles for the Lukan audience.

In the investigation of the different portions of Luke 1–2 we have assessed the material and now we must sum up its theological value in regard to Mary. She typifies the hopes of true Israel, embodies the hope of Israel, and exemplifies the proper response to God's plan of salvation. As Elizabeth's two blessings indicate, God has worked both through Mary's faith response and through her motherhood to bring about the birth of the Savior. Mary's central role in Luke's infancy narrative is a result of God working through Mary's spiritual and physical being. We have noted her central role in various places in the text: (1) the Evangelist composes a scene where Mary, not Joseph, receives revelation; (2) she sings the Magnificat; (3) by Elizabeth's own words Mary is shown to be a more crucial figure than Elizabeth herself (1.41–45); (4) Simeon addresses Mary specifically (2.35); (5) Mary alone speaks for the family at Luke 2.48; (6) while many wonder at the events surrounding Jesus' birth, twice Mary is said to ponder their significance (2.19, 51); (7) Mary in a unique way will feel the effects of Israel's rejection of her son (2.35); (8) Mary links the various sections of this infancy narrative (1.39, 56, 2.5, 22, 39, 41; in Luke 2 Joseph and Mary link the events).

Mary reflects the overlap between the old and new ages – she continues to fulfil the requirements of the law, but believes in the new things God will do through her. Luke 1–2 reveals that in the context of Judaism, God can and does reveal the equality of male and female as recipients and proclaimers of God's revelation. True Israel is called to believe in what God is doing and also to see the blessedness of the motherhood of Mary (cf. Luke 1.42, 2.34). By presenting Mary as an example of true Israel, Luke is able to describe, through one individual, both the struggles of relating a Jewish heritage to God's eschatological activities, and the struggles of relating material blessing and the physical family to spiritual blessing and the family of faith. Significantly, from the beginning of his Gospel, Luke stresses that physical and spiritual blessings are both part of the new thing God is doing. It is not a case of being either Jesus' mother or His disciple, but of orienting her motherhood to the priorities of faith in God's new activity through Jesus. Her struggles in this emerge in Luke 2.41–52. As part of Luke's presentation of the reversal the Gospel brings about, Luke stresses the way women rejoice and are liberated as God acts. Elizabeth is liberated from the curse of barrenness and the reproach of Jewish men; Mary is liberated to sing and prophesy even in a situation where she would appear to be of questionable character; Anna is motivated to witness to those looking forward to the redemption of Jerusalem. The male characters in this narrative, however, either remain silent (Joseph), are struck dumb (Zechariah), or ask to be dismissed in peace (Simeon). While other figures in the infancy narrative fade into the background, Mary with her son are carried over into the ongoing story of the Gospel. In fact, she is the one female figure who reappears by name in Luke's second volume, and to it we will now turn.

D. The Book of Acts — women in the primitive Church

It would not be true to say that Luke features women and their roles in his Book of Acts to the same degree as he did in his Gospel. Nevertheless, there are certain traces of Lukan male–female parallelism, and perhaps male–female role reversal in the material not directly focusing on women, and women figure prominently in some of the redactional summaries. It is also probably not accidental that in the few texts where Christian women do receive attention, Luke gives us something of a survey of the different roles they played in the earliest days of Church history, as his invitation, based on historical precedent, to his audience to 'go and do likewise'.

1. Incidental references to male–female parallelism, male–female role reversal, and female prominence

There are certain incidental features of Acts that appear to reflect Luke's penchant for male–female parallelism. We find examples of it both inside and outside the Christian community. Ananias and Sapphira (Acts 5.1–11) are in some respects negative counterparts to Priscilla and Aquila, even though they apparently were members of the Christian community. Luke is exercised to show that both husband and wife were equally culpable (cf. vv. 2, 8b), the former attempting to deceive Peter, the latter lying openly to him. The actions of this couple stand in contrast to the exceptional generosity and honesty of the only other Christian *couple* to whom Luke gives significant attention – Priscilla and Aquila. Perhaps Luke chose to present Christian couples who were polar opposites in order to provide examples for Christians to avoid or to emulate. Luke stresses the parallels in intention and activity of the male and female members of both couples.

It is also noteworthy that Luke gives examples of male–female partnership outside the Christian community, especially when he refers to governing authorities. The examples of Felix and Drusilla (24.24) and Agrippa and Bernice (25.13–26.12) come to mind. Luke's mention of Agrippa and Bernice three times (25.13, 23, 26.20) is hard to understand since they play no real part in the story. Perhaps Luke has a concern to show that the Word goes out to men and women of all social classes, and that prominent women who hear the Gospel sometimes heed it (cf. Luke 8.3; Acts 16.11–15).

An examination of Luke's summaries reveals that he wishes to stress both male–female parallelism and the reception of the Gospel by prominent women. For example, in the process of recording the swelling tide of conversion (2.41, 47, 4.4), Luke points out specifically at 5.14: μᾶλλον δὲ προσετίθεντο πιστεύοντες τῷ κυρίῳ πλήθη ἀνδρῶν τε καὶ γυναικῶν. When Saul decides to persecute the Christians in Damascus, he plans to seize ἄνδρας τε καὶ γυναῖκας (9.2, cf. 8.3). This should imply to Luke's readers that the women were significant enough in number and/or importance to the cause of The Way that Saul did not think he could stop the movement without taking women as well as men prisoners. We find this sort of parallelism at 17.34 as well where Luke gives us the name of one male (Διονύσιος) and one female (Δάμαρις) who were among those converted at Athens.[77] In fact, two gender-specific groups serve as a parenthesis around two particular names.

Luke's interest in prominent women converts is seen at 17.4 where we find mentioned γυναικῶν τε τῶν πρώτων οὐκ ὀλίγαι. At 17.12 we find καὶ τῶν Ἑλληνίδων γυναικῶν τῶν εὐσχημόνων. These women are apparently among those who 'searched the Scriptures' (17.11), even though Jewish women (or God-fearing proselytes) normally were not allowed to study the *Tanak*. Thus, Luke may be pointing to the new freedom given to women by the Gospel even as they were in the process of accepting it.[78] Interestingly, in each passage it is the women, not the men, who are qualified by words indicating their importance or eminence.

One of the major themes in Luke's Gospel is the idea of reversal of roles or expectations — the last become first, the first becoming servants. Luke carries this theme over into his second volume to some extent; for instance, in Acts 6.1–7. Stephen and Philip, who are among the prominent preachers and teachers of the Word in the early part of Acts (cf. 6.8–8.40), are among the seven chosen to supervise the food distribution to the widows or even to wait on tables. Thus, leading men are chosen for a task that normally a male servant would fulfil in a Palestinian Jewish setting, or a woman would fulfil in a Hellenistic or Roman setting.[79] In the eyes of the Hellenists, for a prominent man to fulfil such a task would be demeaning and a reversal of roles with a man doing a woman's or servant's work.

2. Women as prominent converts and μητέρες συναγωγῆς

At various points in my earlier monograph I noted Jesus' tendency to rely on the system of standing hospitality.[80] It was suggested that this reliance implied an endorsement of certain roles commonly assumed by women. Perhaps now we may tentatively hypothesize that this reliance and Jesus' instructions to His closest friends to rely on this system (cf. Matt 10.5–32; Luke 9.2–5, 10.1–16), not only set a precedent for the traveling missionaries in the early Church, but also established a practice from which came the house church. If this supposition is correct, then it explains why prominent women are mentioned wherever house churches are mentioned in the NT. Women converts of some means who initially were offering occasional lodging and hospitality to fellow Christians, became the Christian equivalent of a μήτηρ συναγωγῆς[81] as their homes became regular meeting places of the converts in their area. In a sense, the Church owed its continuing existence to these prominent women who provided both a place for meeting and the hospitality required by the community. A woman's customary role of providing hospitality to visiting guests became a means by which they could support and sustain the Church.

Luke's interest in lodging and hospitality has long been a recognized feature of both his Gospel and Acts.[82] D. W. Riddle suggests that these people and places are mentioned, not in order to historicize an otherwise non-descriptive narrative or to give it the feel of authenticity, but in order to recognize those who helped in the transmission of the Gospel in those early days.[83] Luke's second volume is about the spreading of the Gospel and those who made it possible; these places of lodging and hosts are mentioned as vital supports to that movement. However, it is not just a matter of these families providing temporary lodging for traveling Christian preachers and prophets, but a matter of providing a place where the Gospel could be preached and oral and written traditions could be collected. Thus, we may see hospitality not only as the physical support that kept the message going, but also as the medium in which the message took hold and was preserved. Riddle suggests:

> These examples of hospitality suggest that the custom may account for a notable phenomenon of those days: the acceptance of the travelling preacher's message by entire households ... That the primitive churches were house-churches is a detail of this, and an aspect of early Christian hospitality.[84]

Christian hospitality was obviously a vital factor both in the intensive (home becomes house-church) and the extensive (home-as-lodging for missionary and the Word) growth of the early Church. Inasmuch as women were mainly responsible for the hospitality of that day in a situation where the house was the center for the Church, women quite naturally were in the forefront of providing the *modus vivendi* for Christian life and growth, and the spread of the Gospel. Probably, it is no accident that at the only two points in Acts where Luke clearly tells us of a church meeting in a particular person's home (12.12, 16.40), not just a place of lodging or hospitality, it is in the home of a woman. Perhaps Luke chose these examples in order to point out the role women, particularly prominent well-to-do women, played in the growth of the early Church.[85]

3. Mary, mother of John Mark

As has been the case throughout this chapter, we are not concerned to raise or answer the question of the historical value of this material. Rather, we wish to ask how Luke is using his source material and what sort of teaching or examples he is providing for his audience.

Luke tells us that Peter went to the house of Mary, the mother of John called Mark (Acts 12.12–17). Luke portrays Mary as a widow whom Luke's audience would know primarily because of her son. Luke means us to see Mary as financially well-to-do; for many (ἱκανοί) could meet in her house which has a τὴν θύραν τοῦ πυλῶνος (v. 13), and a παιδίσκη named Rhoda.[86] Mary's house is portrayed as a place for συνηθροισμένοι καί προσευχόμενοι implying that it was a regular meeting place. Perhaps we are meant to think of this as a prayer meeting primarily attended by women since (1) a woman answers the door in the middle of the night, and (2) Peter's words make clear that James and 'the brethren' are not at the meeting (v. 17).[87] If so, then it should not be overlooked that Peter entrusted his parting words to a group of women.

Luke may be implying that this particular prayer meeting included Rhoda, the servant girl, for it says she came to answer the knock at the door implying that she was within the house at the prayer meeting.[88] Luke may be indicating the equalizing effects of the Gospel so that not only women, but even slaves, were accepted as participating members of the new community (cf. Acts 1.14). Unfortunately, when Rhoda relates her good news, she receives a response similar to that which Jesus' female followers received at Easter (cf. Luke 24.11). Rhoda's audience thought she was mad (μαίνη). Possibly, Luke is providing an example of latent prejudices against a woman's, particularly a female servant's, word of witness. Nevertheless, in the story Rhoda's perseverance pays off, her word is vindicated, and because of her persistence, a crucial message is passed to the Christian community to be sent on to its leaders.

Thus, the witness of a woman is shown to be trustworthy, and Luke presents Rhoda as an example for his audience. Also, that Luke points out that Mary would hold such a meeting in a time of mounting opposition in Jerusalem to the Christian movement is evidence that Luke is portraying one woman's courageous contribution to the community of faith. Perhaps here, as in Luke 24.11, Luke intended a rebuke to those in his audience who had a tendency to devalue the word or work of women.[89] Finally, this pericope also presents God's answer to the prayer of Mary and others, and thus reveals His confirmation of the activities in which Luke indicates early Christian women were engaged.

4. Lydia

As noted in chapter 1, women were allowed to play a significant part in Macedonian society from the Hellenistic age onward. It is not surprising that Luke should wish to relate a story about prominent Macedonian women who not only were converted to Christianity, but also assumed important roles in the Christian community.

As elsewhere in Acts, Luke chooses what may be called representative examples of conversions in the area covered by his narrative.

It is probably not accidental that he focuses primarily on the conversion of one woman (16.12–15, 40) and one man (16.23–39). It appears that Luke's intention is once again to convey a certain male–female parallelism, not for its own sake, but in order to stress the quality of man and woman in God's plan of salvation, and their equal importance to the new community.[90]

The structure of Acts 16.12–40 is important to our discussion, for it reveals how vital it was that Lydia provide a meeting place for Christians.[91] The Gospel is seen to triumph in the midst of the Jewish meeting place (16.14–15), and in the midst of a Roman stronghold (in the city, cf. 16.18–19, and in their prison, cf. 16.25–26). It is seen to triumph over natural and supernatural powers, whether it be magistrates and their jails, or demons. Luke is at pains to show that the Gospel and its followers can exist within the confines of a place of Roman authority by creating its own space 'in house'. That Luke portrays a woman, Lydia, providing such a meeting place for Christians in the city is crucial. Thus, he shows that the faith, while not subservient to Rome, is not fundamentally at odds with the Roman empire or its authorities.

The story of Lydia is extraordinary in many regards. In some ways she should not be seen as a typical Macedonian woman, for Luke portrays Lydia as having come to Philippi from her native city of Thyatira, famous for its production of clothing goods with a distinctive and very popular royal purple dye.[92] Perhaps we are meant to think she had moved to an environment where she could better take advantage of imperial Roman tastes and needs.

One of the significant messages it seems Luke is trying to get across is that Paul, in contrast to his Jewish background, is willing to begin a local church with a group of women converts. That women could constitute the embryonic church, but not the embryonic synagogue, reveals the difference in the status of women in the two faiths at that time, and it seems likely that Luke intended us to draw this contrast by mentioning the προσευχήν in v. 13 and the church meeting in v. 40 in Lydia's house.[93]

Luke tells us that on the sabbath, Paul and his companions went down to the riverside outside the city gates, sat down (assuming the posture of a Jewish rabbi), and taught the women gathered at the place of prayer. Among them may have been some Jewesses, but there was one prominent God-fearer (σεβομένη τὸν θεόν) who had also brought along members of her household.[94] Just as Paul's coming to Macedonia was due to revelation (God's work), so Lydia's conversion is to be seen as God's work — ὁ κύριος διήνοιξεν τὴν καρδίαν προσέχειν τοῖς λαλουμένοις ὑπὸ τοῦ Παύλου (v. 14, cf. Luke 24.45). Luke intimates that God intended Lydia and her household to be the first converts in Macedonia so that the initial European church would have a good home. Lydia responded to God's work in her life by begging Paul and his company to take advantage of her hospitality,[95] basing her plea on Paul's acceptance of her as a sincere convert to Christianity. Perhaps Luke means us to see here a portrait of a woman who had grasped from the first that whatever barriers being a Gentile and a single woman might erect in regard to housing non-Christians (particularly Jews) in her home, these barriers were no longer obstacles to Christians, even Christian males whom she had just met.[96] Luke intimates faith was the only door she had to pass through to be accepted as a disciple and a hostess of disciples.

Lydia's significance was not confined to her being a disciple or hostess to traveling disciples. Luke wishes us to understand that what began as a lodging for missionaries, became the home of the embryonic church in Philippi. This is intimated by the fact that when Paul and Silas emerge from prison they go to Lydia's house to encourage the brethren (16.40), rather than to the Philippian jailor's house where they had also been entertained (16.34). Once again, we see how a woman's fruitful role of providing hospitality played an integral part in the establishment and continuance of a local church.[97] The manner of Luke's telling of this story reflects clearly his interest in showing the advantages to various under-privileged groups in embracing Christianity. Here a woman progresses from being a marginal member of a Jewish circle in which she could never receive the covenantal sign, to being a central figure in the local Christian church and the first baptized convert in Europe.

5. Women as deaconesses

No one is certain when the office of deaconess began in the Church. At the very least it seems probable that the office had its origins in Apostolic times,[98] and perhaps the first traces of its existence may be found in the NT (cf. Rom 16.1, 1 Tim 3.11). What seems more certain and demonstrable is that women were performing in NT times the functions later associated with the office of deaconess. Possibly, we find Luke's development of the idea of women serving the community by providing material aid in Acts 9.36–42.

In Acts 9.32–42 we find a sequence of two miraculous deeds by

Peter – one performed for a man, one for a woman. The account of the healing of Aeneas is very brief (vv. 32–35), and we may conjecture that Luke included it merely to create a certain male–female parallelism which reveals how the Gospel ministers equally to both sexes. Aeneas, a paralytic, bed-ridden for eight years, is healed by Peter's proclamation that Jesus heals him (similarly v. 40). We are told that πάντες οἱ κατοικοῦντες in the area of Lydda and Sharon saw that Aeneas was healed and ἐπέστρεψαν ἐπὶ τὸν κύριον. We may compare this conclusion to the end of the Tabitha story where it is stated, καὶ ἐπίστευσαν πολλοὶ κύριον (v. 42). This is the only detail of the Tabitha story which is somewhat less spectacular than the Aeneas story in fact or effect. In Acts 9.32–42 there is a clear crescendo in the miraculous – whereas Aeneas is healed of paralysis, Tabitha is raised from the dead (cf. v. 37, ἀποθανεῖν). In other respects as well, the story and person of Tabitha are presented in a more positive light than the story and person of Aeneas. While it appears that Aeneas was a Christian (cf. 9.32), he is not specifically called a disciple as is Tabitha. Further, there is no real interest in Aeneas himself, only in the fact of his healing. By contrast, the story of Tabitha relates in a specific way what Tabitha did and why she was important to the community (cf. vv. 36, 39). There is an obvious interest in her person reflected in the mentioning of the details of the funeral preparations (vv. 37, 39). Finally, the story indicates that Peter recognized how important she was to the community, for he makes a point of presenting her to the disciples (v. 41), which did not happen in Aeneas' case. This story may be taken as an example of the Lukan interest in giving a woman more prominence than a man.

Perhaps the main reason for the Tabitha story is that Luke wishes to reveal how a woman functioned as a deaconess, a very generous supporter of widows. It is interesting that at the outset of the story Luke presents her credentials, and they are the sort one would look for in a deaconess. We are told that Tabitha, also called Dorcas,[99] was a female disciple (μαθήτρια), a term used nowhere else in the NT.[100] Perhaps Luke reserved this term for her because among the Christian women he mentions she best exemplified the behavior of a true disciple. We are told that Tabitha literally was 'full of good works',[101] which meant that she was engaged continually in performing good works. In addition, we are told that she gave money or material aid to the needy, and v. 38 implies that this was a service given solely to community members.[102] Some of her good works involved making outer and under garments for needy women. Luke seems to depict Tabitha as at least moderately well-off and single (unmarried or widowed).[103] That Tabitha's service has been to αἱ χῆραι (v. 39), indicates a specialized and ongoing ministry, not just an occasional good deed to friends or neighbors. The description of Tabitha is reminiscent of Luke 8.3 and Acts 6.1–7, and thus it seems that Luke depicts Tabitha as fulfilling a task similar in kind to the work of the Seven.

Possibly, Luke here paints a portrait of a woman commissioned for ministry, for Tabitha's efforts are depicted as an ongoing concern directed to a specialized group of recipients. It is possible that Luke intimates Tabitha is in charge of an order of widows.[104] Thus, she would be presented as a model of one who builds up and maintains the community by her service and living example of the power of the Gospel. It is the presentation of Tabitha as a model disciple that differentiates this story from that of Aeneas.[105]

6. Women as prophetesses

Luke's passing reference to Philip's daughters (Acts 21.9) seems to be made partly because of his interest in the theme of fulfilment (Luke 1.1, 20, 4.21, 21.22–24, 22.16, etc.). In the daughters of Philip it appears Luke mainly means us to see the first recognized and recorded examples of Christian prophetesses in the Apostolic age. But, what sort of prophetesses are portrayed here? Were they of the sort we find in Paul's correspondence with the Corinthians (1 Cor 11.5), and thus perhaps involved in ecstatic utterance? Or, are we to see them as female counterparts to Agabus (Acts 11.28, 21.10–11), and thus a continuation of the type of prophet we find in the OT? Or, are we to see them as some combination of these two types?

A survey of all Luke's references to prophets and prophesying in his two volumes leads to the following conclusions:

(1) Prophets and their functions are significant themes throughout Luke–Acts and relate closely to Luke's stress on fulfilment and the Holy Spirit.[106]

(2) Luke makes a point of establishing that his most important, or at least his exemplary, characters are prophets: John the Baptist (Luke 1.76, 7.26, 20.6); Jesus (Luke 4.18–24, 7.16, 39, 9.19, 13.34, 22.64, 24.19); Peter (Acts 1.20, 2.4–21, 5.3, 9, 11.15–17); Paul (Acts 13.1, 9–11, 17.2–3, cf. 24.14, 26.22–27, 27.10, 23–24, 31, 34); Elizabeth (Luke 1.41–45); Mary or Elizabeth (Luke 1.46–55); Anna (Luke 2.36–38); Agabus (Acts 11.27–28, 21.10–11); Judas and Silas (Acts 15.32).

(3) Luke appears to limit the term προφήτης to a select group; i.e., some of the church leaders (cf. Acts 15.22, 32).[107]

(4) Prophecy is a gift of the Holy Spirit, and while it may be accompanied by glossolalia, it is not identical with that phenomenon (cf. Acts 19.6).

(5) Most of the prophecies recorded in Luke−Acts are citations of OT prophecies that are seen as referring to Jesus, to some event in His life, or to some event that results from His ministry (e.g., the giving of the Spirit).

(6) NT prophets are seen as engaged primarily in discerning the fulfilment of the predictive prophecy of the OT, rather than in giving new predictive prophecy of their own, though the latter is somewhat in evidence (cf. Acts 11.28, 27.10, 23−24, 31, 34).

(7) Prophets are shown to have a supernatural ability to discern people's character (Luke 7.39−50; Acts 6.3, etc).

(8) There are false prophets but they are not as powerful as Christian prophets (Acts 13.6; cf. Luke 6.26).

(9) Israel's continual character is summed up by the term prophet-killer (cf. Luke 11.48−51, 13.34; Acts 7.52).

At this point we may quote Ellis: '... Christian prophecy in Acts is represented as an eschatological power of the Holy Spirit from God (Ac 2.17) or from the risen Jesus (Ac 1.8, 2.17, and 3, cf. Psa 68.19[18], Eph 4.8). Although prophecy is a possibility for any Christian, it is primarily identified with certain leaders who exercise it as a ministry.'[108] As Ellis suggests, Philip's daughters are probably depicted as included among these leaders, since they appear to be more than just occasional prophesiers.[109]

It is not clear how we should take παρθένοι. If it means 'virgins' then Luke may be attempting to say that early on there was an order of single women who had a certain ministry to the Church.[110] Because of the conjunction παρθένοι and προφητεύουσαι it would seem that Luke is not just making an abstract or irrelevant statement about the virginity of Philip's daughters.[111] These are the two main facts he relates about these women and it seems natural to suppose that Luke gives us these facts because they are related to their roles and their spiritual example for the Church. The participial form, προφητεύουσαι, points to an activity or gift rather than an office, but in view of Luke 2.36 it is doubtful that Luke deliberately tried to avoid calling them prophetesses. Perhaps we should not make too rigid a distinction between these women's functions or gifts and their office. However, it may be that Luke intends his audience to see a connection between these women being virgins and their having particular gifts and roles. It is probably not coincidental that most of the women we find in Acts playing a significant role were either single or widowed.[112]

7. Women as teachers

In Acts 18.1–3, 24–26 we have a story about a husband and wife team of Christian missionaries and teachers. Luke's concern is not so much with *what* Apollos was taught by Priscilla and Aquila (the content of the teaching is never clearly mentioned), or the results of that teaching, but that he was taught 'more accurately' by this couple. This suggests that his concern is not doctrinal but personal — he may wish to indicate the role of this couple (and particularly of Priscilla).

The person we are most concerned with is Priscilla, not Aquila, and it is noteworthy that four out of the six times the two are mentioned in the NT, Priscilla's name comes first (Acts 18.18, 26; Rom 16.3; 2 Tim 4.19) in most of the best manuscripts (ℵ, B, *et al.*). Quite clearly Priscilla's name being predominantly first is unusual and perhaps significant.

As W. Bauer points out, it was not unheard of in antiquity for a woman's name to precede her husband's,[113] but it certainly was not usual to mention the woman first in Jewish and even Christian circles. Luke himself is careful to distinguish Aquila from Priscilla in Acts 18.2. It is only Aquila who is a Jew from Pontus, thus possibly implying that Priscilla was from the city they had recently left — Rome.[114] Thus, it has been suggested that there is a special significance in the prominence of Priscilla's name over Aquila's. The suggestions usually have been that Luke intends his audience to think of Priscilla as of higher social rank,[115] or of more prominence in the Church,[116] or both, than her husband.[117]

There are good reasons for thinking that Luke depicts Priscilla and Aquila as being Christians before they met Paul. As E. Haenchen remarks, 'That a Jewish couple expelled because of the conflict with Christians in Rome deliberately gave a Christian missionary work and shelter is far more improbable than that Paul found lodgings with Christians who had fled from Rome.'[118] If Luke means us to think of Priscilla and Aquila as already Christians, then we also see why Paul immediately leaves them in Ephesus — to lay some foundations for his later evangelistic work in that city. Haenchen adds, '... the interest which the author obviously takes in Aquila and Priscilla ... shows that they were so important to the history of the Christian mission that Luke could not overlook them.'[119]

What role do we find Priscilla and Aquila taking? Though Priscilla and Aquila's instructions may have included various matters of Christian doctrine, it is probable that Luke implies that it included instruction in the Christian practice of baptism, since the one deficiency in Apollos' knowledge clearly indicated in the text is that he knew only the baptism of John. τὴν ὁδόν τοῦ θεοῦ is likely to involve a matter of practice.[120] Probably, ἀκριβέστερον is an elative comparative rather than a true comparative.[121] If this is true, then τὰ περὶ τοῦ 'Ιησοῦ is to be contrasted with τὴν ὁδὸν τοῦ θεοῦ, the latter referring to matters of Christian initiation (i.e., Christian baptism), and the former to the story of Jesus. If so, then Apollos was a Christian who needed some advanced instruction primarily on a matter of practice (the 'way' of Christian baptism).

We are now in a position of discuss Priscilla's part in these matters. It is stated clearly that both she and Aquila instructed Apollos (ἐξέθεντο) and her name is mentioned first, so that if anyone is indicated by Luke as the primary instructor, it is Priscilla.[122] By 'more accurately' Luke depicts Priscilla as expounding the matter further than basic Christian teaching, or at least in a way that involves the whole panorama of Christian teaching, so the place of the part would be seen in relation to the whole. Apollos is depicted as already having basically a correct framework and knowledge about τὰ περὶ τοῦ 'Ιησοῦ. Further, Apollos is not just any convert to the faith but a man 'well versed in scripture', and this presupposes that Luke wants his audience to see that Priscilla and Aquila were also adept and knowledgeable enough in scripture to teach Apollos in such a fashion that he would accept it from both a woman and a man. Obviously, since Luke does not care to expound on exactly what was taught, it is the fact of the teaching and the identity of the teachers and pupil he wishes his audience to note. There may be special considerations involved, i.e., Priscilla and Aquila are portrayed as a team, and perhaps a team ministry is different from a woman acting alone. It appears, however, that Luke depicts Priscilla as taking the initiative here, if either one did, and her being married does not seem to be a determining factor. The fact that this act took place in at least semi-privacy is probably not very significant in terms of its possible implications for correct church practice, since there is no indication that Luke was trying to avoid having Priscilla teach Apollos in a worship context.[123]

Not all the implications of Acts 18.24–26 are clear, but certainly Luke portrays Priscilla as a συνεργός of Paul in the Gospel. As John Chrysostom says, 'He sailed for Syria ... and with him Priscilla – Lo, a woman also – and Aquila. But these he left at Ephesus with good reason, namely that they should teach.'[124]

8. Conclusions

At the beginning of this section we remarked that Luke does not feature women to the same degree in this second volume as he did in his first. While there is no need to modify this statement, we should go on to add that in Acts, Luke gives us five important glimpses into the roles he affirms for women in the Christian community. Further, he indicates his interest in women and their roles in some of his redactional summaries and his male–female parallelism.

Luke's five vignettes about Christian women are interesting and important because they reveal the variety of roles Luke intimated women could, and perhaps did, assume in the primitive community. In the mother of John Mark and in Lydia we see women assuming the role of 'mother' to the fledgling Christian community in Jerusalem and Philippi respectively. This involved providing both the home and the hospitality needed for the local Christian missionaries passing through. Thus, Luke implies that women who do such things aid both the intensive and extensive growth of the Christian community.

The role we see Tabitha playing in Acts 9 is similar to that of Lydia and the mother of John Mark in that it entails providing material aid to the believers. In Tabitha's case, it appears to be a more specific ministry to widows. We conjectured that because of the specific and ongoing nature of her good works, we may have here evidence that Luke argued that women should be, and perhaps were, commissioned by the local community as deaconesses in the primitive Church. Certainly, Tabitha is depicted as serving in some of the capacities later associated with that office so that even if she was not labeled or commissioned as a deaconess, Luke may still be presenting her as a prototype of a deaconess. That Luke calls her a female disciple, a word used nowhere else in the NT, may be his way of indicating to his audience that the actions in this story are exemplary of how Christian women ought to be and act. Nevertheless, he shows no desire to confine women to roles that only involved providing material assistance, for he also mentions women who prophesied and women who taught.

Luke's mention of Philip's prophesying daughters is tantalizingly brief, but it is sufficient to indicate that Luke affirmed women were involved in this important activity that had its roots in OT practice but also manifested the new gift of the Spirit (Acts 2.17). Prophesying was not the activity of every early Christian and a good case has been made by Ellis for seeing it as primarily identified in Acts as the task of certain church leaders. If so, then perhaps the reference in Acts 21.9 to the fact that Philip's daughters prophesied is more important than it might at first appear. We also learned from Acts 21.8–9 that Philip's daughters were virgins. Possibly Luke mentions this because he thought that in a woman's case being single was a prerequisite for the task of prophesying (or the office of prophetess, cf. Luke 2.36–37), or, less likely, because he intended to depict Philip's daughters as being part of an order of virgins. Here we also see Luke indicating that roles other than the traditional ones of wife and mother were possible and appropriate for Christian women, and perhaps in Philip's daughters we may see early examples of the sort of roles these women were assuming.

Perhaps most important of all is Luke's reference to Priscilla in Acts 18. Apart from Jesus' mother, she alone among the Christian women mentioned by name in Acts is referred to in several other places in the NT. Her significance is not confined to the fact that it is intimated she is more important or more prominent than her husband, or that she was one of Paul's co-laborers in and for the Gospel. Priscilla is presented as a teacher, and not just a teacher of other women or some nameless converts, but as someone adept enough to give Apollos, a leading male evangelist (Acts 18.24–8; 1 Cor 1.12, 3.4–6), a 'more accurate' instruction possibly about the important matter of Christian baptism. By including this story, Luke reveals the new roles women ought to be assuming in his view in the Christian community. Luke's portrayal of Priscilla is unreservedly positive, thus, it is fair to assume that Luke is presenting her as a model for the behavior of at least part of his audience.

By the very fact that Luke portrays women performing these various roles, he shows how the Gospel liberates and creates new possibilities for women. It is probably true that Luke is not interested in woman and their roles for their own sake; rather, the incidental evidence and the five vignettes we have studied in Acts reveal how the Gospel manifested itself and progressed among the female population in various parts of the first-century Mediterranean world. In Jerusalem (1.14, 12.12–17), in Joppa (9.36–42), in Philippi (16.11–15), in Corinth (18.1–3), in Ephesus (18.19–26), in Thessalonica (17.4), in Beroea (17.12), and in Athens (17.34), we find women being converted or serving the Christian community in roles that normally would not have been available to them apart from that community. Thus, Luke chronicles the progress of women as part of the progress and effects of the Christian Gospel. Though it is not perhaps one of his major themes in Acts, nonetheless he takes care to reveal to his audience that where the Gospel went, women, often prominent, were some of the first, foremost, and most faithful converts to the Christian faith, and that their conversion led to their assuming new roles in the service of the Gospel.

Why then did Luke go to such lengths to stress and indeed support the role of women in the earliest Christian churches? It is a reasonable hypothesis that when Luke wrote in the last quarter of the first century there was still considerable resistance to such ideas among his audience, and so the case had to be made in some detail. Though we have not seen evidence in this chapter to warrant the conclusion that Luke totally rejected the patriarchal framework of his culture, he is exercised, like Paul, to stress a transformed vision of such a framework and to uphold a model of servant leadership (Luke 22.24–30). At the same time, however, Luke stresses the viability of women performing various tasks of ministry for the community. Luke and Paul stand together in maintaining a tension between the reformation of the old order and the affirmation of the new ἐν χρισστῷ.

5

WOMEN IN THE CHURCHES OF MATTHEW, MARK, AND JOHN

The literature covered in this chapter is diverse not only in its generally accepted date, but also in its audience. Mark's Gospel may have been written as early as AD 66–8 in and for a Roman congregation. The Fourth Gospel may date as late as AD 96–100 and could hail from an Asian province. The First Gospel probably dates between these two extremes, and if it is dependent on Mark, then we should date it at least a decade after that Gospel. Finally, the Gospel called Matthew's has a certain Jewish Christian flavor and may have been written to a Syrian audience.

How does all this affect the Evangelists' presentation of women in the Gospel story? To anticipate our conclusions it appears that: (1) Mark has only a moderate interest in women and their roles; (2) the First Evangelist has some interest in this theme but also wishes to stress informed and reformed male leadership for the community that follows Jesus; (3) the Fourth Evangelist has a real interest in portraying certain key women in the story (Mary, Mary and Martha, Mary Magdalene, even the Samaritan woman) as models of awakening faith and as witnesses for the Johannine community at the end of the first century. Once again, we must stress that our focus is not on sources or the thorny historical problems all this material raises, but on what and how the Evangelists present material that bears on the question of women and their roles in the earliest churches.

A. Mark

1. The ministry and passion

At first glance, this Gospel (probably the earliest) appears to reflect little interest in women and their roles in the early Christian community. Indeed, Mark might even be accused of painting a negative picture of Mary and Jesus' family, including his sisters (cf. 3.21, 31–35, 6.1–6). Yet quite clearly he was one who was well aware of the conditions and problems the women in his predominantly Gentile audience faced (as 10.12 indicates; cf. also 13.17 and par.). On closer examination, Mark's critique of Jesus' family appears to be part of his overall attempt to distinguish clearly between the physical family and the family of faith (cf. 3.31–35, especially 10.29). As Mark 10.29 makes clear, the Evangelist has nothing against mothers and sisters being in the Kingdom. They certainly have a place and they are even commended directly or indirectly for their faith and actions (cf. 5.34). Further, Mark records how Jesus gave loving attention to women and their needs.

In Mark 1.30 we find Jesus healing Peter's mother-in-law and in 5.25–34 Jesus takes the time to heal a suffering woman. It is important to notice the climax of this last story: 'Daughter, your faith has made you well' (v. 34, cf. the parallels). It becomes apparent that Mark has no problem affirming women of faith, but in the Mary pericopes what we see is the inherent tension between the old orientation and the new – the physical family and the family of faith. Mark 5.35–43 recounts Jesus' raising of a little girl, but notice this is immediately followed by the misunderstanding narrative at Nazareth. What is even more striking is that on the one hand we have a woman being praised for her faith (5.25–34), a foreign woman being commended for her response to Jesus (7.24–30), a widow being set up as an example for others to follow, while on the other hand the Twelve are being criticized repeatedly for their lack of understanding and belief (cf. 4.40, 6.52).[1] This is particularly telling because Mark focuses on the Twelve as *the* disciples of Jesus who receive extra, private instruction. To them are given the 'secrets of the kingdom' (4.11ff., 34, 8.27–33, 10.32–34).[2] Yet, they do not respond in faith as well as a woman who probably had magic-tainted faith even in the supposed healing properties of Jesus' robe! In short, we see here not only male–female reversal in Mark, but also male–female disciple reversal.

None of this leads us to say that Mark disparages the physical family. Notice how his arrangement of pericopes in Mark 10 (marriage, vv. 2–12; children, vv. 13–14; parents, vv. 15, 19) along with the teaching itself inculcates the value of marriage and family. Notice also that the gist of the teaching on divorce is, in fact, no divorce in the Markan redaction. This could not but give a securer place to wives in Christian marriages, though 10.29 might be there to offset this stabilizing teaching. Against such a deduction, however, Mark probably intended his audience to understand 10.29 to refer to leaving one's non-Christian family.

Another factor which Mark places unique stress on, even to the point of inserting editorial remarks into the text, is the matter of clean and unclean (7.1–3). Mark's point is to show that only moral impurity defiles a person. Now, this teaching, while focusing on food (19b), has clear implications for other ideas about ceremonial cleanness. If such teaching was understood to mean that ceremonial uncleanness was not a problem (only moral uncleanness, cf. the list in vv. 21–22), then women could not be banned from worship or Christian service during the time of their monthly period. We know that this sort of ceremonial uncleanness was considered a major impediment to a woman's full participation in synagogue worship.[3] Doubtless, the implications of Mark 7.1–23 would have been felt most by the Jewish Christians in Mark's audience, but it had implications for all – it made possible, though it did not mandate, the full participation of Christian women in the early Church.

Perhaps most important of all is Mark's focus on women in his passion and resurrection narratives. Here we discover that it was Jesus' women friends and traveling companions, not the Twelve or even the Three, who became the primary witnesses to the most crucial events in Jesus' life. At this point we will focus only on some of the main features highlighted by Mark.[4] First, his anointing narrative (14.3–9 and par.) presents an act by a woman that is objected to by some, but serves as a prophetic foreshadowing of Jesus' death and burial. Most important is the fact that Mark includes 14.9 (cf. Matt 26.13) where a woman's act of devotion will be proclaimed along with the Gospel in memory of her throughout the world. Here we see the author indicating that a woman's part in the Gospel story is so crucial that her deed is to be celebrated repeatedly in memory of her. Is Mark deliberately using sacramental language here (cf. 1 Cor 11.24)? Second, Mark recounts not only that Judas would and did betray Jesus (14.10–11, 43ff.), and that Peter would and did deny Jesus (14.27ff., 66ff.), and that the Three let him down in Gethsemane (14.32–42), but also that καὶ ἀφέντες αὐτὸν ἔφυγον πάντες (14.50). In context, this surely refers to the remainder of the Twelve. In short, Mark portrays, indeed stresses, the failure of the male leadership trained by Jesus – they have become not just last, but lost.

Third, it is particularly striking that Mark, in contrast to the Fourth Evangelist, nowhere in chapter 15 portrays the Twelve or other male disciples as participating in Jesus' death or burial or post-Easter events. Fourth, instead, Mark focuses deliberately on the role the women played at the cross and at the tomb both before and after Easter. Notice how he goes to some lengths to mention their names not once but three times in various places (15.40, 47, 16.1), and stresses the qualities about them that manifest their discipleship. Thus, at 15.41 we hear αἳ ὅτε ἦν ἐν τῇ Γαλιλαίᾳ ἠκολούθουν αὐτῷ καὶ διηκόνουν αὐτῷ (contrast Matthew and Luke). Surely following and serving are the very terms that connote a disciple in the Markan outline, and as if to make clear that ἠκολούθουν has theological significance he distinguishes that following from the many other women who merely συναναβᾶσαι αὐτῷ εἰς Ἱεροσόλυμα. Mark also adds that these women witnessed (θεωροῦσαι) these crucial events of Jesus' life.[5]

What is the point in all this? Probably, Mark wishes to establish the credibility of these named women, for they were to be the validating witnesses of the most crucial elements in the Christian kerygma – Jesus' death, burial, and resurrection (1 Cor 15.3, 4). I agree with H. Schlier and others that it is these women who provide the link between these events because they are mentioned by name as authenticating witnesses.[6] É. Dhanis has rightly pointed out how catechetical interests affect Mark's presentation of these events.[7]

Now it is precisely for these reasons that it seems most unlikely that Mark intended to end his Gospel at 16.8 – on a note of fear and flight which thereby invalidates Mark's crucial validating witnesses. If Mark 16.8 was the original conclusion, then Mark intended to reveal the women's lack of understanding and at least temporary disobedience as a climax or a model post-Easter reaction to the Gospel. All that Mark carefully builds from the crucifixion, to the burial, to the empty tomb in regard to the women's important witness of these events is called into question. This makes it unlikely that Mark 16.8 is the intended conclusion. He cannot have wished to destroy in one final event what he created in a sequence of three key events from 15.40 on. Though Mark's Gospel begins abruptly, it begins with the Gospel, and we may expect it to end in similar fashion. We will now look more closely at Mark's resurrection narrative in 16.1–8.

2. The resurrection narrative

E. L. Bode states, 'The only Easter event narrated by all four evangelists concerns the visit of the women to the tomb of Jesus.'[8]

This observation indicates that all four Gospel writers saw this event as essential to their resurrection narratives.

The Marcan account of the women's second visit to the tomb is replete with textual, exegetical, and theological difficulties. The textual problems are the least serious and will be treated first. Despite the arguments of W. R. Farmer, reviving the view of J. W. Burgon,[9] it is not likely that Mark 16.9–20 was the original intended conclusion of the Second Gospel for the following reasons. First, Farmer's view fails to explain adequately how it was that the best witnesses and versions in various geographical areas happen not to have these verses (cf. syr[s], only similar to B in its omission of 16.9–20), while it is mainly the secondary or tertiary witnesses (except in the West) that include these verses. Second, the evidence of the shorter ending argues strongly against the longer ending.[10] Third, there are too many non-Marcan phrases and too many reminiscences of other Gospel accounts to maintain the Marcan nature of 16.9–20.[11] It appears that 16.9–20 was not originally composed to follow 16.8, but is a mosaic of other Gospel narratives of the resurrection appearances and other accounts adapted and added here to finish the story.[12]

Despite a trend in the past thirty years to argue that Mark 16.8 is the ending of this Gospel, there are good reasons to doubt such claims. The objection that grammatically it is unlikely that anyone would end a work, much less a Gospel, with ἐφοβοῦντο γάρ has been shown by several scholars to have little weight. H. J. Cadbury is able to provide clear examples from the papyri that ending a sentence, paragraph, or work with γάρ is not unknown or even irregular.[13] It seems probable, however, that if Mark had intended to conclude at this point he would have used a verb in the aorist, rather than the imperfect which suggests something more was intended.[14] Another difficulty arises over the meaning of this concluding verb. Apparently, this verb involves an element of fright or terror. Against this it has been argued that this verb may refer to reverential awe, rather than fear of a negative sort. Various studies of Mark's usage of these verbs of fear have concluded that what he intends is to indicate the natural and normal reaction to the supernatural, especially when it breaks in unexpectedly (cf. Mark 5.42, 9.26).[15] Mark, however, is capable of using the verbs of fear and amazement in perfectly ordinary ways, and one could just as well argue that the usage in 11.18 (ἐφοβοῦντο γάρ αὐτόν, πᾶς γὰρ ὁ ὄχλος ἐξεπλήσσετο ἐπὶ τῇ διδαχῇ αὐτοῦ) gives us our closest parallel to the usage in 16.8. Further, the view held by Lightfoot and others fails to deal with the fact that γάρ is used twice in 16.8. In the first place, we are told they fled from the tomb for trembling and astonishment (or bewilderment) took hold of them.[16] Second, we are told they said nothing to anyone for they were afraid. We must ask whether or not Mark is saying that reverential awe led the women to flee from the tomb. Further, while on one level silence and a reverential awe in the face of mystery might be a sufficient and appropriate response to a miraculous act of God, in this case silence is not golden. We are now on the other side of the resurrection and keeping the Messianic secret is no longer the order of the day (cf. 9.9).[17] The appearances of the risen Lord are crucial extensions of the resurrection so far as the Church is concerned, for it is these appearances which were responsible for the regathering of Jesus' followers. The going forth into Galilee motif in Mark has no resolution without at least some account of appearances. It is unlikely that Mark, writing to the Christian community, would fail to reaffirm that it was the risen Jesus Himself who was responsible for the foundation and existence of that community. Finally, the view of Lightfoot and others fails to answer why, as early as the first half of the second century, someone felt compelled to add a long ending to 16.8, and someone else (perhaps later) added a shorter ending where our Gospel apparently breaks off.[18] Thus, it seems unlikely that Mark 16.8 was the original ending of this Gospel.[19]

Thus, either Mark's original ending is lost without a trace, or perhaps there are traces of it even in the NT. The former view is probably a counsel of despair, since Matthew and Luke were dependent on Mark and all go on to relate resurrection appearances as does Acts 1.[20]

An older, but not improbable, conjecture is that of E.J. Goodspeed who points out correctly that Matthew, unlike Luke, takes over virtually everything he finds in Mark.[21] In Matthew, unlike Luke, we have the 'going forth into Galilee' motif so prominent at the end of Mark's Gospel (14.28, 16.7). Further, in Matthew '... in the reference to the "mountain where Jesus had appointed them" there seem to lurk some allusions to the story of the Transfiguration for which Mark is demonstrably Matthew's source.'[22] Taking into account the unique material incorporated by the First Evangelist into the Marcan narrative (i.e., the bribing of the watch, 28.11–15), we note that Matt 28.9–10 and 16–20 form what could be a natural conclusion to Mark's Gospel. Matt 28.9–10 implies that the women reported what they saw, brings to light the Galilean appearance promised in Mark 14.28 and 16.7, and contains the recommissioning of the Twelve intimated in the pre-resurrection narrative of Mark and Matthew. Thus, perhaps the original conclusion of Mark's Gospel can be found in Matthew. We can now examine what Mark 16.1–8 relates about women and their roles in the events at the tomb.

Mark's resurrection narrative begins by telling us that Mary Magdalene, Mary the mother of James, and Salome brought spices the day after the Sabbath in order to anoint Jesus. At some point in the early hours of the morning (the first day of the week) the women departed for the tomb. That the women bring spices indicates that there was no question in their minds that Jesus was dead. They had come to perform a devotional anointing, not to receive a revelation. Mark, however, wishes to indicate that before anyone claimed to see the risen Lord, the word came that He had triumphed over the grave. We will not pause to dwell on the Marcan kerygmatic formulation of the angel's message except to say that Mark is attempting to indicate continuity between the earthly and the risen Jesus, and to confirm the value of the empty tomb tradition. It was this same Jesus who was born in Nazareth and died on a cross that was now risen and now went before them into Galilee. Confirmation of this truth comes by inspecting the empty tomb. This was the real value of the empty tomb. Apart from the word of revelation, the empty tomb was open to various interpretations, not all of them positive (cf. John 20.13). But as a confirmation of or witness to the truth of the word that Jesus was risen, the empty tomb was an important fact.

What is significant is that the women were not simply eye-witnesses of an empty tomb that, taken in isolation, was ambiguous. Indeed, first they were ear-witnesses of the Easter message which gave them the key to a proper interpretation of the empty tomb.[23] Thus, the women had both heard and seen. They could testify not only to an empty tomb but also to a risen Jesus.

The Evangelist claims that the women's task was specific and limited – they should go and proclaim the truth to Jesus' disciples and especially to Peter.[24] In Mark's scheme the key purpose of the women's commission was to restore and reinstate the disciples so that they could become the authoritative witnesses to the world.[25] This does not disparage the women's witness, but it does indicate Mark's endorsement of the view that the male leadership of Jesus' community (in particular, Peter) is recommissioned by divine command, despite their abysmal failure during the Passion events. Certainly, Mark is no feminist, but he is also no anti-feminist. His vision, like that of Luke and Paul, seems to include new roles for women and also a reaffirmation of certain traditional structures.

The women's reaction to the angel's words was to flee from the tomb (v. 8). If Mark 16.8 is not the original ending of this Gospel, then we should not build too much on the words καὶ οὐδενὶ οὐδὲν εἶπαν, ἐφοβοῦντο γάρ.[26] Thus, while recognizing that these women were badly frightened by the occurrence at the tomb, 16.8 probably does not imply a total and eternal silence of these women in disobedience to the angel's command. If we note the parallel construction in v. 8,[27] then it is possible that Mark intends for us to relate the two sentences which each follow καί as well as the two γάρ clauses. The implication would be that for the circumscribed period of time the women fled from the tomb, they said nothing to anyone. The limitation on the period of silence is especially likely if this remark was originally parenthetical and the story continued.[28]

What can we deduce about women and their roles from this passage? The women went to the tomb to perform a role that was traditionally theirs – anointing of a corpse. In the Marcan redaction, they left the tomb charged with performing a most untraditional role – relating to Jesus' disciples the angel's Easter message and, by implication, the angel's command to go to Galilee. Did Mark intend to provide a precedent for Christian women to instruct even an all male audience? Put in a different way, is Mark claiming that the circumstances of salvation history are such that they bring about the reversal Jesus preached – the first become last, and the last, first? We have noted before that Mark says there were women witnesses to the three crucial events later confessed in the creeds – death, burial, and the resurrection (by revelation of the empty tomb). Dhanis has shown that Mark's narrative of these three events is bound together and given continuity by the triple mention of these women whose witness validated each event. Mark thus reveals that these women are the foundation of the confession of the first three articles of the traditional creed (cf. 1 Cor 15.3–4). This contention is supported by noting how Mark's narrative reveals a correspondence between the angel's words and the women's witnessing – 'You seek Jesus the Nazarene (cf. 15.41 – they followed Him in Galilee), the crucified one' (cf. 15.40 – the women witnessed the crucifixion). It is possible that Mark went on to make clear that the women received a reassuring appearance of Jesus before they could properly carry out their task (cf. below on Matt 28.9–10). Further, as Catchpole says,

... Mark 16.7 and 8b do not have to be related as command and disobedience ... to command, but as command and an obedience ... which brings the message to certain specified persons while at the same time realizing correctly that the public at large are not meant to be brought within its scope. Of course this indicates indirectly that disclosure to the world at large is going to happen by means of the preaching of the disciples rather than through the women.[29]

Thus, while Mark probably intends this passage to give a precedent for women to bear witness to the Easter events, and affirms the worth of women witnessing to men, even the male leaders of the community, at the same time the commission given to them may reaffirm these women's subordinate positions in relation to the community's original male leaders. The women's witness is an indispensable foundation for the Gospel tradition, but the Apostles are the official (or primary) witnesses to the world.

B. Matthew

The First Evangelist's interest in Peter and in matters of ecclesiology are too well known to need rehearsing. He alone tells us the ἐκκλησία is founded on Peter. But it is less well known that he, almost exclusively amongst the Evangelists, characterizes the male disciples (and Peter in particular) as ὀλιγόπιστοι (cf. Matt 14.31, 8.26, 6.30, elsewhere only at Luke 12.28). By contrast, of only one person in this Gospel is it said μεγάλη σου ἡ πίστις — a foreign woman (15.28).[30] Thus, the theme of male–female reversal is somewhat in evidence even in the most Jewish of all the Gospels, but as we shall see in most regards it is the most traditional of all the Gospels.

1. The Birth Narratives

New Testament scholars have grown accustomed to the dictum that the development of the Gospel tradition began with the last events in Jesus' life and gradually worked its way back to the birth stories. In short, it is normally maintained that the birth narratives were the last to be put into a relatively fixed written form. If so, then it is reasonable to expect the birth narratives to tell us something of the attitudes about women that the Evangelists wished to inculcate when they presented these stories, attitudes that would reflect what women's roles were in the last twenty or so years of the first century.

In Matthew's birth stories, the main focus is on Jesus, but various women do play secondary roles. The first mention of Mary in the NT is found in the genealogy (1.16): 'Jacob begat Joseph the husband of Mary of whom Jesus was born, who is called Christ'.[31] What the First Evangelist intimates by this phrase is: (1) that Jesus is legally in the line of David through Joseph, but (2) that physically Mary is Jesus' only human parent. Indeed, both the genealogy and the following pericope (1.18–25) can be seen to focus primarily on Jesus as the son of David and Son of God, themes present elsewhere in Matthew.[32] Matthew 1.18–25 may be taken as an explanation of how Jesus could be born of Mary and not of Joseph, and yet still be in the Davidic line.[33] The genealogy and the pericope which follows assume and to some extent explain the virginal conception perhaps in an attempt to answer the difficulties consequent upon Jesus' irregular origins.[34]

What is unusual about the Matthean genealogy is that it mentions not only Mary but also four other women.[35] There are several hypotheses to explain why the First Evangelist includes Tamar, Rahab, Ruth, and Uriah's wife: (1) because he is attempting to identify Jesus with Gentiles or sinners; (2) because these women were subjects of controversy in the Jewish debate about the Davidic Messiah; (3) because they were involved in 'irregular' unions and yet they were vehicles of God's Messianic plan; and (4) because he wished to show that not only Jesus but also other great Davidic kings had irregularities in their past history and yet were God's chosen ones. None of these views is without problems; however, it seems probable that view (3) is the most accurate.[36] If so, then the First Evangelist calls attention to Mary as an instrument of God's providence even prior to 1.18–25. The genealogy also points out Jesus' indebtedness to women as well as to men for His Davidic ancestry, and to Mary especially for His humanity.

With the mention of Mary and the other women in the genealogy, one might expect the First Evangelist to give special attention to Mary's role; however, he goes on to focus almost exclusively on Joseph.[37] It is not without purpose that only Joseph, apart from Jesus, is given the title 'son of David'. It is through Joseph and the naming of his son that Jesus becomes, like His father, a son of David.[38] The focus on Joseph and Jesus continues as the birth narrative develops. It is Joseph who initiates the actions that take place after he is instructed three times by an angelic messenger (1.24, 2.13, 19). He is seen as the head of his family and the one who will guide and protect Mary and Jesus. It is Joseph, not Mary, who receives these divine revelations and is presented as the model disciple or son of Israel, being obedient to God's word as he receives it.[39] It is when we turn to the second theme, Jesus as the Son of God, that Mary comes to the fore through her relationship with Joseph and her role as Jesus' mother. Even here, however, the story is couched in light of what has happened to Mary, but is focused on Joseph's reaction to Mary's pregnancy. We now turn to the details of the narrative to understand how Mary's role and her virginal conception were viewed by this Gospel writer.

What are we to make of πρὶν ἢ συνελθεῖν (1.18)? Here we have a genitive absolute agreeing with the subject.[40] Two possible meanings are: (1) 'before they had marital union', or (2) 'before they married or cohabited'. If the former is meant, then it would imply that Mary and Joseph consummated their marriage after the birth of Jesus.[41] If the latter is accepted, then there need be no such implication – it would simply be a statement about Mary's pregnancy during betrothal. There is, however, a third possibility – both marriage and its consummation are intended by this general phrase. It is difficult to imagine a Jew or Jewish Christian separating these two ideas. Thus, it seems likely that sexual union is at least implied. This phrase is, however, mainly a way of explaining that God alone was responsible for Mary's conception and that Jesus is the result of God's, not Joseph's, creative act. As I. Broer notes, the First Evangelist is concerned with Joseph's conduct only until the birth, to affirm that the virgin has given birth as the prophet foretold.[42] Thus, Jesus as a son of David and as the Son of God is seen as a fulfilment of OT prophecy. This being so, Mary is fulfilling the role which would be the Jewess' greatest honor – being parent to a first-born son who is the Davidic Messiah. Through her, Israel's national destiny is fulfilled.[43]

Matthew 1.18 goes on to say Μαρίας ... εὑρέθη ἐν γαστρὶ ἔχουσα ἐκ πνεύματος ἁγίου. It seems clear from the text that the author wishes to show that Joseph discovered Mary was pregnant, for the action in v.19 is precipitated by the εὑρέθη in v.18.[44]

The Evangelist portrays Joseph as caught between the holy law of God and his love for Mary. He did not wish to expose her to ridicule by public divorce,[45] yet his allegiance and submission to God's will came first. How could Jesus be his son in any case? The Evangelist adds the angel's annunciation to answer this question for his audience. His intention is to paint a theological picture of Joseph as a model disciple who gives up a Jewish father's greatest privilege (siring his first-born son) in order to obey God's will (cf. 1.24). The attempt to rehabilitate the image of Joseph is perhaps part of the Evangelist's larger purpose of demonstrating the respectability of Jesus' origins.

Matthew 1.25 concludes this pericope and has often been a point of debate between Protestant and Catholic scholars. It seems correct to assert that the focus of this text is on the fact of Mary's virginity *ante partum* and, as the imperfect verb implies, the duration of Joseph's abstinence from intercourse prior to Jesus' birth.[46] Nonetheless, the imperfect probably implies subsequent sexual relations between Mary and Joseph even more than the punctiliar aorist, for the phrase 'he used not to' or 'he was not knowing her' implies a certain duration of time delimited by the ἕως οὗ. This implies that the previously abstained from action did or will take place after that duration is over.[47] Attempts to redefine ἕως as 'while' or 'without', or to see it as the beginning of a new phrase are unconvincing in view of the grammatical and lexical evidence.[48] Thus, Mary's virginity *ante partum* is affirmed in Matt. 1.18–25, but Mary's virginity *post partum* is probably ruled out by this text.

Speaking purely on the level of the Evangelist's theological presentation, we may note that he focuses on Joseph's role to show how Jesus also became a son of David. It is Joseph, not Mary, who connects the sections and ties this infancy narrative together (a role Mary plays in Luke's infancy narrative). Joseph is pictured as a model of obedience to God's will (1.24), and as an object three times of God's revelation (1.20, 2.13, 19). He is both presented and addressed by God through the angel as the head of his family – the one who guides and protects them. Mary is seen as submissive to Joseph's leading into and out of Egypt. In fact, she not only is submissive, but also silent. Thus, the Evangelist reaffirms the traditional Jewish roles of headship and subordination despite the fact that Mary is singularly honored by a special relationship with God and His son. This may be due to the Evangelist's audience.[49] It is only in Luke's infancy narrative that we see the different emphasis on Mary's role as mother and servant of God and His son.

2. Women in Jesus' ministry

In various other places in the Matthean editing of different source material we find the ideas mentioned above confirmed. Thus, for instance, in the Sermon on the Mount, Matthew places extra responsibility on the male leadership of the community for maintaining its moral integrity. If my exegesis of Matt 5.27–32 is correct,[50] then this passage is about the restriction of male aggression, and it is notable that there is no attempt here to make women scapegoats in a situation involving sexual sin. It is possible to take the famous exceptive clause (5.32) to mean that the male privilege of divorce is reaffirmed, while no parallel privilege for women is mentioned. Against this, however, I have argued in detail that πορνεία, especially in Matt 19.1–10, may refer to incest.[51] In any event, this material continues to affirm male leadership, but it is a reformed view that is urged – one that does not make women scapegoats for sexual sin, and one that understands that such leadership means more responsibility, not more privilege, especially in regard to the moral integrity of the community, Part of this responsibility placed on men is permanently to remain either married or continently single for the sake of the Kingdom (cf. 19.10–12).[52]

The Matthean redaction of various Marcan stories involving women gives little or no indication of any notable attempts to highlight women or their roles beyond what was present in the source (cf. 8.14–17, 9.18–22, 22. 23–33, 12.42; cf. Luke 11.31). The First Evangelist does include some of the radical sayings that indicate the way of Jesus would cause division, not harmony, in the physical family (10.34–37). Again at Matt 12.48–50 the Evangelist has Jesus distinguish 'disciples' from his own family very distinctly, even more than in his Marcan source. Further, he is not averse to adding material which may reflect negatively on a woman. Thus, at Matt 20.20–2 it is not James and John (cf. Mark 10.35–40) but their mother who requests the special seats in the Kingdom, though she is requesting them for her sons, not for herself. The parable of the wise and foolish virgins, unique to this Gospel, represents both positive and negative impressions of women as symbols of preparedness for the coming Kingdom (or King?) or the lack of preparedness.[53]

In the passion narrative, the First Evangelist seems to highlight even more than Mark the perfidy of the Twelve (cf. Matt 26.56, 69–75, espec. 27.4–5 on Judas). Yet he does not highlight the discipleship or witness of the women at the cross as much as Mark. According to Matt 27.55 it is not said that the women followed Jesus while in Galilee, but only ἠκολούθησαν τῷ ᾽Ιησοῦ ἀπὸ τῆς Γαλιλαίας διακονοῦσαι αὐτῷ. Here the women simply traveled with Jesus when he pilgrimaged up to Jerusalem. This impression is avoided in Luke by his unique pericope, 8.1–3, and in Mark by 15.41. Nonetheless, the First Evangelist may highlight women as witnesses at the tomb more than Mark and present on the whole a more positive portrait of the women's involvement in the Easter events.

3. The resurrection narrative

Since the First Evangelist is probably dependent upon his Marcan source for information about the empty tomb (except for the material about sealing and guarding the tomb, added for apologetic reasons) our task is to note how Matthew has modified his source in ways that affect his portrayal of women. We are first told that the women go to *see* the tomb; there is no mention of spices or intention to anoint. It is argued that this change is due to the insertion of the sealing of the tomb.[54] While this is plausible, it does not explain why Matthew includes the 'seeing'. Perhaps the best explanation for the 'seeing' motif is given by F. Neirnyck who argues that Matt 28.1 serves as a title – the witnessing of the women.[55] This accords with the First Evangelist's use of θεωρέω in 27.55 (cf. Mark 15.47, 16.4), and it also makes sense in view of the role the women are about to be assigned. The Evangelist is suggesting that, seen from the point of view of God's providential plan, the women come 'to witness' the empty tomb and go forth to witness about it, whatever their own original intentions might have been. If Neirynck is correct, then it probably rules out the view that the Evangelist intended us to think that the women witnessed the opening of the tomb (and thus the resurrection?).[56] The Evangelist probably hints that only the angel saw the resurrection, and that through the angel's words and the empty tomb the women learn of the resurrection.

The angel's address to the women begins abruptly (note the guards alone have been mentioned in v. 4), because the First Evangelist has incorporated his guard story into the Marcan narrative. The following differences between the Matthean and Marcan account of the angel's message are of significance to this study. (1) The Evangelist places no stress on the women's developing reactions to the events, reserving his comments on their feeling to one place after the angel's message. Matthew avoids Mark's wonder or astonishment vocabulary, leaving out Mark's μὴ ἐκθαμβεῖσθε and substituting μὴ φοβεῖσθε ὑμεῖς. (2) The ὑμεῖς is emphatic and brings out the fact that the women, perhaps in contrast to the guards, have no reason to be afraid.[57] (3) In Matthew, the angel not only tells the women *what* he knows of their intention (as in Mark), but also *that* he knows of their intention (οἶδα γὰρ ὅτι). (4) The command to tell Peter in particular is omitted. (5) There is an addition of καθὼς εἶπεν after 'He is risen' stressing that Jesus foretold it. Later, after the statement about Galilee, Matthew has ἰδοὺ εἶπον ὑμῖν instead of Mark's καθὼς εἶπεν ὑμῖν (Matt 28.7 – Mark 16.7). The angel thus speaks on its own authority in Matthew to some degree. Is there some hint here that the women are not merely messengers but intended recipients of the resurrection proclamation? (6) The women are told to go quickly (ταχύ, v. 7) to tell the disciples, and they do so (v. 8). Thus, their complete obedience is made clear. This is a non-Marcan feature. (7) In Matthew, part of the message the women are to take to the disciples is ἠγέρθη ἀπὸ τῶν νεκρῶν (not mentioned in Mark directly as part of what they are to say). The women are to proclaim the resurrection as well as where the risen Jesus can be seen. Further, if ὅτι in Matt 28.7 is recitative (as it seems to be in Mark 16.7), then there is no contradiction between a promise that Jesus will be seen in Galilee and the fact that He is seen by the women in Jerusalem. The appearance promised in Galilee is a promise for the Eleven alone. The women are given no clear indication that they too will see Him. The First Evangelist, unlike Mark, seems to suggest that to *hear* that He is risen is sufficient, for they have been faithful through these passion and resurrection events. The Eleven, however, needed more. If we are correct in seeing part of Mark's lost ending in Matt 28.9–10,[58] this favors the view that the ὅτι in Mark is also recitative and there is a clear distinction in both Matthew and Mark between promise and authoritative appearance to the Eleven in Galilee, and surprise appearance to the women alone in Jerusalem.

The reaction of the women to the angel's words in Matthew is both similar to and different from Mark's account. In both, the women leave the tomb rapidly, but the First Evangelist adds ταχύ and omits ἔφυγον. He tells us the women left *with* fear and great joy, not *because* of it. This modification of Mark is perhaps made in light of what is to follow in vv. 9–10 and is an attempt to soften, if not eliminate, Mark's negative tone. The First Evangelist intends us to think that the women's emotions are mixed and their running is not only out of fear of their experience at the tomb, but also from a desire to ἀπαγγεῖλαι τοῖς μαθηταῖς αὐτοῦ (v. 8). The First Evangelist omits entirely the silence due to fear which we find in Mark 16.8, and thus we have a much more positive portrayal of the women in this angelophany than in Mark's, and the women's role seems to be more significant in Matthew than in Mark. In Matthew, we are told directly that the women must say that Jesus is risen from the dead.

There is a certain amount of contrast between the picture the First Evangelist paints of how the women react (28.9–10) and how the male disciples react (28.16–17) to Jesus' appearance. When the women see Jesus, they eagerly grasp His feet and worship Him (28.9).⁵⁹ When Jesus appears to the men we are *not* told they worshipped Him, but that some have doubts (οἱ δὲ ἐδίστασαν, 28.17). This reversal can be recognized as part of a larger pattern when we see it in the following Matthean context: (1) the women receive the first appearance; and (2) it is only as a result of the women's testimony that the men go to Galilee and see Jesus.

Perhaps, at 28.10, Matthew implies the women needed to be confirmed in their surprising new task of 'instructing' the Eleven. This last suggestion is confirmed upon examination of the content of the words in 28.10. When the women see Jesus they approach Him and ἐκράτησαν αὐτοῦ τοὺς πόδας. This is similar to what we find in John 20.17; in fact, there are reasons for seeing Matt 28.9–10 and John 20.13–18 as two versions of the same story.⁶⁰ While the First Evangelist may mention the grasping because of apologetic reasons (i.e., demonstrating to the women and the Evangelist's audience the physical reality of the risen Jesus) more likely we are to see this as an expression of the women's eager desire to be near to Jesus once again.⁶¹ Elsewhere in Matthew this gesture represents supplication (8.2, 9.18, 15.25, 18.26, 20.20), but here the women are not asking for help, they are giving adoration to their beloved Master (cf. Acts 10.25).⁶² The women's response is instantaneous once they hear the Master's voice (possibly another indication that this is a form of John 20).⁶³ The word ἐκράτησαν is joined to προσεκύνησαν by a καί indicating that they are two coordinate activities.

The Evangelist does not have Jesus make a verbal effort to reassure them that He is risen; rather, the μὴ φοβεῖσθε in v. 10 is followed by a reiteration of the women's task. It is interesting that in Matthew we are not told how the women's words are received. Perhaps the Evangelist wishes to spare the Eleven at this point, or did not wish to imply that the women's efforts went for nothing.

In comparing Matt 28.9–10 to 16–20, we see that only the women followers of Jesus are portrayed as post-resurrection models for the Evangelist's audience. Their devotion is sincere, their joy great, their obedience perfect. They worship Jesus. By contrast, there is no such outward expression of devotion by the men, rather it is said that some of Jesus' chosen leaders doubted. In the reactions to these two groups we see a certain amount of male–female contrast. In the action of Jesus, the Evangelist presents male–female parallelism – He appears both to a group of female followers and to the male disciples (first the sisters, then the brothers). He gives a commission to both groups. But in the difference of the commissions we may see a pattern of male headship emerging. The women are given a crucial, but temporary, task in service to the community of disciples. They are told to leave Jesus, go to the disciples, and instruct those who are already brethren. In the Matthean theological schema the men are given the permanent task and authority to make disciples, and the promise of Jesus' continual presence. The commission of the women both affirms the women's new roles in the community, and reaffirms the Eleven's headship role. Matt 28.16–20 makes explicit what was implicit in the commanding of the women to tell the disciples to go to Galilee (28.7, 10).

In conclusion, the Matthean resurrection narrative proves to be an interesting combination of motifs involving male and female disciples. On the one hand, we have a pattern of reversal in which the women are presented as better models of discipleship than the men, and the women (rather than the men) receive the first appearance of Jesus. Another part of this pattern of reversal is that the women assume the role normally allotted to men of instructing Jesus' male followers. On the other hand, the women's task is limited in nature and serves the purpose of reassembling the Eleven (and possibly others) so that they can be recommissioned as leaders of Jesus' resurrection community and as evangelists given authority to make disciples of all nations. Thus, we see how both women's new roles and a somewhat reformed view of headship for the male followers of Jesus can be affirmed in one breath by the First Evangelist. In Matt 28.1–10 we have the crucial and historically credible admission that the Church owed its testimony to the empty tomb to Jesus' women followers, and that it was they who were surprised and blessed by Jesus' *first* post-Easter appearance.

C. John

In some ways, the Fourth Evangelist presents us with the most developed picture of women and their roles among those who responded to the call of the Gospel. In fact, he presents several women as more perceptive spiritually than certain men, and shows their progress toward a fully formed Christian faith. On the whole, the Fourth Evangelist seems to share the full agenda of affirmation of women and their roles that we found characteristic of Luke.

1. Mary, mother and disciple (John 2, 19)

The figure of Jesus' mother is one which almost frames the Gospel story (John 2 and 19 only). In John 2 we see the tension between Jesus' physical family and the family of faith that we noted especially in Mark. Not only is Jesus' mother called 'woman', not 'mother', but Jesus' response to Mary (2.4) should be seen as his disengagement from her parental authority (a theme in evidence in Luke 2.41–52).[64] Mary must learn to see Jesus first through the eyes of faith, and only then with a parent's eyes. Nonetheless, John 2 does depict Mary having a partial faith in Jesus' ability to do 'something'.

John 19 should be seen as the Evangelist's way of saying that beneath the cross the family of faith and the physical family can be reconciled, by the latter being incorporated into the former. The beloved disciple should be seen as the representative of the (Johannine) community of faith that takes charge of and cares for Jesus' mother. She is to become a spiritual mother in and to the Johannine community, but not the 'mother of the Church' since the community embodied in the beloved disciple exists prior to her incorporation into it (according to John's portrayal of Mary's journey of faith).[65] There is some reason, however, to think that the Evangelist portrays Mary and the beloved disciple as archetypal disciples, male and female standing together beneath the cross as examples for all.

2. The Samaritan woman (John 4)

The story of the Samaritan woman is particularly striking as a narrative of the progress of a soul toward an adequate faith in Jesus. In the end, this woman seems to fulfil the role of disciple better than any of the Twelve for she goes forth to share the Good News about Jesus. In verse 39 we are told, τὸν λόγον τῆς γυναικὸς μαρτυρούσης. She provides Jesus' real spiritual food, while the disciples can only bring back physical sustenance from the village. Here is a clear example of male–female reversal. John 4 is all the more striking because it positively portrays a Samaritan woman, who would be considered unclean and unacceptable to Jesus' Jewish disciples. Further, if the Fourth Evangelist intended to compare the Samaritan woman to Nicodemus (John 3), then we see portrayed a woman who more nearly approximates a true faith in Jesus than even a member of the Jewish ruling class. Thus, we find another example of a woman on the way to becoming a full-fledged disciple portrayed as a model to the Evangelist's audience. If, as I think, this Gospel is directed primarily to non-Christians, then this author is probably showing his audience how they should respond to Christ, using women as examples.

3. Mary and Martha (John 11–12)

The portrait of Mary and Martha in John 11–12 is similar to that found in Luke 10.38–42. For our purpose, Martha is the critical figure, for she is depicted as having a dialogue of faith about Jesus (11.21ff.). Martha is said to believe that even after Lazarus' death, Jesus can still help him. Yet, it is also evident that her confession of faith is correct, but not comprehensive. Even after affirming Jesus' 'I am' saying (v. 39) she still does not expect resurrection in the present. Nevertheless, she makes the least inadequate confession of faith to this point in the Gospel (11.27). Here is another example of a woman seen on the way to being a full-fledged disciple. In John 12, Mary is depicted as a model of a servant, and indeed as performing a proleptic and prophetic burial act. Probably, in John, more than in the Synoptics, the fact that this is to be seen as a proleptic burial act is brought out by the language of v. 7.[66]

4. The passion narrative (John 18–19)

In the Johannine passion narrative there is not the same emphasis on women as authenticating witnesses as in the Marcan account, but there is a witness list mentioned at 19.25. We are told that these women were near to the cross, presumably near enough to hear and see the final moments of Jesus' life. There is no mention of the women making a trip to the tomb to witness Jesus' burial, unlike in the Synoptics. Instead, two Jewish males are mentioned. This suggests that the Evangelist, unlike Mark, is not concerned to link the women's authenticating witness to all three of the crucial elements in the creed – death, burial, resurrection. Nevertheless, the Fourth Evangelist presents the most developed picture of the women's visit to the tomb on Easter morning.

There are certain interesting parallels between John 19.25–27 and John 20. It is as if the Fourth Evangelist deliberately set out to give us a narrative about the two leading women in the early Christian community, Mother Mary and Mary Magdalene, who represent the two circles of Jesus' physical and spiritual families. More frequently noted are the parallels between Mary Magdalene and Thomas, and the contrasts between her and the beloved disciple (and/or Peter). These points of contact between John 20 and what precedes and follows should be remembered as we examine the exegetical details of the resurrection narrative.

5. The resurrection narrative (John 20)

In one sense John 20.1–2, 11–18 is a moving drama of the progress of a soul. It relates how Mary Magdalene went from (1) a state of abject sorrow and preoccupation with the dead body of Jesus which she still identified as the Lord, to (2) a sudden state of euphoria because Jesus was alive, a euphoria which involved clinging to Jesus' physical nature in a way that limited her understanding of her Lord, to (3) a state of understanding so that she was able to leave her preoccupations behind and become an 'apostle to the Apostles'.[67]

John 20.3–10 (cf. Luke 24.12, 24) is an interlude which does not concern us directly except that possibly the beloved disciple's faith is contrasted to Mary's sorrow and apparent spiritual insensitivity. The beloved disciple ἐπίστευσεν. In the Johannine schema this may mean that the beloved disciple believed what Mary had said or, more likely, that something miraculous had happened to Jesus or His body without specifically implying a belief in the resurrection. In fact, we are told that Peter and the beloved disciple did *not* understand from Scripture that Jesus had to rise from the dead. This may mean that the beloved disciple believed in the resurrection from the visible evidence. Elsewhere in John, πιστεύω does not imply complete belief in the risen Lord or even that Jesus is the Messiah (cf. 2.23–24, 12.42–43, 20.8, where we are not told what was believed).[68] Thus, we should be cautious in making dramatic contrasts between the reactions of Mary and the beloved disciple to the moved stone and the empty tomb.[69] What the beloved disciple believed is uncertain especially in view of v. 9 and also in view of the fact that he went home and apparently said nothing to either Peter or Mary (v. 10). We will now examine vv. 11–18 as a literary unit constructed by the Evangelist in order to see how he portrays Mary.

From v. 11 we begin to see a gradual process of revelation to Mary. We recognize a certain similarity between Mary's activity in v. 11 and

Peter's in v. 5. Peter παρακύψας sees (βλέπει) the grave clothes. Mary παρέκυψεν ... καὶ θεωρεῖ two angels sitting like bookends in the tomb where Jesus was laid. Theologically they serve as a supernatural parenthesis indicating God's activity is involved in this emptiness between them. There is a void, but it is not devoid of meaning. They indicate that Jesus' body is no longer in the tomb and thus one should no longer focus on the past, the tomb, or Jesus' dead body. Their virtual silence is preparatory for the significant dialogue that follows, emphasizing it by means of contrast. This revelation is of a more positive and living nature than what Peter received. He saw vestiges of something which might have meant no more than that an orderly conclusion to Jesus' life had taken place – God took Him up into heaven. Mary saw something which pointed to God's present activity. She does not react to the angel's presence, however, but simply continues to cry. Apparently, the Evangelist wishes us to think that anything less than Jesus Himself could not change her mood. In this she is like Thomas (cf. 20.25). The Evangelist has the angels attempt to draw her out of her sorrow by saying γύναι, τί κλαίεις? Mary's problem is that her mental horizons are fixed in the past. The body that was in the tomb is still called κύριόν μου (v. 13). Significantly, it is only when Mary turns away (ἐστράφη, v. 14, στραφεῖσα, v. 16) from the empty tomb (and the past) that she sees Jesus. R. H. Fuller intimates that there may be in this an implied criticism of the empty tomb tradition if used apart from the appearance traditions.[70]

The Evangelist has Jesus open the dialogue with the words, γύναι, τί κλαίεις? Perhaps we are meant to be reminded of the γύναι of John 19.26. In that narrative we may note the progress from γύναι (v. 26) to μήτηρ (v. 27). In similar fashion here we note the progress from γύναι (20.15) to Μαριάμ (20.16). Just as the mention of μήτηρ indicated the point of recognition and acceptance by Jesus of His mother into the family of faith, so Μαριάμ is the point where Mary first recognizes Jesus and is recognized in such a way that her place in the family of faith is implied. 'He calls his own sheep by name ... and his sheep follow him because they know his voice' (cf. 10.3 – 4).[71] In addition, we may note the presence of the language of the family of faith in both texts: (1) 'Woman behold your son ... behold your mother' (19.26 – 27); (2) 'I am going to my Father and your Father, go tell my brothers' (20.17).[72] But Mary Magdalene is being favored in a way that Jesus' mother was not, for she is the first to see the risen Jesus, and she too had been at the cross with Jesus' mother.

By including the question τίνα ζητεῖς the Evangelist has Jesus hint that Mary is seeking some*one* (a living person), not some*thing* (a corpse).[73] Yet, Mary's thoughts are still riveted on a body. She makes the blunder of mistaking Jesus Himself for a gardener who might have stolen Jesus' body. The irony is obvious, but there are certain parallels to other appearance stories of the recognition type (Emmaus; possibly John 21).[74] Jesus finally calls the Magdalene by her name, but her spiritual pilgrimage is not over when she recognizes Jesus. Her reply (ραββουνι) indicates that she still thinks of Jesus in terms of her past relationship with Him. This is verified by the translation the Evangelist gives of the word διδάσκαλε; thus, we probably are not meant to see this as a confession that parallels that of Thomas (cf. 20.28, ὁ κύριός μου καὶ ὁ θεός μου).[75] The reaction is natural, as is the 'clinging' that follows.

There are certain parallels between the story of the appearance to Mary and John 20.24–31. Consider the following: (1) both narratives focus on a special appearance to or at least for an individual by Jesus; (2) in both, the one receiving the appearance has a strong conviction that Jesus is not alive, and thus a strong preoccupation with the Jesus of the past (in Mary's case there is a fixation with Jesus' body; in Thomas' case with His wounds); (3) in both, there is a need to touch or hold on to Jesus; (4) in both, Jesus appears suddenly; (5) in both, the point is to lead an individual to overcome his or her doubts and believe in Jesus in the right way (cf. John 20.17, μή μου ἅπτου, to John 20.27, μὴ γίνου ἄπιστος). We may see in these two narratives a deliberate male–female parallelism as the Evangelist attempts to indicate Jesus' desire to recover both His 'brothers' and 'sisters'. There are certain important differences in the stories, however. The command to touch in one case and its prohibition in the other, are not so much a denigrating of Mary in comparison to Thomas, as a reflection of the relative needs in each situation. One must remember that in the Evangelist's portrayal of these events, Thomas had heard of previous resurrection appearances, whereas Mary had knowledge only of Jesus before His death to guide her response. This is why there is no recognition motif in the Thomas story, but there is in Mary's. Interestingly, Mary is given an apostolic task and Thomas is not. Further, Thomas' unbelief is more flagrant and more reprehensible than Mary's and he alone is chided for it. In both cases, however, only an appearance of Jesus suffices to alter the mood of the recipient.

Some of the above remarks about Mary's spiritual state when she exclaims, 'Rabboni!', are verified perhaps by Jesus' cryptic words, μή μου ἅπτου, οὔπω γὰρ ἀναβέβηκα πρὸς τὸν πατέρα. Some of our conclusions depend on whether we translate μή μου ἅπτου as 'don't touch me', or 'stop touching (clinging to) me'. In either case, it is implied that Mary is trying to approach Jesus in some way; otherwise, this would be an odd statement. The tense of ἅπτου is probably meant to imply a cessation of an action in progress; thus, we should translate 'stop holding on to me'.[76] Why, in the Johannine schema, is it that Mary is not allowed to hold on to Jesus, while later Thomas is bidden to put his finger in the nail prints of Jesus' hands? In John 20.27, the purpose of the touching is to lead Thomas to a more perfect faith. In John 20.17, however, the wrong sort of clinging to Jesus' physical being is involved. It assumes that relating to Jesus after the resurrection is only a matter of renewing pre-resurrection relationships.[77] It is not a case of Mary being irreverent;[78] rather, she still looked to the past and must be led to a higher, more spiritual way of holding on to Jesus. Further, she needs to get on with the task He is about to assign to her − instructing the brethren.[79]

The idea the Evangelist wants to convey is that Jesus does not wish Mary to take advantage of what will only be a temporary possibility (and is thus not to be depended upon). The Evangelist thus indicates to his audience the dangers of the wrong sort of attachment to the earthly Jesus. In view of the οὔπω clause, the ἀναβαίνω of v. 17 is probably to be taken in the sense of a future certainty expressed as a present reality.[80]

One key to seeing this verse as the Evangelist intends can be found in the journeying motif. Frequently in the Fourth Gospel Jesus is regarded as journeying back to the Father from whom He came (cf. 7.33, 13.3, 14.12, 28, 16.28). As P. Minear rightly pointed out, Mary's concern is with where Jesus' body is, even when she recognizes and seizes Him. She is seeking Jesus in the wrong sense, for the Evangelist is asserting that it is not a knowledge of where Jesus is but where He is going that truly leads to finding Jesus and to having a permanent grip on Him. The Evangelist has Jesus speak to Mary of the ascension as the proper answer to her 'where' question. Until Jesus ascends He cannot be where all His disciples can have access to Him. Thus, the successful conclusion of Mary's 'pilgrimage of faith was precluded by ignorance of "the end".'[81] The Evangelist indicates Mary finally learns this by the fact that she gives up the wrong sort of clinging to Jesus and journeys to the disciples to proclaim her risen Lord. Knowledge of Jesus' true destination gives her the freedom to play a part in revealing the destiny of Jesus and His followers. Just as Jesus must journey to the Father before His disciples can journey to the nations, so too Mary must learn of Jesus' journey to the Father before she can journey to the disciples. The two disciples' journey to Emmaus (v. 10) is an antithesis to Mary's journey and reveals that they do not yet know of Jesus' destination.

In this context, it is significant that Jesus says to Mary, 'Go to my brothers'.[82] The word 'brothers' indicates Jesus is trying to re-establish a close family relationship with His disciples, not distinguish Himself from them. Mary is given the role, usually taken by Jesus' 'brothers', to bear witness. She is to be an 'apostle to the Apostles'. Not until v. 18 is it clear that Mary has 'grasped' who Jesus really is, and that she can no longer cling to the past, or her past basis of relating to Jesus, or even His present glorified body.

The words, 'Mary Magdalene went proclaiming (ἀγγέλλουσα)[83] to the disciples' very effectively tells us that she is now looking forward to the task at hand, knowing that the Jesus she has left at the tomb will not go away and leave her comfortless again. He had talked of spiritual family relationships in the present tense; this meant that her relationship with Him would continue, albeit transposed into a higher key. Thus, she tells the brethren, ἑώρακα τὸν κύριον. Thus, we see how the Gospel events as well as the Gospel message have a tendency to cause reversals. Ironically, Jesus has begun to re-establish fellowship with His 'brothers' by first establishing fellowship once again with one of His 'sisters'.

There is little doubt that the Fourth Evangelist wishes to portray Mary Magdalene as important, perhaps equal in importance for Jesus' fledgling community as Mother Mary herself. Probably, the reason why Mary Magdalene is presented first in all the lists of women (save John 19.25) is because early on in the tradition it was indicated that she had been the first to see the risen Lord. Whatever the historical accuracy of this judgment, certainly the Fourth Evangelist seeks to portray Mary Magdalene as the first witness and so as a positive image and model of women whose testimony was valued and valid. Perhaps this was a message the Fourth Evangelist's audience needed to hear in the last decade of the first century, due to the frequent disparagement of women as valid witnesses in various contexts in the first century.

It must be added that this Evangelist also affirms the ongoing male leadership of the community. It is on them that Jesus breathes the Spirit in John 20.21–22, and if John 21 is by the same author, he also stresses the recommissioning of Peter as *the* tender of the sheep (21.15ff.). Peter follows his Lord's example, becoming a martyr, and providing the ultimate example of love and self-sacrificial leadership (cf. John 15.12–17).

D. Conclusions

We have come to the end of our discussion of the editorial tendencies of three Evangelists in regard to women and their roles. What this survey has revealed is that the First and Fourth Evangelists, as well as Mark, all manifest some of the themes we noted in Paul and in Luke–Acts, e.g., male–female parallelism, male–female role reversal, use of women as exemplars of faith, or as legitimate witnesses to the Gospel events. However, we noted that at the same time the male leadership of the community is still reaffirmed even after their disastrous behavior during the events recorded in the passion narratives. Even before the resurrection material, there are hints that it is a reformed patriarchy the Evangelists have in mind, one that means more moral responsibility, not more privilege.

The First Evangelist seems to be the most tradition-oriented of all, perhaps due to his Jewish–Christian audience, but even he does not endorse sexual stereotypes and holds up women as examples of faith, even at the expense of some male disciples. Mark's material places special stress on women as the validating witnesses of the crucial doctrines of the creed. The Fourth Evangelist, probably writing last of these three authors, places special stress on various women as models of the process by which one comes to a fully formed Christian faith. Perhaps of these three writers, only for the Fourth Evangelist is this as much a crucial part of the agenda as it is for Luke. Once again, it is plausible that the reason why these authors feel it is important as at least part of their agenda to give significant attention to women and their roles is because when they wrote there was significant resistance to such ideas perhaps especially amongst Jewish Christians. If this resistance was indeed a pervasive reaction to women assuming vital roles in the earliest churches, then it is to the Evangelists' credit that they did not try to obscure this fact, indeed, they often focused on it. As we shall see, this sort of honesty and commitment was to be almost universally lacking in the post-NT literature that led up to the Council of Nicea in AD 325.

6

TRAJECTORIES BEYOND THE
NEW TESTAMENT ERA

The study of women and their roles in the earliest churches would not be complete without some attempt to glimpse how things proceeded after the period when the NT documents were written.[1] This is especially important not least because there probably was no canon of twenty-seven books recognized before the time of Athanasius' famous *Festal Epistle* of AD 367. This means that many documents, both orthodox and heterodox, being written until well into the fourth century, were considered to be of great authority and even had the possibility of being recognized as canonical and so of final authority.[2] It also means that documents later labeled orthodox and heterodox may reflect conditions not only in the Church during the period that led up to canonization, but also in groups on the fringe of or outside the Church. Thus, it will be important to examine the references to women and their roles not only in the Ante-Nicene Fathers, but also in the apocryphal material.

Since our study is about the earliest churches, we will examine material that can be dated with reasonable certainty to a time before AD 325. This means that we will not be dealing with the period when monasticism and Mariology were perhaps the two main forces dominating what roles and images the Church saw as appropriate and exemplary for Christian women.

We have already noted the anti-feminist bias of various readings in the so-called Western Text of Acts.[3] This suggests that there might be some justification for W.M. Ramsay's judgment that there was a growing dislike for women assuming prominent roles in the Church during the post-NT era.[4] It will be important to see whether or not there is other evidence to suggest this was the case.

In the past half century there have been various surveys of relevant data about women in the period AD 80–325 by J. Leipoldt, F. Blanke, J. Daniélou, G.H. Tavard, R. Gryson, L. Swidler, and E. Schüssler Fiorenza to name but a few.[5] Thus, rather than follow the path others have trod, I will divide up the discussion topically and pursue the trajectories of various relevant issues.[6]

A. Asceticism and views of human sexuality

There is little question that various of the writers in the Ante-Nicene period had a deficient view of human sexuality usually coupled with an exaltation of celibacy, singleness, or even continence in marriage. This deficiency is not merely exhibited by Gnostic writers, or those associated with Montanism (including Tertullian), but even amongst Christian writers whose orthodoxy or orthopraxy was not in question. In the Gnostic literature we hear repeatedly that matter itself, and therefore human flesh and the deeds of the flesh, are evil,[7] but even in non-Gnostic writers, the original sin is sometimes assumed to be pleasure. Sexual intercourse is thought of as tainted if not fully sinful, and Christian marriage is seen as second best as a state of being for Christians. To the degree that an author thought women were defined and delimited by their sexuality, to that degree they fell under suspicion of being temptresses or sources of sin.

In the earliest part of the Ante-Nicene period we find little evidence of these stereotypes. Thus, in the *Epistle of Barnabas* 20.1 (c. AD 70–110), we hear the usual condemnation of sexual sin in the form of adultery, but this is no more than what we find in the canonical literature. In *1 Clement* 33.5–6 (c. AD 96) we find a repetition of Gen 1.26–28 which is followed by the words: ἴδωμεν, ὅτι ὅυ ἐν ἔργοις ἀγαθοῖς πάντες ἐκοσμήθησαν οἱ δίκαιοι (33.7).[8]

The *Shepherd of Hermas* (c. mid second century) was probably written in Rome.[9] This tract, in the form of an apocalypse, is about sins committed after conversion and baptism, and the remedy for them. In *Mand.* 4.1.3–11 the discussion centers on the subject of the wife who commits adultery. Because of the one-flesh union, the husband, if he knows of her sin or she does not repent, becomes a partaker in that sin. The remedy for an unrepentant wife is: 'Απολυσάτω, φησίν, αὐτὴν καὶ ὁ ἀνὴρ ἐφ' ἑαυτῷ μενέτω.[10] In view of what follows, the author obviously holds to the idea that the one-flesh union remains even after the 'putting away' so that the man is not free to remarry. To do so would violate that first and ongoing marital union. Lake is right that here we see an example where the Christian precept against divorce is superseded by the Christian precept against having intercourse with immoral persons.[11] In other words, sexual purity is more crucial than the marital bond. Notice too, on the question of remarriage after the death of the Christian partner we read in *Mand.* 4.4.2 that while remarriage is not a sin, δὲ ἐθ' ἑαυτῷ μείνῃ τις, περισσοτέραν ἑαυτῷ τιμὴν καὶ μεγάλην δόξαν. While the author may see fleshly desires as always tainted, the flesh itself is not inherently evil. It can be kept pure and undefiled and, in contradiction to some Gnostic teaching, the author insists that flesh and spirit are in communion (κοινά) and neither can be defiled without the other (*Sim.* 5.7.4). This seems to go against later tendencies toward a body/soul dualism even among orthodox thinkers, and may suggest the earliness of this document.

In another *Similitude* (9.11.3) we hear of a practice that seems to have been extant in some Christian communities in the second century, namely, sleeping with a or several women, ὡς ἀδελφός καὶ οὐχ ὡς ἀνήρ. This apparently entailed some sort of spiritual marriage but without sexual sharing. In the *Shepherd of Hermas*, however, an actual relationship is not being described but it appears clear that the author is familiar with such practices, and it reveals his own ascetical tendencies. This tendency is also in evidence at *Sim.* 9.15.1ff., where women are seen as types of the extremes of good and evil, holiness and unholiness. This siren/saint stereotype was to become a familiar one, and it seems likely that it made life difficult for ordinary Christian women, especially married women who were looking for examples that fit neither of these extremes.

Sometimes second-century material moves from suspicion to outright declaration that women are evil due to their sexual natures. Thus, in *T. Reuben* 1.5ff. we hear, 'For evil are women, my children; and since they have no power of strength over man, they use wiles by outward attractions, that they may draw him to themselves ... the angel of the Lord told me and taught me that women are overcome by the spirit of fornication more than men ...'[12] Here and elsewhere in *T. Reuben*, fear of fornication leads to fear of women, and a projection of their sin on the woman to such a degree that she becomes synonymous with it. In Gnosticism there are often these sorts of associations of flesh/sin/women, but it is surprising to find it so clearly in a Jewish–Christian document.

Tertullian (AD 160–225), even before his Montanist period (c. AD 213), usually has a rather negative view of human sexuality in general, and women in particular. Besides holding Eve responsible for the original sin and identifying all women with Eve ('You, O woman, are Eve ... the gate of the devil, the traitor of the tree. You are the one who enticed the one whom the devil did not dare approach' [*De Cultu*

Feminarum I.1]), Tertullian adds, '... you broke ... the image of God, man (hominem); because of the death you deserved the Son of God had to die.' Yet despite this, at least in his pre-Montanist period, he docs not categorize material intercourse as evil (cf. *De Monogamia* 9), indeed he speaks of the happiness of marriage which the Church unites and says of the married couple, '... they are companions; there is no separation of spirit and flesh' (*Ad Uxorem* II.9). There is no separation of husband and wife even when one dies, and so there can be no question of remarriage. There is then some evidence of a positive view of Christian marriage in Tertullian's works but there is as much or more evidence of a negative view of women's sexuality as well as a tendency to blame all women for Eve's error, and an indication that only man is fully created in the image of God.

Clement of Alexandria (AD 150–215), whose writings not surprisingly sometimes breathe the same sort of atmosphere as Philo, also manifests a deficient view of human sexuality as well as some dubious exegesis to back it up. Thus, for instance, in his exegesis of Genesis 3, Clement sees the original sin as ὑποπίπτων ἡδονῇ, the serpent being an allegory for pleasure (*Exhortation to the Greeks*, ch. 11).[13] In chapter 12 of the same work, pleasure is seen to be embodied in woman and quoting Hesiod, *Works and Days* 373–4, he says, 'Let not thy heart be deceived by a woman with trailing garment, coaxing with wily words to find the place of thy dwelling.' Nevertheless, in the very same chapter, Clement draws an analogy between the Bacchic rites and especially the procession, and Christian activities, and says of Christian women, 'ἀλλ' αἱ τοῦ θεοῦ θυγατέρες ... αἱ καλαί, τὰ σεμνὰ τοῦ λόγου θεσπίζουσαι ὄργια ... ψάλλουσιν αἱ κόραι'.[14] It is hard to know how much should be made of this, but it does appear to indicate that women played a vocal role in Christian worship at least in so far as singing was concerned. In the exhortation 'to the newly baptized' (1.20–21), there is an exhortation to modesty when meeting and greeting women. One's eyes should be cast to the ground.[15] Looking at another's physical beauty or form is apparently suspect. All in all, Clement seems to fall short of having a satisfactory and fully biblical idea about human sexuality, but in this shortcoming he differs little from other authors also influenced by Hellenistic ideas (e.g., Musonius Rufus).

In the *Stromata* 2.23 and 3.1, Clement is concerned to reject certain Gnostic ideas but in the process he manifests some of their same tendencies. Thus, for instance, he says in chapter 23, 'Since pleasure and lust seem to fall under [the same category as] marriage, it must also be treated of.' Marriage is said to be 'sacred' but '... it is the diseases of the body that principally show marriage to be necessary'.[16] In *Paed* 3.3 he associates men with action, maturity, and non-castration; women with passivity, immaturity, and castration.

Clement is not against marriage and sexual union *per se*, but his 'ideal is not to feel sexual desire, and let sexual union be determined wholly by will'.[17] Clement is not of the opinion that continence in marriage is a good thing; rather, he says of those who practise this that they 'conjugii divisores'. Yet, at the same time, he takes the allusion in 1 Cor 9.5 about the other apostles who had a right to take their Christian wives to mean that they treated their wives 'non ut uxores, sed ut sorores circumducebant mulieres' (*Paed* 3.6). He goes on to speak of those wives ministering where the husbands could not – in women's quarters, in discussions with other wives. Clement rejects the idea that marital relations are a result of the Fall; indeed, he calls this blasphemy against creation. Clement's ideal is ἀπαθεία – marriage and relations controlled by will, not desire. Thus, a Greek ideal is imported into Christian marital teaching.

Clement's teaching reflects ambivalence about marriage and sexual relationships. Clearly, he is willing to use stereotypes of women as temptresses and to urge continence and celibacy as a good thing, but just as clearly he wishes to refute the Gnostics. Thus, he cannot allow that human sexuality, marriage, or intercourse is inherently evil. The result is a rather lukewarm, but necessary, endorsement of marriage. Here we see the attempt to confine women (or at least wives) to the home and familial roles. To the extent that such roles are seen as second best to celibacy, to that extent the importance of women who engage in such roles is attenuated. Nonetheless, here too we seem to see the first inkling of a gender-specific ministry of women to other women.

Origen (AD 185–254) was a student of Clement and probably his successor as head of the catechetical school in Alexandria. His self-castration is a literal fulfilment of Matt 19.12, and there are other clear indications of his deficient view of human sexuality and his ascetical tendencies. Origen, like his mentor, is exercised to repudiate Gnostic false teaching.[18] In Origen, virginity is clearly exalted as the ideal state for the Christian, the only state of absolute purity. We are told clearly that marriage is allowed under the new covenant due to human weakness (*Comm. Mt.* 14.23), but everyone who asks could be given the gift of celibacy, for there is 'perfect purity in celibacy and chastity' (*Comm. Mt.* 14.25). This did not necessarily lead to single women having more viable roles in the Church, for Origen also asserts, 'It is not proper for a woman to speak at the assembly, however admirably or holy what she says may be, merely because it comes from female lips.'[19] H. Crouzel has demonstrated in his exposition on Origen's teachings that Origen takes a rather Gnostic view of creation. First there was a spiritual creation of human souls in God's image, but then there was a necessity of a second creation after the Fall which involved the human body and sexuality. The soul is made impure by being clothed in a human body, and sexual activity is seen as a source of spiritual impurity, not least perhaps because it results in producing more fallen human beings with impure bodies.[20] When human sexuality is a result of the Fall, sexual intercourse can only be at best a *remedium concupiscentiae*. In Origen, marriage is not seen primarily as a lesser good than celibacy; rather, it is seen as a lesser evil than being profligate. It is not surprising then to learn that women, who were chiefly identified with certain roles that were a product of their sexuality (wife, mother, homemaker), were seen by Origen as inferior beings to men.[21] Sexuality is not something to be transformed, but transcended, if one is to be pure − especially was this seen to be the case with women. Instead of mortification of the sinful nature, mortification of the flesh itself was seen to be necessary for being truly pure.

In some regards, the beginnings of the monastic movement seem to be grounded not only in this deficient view of human sexuality, but also in a transformed vision of how the Kingdom comes. Instead of a horizontal eschatology that looked forward to Christ's return and the redemption of the believer in the body, we have a vertical, other-wordly eschatology gaining momentum in the second and third centuries AD. In this view, the Kingdom came and thus redemption is to be found by withdrawal from the world; by mortification and denial of the flesh (fasting, sexual abstinence, and finally flagellation); and by purely spiritual communion with the Godhead above (either individually or as a group). This seems to have been a product of several elements: (1) the adoption of a Greek body/soul dualism; (2) the waning of eschatological fervor; (3) as a result of (1) and (2), a deficient view of creation and of human sexuality and its place in the order of recreation. It must be borne in mind, however, as Everett Ferguson pointed out to me, 'The early Church's statements must be understood in the context of pagan licentiousness on one hand, and on the other the strong current of asceticism (a reaction?) which was flowing in non-Christian circles in the second century. In an atmosphere where asceticism was equated with spirituality, the Church could not afford to appear less "spiritual" than its rivals.'[22]

It is not without importance then that when we examine the life of St Anthony of Egypt (AD 251?–356), thought to be the founder of the monastic movement, we hear that when he decided to give up all his possessions and retreat into the desert, he placed his sister in a 'house of virgins' which was already in existence.[23] This suggests that monasticism of some sort was being practised by women (the order of virgins?) in the middle of the third century or earlier. Consistent with this is the report that Pachomius (AD 290–346), the writer of the first monastic 'rule', built a convent for his sister at which she became the Abbess.[24] The record is also clear that by the end of the fourth century there were various monasteries and convents especially in Egypt, but apparently also in Syria. What this may suggest is that women with spiritual gifts sought refuge in a setting where they could practise their piety. Perhaps they did not wish to be confined to the home or minimal roles in the Church. When we examine the matter of Church orders, we will see the furtherance of this sort of gender-specific grouping of Christians between AD 80–325. Monasticism may have arisen as a solution by and for women, but in any case this sort of separation was not in the end going to effect their equality.

One of the more interesting developments in early Church history is the hermeneutical move in which OT institutions and ideas are used to describe, reorient, or even replace NT teachings and practices. This phenomenon is in evidence in the writings of Dionysius the Great (AD 190–264), Origen's second successor at the catechetical school in Alexandria. It seems clear from Mark 7 and elsewhere that at least as early as AD 68–70 it was assumed that Jesus taught that all the OT regulations about clean and unclean were either fulfilled or no longer applicable to His own disciples. Yet, Dionysius in his *Epistle to Bishop Basilides Canon* II says that women, during their menstrual period, should be prohibited from approaching the Table of the Lord and partaking of His body and blood when they are not 'perfectly pure both in soul and body'. In this Canon, the Table of the Lord is equated with the Holy of Holies, and so on OT grounds women are expected to refrain from entering the house of God during their menstrual period. This can only be seen as a step backward, and a contradiction of Jesus' teaching about the 'new situation' since His coming. It appears likely that, as the Church became increasingly viewed as a 'temple', and ministers became increasingly viewed as 'priests', and the Lord's Supper became increasingly viewed as a 'sacrifice', Christian worship and ministry reverted to the OT order of things in which males assumed all the priestly functions.

B. Gnosticism

The study of Gnosticism's bearing on women and their roles has been brought to the fore by the works of E. H. Pagels and others.[25] What has become apparent is that one cannot always generalize about Gnostic practices that seem to vary from group to group. Nevertheless, despite various diversities, certain constants seem to be reflected in Gnostic thought about women. First, the doctrine of the syzygy always seems to involve the union and unity of an eon with its female counterpart. Second, dualism with either the denigration of the material world and so human flesh, or the view that things of this world are adiaphora, is characteristic. Thus, for instance, Severus argues, 'those who consort in marriage fulfil the work of Satan'.[26] In the *Gospel of the Egyptians* (a second-century document of which we have only fragments in various Church Fathers) we hear, 'When Salome asked "How long will death have power?" the Lord answered, "So long as you women bear children ..." '[27] Elsewhere in the same document we hear that the Kingdom will come, 'when you have trampled on the garment of shame and when the two become one, and the male and female is neither male nor female'.[28] Again, in this same document Jesus is reported to have said, 'I have come to destroy the works of the female, by the "female" meaning lust, by the "works", birth and decay.'[29]

Now, it is not surprising to discover that with such a view, salvation for all involves liberation from bodily passions, if not from the body and the world itself. In various expressions of the Gnostic system, the female represents all that is earthly, worldly, subject to change and decay; while the male principle is associated with eternal life, the Holy Spirit and the world to come. Thus, in a sense, the unsaved (men or women) are all female. Clement (*Theodotus* 68) cites the following Gnostic saying: 'As long as we were children of the female only – as of shameful copulation, imperfect, reasonless ... we were children of woman; but once we were formed by the Savior, we have become children of man ...'[30] Salvation, then, is discussed in terms of andronization (cf. *Gnostic Gospel of Thomas* log. 112). We must bear in mind that principles, not persons, are involved in the terminology used, but when femaleness is equated with mortality, decay, weakness, and corruption, this could not but reflect back on one's image of women.[31] Here and elsewhere Gnosticism partakes of the patriarchal orientation of the dominant civilization, even when women were allowed significant roles in certain Gnostic communities.

The Carpocratians stand at the other end of the scale from Marcion, Severus, and the author of the *Gospel of the Egyptians*. Libertinism, not asceticism, can lead to liberation from the body, though the body itself is not evil, but only adiaphora. Perhaps then, it is not surprising that the Carpocratians did not hesitate to see women, especially Salome, Martha, and Mary Magdalene, as the sources and guarantors of their secret teachings. Further, Epiphanes, the child of Carpocrates, sounds a clearly egalitarian note insisting, '... no distinction should be made between female and male'.[32] One is never quite sure whether this is because the sexes are considered equal, or if femaleness is equally unimportant as maleness.

Valentinian Gnosticism is the most familiar form of Gnosticism. Here there is no antithesis of male and female principles; rather, they are seen as complementary, making the universe a whole. The two principles were united originally, and indeed were part of the God-head. They will be reunited when the female spirit is andronized or absorbed back into the male. Now, it appears that the female eons have names associated with the union of male and female, but the male eons are named for Christian virtues. R. Baer also points out, 'The Valentinians did not identify the female with any absolute principle of evil, but rather with the fallible part of God ...'[33] This in itself suggests a patriarchal orientation.

It is in the teachings and practices of Marcus, a follower of Valentinian, that we hear of an androgynous Adam and of salvation amounting to the removal of separation between male and female. As Fiorenza indicates, this is close to the teaching of the *Gospel of Philip*.[34] It is not certain that androgyny is, in fact, the salvific goal even in the teaching of Marcus or the *Gospel of Philip*, as in some respects, reunion sounds rather like reabsorption of the female principle by the male one.

In any event, Gnosticism in any of its forms cannot be seen as a heretical theology that was *anti-patriarchal* in orientation. As Fiorenza rightly concludes:

> Salvation in the radically dualistic gnostic systems requires the annihilation and destruction of the female or the 'feminine principle'. In the moderately dualistic systems, salvation means the reunification of the male and female

principles in an androgynous or asexual unity.... The female principle is secondary, since it stands for the part of the divine that became involved in the created world and history. Gnostic dualism shares in the patriarchal paradigm of Western culture.[35]

Women may have had some new roles in Gnostic communities and in some Gnostic communities there may have been more sexual freedom, but there is insufficient evidence to suggest that the prominence of women in Gnostic circles was the key factor which caused the Church to turn to a more patriarchal orientation and in particular, to a more patriarchal ministry. It is quite believable that it was *an* important factor that could have nudged the Church in that direction, especially when some Gnostic communities claimed to base their theology on the traditions passed on by Christian women of the apostolic age.

C. Prophecy, prophetesses, and Montanism

Without question, the prophet was a major figure in the early Church well into the second century. The role of prophet raised in an acute way the question of whether the Church's leadership should be raised up purely by the Spirit or by some institutional procedure. This problem was magnified by the fact that there is evidence from the early second century that leadership roles and structures differed somewhat from region to region.

One of the earliest extra-canonical sources of information about Christian prophecy is the *Didache* (chapters 11–13). In the *Didache* prophets are grouped with apostles and teachers, all of whom seem to be itinerants. They are distinguished from ἐπισκόπους καὶ διακόνους (15.1), whom the local church are exhorted to χειροτονήσατε ἑαυτοῖς. Second, a prophet is not to be tested in regard to his utterance, lest blasphemy of the Holy Spirit be committed (11.7). This implies that what a prophet says, he says as the *vox Dei*, and it is not to be questioned much less judged. The test for discerning the true from the false prophet involves examining their behavior: (1) if one asks, ἐν πνεύματι, for money or food, then this is a sign of the false prophet; (2) if one does not practise what one teaches, then this is also a sign. Nobody has satisfactorily explained what ποιῶν εἰς μυστήριον κοσμικὸν ἐκκλησίας (11.11) means, but it seems to involve more than mere prophesying, perhaps some sort of miracle or symbolic prophetic act like the OT prophets performed. Though the prophet might be an itinerant, he was to be permitted to settle in a Christian community (13.1) and was entitled to be given the first fruits of the harvest, for εἰσιν οἱ ἀρχιερεῖς ὑμῶν (13.3). This implies that they did not have to do manual labor, but a true prophet should be supported by the community. However, 13.4 makes clear that the author does not think there are prophets in every Christian community.

The provenance of the *Didache* is unknown, but it seems to be addressing a community away from any large city or center of the faith. Thus, it is interesting to find evidence of prophecy, or at least the interpretation of prophecy, in *2 Clement* 2 which is usually assigned a provenance of Rome or Corinth.[36] What this suggests is that prophecy was by no means a purely urban or local phenomenon in the Church, but rather a widespread one.

The *Shepherd of Hermas*, like the *Didache*, is also concerned about false prophets (*Mand.* 11). A true prophet is distinguished by the fact that he does not spend his time answering people's questions about their future, but instead simply proclaims the truth under the impetus of the Holy Spirit (11.5). Again, the way to test a prophet is by his life and character (cf. 11.7–12), by the company he keeps (11.13), and by his deeds (11.16). The author's view of inspiration is that God's words come to the prophet when God wills, not upon human request, and it comes in the assembly after prayer has been made (presumably for a word from God). The *Shepherd of Hermas* speaks of the moment when ὁ ἄγγελος τοῦ προφητικοῦ πνεύματος (11.9) comes upon the prophet.[37] It is noteworthy that the author seems to see prophecy as a function of worship and something which is addressed to the congregation. By contrast, the false prophet tends to shun such an assembly and prefers to speak in a context other than worship. The *Shepherd* suggests that prophecy was a very live issue in the middle of the second century, perhaps particularly in Rome.

The importance of such material should be obvious in view of our earlier discussions of prophetesses in Corinth and Caesarea.[38] Before the close of the first century, however, there appear to have been some problems with, and some serious misgivings about, some prophetesses. Thus, in Rev 2.20–23 we hear of a prophetess in Thyatira leading some to eat food offered to idols. Apparently, she was a valued member of the congregation in Thyatira, allowed to teach, and allowed to repent of her errors. For our purposes, what is especially important is that Thyatira is in the region where the Montanist movement arose or was at least located. Here we see another area of the Church involved in prophecy, and in this case we are specifically told that at least one woman was involved.

One of the most intriguing documents of the second century is the *Acts of Paul*. This document was known by Tertullian, apparently as early as AD 200 which means it must have been written earlier. There is no reason to doubt Tertullian's assertion that the document comes from an elder in Asia Minor, as it appears to be familiar with activities in that area.

Incorporated into the *Acts of Paul* is a still earlier document, the *Acts of Paul and Thecla*, which comes from the second half of the second century but probably before AD 190 when the *Acts of Paul* seems to have been put together. The motive for making this collection seems to have been to combat, not promote, heresy. It is difficult to say how much historical truth is preserved in these legends, but the document does reflect the fact that women in the churches in Asia Minor had a certain amount of freedom and ability to exercise the gift of leadership,[39] as was true in the Montanist movement in the same region. Tertullian says the author of the *Acts of Paul and Thecla* was condemned and relieved of his office for circulating this document and misrepresenting Paul's view of women. 'How credible would it seem, that he who has not permitted "mulieri" even to learn ... should give "femininae" the power of teaching and baptizing! "Let them be silent" he says ...' (*On Baptism* 17).

Despite Tertullian's reaction, the *Acts of Paul and Thecla* was apparently a popular document in the third century and later, for it exists not only in the original Greek, but also in Latin, Syriac, Armenian, Slavonic, and Arabic.[40] Precisely because of the popular character of the document it may well have had an ongoing impact on the Church as a favorable testimony for women assuming important church roles. Even if this is so, it promoted the view that women must renounce or abandon their femaleness or at least their gender-specific functions of wife or mother to assume such a role. In Paul's first major speech in this document (a sort of Pauline beatitudes) he says,

> Blessed are they who have kept the flesh pure for they shall become a temple of God.
> Blessed are the continent, for to them God will speak ...
> Blessed are they who have wives as if they had them not, for they shall inherit God.

> Blessed are the bodies of the virgins, for they shall be well pleasing to God, and shall not lose the reward of their purity ...[41]

The virgin Thecla is captivated by this speech. Paul goes on to announce that he preaches a Gospel of salvation from all pleasure (*Paul and Thecla* 17). Thecla eventually follows Paul around Asia Minor but not without a trial by fire and another by lions. In Antioch she baptizes herself *in extremis* while in a seal pit in the arena (*Paul and Thecla* 34). When she is rescued from this ordeal she goes forth and instructs a woman and her maid servants. Again, she joins Paul who commissions her: 'Go and teach the Word of God' (*Paul and Thecla* 41), which she does in the region of Seleucia.

Thecla gives up marriage in order to take on a life of virginity, prayer, and teaching. Here we see evidence that for a woman to exercise the ministry of the Word she had to give up or even renounce her sexuality. Thecla is not said to be a prophetess, but other women in the *Acts of Paul* (Myrta, in *Paul in Corinth* 1.33ff.), are portrayed as prophetesses. The final editor of this material may not have strongly differentiated between the two functions.[42]

The *Acts of Paul* is not the only example from the apocryphal Acts that indicates women had prominent roles in the early Church. The *Acts of John, Peter, Andrew, Thomas, Xanthippe* are generally from the same time period (AD 160–225) and from the same area with the exception of the *Acts of Thomas* which comes from Syria and is in Syriac. All these apocryphal Acts exalt Christian celibacy and virginity, manifest various ascetical tendencies and attitudes, and show spiritually gifted women in significant church roles though at the expense of their traditional female roles in the family.[43]

That prophetesses were considered a threat or problem in certain Christian churches in the second century is probably demonstrated by the *Kerygma of Peter*. Though incorporated into the later Pseudo-Clementine material, it appears that the *Kerygma* goes back at least to the second half of the second century. Its Encratite and Docetic cast may indicate Gnostic influence or reaction to Gnostic influence which favors a late second-century date.[44]

The *Kerygma of Peter* focuses on the 'true prophet' who brings divine revelation to the world through men such as Adam, Moses, and Jesus.

> Female prophecy appears as the opponent of the true prophet ...; she accompanies him as a negative, left-hand

syzygy-partner in his passage through time. Her first representative is Eve, the mother of mankind, who was created at the same time as Adam .... What she proclaims suits the taste of the transitory cosmos ...; she pretends to possess knowledge, but leads all who follow her into error and to death ...[45]

It is important to remember that the speaker is supposed to be Peter, the representative of the Church, and that apparently this document 'was very popular in the early Church'.[46] It may be of some relevance that there is also an anti-Pauline cast to some of this material in so far as Paul is seen as the representative of female prophecy (H. 2.17.3), and a rival of Peter who stands with and for male or 'true' prophecy. Several excerpts are worth repeating here:

> Along with the true prophet there has been created as a companion a female being who is as far inferior to him as metousia is to ousia, as the moon is to the sun, as fire is to light. As a female she rules over the present world, which is like to her, and counts as the first prophetess; she proclaims her prophecy with all amongst those born of women ... (H. 3.22).

> For whilst the present world is female and as a mother brings forth the life of her children, the aeon to come is male and as a father expects his children ... (H. 2.15).[47]

Whether or not this document is orthodox in origins, it received a sympathetic hearing at least in the Egyptian part of the Church, and may well have been used to put a stop to women prophetesses or at least to curtail their activities. It may be no accident that this document seems to have been in circulation during the period when Montanism had its greatest influence.

Depending on whether one believes Eusebius or Epiphanius, Montanus began to prophesy in Phrygia either in AD 172 or 156–57. He led an apocalyptic movement expecting the Heavenly Jerusalem to appear soon, by descending on Phrygia during Montanus' lifetime. The sign that the end was coming was the outpouring of the Paraclete on Montanus and two prominent women involved in the movement – Prisca and Maximilla. The Montanists were decidedly ascetical and rigoristic. The movement was sufficiently powerful to spread to Roman Africa and win an important convert in Tertullian (c. AD 206–213). In its African incarnation, the movement became even more rigorous in its discipline, fasting, and condemnation of second marriages. Before it ever reached Africa, however, it had been condemned by synods in Asia Minor and reluctantly by Pope Zephyrinus of Rome (AD 200).

Now, it must be noted that unlike Gnosticism, Montanism was fundamentally orthodox in its theology. To be sure, it erred in regard to an imminent parousia in Asia Minor, and it also had a deficient view of human sexuality, but these same traits were characteristic of other orthodox groups and writers. Hippolytus maintained some of the Montanists were guilty of Binitarianism, but his basic argument against them pertained to their fasts and feasts.[48] In short, the objection Hippolytus is able to prove involves heteropraxy, not heterodoxy. He is particularly concerned about their claims to authority based on direct inspiration, not church tradition.

> But this initial clash between the authority of Church officials who mediate the message of God from the past with the free spirit of new ongoing, and uncontrolled 'revelations' was an instance of a fundamental type of conflict. The Montanist controversy illustrates one type of basic disagreement that has remained with us throughout history. The hierarchically controlled Church is faced with the accusation that it has maintained order and continuity at the price of suppressing or at least restraining the spontaneity and effervescence of the Spirit.[49]

One thing that especially galled the Church Fathers about the Montanist movement was that women were allowed leadership roles. This objection no doubt intensified once Montanus died and Maximilla became the *de facto* leader. Besides Hippolytus, who speaks of 'victims of error being ... captivated by wretched women named Priscilla and Maximilla whom they supposed to be priestesses' (*Refutation* 12, 1.4–6), there were other Fathers who objected on similar grounds. Origen objected, but apparently because he had some sympathy with the ascetical tendencies of the movement he simply insisted that their women prophets only speak in private, not in the assemblies (cf. to Tertullian, *De anima* 9).[50] Irenaeus (AD 130–200), Bishop of Lyons, was fearful that the spirit of prophecy would be rejected by and in the Church because separatist groups such as the Montanists 'wish to be pseudo-prophets ... but ... set aside the gift of prophecy from the Church' (*Against Heresies* 3.11.9). In some regards Irenaeus was prophetic in his anxiety, for both women and prophecy in the Church were affected negatively when the Montanist movement was condemned. All Montanist books were burned by imperial decree in AD 298 which meant that thereafter the Church could read of Montanism only through approved, polemical sources.

It would be wrong to assume that prophecy died out with the Montanist movement. For one thing, there were approved orthodox men and women who continued to be revered as prophets and prophetesses. Thus, in the *Acts of the Martyrs* we hear of Perpetua and Felicitas being martyred during the Severian persecution of AD 202 or 203. Perpetua was a married woman and a prophetess (or at least one who received visions). If one examines the *Passio Perpetuae et Felicitatis* 1.3–6.3, one discovers the idea that through a vision Perpetua was andronized. Clearly, her femaleness was seen as an obstacle to her becoming a true martyr, and so it had to be transcended or transformed into maleness. Nevertheless, here we have ongoing evidence of prophetesses who could even be celebrated as Christian martyrs and saints of the Church.[51] This evidence is important because it appears in a document from the third century that the Church seems to have embraced. Eusebius apparently collected many 'acts of the martyrs' documents for general church use in the fourth century.

It has been conjectured that 'the episcopal hierarchy ... replaced early Christian prophecy'.[52] Whether or not this can be demonstrated, there was an attempt to see orthodox male church leaders as prophets as early as the second century. This is the case with Polycarp (*Martyrdom of Polycarp* 16, 'an apostolic and prophetic teacher, and bishop'), and Melito of Sardis (Eusebius, *H.E.* 5.24.5). The importance of this should not be under-estimated, for these sources were from the third and fourth centuries (though the original form of the *Martyrdom of Polycarp* probably appeared in the latter part of the second century) and may be attempts to claim the prophetic function for the institutional Church and for approved men in particular. The evidence from the third and fourth centuries, however, is not sufficient to warrant the conclusion either that charismatic prophecy died out in this period, or that women were forbidden from prophesying in the Church. In fact, it appears that Didymus the Blind (late fourth century) was still battling against women prophetesses assuming important roles in the Church.[53] The evidence is sufficient, however, to suggest an attenuation of recognition of the legitimacy of such a function unless it was associated with a church official. This could not but constrict and restrict orthodox 'women of Spirit'[54] during the century leading up to the Council of Nicea. A similar attenuation will now be demonstrated in regard to other church functions.

D. Church order

In a limited space it is impossible to delve into all the varieties of church polity found between AD 80 and 325. Without question there will be continuing debate over such matters as the nature and viability of apostolic succession, and whether the Ignatian picture of the monarchical bishop represents a regional concept or one that was more widespread. It is impossible to say how directly the development of these ideas affected women's attempts to minister for Christ, for women are not mentioned in relationship to these struggles in any full or revealing way. It is possible, however, to chronicle gender-specific orders in the Church and their development.[55]

1. Deaconesses

We have already traced the origins of this 'order' of ministry in the NT period.[56] But perhaps our first piece of extra-biblical evidence is found in non-Christian literature — a letter of Pliny to Trajan (who reigned AD 98–117) where he speaks of the torture of two 'ancillis' who were called 'ministrae' (10.96–97).[57] Tertullian may also be referring to deaconesses in his *On Exhortation to Chastity* 13 end, when he refers to men and women 'in ecclesiasticis ordinibus' who owed their position to their chastity. It is possible, however, that this is a reference to the order of widows or virgins.

More clearly, Clement of Alexandria (*Stromata* 3.6.53.3–4) speaks of 'feminis diaconis' but the context is a discussion between Paul and Timothy (1 Tim 3.11). Clement's student, Origen, refers to 'feminas in ministeris Ecclesiae constitu' (*Commentary on Romans* 16.1, 2) which seems unambiguous about there being deaconesses. The question in all these cases is: how are their roles understood? In the *Apostolic Tradition*, attributed to Hippolytus (c. 170–235) we are told of a ceremony of laying on of hands for deaconesses that is an exact duplicate of the ceremony for deacons.[58]

More important is the material from the *Didascalia* (of Syrian provenance) from the earlier half of the third century. At 3.12 deaconesses are said to have the responsibility of instructing new female converts on how to live a Christian life. At 2.26.5–8 we have an exhortation to honor church officers including deaconesses who are a 'type of the Holy Spirit'. In the *Apostolic Constitutions* (c. AD 350–400), also of Syrian provenance, we hear again that the deaconess is to receive the newly baptized female (3.16). The bishop is to 'ordain also a deaconess who is faithful and holy, for ministering to the women' (3.15.2). In the same section she is allowed to anoint women with oil after the deacon has done so in preparation for baptism. The ordination ceremony for the deaconess is described briefly (7.3.19–20) and includes the following prayer the bishop is to repeat after laying hands on the deaconess:

> O Eternal God, the Father of our Lord Jesus Christ, the Creator of man and of woman, who didst replenish with the Spirit Miriam, and Deborah, and Anna, and Huldah; who didst not disdain that Thy only begotten Son should be born of a woman; who also in the tabernacle of the testimony, and in the temple, didst ordain women to be keepers of Thy holy gates, – do Thou now also look down upon this Thy servant, who is to be ordained to the office of a deaconess, and grant her Thy Holy Spirit, and 'cleanse her from all filthiness of flesh and spirit,' that she may worthily discharge the work which is committed to her to Thy glory, and the praise of Thy Christ, with whom glory and adoration to be Thee and the Holy Spirit for ever. Amen.[59]

All of this should be compared to *Canon* 19 from the Council of Nicea (AD 325) which numbers deaconesses among the Kanoni.[60] The evidence thus far reviewed suggests a viable order fully endorsed by the Church. Yet, in the fifth and sixth centuries at least three Councils, one at Orange (441), one at Epaon (517), and one at Orleans (533), mandated the ordination of deaconesses be stopped entirely and the Council of Orleans seemed to suggest that there should be no more deaconesses at all – not even unordained ones.[61] It is difficult to say what the factors were which led to these decisions, but the effect was to prevent various women, especially older women, from being officially recognized and in some cases even functioning in the capacity of deaconesses. The order had probably begun as a means of practical service, but eventually had involved sacral functions at baptism (possibly to prevent scandal since often baptism was in the nude). Thereafter, it involved the teaching of new female converts, again as a matter of decorum. In due course, principles drawn from the (mis)interpretation of such texts as 1 Cor 14.33b–36, 1 Tim

2.1ff., appear to have won the day over other considerations, thus impoverishing the Church of vital female workers from the fourth century onwards.

2. Widows

The NT, like the OT, manifests a clear concern for widows (Acts 6.1–3, 9.36–43). It may also reveal the beginnings of an order of widows (1 Tim 5.3–16). It is not clear whether the list of approved widows, who were known for their good character, is simply a list of those being supported by the Church (which seems to be the main burden of the passage), or is a list of those commissioned by the Church for specific religious functions. Nevertheless, at least by the second century there was a viable order of widows with religious functions.

In the correspondence of Ignatius with Polycarp (4.1–3), Ignatius exhorts that the widows (χῆραι) should not be neglected and that Polycarp should personally consider himself their protector (Hermas *Man.* 8.10, *Sim.* 9.28.3). It appears from Polycarp's letter to the Philippians (6.1) that he took this advice, and here we find that widows and orphans are grouped together (possibly because they appear together in the Bible, cf. Deut 14.29, 16.14). At the end of another letter, Ignatius greets τὰς παρθένους τὰς λεγομένας χήρας (*Smyr.* 13.1). Now, if Ignatius had said the reverse of this, we might deduce that he was referring to real widows who had committed themselves to a life of chastity and church service henceforth. Since, however, it is the virgins who are called widows, this may suggest that χήρας is a *terminus technicus* for all unmarried women dedicated to chastity and the Lord's work, including those who have never been married (which seems to be the thrust of this passage).

Tertullian, in his essay on the veiling of virgins (ch. 9), speaks of a virgin less than twenty years old being enrolled with the widows, but it is clear he is not in favor of virgins becoming widows. He also mentions that apparently married women and even mothers and teachers of children were being elected to the order of widows (or virgins?) so that they might be trained to aid not only their own family but also other church members. Obviously, Tertullian is displeased with all this, for at the beginning of this same section he repeats 1 Cor 14.34, 35 and says women are not allowed to teach, baptize, or exercise any male functions, much less hold a sacred office. Nevertheless, he does bear witness to the reality of an order of widows/

virgins, or widows that included virgins, and even married women in his day.

In the early third century the *Didascalia* (3.8.3) exhorts widows to fast, to visit the sick, and to pray over and even lay hands on them. It is difficult to know how much of this reflects a regional practice in view of some of the unique features of this and other Syrian documents. Hippolytus (AD 170–236) says widows were appointed by word, but not ordained by the laying on of hands, because a widow does not offer a sacrifice or have a ministry (*Apostolic Tradition* 10, cf. 30).[62]

Certainly one of the most interesting aspects of the passages dealing with widows is the image used of the widow as an altar. C. Osiek has provided a detailed study of the relevant passages that allude to the widow (sometimes in conjunction with orphans) as a θυσιαστήριον.[63] After examining passages from Polycarp (*Phil.* 4.3), Tertullian (*To His Wife*, 1.7.4), Methodius (*Symposium Disc.* 5.6, 8), the *Didascalia* (2.26.8, 3.63, 3.14.1, 4.5.1, cf. 3.7.2, 4.3.3), and the *Apostolic Constitutions* (8.74.4) as well as texts that go beyond the parameters of this inquiry, she concludes:

> Since the majority of the references that give any explanation or elaboration at all do so in terms of offerings, it can be stated with certainty that the original basis for associating widow and altar, at least in the Christian texts, is the depositing of the gifts of the faithful upon the altar and their distribution to widows as recipients of charity ... Prayer as the special ministry of widows may have further encouraged the association of widows with an altar ... Prayer was an act of spiritual sacrifice, and righteous persons were an altar.[64]

She is also able to demonstrate that in the fourth and fifth centuries there was an attempt to restrict the activities of widows, even to the point of using the altar symbolism to indicate that widows should stay in one place, at home, to do their praying. She conjectures that:

> The more hierarchically structured Christian churches of the second and third centuries often felt themselves to be in a state of siege because of the threat posed by the more 'charismatic' or loosely structured communities that more often than not seem to have allowed a great deal of freedom and responsibility to women. ... Gnostic, Montanist, and Marcionite communities existed down the street from orthodox

communities in eastern cities. Though the churches that produced the Didascalia and Apostolic Constitutions had deaconesses, their role was carefully restricted to certain functions with women that it would have been socially improper for a man to perform; going into homes to visit the sick and instruct women, keeping order among women in the assembly, assisting in the disrobing process and anointing of a woman's body at baptism.[65]

3. Virgins

We now turn to an order which, though perhaps not formally recognized until after the peace brought about by Constantine (c. AD 320)[66] between State and Church, nonetheless existed *de facto* before that — the order of virgins. The emphasis on virginity in the early Church did not begin in the fourth century but much earlier. The growing emphasis can be traced by examining references to Mary as a virgin in the period AD 80–325.[67] It may be that the traditions about Mary's virginity at the time of conception of Jesus gave impetus to the stress on virginity in the second and following centuries, but the Church already had ascetical tendencies as early as the time when Paul wrote 1 Corinthians 7 and when Luke took note of Philip's virgin daughters.[68]

By the time the *Shepherd of Hermas* was written, we already appear to have indications of the strange practice of the *virgines subintroductae*. As Tavard points out, there were unmarried deacons, priests, monks, and apparently bishops, who were sharing homes and even beds 'chastely' with these virgins. Paul of Samosata, Bishop of Antioch in AD 260, apparently lived with several such women, and Cyprian in Africa also knew of this practice (*Epistle* 61 [62] to Pomponius). Paul, however, was deposed for aberrant Christology in AD 268, whereas Cyprian seems to be writing to orthodox Christians. This practice was considered suspect and was condemned not only by Cyprian, but also by Chrysostom, Ambrose of Milan, and the Council of Antioch (AD 268).[69]

The Council of Antioch also deposed Paul of Samosata because, according to Eusebius' account of the decree, 'Even if we grant ... [he] does nothing licentious, he should have taken care to avoid the suspicion to which such practices give rise ...' (*H.E.* 7.30).[70] What is remarkable about this is that the condemnation is purely on pragmatic grounds. The Council did not argue that such chaste marriages were utopian ideals which could not be realized. Apparently, the Church so much believed in the grace that accompanied chastity and virginity and they did not think even the practice of *virgines subintroductae* was objectionable on grounds of theological or ethical feasibility. The Council of Nicea (AD 325) seems to have left the door open for clergy to continue this practice providing it was a relative or person beyond suspicion.

. The degree to which virginity was held in high esteem in the Church is shown in a fascinating work called the *Banquet* by Methodius of Lycia (d. 311?), written apparently in the last thirty years of the third century. In it are eleven speeches on virginity set in the framework of a fictional all-female banquet. In *Discourse* 1.1 we hear:

> Virginity is something supernaturally great, wonderful, and glorious; and, to speak plainly and in accordance with the Holy Scriptures, this best and noblest manner of life alone is the root of immortality, and also its flower and first-fruits; and for this reason the Lord promises that those shall enter into the Kingdom of heaven who have made themselves eunuchs, in that passage of the Gospels in which He lays down the various reasons for which men have made themselves eunuchs. Chastity with men is a very rare thing, and difficult of attainment, and in proportion to its supreme excellence and magnificence is the greatness of its dangers.[71]

As the work progresses it becomes apparent that the author thinks the soul is the image of God in humanity and thus the body is a mere hindrance to true sanctification and spirituality (cf. 6.1). On the basis of a schema of Christological interpretation, the author interprets Ps 45.15, 16 to mean that the Spirit praises virginity next to the King's spouse (i.e., the Church), and that virgins have a place second only to the corporate Bride in the Kingdom of heaven (7.4, cf. 4.5). Similarly, virgins are called a golden altar in the holy of holies (5.8), while widows are only compared to brazen altars. At several points we seem to have excerpts from the ritual procedure that was apparently used when someone became a part of the order of virgins (cf. 11.2) as well as a discussion of their vows being compared to various sacred OT vows (e.g., Nazaritic, cf. 5.4, 5). In a *heilsgeschichtliche* argument, Methodius argues that the age of virginity has now dawned, superseding even the age of marital continence.

God no longer allowed man to remain in the same ways, considering how they might now proceed from one point to another, and advance nearer to heaven, until, having attained to the very greatest and most exalted lesson of virginity, they should reach to perfection; that first they should abandon the intermarriage of brothers and sisters, and marry wives from other families; and then that they should no longer have many wives, like brute beasts, as though born for the mere propagation of the species; and then that they should not be adulterers; and then again that they should go on to continence, and from continence to virginity, when, having trained themselves to despise the flesh, they sail fearlessly into the peaceful haven of immortality.[72]

As we have seen in our earlier examination of Clement of Alexandria, Origen, and Tertullian, Methodius is by no means alone in his exaltation of virginity. Tavard, by arguing for the fourth century, may be too conservative and late in the time when he sees virginity having become the Christian ideal.[73] The fact is, in Greece, Egypt, Africa, and elsewhere in the third century, virginity was considered the highest possible state of the Christian, literally a form of heaven or angelic purity on earth. Rather than the Kingdom coming at the end of time, it had come down from above, like the heavenly Jerusalem, in the state of virginity. The impact of this ascetical piety on women must have been that women were given two basic choices in the Church of the late third, early fourth century — to pursue some sort of celibate ministry for the Church as a virgin, widow, or deaconess, or to marry and be restricted to the roles that one's sexual identity dictated — those of wife and mother. Nowhere do we hear of a healthy balance where both one's human sexuality and spiritual gifts are affirmed, where both marriage and ministry are pursued. Certainly by the fourth century, life in the Church had become a clear either/or proposition with women in ministry being linked to a transcending or abandoning of any affirmation of their sexual identity. In our last section we will examine some examples, types, and images that further inculcated this development.

E. Types, examples, and images

To do a detailed study of Mariology and its early development would warrant another book. Here we intend to highlight the image of Mary inculcated by several authors in the second through fourth centuries. We have already seen that the image of Mary was not unreservedly positive during the NT era (cf. Mark 3.21ff.; Luke 2.41–52).[74] There is, however, apparently no comparable criticism of Mary in the extra-canonical literature between AD 80–325. Instead, there is an exaltation of Mary and especially of her virginity.

Even as early as Ignatius, we see a fixation on Mary's role in Jesus' birth and her virginity to the exclusion of her other roles in the Gospel story (cf. *Eph.* 7.2, 19.1; *Smyrn.* 1.1). It is not surprising that a pseudepigraphal letter later appeared involving Ignatius and Mary. Indeed, a measure of her growing importance to the Church is the amount of apocryphal material highlighting Mary written during the second to fourth centuries. For some reason, the Gnostics tended to focus on Mary Magdalene (cf. the *Gospel of Mary*, the *Questions of Mary*), though their interest in Jesus' mother seems indicated in the document, *Genna Marias.*[75]

Among orthodox apocryphal documents, the *Protoevangelium of James* deserves pride of place, being from the middle of the second century and written for the glorification of Mary. The work also manifests an early attempt to see Mary as *semper virgo*[76] and attributes to her the same qualities her son had.[77] Thus, we hear of Mary's miraculous birth, her Davidic descent (10.1), and her presentation in the Temple (7.1). In most of these details, the other infancy gospels followed suit and embellished the stories further, as did many Church Fathers including Clement of Alexandria, Epiphanius, Ephraem Syrus.[78] Tertullian possibly took issue with the idea of the perpetual virginity of Mary (cf. Tert. *de Monog.* 8), but this view became dominant even as early as the end of the second century. This set off various attempts in the latter part of the fourth century to explain the brothers and sisters of Jesus as cousins or step-brothers and step-sisters.

Various gaps in Mary's biography also generated insistence on her Davidic descent which had to be demonstrated in view of a virginal conception (ruling out descent through Joseph, cf. Ignatius, *Eph.* 18.2, *Tral.* 9.1, *Smyrn.* 1.1; Origen, *Contra Celsum* 1.39, 2.32). The gaps also led to pious speculation about a resurrection appearance to Mary which seems to go back to Tatian's time (c. AD 160).[79]

Great interest also developed in how Mary passed from this world, even to the point of trying to locate the very house in which she died (the *Dormitio Mariae*).[80]

As far as images of Mary or the viewing of Mary as a type, we see early evidence of her being seen as an anti-type of Eve. In Justin (d. 160), we hear, 'For Eve who was a virgin and undefiled, having conceived [by] the word of the serpent brought forth disobedience and death. But the Virgin Mary received faith and joy when the angel Gabriel announced the good news ...' (*Dialogue with Trypho* 100).[81] This sort of comparison and contrast is also seen in Irenaeus (*Against Heresies* 5.19.1, 1.30.7–11). A developed Church/Mary typology or Mary as the Church's Mother we do not seem to find between AD 80–325, though there are various opportunities for it. For instance, in Methodius (*Banquet* 7.4), in the exposition of Revelation 12 about the woman clothed with the sun, we are told this is the Church, not Mary. Again, in Cyprian (*Dress of the Virgins*, ch. 3, c. AD 249) we hear of Mother Church who produces virgins as her fairest flower, but not Mary as Mother to or of the Church. Interestingly, Rahab is seen as a prefigurement of the Church in the treatise on the *Unity of the Church* 8.

Thus, we may sum up this discussion by saying that Mariology was certainly not in full flower before AD 325, but it was well on its way in that direction. The presentation of Mary in an exclusively positive light could only further this image and, from the time of the *Protoevangelium of James*, the stress on Mary as *semper virgo* is a major theme. This would only further the general trend towards the exaltation of virginity and celibacy for women.

We have noted at some length the importance of Mary Magdalene in the Gospel traditions.[82] If the tradition of the Church spent a good deal of time exalting Mary, the same may be said of the Gnostic traditions in regard to Mary Magdalene. Indeed, so much was this the case that apologetes in the Church (cf. *Epistula Apostolorum*) used the more traditional figure of Martha to counter the image of a somewhat liberated Mary Magdalene in the Gnostic literature.[83]

In the *Gospel of Thomas* we find Mary Magdalene as an interlocutor of Jesus (log. 21). In the *Gospel of Mary* (second century), she is not only a proclaimer of God's revelation, but also an encourager of the male disciples. The hostility of Peter toward Mary Magdalene may reflect the tension in the Church about women assuming important roles.[84] In the *Pistis Sophia* from Egypt (mid third century?), Mary Magdalene asks Jesus a series of questions; in fact, thirty-five of the forty-six questions asked are from her. At one point, Mary Magdalene and John are given the choice seats in the Kingdom, on the right and left of Jesus. In the *Gospel of Philip* (early or mid third century at the latest),[85] Mary Magdalene appears as the companion of Jesus whom he loved more than the other disciples and whom he kissed often.[86] In view of this sort of material from the Gnostic corpus, it is not surprising to find a harsh reaction in the *Epistula Apostolorum*. As F. Bovon says, this literature:

> ... insiste tour a tour 1° sur la vertu et la pureté de Marie-Madeleine; 2° sur l'affection de Jesus pour cette femme; 3° sur le contact premier, immediat et privilégié qu'elle entretint avec le Ressuscité, source de revelation; 4° sur la jalousie des disciples face à ce privilège pascal; 5° sur la responsabilité dont elle fut chargée, de regrouper les disciples et de les envoyer en mission; 6° sur le caractere viril, enfin, au sens spirituel, de cette femme choisie et choyée.[87]

Various interesting female figures are used in the literature between AD 80–325 as positive examples for a Christian audience. For instance, Clement (*1 Cor 12.1–8*) sees Rahab as a notable example of faith and hospitality and indeed ὅτι οὐ μόνον πίστις καὶ προφητεία ἐν τῇ γυναικὶ γέγονεν (12.8). In general, early extra-canonical writers seem to have less difficulty with the idea of women being examples and playing leading roles in the church community perhaps because some of them, like Clement, were able to partake of the ethos we noted during the NT period.[88] Clement goes out of his way to present notable women of faith as examples for his audience, referring to Judith and Esther and arguing πολλαὶ γυναῖκες ἐνδυναμωθεῖσαι διὰ τῆς χάριτος τοῦ θεοῦ ἐπετελέσαντο πολλὰ ἀνδρεῖα (55.3).

Finally, a few words should be said about the image of the Church. The language of bride or bride-to-be in Eph 5.22–33 is a notable theme in the literature and probably led in various directions, e.g., the Church being called a woman or a mother. The latter we have seen in our discussion of Mary, but an even more basic use of the general imagery is found in 2 Clem 14.2 where we have an exegesis of Gen 1.27: 'God made humanity male and female', followed by 'the male is Christ, the female is the Church' (τὸ θῆλυ ἡ ἐκκλησία).

In the *Shepherd of Hermas*, *Vision* 1.1–2.4 opens this work with images of two women. The second woman is clearly the Church seen as an older lady (κυρία). Tavard suggests, however, that Rhoda (*Vision* 1) is also a symbol, in particular of the Church at Rome.[89]

Whether or not this conjecture is correct, we do have an interesting image of the Church as a woman looking young or old depending on whether or not the faithful repent of their sins. It is thus not a static image but it used interchangeably with the image of the Church as a tower (*Vision* 3). All of this suggests that biblical images were taken to be touchstones, not exhaustive representations, of how the Church could be depicted. It is this same flexibility we have already noticed in the mentioning of women in the earliest period.

F. Conclusions

Our study suggests that the crisis of the latter part of the second century over Gnosticism and Montanism took more of a toll on women in ministry with (and not just apart from) men than we may have imagined. This, combined with the increasing stress on asceticism, and coupled with a deficient view of human sexuality, led to a significant attenuation of women's roles in the churches by AD 325. We cannot say that women in ministry had been eliminated by that time, but we can say that forces within and without the Church contributed to a decline of women's possibilities for ministry, and to a shunting of women into a separatist track. This led women either to withdraw into the desert or convent and devote themselves to prayer and being examples of chastity, or to restrict themselves, in the case of deaconesses, to working with women or children. Their work would involve ministry of the Word or the sacrament of Baptism, and providing prayer and practical help for women and children.

The order of widows appears to have been a gender-specific exercise, except possibly in matters of prayer or help to the sick and needy. Even these separate but unequal forms of ministry were to be curtailed, or eliminated, in the latter half of the fourth century.

When ascetics withdrew into a community or into the desert they in fact removed themselves from being a viable influence on the Church in any ongoing way (apart from their example and their prayer life). This meant that many of the most committed Christian women went into a form of Christian living that precluded them from outreach, evangelism, and other functions of the Body of Christ. The net result, whether due to the Church's deliberate action or reaction to crises, was a considerable strengthening of patriarchy in the leadership structure of the Church by the time of Nicea (AD 325). Unfortunately, this affirmation of patriarchy was not in the mould of the sort of reformed patriarchy we saw in the Pauline epistles. One can only call this a retreat or regression back to a more Old Testament image of the nature of Church and ministry, a regression toward greater conformity with the patterns of the dominant secular culture. The Church, as it moved forward into the early Middle Ages, moved backward in its social structures. Perhaps the group most adversely affected by this regression were the devout Christian women, many of whom would never get a chance to use the gifts God had granted them. It is a matter the whole Church still has not rectified fully.

CONCLUSIONS

Since we have drawn conclusions at the end of each chapter, it only remains here to make some final remarks. We may begin by reiterating what was suggested in the introduction.

> It appears that the New Testament evidence shows a definite tendency on the part of the authors addressing the earliest churches to argue for, or support by implication, the new freedom and roles women may assume in Christ. At the same time, the evidence indicates an attempt at *reformation*, not repudiation, of the universal patriarchal structure of family and society in the first century in so far as it included the Christian family and community. It is crucial to see that this reformation was to take place 'in Christ'. In the New Testament material there is no call to social revolution or the overthrow of a patriarchal society outside of the Body of Christ. *Reformation in community*, not renunciation in society, is the order of the day.
>
> This significant, though not radical, reformation in community and affirmation of women was not quickly or universally accepted even in the Christian Church. When the author of Luke—Acts wrote in the last quarter of the first century these views still had to be argued. The same is true even later when the final form of the Fourth Gospel appeared. Even a cursory review of post-New Testamental and pre-Nicene material suggests that, as problems arose with heresy, the resistance to both the *reformation* and *affirmation* mentioned above intensified.

It seems to me that the evidence we have examined more than adequately documents this thesis. But now we are in a position to say more.

Note that it is the *later* material from the first century – Luke–Acts and the Fourth Gospel – which argues most strongly for the viability of new roles for women in the early Church. This means that it is impossible to deduce some evolutionary schema from the radical feminism of Jesus to the reinculturation of the Church and its capitulation to an unreformed patriarchy by the end of the first century. Nor is it likely that Paul should be seen as a development away from the pristine insight of Jesus on these matters. The same sort of tension between the choice of twelve men as the new community *in nuce* coupled with a clear interest in and affirmation of the new faith of and roles for women that existed in Jesus' ministry is also present in Paul's epistles. Both Jesus and Paul affirm a transformed vision of the old patriarchal schema coupled with an affirmation of women's new roles in the community of faith.

The tension between the family of faith and the physical family is also maintained by the Evangelists. The First Evangelist has more emphasis on a somewhat revised traditional orientation, and Luke's agenda places more stress on the new roles and possibilities for women. However, not one of the Evangelists neglects or obscures either side of the tension. Deliberate neglect of women and their roles along with a reassertion of Old Testamental patriarchalism is not found before some of the second-century Christian literature. None of the relevant New Testament material fits neatly into either of the modern patriarchal or feminist categories. Such stereotypes do not do justice to the evidence, and do not advance the discussion of this complex subject. It is relatively clear, however, that in the period between AD 80–325 there is justification for seeing an increasingly non-Christian patriarchal orientation taking over the Church.

This investigation raises significant questions about what sort of societal and community pressures may have prompted or encouraged the balancing of tensions we have seen in our study. What were the forces that led to a reformed patriarchal orientation?

In examining the *external* pressures that may have been at work, several pieces of information are relevant. First, as R. L. Wilken has shown, early Christians lived under the suspicion that they were practitioners of a 'superstition,' i.e., a religion which not only was foreign in origin but also undermined the social and civic order and the very foundation of Roman society. Romans valued religion largely because of its usefulness for sustaining the Roman commonwealth, and Christianity did not fit this description. According to Wilken,

Given this attitude that religion is a patrimony from the past which sustains the life of the state, it was inevitable that the piety of the persecutors would conflict with the new movement that had begun in Palestine. The Christians were seen as religious fanatics, self-righteous outsiders, arrogant innovators, who thought that only their beliefs were true.[1]

Both the exclusive claims of Christianity and its perceived lack of support for any nation's institutions or culture, placed Christianity in a very bad light in the eyes of most Romans.

Second, as Meeks has suggested,[2] with some notable exceptions first-century Christianity was mainly a lower and working class phenomenon. Furthermore, all indications are that Christianity was *perceived* as a religion largely supported by women, slaves, and even minors. Celsus was surely not the first to notice how many of those who were usually thought to be the subordinate members of society were involved in this new religion.[3] If we take at face value Paul's reminder in 1 Cor 1.26 that not many in his audience were powerful or of noble birth, then we see that Paul and probably the other NT authors as well mainly addressed a group of people who had *least to lose* by a change in the status quo, whether social, political, economic, or even religious. To put it the other way around, the early Christians were those who had *most to gain* by a change in their status. This being the case, in an environment where Paul was concerned that Christianity (as a fledgling and minority religion) present no scandal but the scandal of the Gospel, it is not surprising to hear exhortations such as we find in Romans 13 to support the governing authorities, for wives to submit to their husbands,[4] or even for slaves to remain in the socio-economic state in which they were called (1 Cor 7.17ff.). What is surprising is that Paul believes there is a theological rationale for such exhortations. Perhaps one should conclude that societal pressures provided the occasion and impetus for such exhortations, but not the rationale for them.

Third, early Christianity was largely an urban phenomenon, and Paul was writing to Christians who had not withdrawn from the world like the Qumran community. Thus, advice on how to live in and with the societal pressures and norms of the day is to be expected. Indeed, Paul did not wish for Christians to withdraw from society, but to be witnesses to the dominant culture. Instructions for transformation, rather than capitulation to societal models had to be urged, and this had to be done in a context where Christianity would be perceived as a viable option for urban pagans and Jews. A process of adopting and adapting ideas and practices (whether Jewish or pagan), as well as generating new uniquely Christian ones, was the order of the day. Christians were but a tiny minority in the Roman Empire, and that minority status could not help but affect the way Christians viewed their behavior, since they were also people who believed fervently in proselytizing. The apparently widespread effort by NT authors to balance the old and new, traditional and non-traditional, is explicable because Christianity *was* from the outset a world-affirming, yet world-transforming, religion. Since Christianity was evangelistic by nature, it did not wish to be perceived as a revolutionary group so far as political, economic, and (to some extent) social matters were concerned. Redemption in the end, for Christians, was not a matter of new creation and new community *ex nihilo*, but rather a renewal and transformation of the old creation. This meant that a process of sifting the values of the dominant culture was in order, along with the creation of some new values as well.

But how could early Christians demonstrate that it was not their purpose to undermine the very fabric of Roman society? How could they allay suspicions that they might be the sort who would lead a slave revolt or burn the capital city of Rome? How could they live in the world without being of it and still make a positive impression on their potential converts? Certainly one way of doing this was to participate in the ordinary activities and common social life of the Empire. To some extent this was possible, and there are rather clear indications that Christianity was perceived as another 'club', similar to the *hetaeria* which met for meals, social functions, and religious activities including burial rituals. It was only natural that members of the dominant culture would draw this conclusion about Christianity whose members largely met in private homes and had no public shrines. Yet, though Christianity resembled various other groups in the Empire, this did not place it above suspicion so far as those in power were concerned. The *hetaeria* were suspected of being sources of clandestine and subversive activities including repugnant secret rituals. These *hetaeria* were a phenomenon of the merchant and lower classes of society who did not have access to the social circles that the well-to-do and noble of society had. The letters of Pliny clearly show that the perceived categorization of Christianity as being among the political, burial, or social clubs was not necessarily a plus for the new religion.

Christianity also operated at a distinct disadvantage because not only was it a religion which was not associated with a particular nation, shrine, well-known religious location, particular season, or function of nature, but also it appeared to distance itself deliberately from the only 'recognized' nation and religion it had clear associations with — Palestine and Judaism. To make matters worse, Christians refused to recognize the legitimacy of other people's religious practices. This had definite social, economic, and political ramifications. Minucius Felix was undoubtedly not the first or only one to complain about Christians: 'You do not go to our shows, you take no part in our processions, you are not present at our banquets, you shrink in horror from our sacred games.'[5] To this list we may add that Christians refused to worship the Emperor, and in some quarters they refused to join the Roman army. In short, Christians were seen as distinctly anti-social! Their refusal to participate in most of these activities was specifically religious in nature, i.e., pagan worship and rituals were required in most of these state functions. This was also true of the merchant guilds that existed all over the Roman Empire.

Thus, it was imperative for Christians to appear to be good citizens in the few areas where they could endorse the values of the society. These areas were chiefly in obedience to governing authorities and the endorsement of traditional family values. The surprise, then, is not that some traditional values were strongly asserted by Christian writers both during and after the NT era, but that new roles for women and new evaluations of slaves (cf. Philemon) were also developed. I can only conclude that both the old *and* the new roles for women in the Christian community must have been considered *essential* to early Christianity, for the pressures to conform to other religious and social groups were considerable, especially on a proselytizing religion that refused to withdraw from the urban environment and dominant culture.

But what of the *internal* forces which prompted the balancing of the old and new in regard to women and their roles in the Christian community? What internal pressures were at work to cause, and what pressures to resolve, the conflict between cultural norms and community values? Answers to these questions seem harder to come by.

It has become a matter of course to argue that the loss of belief in an imminent Parousia caused a gradual process of accommodation by the Church to the values of the dominant culture. In fact, Käsemann once defined early Catholicism as '... that transition from earliest Christianity to the so-called ancient Church, which is completed with the disappearance of the imminent expectation'.[6]

Now I do not deny that there were various early Christians who believed in an imminent Parousia in the first century, and that this number probably diminished as the first century came to a close. I maintain, however, that it is difficult to demonstrate that the concept of the imminent Parousia was the main factor causing NT theology and ethics to develop in the ways they did, much less to prove that this concept explains why the post-New Testament, Ante-Nicene Church seems so different from what we find depicted in the NT. In fact, it seems to me that a much more significant shift within the Church's thinking that affected views of women and their roles is the shift from a balanced 'already–not yet' eschatology (future oriented *and* horizontal in approach) to an 'over-realized' eschatology (vertical in approach). This shift, I believe, adequately explains the growing dualism, other-worldly orientation, and world-denying character of early Christianity. Also, it explains why certain more ecstatically oriented groups, who affirmed that 'the future is now', allowed women to have significant roles in their communities (cf. Corinth). Further, it explains why other groups, with a *different* sort of realized eschatology, saw the importance of developing Church institutions and structures which would 'incarnate' the Kingdom on earth. Whether the structures were thought not to matter *or* were seen to be of paramount importance (cf. the case of Ignatius and the monarchical episcopacy), both of these approaches reflect a replacement of a future eschatology with a realized one.

On the one hand, vertical eschatology was capable of being world-denying and dualistic, insisting that flesh and spirit were inherently at odds with each other (cf. the Montanists). On the other hand, vertical eschatology was capable of insisting on the essential goodness of creation, believing that the spirit could be incarnated in the flesh, and even in human institutions. For those who affirmed the former type of realized eschatology, all sorts of social, economic, and political matters became adiaphora; for those who affirmed the latter, such matters could be seen as of paramount importance for the advance of Christianity in the Roman Empire. The former approach would lead to a more private, if not separatist, approach to Christianity, while the latter would opt for a public approach to Christianity involving both culture and cult.

In both subtypes of vertical eschatology, it is the *nature* of their realized eschatology, not their view of the timing of the end, which determines their orientation. As a careful reading of the Ante-Nicene Fathers shows, it was possible for exponents of either approach to believe in an imminent Parousia. This should not surprise us since we find this same phenomenon in the NT. On the one hand the author of Revelation takes a rather world-denying approach to religion and prays for the imminent return of Christ to right all wrongs and to remedy the suffering of the saints. On the other hand, Paul counseled about earthly matters and relationships, the nature of the marriage and government, etc., precisely because he did not believe they were matters of indifference, even though 1 Thessalonians 5 shows he could believe that the end might be near. Not the timing but the *nature* of the eschatological approach is what is crucial. Furthermore, how the creation and so-called creation order fits into one's eschatology (or total theology of redemption) will significantly affect one's view of women and their roles in the Christian community. The way creation and redemption interact in one's eschatology will in large measure determine one's view of social roles and relationships.

Richard Longenecker has put the matter as follows:

> At the heart of the problem as it exists in the Church is the question of how we correlate the theological categories of creation and redemption. Where the former is stressed, subordination and submission are usually emphasized − sometimes even silence; where the latter is stressed, freedom, mutuality, and equality are usually emphasized. What Paul attempted to do in working out his theology was to keep both categories united − though, I would insist, with an emphasis on redemption. Because of creation there are differences between the sexes which exist for the blessing of both men and women and for the benefit of society. Paul does not argue for anything like unisexuality or some supposed androgynous ideal. Heterosexuality is presupposed in all of his letters as having been ordained by God, ... Yet Paul also lays emphasis on redemption in such a way as to indicate that what God has done in Christ transcends what is true simply because of creation.[7]

Now, it seems to me, that Longenecker errs at precisely the crucial juncture. Surely, for Paul, it is not a matter of transcending creation, but of transforming it in Christ. Whatever is done in Christ is a fulfilment, not an abolition, of God's original purposes in creation and His renewed purposes in the work of redemption.

This is so precisely because Paul believed in the redemption, not the replacement, of creation.

Käsemann is much nearer the truth when he says,

> Paul did not take over the present eschatology of the enthusiasts but set over against it eschatological reserve and apocalyptic. He is unable to assent to the statement that the Christian has only to demonstrate his heavenly freedom because the powers and principalities have already become subject to the Christ. According to Rom. 8.18ff., he knows that not only does the creation cry out for the glorious freedom of the children of God, but the Church, too, joins in this cry, even in her worship, because her perfection has still to be accomplished. He knows, we can now say more directly, the tempted condition of the believer who is still living through the pangs of the Messiah, free because he has been called once and for all into sonship but menaced by the last enemy which is death and therefore by the cosmic principalities; these are continually striving to wrench him away from sonship and freedom, and so he is compelled continually to be reestablished in the *nova obedientia*. Present eschatology by itself, and not comprehended within a future eschatology – that would be for the Christian pure glorying in the flesh, such as [sic] enthusiasm has certainly sufficiently demonstrated in every epoch. It would be illusion and not reality. It is precisely the apocalyptic of the apostle which renders to reality its due and resists pious illusion. The Christian Church possesses the reality of sonship only in the freedom of those under temptation – the freedom which points forward to the resurrection of the dead as the truth and the completion of the reign of Christ.[8]

Later, Käsemann affirms:

> The new age is not suspended in mid-air: it takes root on this our earth to which Christ came down. It does not create for itself there an island of the blessed as the Corinthians believe: it creates the possibility of the kind of service which can no longer be universal and alive if it is not carried out in the midst of the old, passing world, thus declaring God's rightful lordship over this earth; that is, preserving the world as divine creation. According to Paul, it is none other than the Spirit

who imposes himself on the everyday life of the world as being the locus of our service of God; while emancipation, even when it appeals to the Spirit, prefers to retreat from this everyday life and the possibilities of service that are given with it, and is thus a perversion of Christian freedom.[9]

This is the vision of the dominant figure of NT theology, Paul, and it adequately accounts for his attempt to balance the 'already/not-yet', the present and future aspects of eschatology, the old roles of women in the physical family with their new roles in the family of faith. Paul espouses a theology of creation affirmed but reformed in redemption. It would appear that few were able to follow Paul in preserving the various tensions between old and new, and some, such as the authors of Matthew and Luke–Acts, had to place more stress on one side or the other of the tension probably because of the problems their communities faced in adjusting to life in the dominant culture.

As we have seen, the study of the post-NT, pre-Nicene evidence suggests an attenuation of the new element in Christianity that allowed women to assume new roles in the family of faith. I would submit that one major reason why this occurred was because the Church substituted one or another form of a realized eschatology for the balanced 'already/not-yet' approach we find in Paul and to a lesser degree elsewhere in the NT. It is inadequate to talk about the Christianizing of the Roman Empire if one does not also talk about the acculturation of the Church. I submit that a main reason for that gradual acculturation was due to the acceptance of one form or another of realized eschatology that either made its peace with the world or assumed that worldly matters and material things were adiaphora. As a result, the Church gradually allowed the dominant culture to set the agenda in economic, political, and social matters (including the role of women). Where, then, does all this leave us today?

A brief word is in order concerning the implications of these conclusions for modern discussions about women's roles in the Church. Nothing in this book suggests that women did not assume, or should not assume, a variety of roles in the Church – teaching, preaching, prophesying, providing material support, hostessing church functions, etc. The question of women's ordination is not discussed or dismissed in the New Testament, but there is nothing in the material that rules out such a possibility. If the possibilities for women in the earliest churches, as evidenced in the NT, should be seen as models for church practice in subsequent generations, then it should be seen that women in the NT era already performed the tasks normally associated with ordained clergy in later eras. These roles seem to be clearly supported by various NT authors.

At the same time, note that there is no evidence in the NT material investigated in this study of any sort of radical repudiation of the traditional family structure. Such structures are revised and reformed in the Christian community. Headship comes to mean head servant, or taking the lead in serving, but this is not quite the same as some modern notions of an egalitarian marriage structure. It is possible to argue that the NT material, even if it involves imperatives, is no longer normative for church teaching on marriage today. However, this raises the problem of using a selective hermeneutic, or of having some standard external to the biblical material itself as the final authority or arbiter of what is appropriate in matters of faith and practice.

One can also argue that it is the direction the New Testament data is pursuing, its trajectory, not its position, that is normative for the Church of subsequent eras. At this point one might suggest an analogy between the NT teaching on slavery and on women and their roles. If the direction of the NT data is the reformation of patriarchy coupled with the affirmation of women's new roles, then could this not lead to a stage in which the Church has reformed itself into a state *beyond* patriarchy? If the cry of the NT authors is *semper reformanda*, does there come a point where reformation entails abandonment or a point where reformation is no longer necessary?

Whatever conclusions one draws on these issues or their implications for modern church practice, surely the starting point for such discussion should be the careful, historical study and exegesis of the biblical material itself. It is hoped that this study will have helped the furtherance of that necessary, preliminary investigation.

NOTES

Introduction

1 S. Goldberg, *The Inevitability of Patriarchy* (New York: W. Morrow, 1973–74). This is not an exegetical or biblical study, but its analysis of the origins of patriarchy and patriarchal culture and religion does have bearing on the discussion (cf. pp. 177ff.).

2 G. W. Knight, *The New Testament on the Role Relationship of Men and Women* (Grand Rapids: Baker, 1977); cf. S. Foh, *Women and the Word of God. A Response to Biblical Feminism* (Philadelphia: Presbyterian and Reformed, 1979).

3 L. Swidler, *Biblical Affirmations of Woman* (Philadelphia: Westminster, 1979); cf. E. and F. Stagg, *Women in the World of Jesus* (Philadelphia: Westminster, 1978).

4 R. and J. Boldrey, *Chauvinist or Feminist? Paul's View of Women* (Grand Rapids: Baker, 1976).

5 Cf. among others, K. Stendahl, *The Bible and the Role of Women* (Philadelphia: Fortress, 1966), p. 32; H. D. Betz, *Galatians* (Philadelphia: Fortress, 1979) 190ff.

6 Cf. A. Oepke, *Der Brief des Paulus an die Galater* (ThHK 9, 3rd ed.; Berlin: Evangelische Verlagsanstalt, 1973) 123; E. Burton, *The Epistle to the Galatians* (ICC; Edinburgh: T. & T. Clark, 1921) 206–7.

7 P. Trible, *God and the Rhetoric of Sexuality* (Philadelphia: Fortress, 1978) 202. I wish to note that Trible's work, apart from the quoted portion, is insightful and challenging, revealing how seriously she takes the task of exegesis and rhetorical criticism.

1 Women in first-century Mediterranean cultures

1 F. W. Cornish and J. Bacon, 'The position of women', *A Companion to Greek Studies* (ed. L. Whibley; Cambridge: University Press, 1931) 615–16.

2 A. W. Gomme, 'The position of women in Athens in the fifth and fourth centuries BC', *Essays in Greek History and Literature* (ed. A. W. Gomme; Oxford: Oxford University Press, 1973) 89–115, only succeeds in establishing that women 'in their place' were respected on the stage, in poetry, and in the art of classical Athens.

3 For an overview of a woman's position, primarily between the ninth and sixth centuries BC in Greece, cf. M. B. Arthur, 'Early Greece: the origins of the Western attitude toward women' *Arethusa* 6:1 (1973) 7–58.

4 Thucydides, *History of the Peloponnesian War* 2.45.2, LCL (1919) 1.340–1.

5 Xenophon, *Oeconomicus* 3.13, LCL (1923) 388–9; cf. 7.5, pp. 414–5.

6 Aristophanes, *The Thesmophoriazusae* 414–417, LCL (1924) 166–7, also 790–800, pp. 200–1. This sort of seclusion apparently existed only among aristocratic women. There are examples of middle- and lower-class citizen-women being involved in various jobs and businesses outside the home; cf. K. J. Dover, 'Classical Greek attitudes to sexual behavior', *Arethusa* 6:1 (1973) 59–73.

7 Cf. the references in n. 6 above stating that they went to the baths, theaters, and markets; Cornish and Bacon, 'Position of women', 614–5; and D. C. Richter, 'The position of women in classical Athens', *Classical Journal* 67 (1971) 7 and notes. Citizen-women could be priestesses in some of the cults in Athens; cf. Pausanias, *Description of Greece, Attica* 27.1–3, LCL (1918) 138–41; and L. R. Farnell, *The Cults of the Greek States* (Oxford: Oxford University Press, 1907) 3.106–16 on their roles in the Attic Demeter festivals.

8 Herodotus 3.119, LCL (1921) 2.146–9.

9 Euripides, *Medea* 230–34, LCL (1912) 302–3. Cornish and Bacon, 'Position of women', 614–5, suggest that Euripides paved the way for the more tolerant views of women found in later writers, e.g., Apollonius Rhodius and Theocritus.

10 G. E. M. de Ste. Croix, 'Some observations on the property rights of Athenian women', *Classical Review* 20 n.s. (1970) 273–8. It appears that the restrictions had been relaxed somewhat by the Hellenistic period and a great deal by the Roman era.

11 Diogenes Laertius, *Thales* 1.33, *Lives of Eminent Philosophers*, LCL (1925) 1.23–5. Lactantius attributes this quotation to Plato, but this seems unlikely in view of Plato's other sayings about women. It has been suggested that this saying is the source of the Jewish three-fold blessing. Cf. Wayne Meeks, 'The image of the androgyne: some uses of a symbol in earliest Christianity', *HR* 13:3 (1974) 167–8.

12 Cf. Robert Flacelière, *Love in Ancient Greece* (trans. J. Cleugh; London: F. Muller, 1962) 115ff.; H. Licht, *Sexual Life in Ancient Greece* (ed. L. H. Sawson; trans. J. H. Freese; London: George Routledge, 1932) 339–63, 395–410.

13 Cf. for instance, Plutarch, *Alcibiades* 39.1–5, *The Parallel Lives*, LCL (1916) 112–15.

14 James Donaldson, *Woman: Her Position and Influence in Ancient Greece and Rome, and Among Early Christians* (London: Longmans, Green and Co., 1907) 59.

15 Cf. Athenaeus, *The Deipnosophists* 13.591, LCL (1937) 6.190–1.

16 Donaldson, *Woman*, 59.
17 Xenophon, *Memorabilia* 3.11.1–18, LCL (1923) 240–9.
18 Xenophon, *Memorabilia* 2.6.36, LCL (1923) 144–5. Socrates is also reported to have had another non-Athenian woman, Diotima of Mantinea, as his instructor in love; cf. Plato, *Symposium* 201.D, LCL (1925) 3.172–3.
19 As quoted in Xenophon, *Banquet* 2.9, Budé (1961) 43–6; but the context of this saying should also be compared.
20 Martin Nilsson, *Greek Folk Religion* (New York: Harper and Row, 1961) 58ff.
21 Martin Nilsson, *A History of Greek Religion* (Oxford: Clarendon, 1925) 241.
22 Plato, *The Republic* 455DE, LCL (1930) 446–7. For a balanced approach to Plato's view of women, cf. D. Wender, 'Plato: misogynist, paedophile, and feminist', *Arethusa* 6:1 (1973) 75–90. See Plato, *Timaeus* 42.A–C, 91.A, LCL (1929) 90–3, 248–9, for his negative remarks on women; also Plato, *The Republic* 452–457E, LCL (1930) 436–55.
23 Diogenes Laertius, *Speusippus* 2, *Lives of Eminent Philosophers*, LCL (1925) 1.374–5.
24 Aristotle, *Politics* 1.2.12, LCL (1932) 20–1.
25 Aristotle, *Politics* 3.2.10, LCL (1932) 193–5, but cf. 1.1.5–7, pp. 4–9.
26 Cf. Cornish and Bacon, 'Position of women', 612, though the discussion here concerns the Greeks of Ionia.
27 Athenaeus, *The Deipnosophists* 13.559, LCL (1937) 6.20–3.
28 Richter, 'Position of women', 1–8, has successfully challenged the extreme form of the seclusion thesis. Cf. M. Hadas, 'Observations on Athenian women', *Classical Weekly* 19:13 (1926) 97–100.
29 Aristophanes, *Lysistrata* 640–650, LCL (1924) 3.66–7, and note b.
30 This widespread practice was known even in Egypt and other locations where women's status was considerably higher than in Greece or Italy. Cf. A. Oepke, 'παῖς', *TDNT* 5 (1967) 639–41; *POxy.* 744–49 (1904) 4.243–4.
31 R. J. Bonner, 'Did women testify in homicide cases in Athens?' *Classical Philology* 1 (1906) 127–32. Bonner's arguments, however, are based on some indirect evidence in Demosthenes, *Against Evergus* 55–61, *Private Orations*, LCL (1936) 1.310–15. There is no indication that these views changed in the Hellenistic or Roman periods.
32 A. Oepke, 'γυνή', *TDNT* 1 (1964) 777. R. van Compernole, 'Le mythe de la gynécocratie – doulocratie argienne', *Hommages à Claire Préaux* (ed. J. Bingen; Brussels; Brussels University, 1975) 355–64, makes clear that the known evidence on this matter, 'ne contient la moindre trace de la présence à Argos d'une gynécocratie' (p. 364).
33 Donaldson, *Woman*, 26.
34 Cf. Plutarch, *Lycurgus* 14.2–3, *The Parallel Lives*, LCL (1914) 1.245–6; Propertius, *Elegies* 3.14.1–13, LCL (1912) 227–9.

On Spartan marriage customs, cf. Athenaeus, *The Deipnosophists* 13.555, LCL (1937) 6.4–5.

35 Donaldson, *Woman*, 27ff. Space does not allow a review of Greek wedding customs. Only citizens could marry and women were passed from the control of their fathers or guardians (κύριοι) to their husbands. In Athens women had no claim on their husband's property. Cf. *Harper's Dictionary of Classical Literature and Antiquities* (ed. H. T. Peck; New York: Harper and Bros., 1897) 1012–16, and Licht, *Sexual Life*, 38–56.

36 *CIG* 1438, 1442, 1446, 1452 (1828) 1.680–6.

37 Donaldson, *Woman*, 33ff.

38 Plutarch, *Lycurgus* 14.1–2, *The Parallel Lives*, LCL (1914) 1.245–6; Plutarch, *Sayings of Spartan Women* 240, *Moralia*, LCL (1931) 3.454–9. Plutarch, writing in the late first century AD, praises Sparta as a place where adultery and polygamy are virtually unknown. It is hard to say how much is his idealisation and how much reflects actual practice in pre-Roman times. Cf. Herodotus 5.39–41, LCL (1922) 3.42–5.

39 Gerhard Delling, *Paulus' Stellung zu Frau und Ehe* (Stuttgart: Kohlhammer, 1931) 19.

40 *CIG* 1435–40 (1828) 1.680–2.

41 Plutarch, *Sayings of Spartan Women* 242.23, *Moralia*, LCL (1931) 3.466–7.

42 Cf. Farnell, *Cults* (1907) 4.389, on Laconian women in the Dionysian cult. Various other cults, such as Magna Mater, had female ministrants. As Farnell, *Cults* (1896) 2.639–40, reminds us, 'In the native Greek cults it is usual to find the female ministrants in the ritual of the female diety.' Cf. Pausanias, *Description of Greece*, *Laconia* 3.12.9, LCL (1926) 2.76–7, on a Spartan temple of Magna Mater.

43 Athenaeus, *The Deipnosophists* 13.573, LCL (1937) 6.96–7. Pindar, *For Xenophon of Corinth*, *Odes*, LCL (1915) 132–45. Xenophon, a native of Corinth, following established traditions, promised to render a troupe of prostitutes to Aphrodite if he won at the Olympic Games. Thus, Pindar calls him, 'Kindly to strangers' (pp. 132–3).

44 Donaldson, *Woman*, 56. Apparently for a long time ἑταῖραι not only were forbidden from participating in the Spartan cults, but also were banned from the whole region.

45 Athenaeus, *The Deipnosophists* 13.574, LCL (1937) 6.100–3. Pausanias, *Description of Greece*, *Corinth* 34.11–35.2 LCL (1918) 1.438–49, tells us of maidens and widows sacrificing to Aphrodite in Corinth.

46 Pausanias, *Description of Greece*, *Corinth* 20.6–9, LCL (1918) 1.352–5. cf. 22.1, pp. 362–3.

47 Pausanias, *Description of Greece*, *Corinth* 33.1–3, LCL (1918) 1.426–9; cf. Farnell, *Cults*, 2.639–40.

48 Farnell, *Cults*, 4.187–9.

49 Plutarch, *Lycurgus* 5.3, *The Parallel Lives*, LCL (1914)1.216–7; and *Numa* 9.6, *The Parallel Lives*, LCL (1914) 1.338–9.

50 Farnell, *Cults*, 3.1.6–16.
51 Martin Nilsson, *Die Religion der Griechen* (Tübingen: J.C.B. Mohr, 1927) 70.
52 Cf. Pausanias, *Description of Greece*, Arcadia 8.31.8, LCL (1935) 4.62–3.
53 Euripides, *Bacchanals* 1050–60, LCL (1912) 3.90–1; Martin Nilsson, *The Dionysiac Mysteries of the Hellenistic and Roman Age* (Lund: C.W.K. Gleerup, 1957) 4, 38.
54 As the Villa Item in Rome shows; cf. K.H. Rengstorf, 'μανθάνω', *TDNT* 4 (1967) 399.
55 Pausanias, *Description of Greece*, Elis 1.13.10–11, LCL (1926) 2.456–7.
56 Demosthenes, *Against Neaera* 122, *Private Orations*, LCL (1939) 6.444–7.
57 W.W. Tarn and G.T. Griffith, *Hellenistic Civilisation* (3rd ed.; London: Edward Arnold, 1952) 98; cf. J.B. Lightfoot, *St Paul's Epistle to the Philippians* (Grand Rapids: Zondervan, 1953) 56; and R. Martin, *Philippians* (NCB, Greenwood: Attic, 1976) 8. For a good survey of Hellenistic women in general, and Macedonian women in particular, cf. Sarah Pomeroy, *Goddesses, Whores, Wives, and Slaves* (London: Robert Hale, 1975) 120ff.
58 Strabo, *Geography* 7.21–24, LCL (1924) 3.342–7.
59 *IG* 62 (1908) IX.2, p.20.
60 *CIG* 1967, cf. 1968a, b (1843) 2.52–3; cf. *IG* (1908) IX.2, pp.xxiv, xxv, for a list of Thessalonian praetores.
61 *CIG* 1957, 1997 (1843) 2.50, 61.
62 *CIG* 1958, 1977 (1843) 2.50–1, 56.
63 *CIG* 1973 (1843) 2.56.
64 *CIG* 1965, 1977 (1843) 2.52, 56.
65 Cf. Herodotus 5.19–20, LCL (1922) 3.18–23.
66 Cf. Tarn and Griffith, *Hellenistic Civilisation*, 56ff.; Pausanias, *Description of Greece*, Attica 6.8–7.2, LCL (1918) 1.34–5; Plutarch, *Alexander* 2.1–4, *The Parallel Lives*, LCL (1919) 7.226–7. G.H. Macurdy, 'Queen Eurydice and the evidence for woman power in early Macedonia', *AJP* 48 (1927) 201–14, shows that there is no evidence to prove that before Eurydice women mingled in political affairs, and there are no traces of matriarchy anywhere in Macedonia.
67 Diogenes Laertius, *Strato* 5.60, *Lives of Eminent Philosophers*, LCL (1925) 1. 512–3.
68 Plutarch, *On Brotherly Love* 489c, *Moralia*, LCL (1939) 6.258–9.
69 Tarn and Griffith, *Hellenistic Civilisation*, 98.
70 Meeks, 'Image', 172ff.; Tarn and Griffith, *Hellenistic Civilisation*, 330.
71 *IG* 329 (1898) XII:3, 80.
72 This was true of mainland Greece as well as Asia Minor; cf. Oepke, 'γυνή', *TDNT* 1 (1964) 786; Pausanias, *Description of Greece*, Arcadia 8.5. 11–12, LCL (1933) 3.370–1.
73 Lucian, *The Syrian Goddess* 17--19, LCL (1925) 4.360–5.

74 Farnell, *Cults* (1909) 5.159–60, 199.
75 *SIG* 985 (1920) 3.113–4.
76 *IG* 499 (1899) XII:2.101. Cf. Martin Nilsson, *The Dionysiac Mysteries of the Hellenistic and Roman Age* (Lund: C.W.K. Gleerup, 1957) 8–9.
77 Delling, *Paulus' Stellung*, 10; Pomeroy, *Goddesses*, 126. In Galatia alone we have the following inscriptions honoring wives and mothers: *CIG* 4058, 4051 (1853) 3.95; 4074, p.98; 4079, p.100; 4101, p.105; 4108, p.106; 4111–4112, p.107; 4121, p.109; 4129, p.111; and espec. 4142, p.114 on ἱέρεια.
78 A.H. Smith, 'Notes on a tour of Asia Minor', *JHS* 8 (1887) 216–67, espec. 256.
79 *IG* 62 (1908) IX:2.20.
80 As is shown by their heir settlement which passed from a mother to her daughter; cf. Demosthenes, *Against Boeotus* 2.6, *Private Orations* I, LCL, (1936) 4.484–5.
81 Donaldson, *Woman*, 124.
82 M. Barth, *Ephesians 4–6* (Garden City: Doubleday, 1974) 656.
83 *POxy.* 1380–1381 (1898ff.) 9.214–5.
84 *SIG* 1267 (1917) 3.390–2. It is primarily in the Isis cult that the female deity is prominent in Egypt; cf. R.E. White, 'Women in Ptolemaic Egypt', *JHS* 18 (1898) 240.
85 J. Leipoldt, *Die Frau in der antiken Welt und im Urchristentum* (Leipzig: Koehler and Amelang, 1955) 15–6, says, '... die Frau sich hier tatsachlich allerlei Freiheiten erfreut.' Cf. Tarn and Griffith, *Hellenistic Civilisation*, 359ff.
86 Diodorus Siculus, *Library of History* 1.27.1ff., LCL (1933) 1.84ff. Sophocles, *Oedipus at Colonus* 337–340, LCL (1912) 1.178–9, makes a similar remark revealing that the liberty of Egyptian women was known widely. Diodorus Siculus, *Library of History* 1.17.3ff., LCL (1933) 1.55, says that Osiris turned over supreme power to Isis and this led to women's prominence in Egypt. Thus, he furthers the trend of giving an aetiological myth as the basis of a social phenomenon. One must add that once the cult developed there can be no doubt that it furthered the rights and status of women.
87 This is the conclusion of Jacques Pirenne, 'Le statut de la femme dans l'ancienne Égypte', *Recueils de la Société Jean Bodin*, vol. XI: *La Femme* (Brussells: Éditions de la Librarie Encyclopédique, 1959) 63–77.
88 O. Rubensohn, ed., *Elephantine-Papyri* (Berlin: Weidmann, 1907) 18–22; *PTeb* (1902) I:1.449–53. In the main the Greeks appear to have avoided such forms of marriage as homology or synchoresis; cf. A. Oepke, 'γυνή', *TDNT* 1 (1964) 778.
89 The commercial texts involving women are assembled and discussed conveniently in Claire Préaux, 'Le statut de la femme à l'époque hellénistique principalment en Égypte', *Recueils de la Société Jean Bodin*, vol. XI: *La Femme* (Brussells: Éditions de la Librarie Encyclopédique, 1959) 127–75. Préaux sees an advance in social and commercial, but not political, rights in this era. She concludes,

'La capacité de la femme grecque (avec κύριος) et celle de la femme
égyptienne (sans κύριος) sont plus étendues que celle de la femme
romaine' (145). Cf. Pomeroy, *Goddesses*, 127. In fact, the Greeks,
horrified by Egyptian women in charge of property matters, added
the rule that a Greek woman had to have a legal guardian's aid to
transact business. On a Greek woman's κύριος, cf. *PGrenf* 22 (1896)
1.62–6.
90 On divorce (c. AD 96), cf. *POxy* 266 (1898ff.) 2.238–43. On women
   as sellers and lenders, cf. *PGrenf* 18–20 (1896) 1.38–44. On women
   being ceded land (c. 132–109 BC), cf. 27, pp. 54–7. On land sold
   by a priestess and her husband (c. 114 BC), cf. 25, pp. 51–3. On
   a woman lending wheat without interest, cf. 18, p. 38. On women
   selling and inheriting land, cf. 21, pp. 44–8 and 33, pp. 62–5.
   Herodotus, when he visited Egypt shortly after 460 BC, reveals that
   even at this time Egyptian women were more liberated in comparison
   to their counterparts in Greece and Rome. He observed with some
   amazement, 'Women buy and sell, the men abide at home and
   weave' (2.35–36, LCL [1920] 1.316–7). He also tells us that this
   is the only place in the world where such peculiar things happen,
   and we may take his word as accurate about the status of women
   elsewhere in the Mediterranean.
91 *PTeb* 766 (1933) 2.207–9.
92 Pausanias, *Description of Greece, Attica* 7.1–12.5, LCL (1918)
   1.34–63. R. E. White, 'Women in Ptolemaic Egypt', *JHS* 18 (1898)
   245ff., comments on women's rise to power in Ptolemaic Egypt.
93 White, 'Women', 264–5, says this principle came not from
   Macedonia, but from Egypt. This tradition may explain the
   brother–sister marriages in royal circles, which could be an attempt
   by the men to deprive women of some of their sole inheritance
   rights. The practice of deifying the queen apparently began with
   Arsinoe Philadelphus. Her cult existed as early as 267 BC, and
   we read of priestesses ministering in this cult (White, 251, n. 1,
   and 252). A. M. Blackman, 'On the position of women in ancient
   Egyptian hierarchy', *BA* 7 (1921) 8–30, has shown that there
   were musicians, priestesses, high priestesses, and prophetesses
   even before Herodotus' time (4th Dynasty, Old Kingdom). White
   (266) asserts that by Ptolemaic times there was a priestess in every
   cult of the Egyptian gods and goddesses. There was a parallel rise
   in the presence and privilege of women in the political arena as well.
   After Arsinoe, queens were deified as a regular procedure in Egypt,
   and frequently their names take precedence over the king in the
   inscriptions (cf. *PGrenf* 25, 27 [1896] 1.51–3, 54–7).
94 Pomeroy, *Goddesses*, 124ff.
95 Plutarch, *The Education of Children* 1.51, 1.8c, 1.9d, 1.14b,
   Moralia LCL (1927) 1.22–3, 38–9, 44–5, 66–7 (c. first century
   AD). Cf. Leipoldt, *Die Frau*, 12–16, 24–71.
96 Donaldson, *Woman*, 77–147; Pomeroy, *Goddesses*, 149–226;
   J. P. V. D. Balsdon, *Roman Women: Their History and Habits*
   (London: Bodley Head, 1962) 45. For a summary of a Roman

woman's legal status, cf. R. Villers, 'Le statut de la femme à Rome jusqu'à à le fin de la République', pp. 177–89, and J. Gaudemet, 'Le statut de la femme dans l'empire Romain', both in *Recueils de la Société Jean Bodin*, vol. XI: *La Femme* (1959).

97 Balsdon, *Roman Women*, 282.

98 Cf. V. Taylor, *The Gospel According to St Mark* (2nd ed.; New York: St Martin's, 1966) 32, and C.E.B. Cranfield, *The Gospel According to St Mark* (CGTC; Cambridge: Cambridge University Press, 1972) 9.

99 J. Carcopino, *Daily Life in Ancient Rome* (London: George Routledge, 1941) 77; cf. Sallust, *The War with Cataline* 39.5, LCL (1960) 68–9. Apparently, slaying a wife was no longer a right by the later days of the Republic, unless she was caught in adultery. However, cf. Valerius Maximus, *Factorum et Dictorum Memorabilium* 6.3.9 (ed. C. Kempf; Stuttgart: B.G. Teubner, 1966) 289–90; Donaldson, *Woman*, 145.

100 Carcopino, *Daily Life*, 80ff.; Donaldson, *Woman*, 87. Only the husband was allowed to divorce during the Republic – yet another indication of women's subordinate position. Though written in the late first or early second century AD, Plutarch, *Romulus* 22.3–4, *The Parallel Lives*, LCL (1948) 1.160–3, probably reflects earlier practice. Cf. Dionysius of Halicarnassus, *Roman Antiquities* 2.25, 4–7, LCL (1937) 1.382–5, on a woman's subordination (c. 50 BC).

101 Livy 34.3.11–12, LCL (1935) 9.416–7; cf. F.H. Marshall, 'The position of women', *A Companion to Latin Studies* (ed. J.E. Sandys; Cambridge: Cambridge University Press, 1910) 184.

102 Carcopino, *Daily Life*, 83; Balsdon, *Roman Women*, 45. Families became increasingly reluctant to turn over their daughter's considerable assets to another family. Cf. Pomeroy, *Goddesses*, 154.

103 Cf. the words of Q. Lucretius Vespillo, the consul in 19 BC, 'So long a marriage as ours ended by death and not by divorce is rare; it has been our lot to have it prolonged for 41 years without a quarrel' (*Laudatio Turiae*, *CIL* 1527 [1876] VI:i.332–6).

104 Suetonius, *The Deified Augustus* 24, 89, LCL (1914) 1.176–9, 258–9. Few of these women over fifty, except perhaps the diseased or demented, had gone through life unmarried. This dispensation simply allowed women not to remarry, a privilege probably given because they could no longer have children.

105 Plutarch, *Pompey* 9.55, *The Parallel Lives*, LCL (1917) 5.134–7.

106 There were various means women could use to initiate a relationship that led to marriage; cf. Plutarch, *Sulla* 35.3–5, *The Parallel Lives*, LCL (1917) 5.438–9.

107 M.K. Hopkins, 'The age of Roman girls at marriage', *Population Studies* 18 (1965) 309–27; Pomeroy, *Goddesses*, 157.

108 Cf. Balsdon, *Roman Women*, 252; and Pliny, *Letters* 5.16, LCL (1915) 1.422–3.

109 Plutarch, *Pompey* 55, *The Parallel Lives*, LCL (1917) 5.260–1, F.E. Adcock, 'Women in Roman life and letters', *Greece and Rome* 14 (1945) 1–22.

110 Sallust, *The War with Cataline* 24.3—25.5, LCL (1960) 42—5.
111 On the Fulvias, cf. Cicero, *Philippics* 2.5.11, 2.44.114, 5.4.11, 6.2.4, LCL (1926) 76—7, 176—7, 266—7, 318—9. Also, Martial, *Epigrams* 11.20.3—8, LCL (1920) 2.252—3.
112 Cf. Valerius Maximus, *Factorum et Dictorum Memorabilium* 8.3.1 (1966) 378. When Maesia's trial took place, theoretically women were not allowed to plead cases.
113 Suetonius, *The Deified Augustus* 84.2, LCL (1914) 1.250—1. Seneca, *De Clementia* I.9.6—10, *Moral Essays*, LCL (1928), 1.382—5.
114 Cf. Balsdon, *Roman Women*, 93ff.; Suetonius, *Galba* 5.2, LCL (1914) 2.198—9.
115 Tacitus, *Annals* 1.8.2, 1.14.3, LCL (1931) 3.256—7, 270—1.
116 Tacitus, *Agricola* 4, LCL (1970) 1.30—3; and *Dialogus* 28—29, LCL (1970) 1.304—9.
117 Plutarch, *Tiberius Gracchus* I, *The Parallel Lives*, LCL (1920) 10.144—7. Thus, Cornelia's example is seen as praiseworthy. Cf. Tacitus, *Dialogus* 28.4—29, LCL (1970) 1.304—9.
118 Suetonius, *The Deified Augustus* 73, LCL (1914) 1.236—9; *CIL* 1211 (1918) I:2.590.
119 Pliny, *Natural History* 18.107, LCL (1950) 5.256—7; cf. 9.67, LCL (1950) 3.206—9. Petronius, *Satyricon* 37, 67, LCL (1969) 64—7, 148—51.
120 Gaius, *Institutes* 1.145, Budé (1950) 28; Gellius, *Attic Nights* 1.12.9—12, LCL (1927) 1.60—1, and 10.15.31, LCL (1927) 2.252—3.
121 Livy 1.20.3, LCL (1919) 1.70—1; Tacitus, *Annals* 4.16.6, LCL (1937) 3.30—1.
122 Matrons cared for the Vestals if they were ill; cf. Pliny, *Letters* 7.19, LCL (1927) 2.46—53.
123 Plutarch, *Numa* 10, *The Parallel Lives*, LCL (1914) 1.342—3.
124 Cf. Tacitus, *Annals* 11.32.5, LCL (1937) 3.302—3; Suetonius, *The Deified Julius* 83, *The Lives of the Caesars*, LCL (1914) 1.112—13; Plutarch, *Antony* 58.3—5, *The Parallel Lives*, LCL (1920) 9.268—71.
125 Plutarch, *Roman Questions* 86, *Moralia*, LCL (1936) 4.130—3.
126 Pomeroy, *Goddesses*, 206.
127 Pomeroy, *Goddesses*, 206—7.
128 Cf. Valerius Maximus, *Factorum et Dictorum Memorabilium* 8.15.12 (1966) 418.
129 Livy 10.31.9, LCL (1926) 4.478—9; cf. Pomeroy, *Goddesses*, 207.
130 Pomeroy, *Goddesses*, 208ff.
131 Cf. Dio Cassius, *Roman History* 56.1—10, LCL (1924) 7.2—25, on the Lex Papia Poppaea of AD 9.
132 Cf. Suetonius, *The Deified Augustus* 89.2, LCL (1914) 1.256—9; Tacitus, *Annals* 3.24, LCL (1931) 3.560—1.
133 There can be little doubt that Augustus saw the neglect of religion as the cause of Rome's difficulties; cf. F. Altheim, *A History of Roman Religion* (London: Methuen and Co., 1938) 355ff.
134 Altheim, *History*, 351—2.
135 Cato, *On Agriculture* 83, LCL (1934) 86—7; Altheim, *History*, 351—2, 390—405.

136 Carcopino, *Daily Life*, 128.
137 Livy 29.14.10, LCL (1949) 8.260–1; cf. 29.10.5, pp.244–5; Donaldson, *Woman*, 94.
138 Livy 39.8.5–39.9.7, LCL (1936) 11.240–5; Donaldson, *Woman*, 95.
139 Petronius, *Satyricon* 44, LCL (1969) 84–7. For, 'No one now believes the gods are gods', see p. 87.
140 Tacitus, *Annals* 2.85, LCL (1931) 3.516–17.
141 Juvenal, *Satires* 6.511–541 (ed. J. D. Duff; Cambridge: Cambridge University Press, 1970) 37–8. The translator also notes the prohibition of the Isis cult within Rome's walls (246). Cf. Pomeroy, *Goddesses*, 221.
142 Pomeroy, *Goddesses*, 214ff. There are reasons to doubt this statement. Cf. S. L. Mohler, 'Feminism in the Corpus Inscriptionum Latinarum', *Classical Weekly* 25 (Feb. 15, 1932) 116.
143 On conversion to Isis, cf. Apuleius, *The Golden Ass (Metamorphoses)*, LCL (1915).
144 Plutarch, *Isis and Osiris* 273e–f, 382c–d, *Moralia*, LCL (1936) 5.128–31, 180–1; *CIL* 3800 (1883) X:1.379.
145 Balsdon, *Roman Women*, 246; Pomeroy, *Goddesses*, 224. Isis was endorsed officially from the time of Caligula onward.
146 *CIL* 2244–2248 (1883) VI:1.617; Pomeroy, *Goddesses*, 223.
147 Pomeroy, *Goddesses*, 224.
148 Pomeroy, *Goddesses*, 223; cf. Valerius Maximus, *Factorum et Dictorum Memorabilium* 1.3.4 (1966) 17.
149 On women in shipbuilding in the time of Claudius, cf. Balsdon, *Roman Women*, 277. H. J. Loane, *Industry and Commerce of the City of Rome (50 BC – AD 200)* (Baltimore: Johns Hopkins University, 1938) mentions extensive inscriptional evidence proving the existence of women owners of fleets (23), dye-making factories (76–7), and brick factories (103–4, 110–11). But cf. Adcock, 'Women', 10. For a summary of the roles of slaves and freed women in rich or imperial homes, cf. S. Treggiari, 'Domestic staff at Rome in the Julio-Claudian period: 27 BC – AD 68', *Histoire Sociale: Revue Canadienne* 6 (1973) 241–55.
150 Pomeroy, *Goddesses*, 198.
151 Columella, *On Agriculture and Trees* 12, preface 9, *De Re Rustica*, LCL (1955) 3.178–9; Cato, *On Agriculture* 143, LCL (1934) 124–5.
152 Pomeroy, *Goddesses*, 229.
153 Cf. the conclusion of J. P. Hallett, 'The role of women in Roman elegy: counter-cultural feminism', *Arethusa* 6:1 (1973) 103–24, espec. 103–7. For helpful bibliographies, cf. S. B. Pomeroy, 'Selected bibliography on women in antiquity', *Arethusa* 6:1 (1973) 125–57, and espec. L. Goodwater, *Women in Antiquity: An Annotated Bibliography* (Metuchen: Scarecrow, 1974).

2 Women and the physical family in the Pauline epistles

1 On the authorship of the Pastorals, see p. 262, and ch. 3, n. 194 on 1 Tim 2.9–15.

2 I owe the progress/problem letter distinction to Allan Chapple, 'Local leadership in the Pauline churches' (Ph.D. dissertation, University of Durham, 1985).

3 Cf. R. and J. Boldrey, *Chauvinist or Feminist?*; P. K. Jewett, *Man as Male and Female* (Grand Rapids: Eerdmans, 1975); V. R. Mollenkott, *Women, Men, and the Bible* (Nashville: Abingdon, 1977); D. Stein, 'Le statut des femmes dans les lettres de Paul', *Lumiere et Vie* 27 (1978) 63–85; H. W. House, 'Paul, women, and contemporary feminism', *BSac* 136 (1979) 40–53; R. W. Graham, 'Women in the Pauline Churches: a review article', *LTQ* 11 (1976) 25–34; A.-M. Dubarle, 'Paul et l'antifeminisme', *RSPT* 60 (1976) 261–80; F. Raurell, 'Saint Paul fut-il misogyne et antifeministe?', *Etudes Franciscaines* 15 (1965) 66–73; G. B. Caird, 'Paul and women's liberty', *BJRL* 54 (1972) 268–81; R. G. Osborne, 'Hermeneutics and women in the Church', *JETS* 20 (1977) 337–47; C. Butler, 'Was Paul a male chauvinist?', *New Blackfriars* 56 (1975) 174–9; R. Scroggs, 'Paul and the eschatological woman', *JAAR* 40 (1972) 283–303; E. A. Leonard, 'St Paul on the status of women', *CBQ* 23 (1950) 311–20; E. Kähler, *Die Frau in den paulinischen Briefen unter besonderer Berücksichtigung des Begriffes der Unterordnung* (Zurich: Gotthelf, 1960).

4 A strong case for Pauline authorship of Ephesians can still be made. Cf. M. Barth, *Ephesians 1–3* (Garden City: Doubleday, 1974) 36–50, Michaelis, Percy, Feuillet, Roller, Sanders, *et al.*, who all support Pauline authorship. Perhaps one of the major arguments against the continuity of content of Ephesians with the undisputed Paulines can be answered if it can be shown that 1 Corinthians 7 and Ephesians 5 are addressing different situations at different points in Paul's career. There are, of course, other weighty arguments against Pauline authorship which we will be unable to deal with in this work. Even if Ephesians is by a Paulinist, rather than Paul himself, its perspective on marriage and women's roles seems to be a legitimate extension of such texts as 1 Corinthians 7. Our working hypothesis, and it is only a hypothesis, is that the arguments against Pauline authorship of Ephesians are not yet compelling.

5 This is the case in 7.1 since ὧν ἐγράψατε is added, and may well be the case in 7.25. On the other hand, the περὶ δέ at 7.25 may be used by Paul to indicate that he is returning to the main discussion after a short digression. If so, then we can see 7.1–40 as one unit with a new discussion beginning not at 7.25 but at 8.1.

6 S. Scott Bartchy, ΜΑΛΛΟΝ ΧΡΗΣΑΙ: *First-Century Slavery and the Interpretation of 1 Corinthians 7.21* (SBLDS: Missoula: Univ. of Montana, 1973) 164; cf. D. R. Cartlidge, '1 Corinthians 7 as a foundation for a Christian sex ethic', *JR* 55 (1975) 220–34, here

221–2. For the view that Paul is engaging in 'apostolic opportunism' in this chapter, cf. H. Chadwick, ' "All things to all men" (1 Cor. IX.22)', *NTS* 1 (1954–55) 261–75, espec. 264ff.

7 As E. Kähler, *Die Frau*, 21, says, '... es in 1. Kor 7 nicht um Aussagen über Mann oder Frau geht, sondern um Aussagen über Mann und Frau!'

8 Bartchy's complete schema cannot be reproduced here; further, it is not necessary to agree with his divisions at every point in order to accept the general format he has discerned (*First Century*, 166–71).

9 J. A. Fischer, 'Paul on virginity', *Bible Today* 72 (1974) 1633–8, here 1637.

10 ἅπτω here may mean 'to touch', but in light of vv. 2ff. it probably means 'to have intercourse with', a well-established Greek usage. Cf. BAG, 102; LSJ, 232. Against the translation 'to marry' offered by Str-B III, 367–8 (cf. *NIV*), is the LXX use of the verb (Gen 20.5, 6; Prov. 6.29) which refers to extra-marital intercourse. Note that Paul uses ἄνθρωπος, not ἀνήρ. The discussion is not solely about the conduct or behavior of a husband and wife, though that is part of the problem. Cf. W. F. Orr and J. A. Walther, *I Corinthians* (Garden City: Doubleday, 1976) 206.

11 Note the position of καλός and its use in v. 8. Cf. H. Conzelmann, 1 Corinthians (Philadelphia: Fortress, 1975) 115; BAG, 401. While καλός may be a comparative here ('it is better'), in view of the context it is probably correct to translate it with 'good' and mean that which is right or praiseworthy. Delling, *Paulus' Stellung*, 69–70, and n. 93.

12 Note that Paul cites a case (v. 5) where such a statement could apply for a brief period even to a married couple if the purpose of the abstention was to further one's devotion to the Lord. Cf. n. 24 below; M. Ket. 5.6, Danby, 252.

13 Cf. J. Jeremias, 'Zur Gedankenführung in den Paulinischen Briefen', *Studia Pauline in honorem Joannis de Zwaan Septuagenarii* (Haarlem: De Erven F. Bohn, 1953) 146–62, here 151–2.

14 Cf. J. J. von Allmen, *Pauline Teaching on Marriage* (London: Faith, 1963) 13–16; Cartlidge, '1 Corinthians 7', 223–4.

15 Cf. F. F. Bruce, *1 and 2 Corinthians* (NCB; Greenwood: Attic, 1971) 66. It is conceivable that these two attitudes toward the body and sexual relations existed in the same group in Corinth, i.e., among the 'Christ' or 'spiritualist' party. The spiritualist could treat bodily functions as either amoral or evil (a hindrance to life in the Spirit). Both views presuppose a body/Spirit or body/soul dichotomy, and both views are contrary to Paul's view of life in the Spirit, especially since he saw the body as playing a role in the eschatological state (cf. 1 Corinthians 15). Cf. D. L. Balch, 'Backgrounds of 1 Cor. VIII: sayings of the Lord in Q; Moses as ascetic ΘΕΙΟΣ ANHP in II Cor. III', *NTS* 18 (1972) 351–64, here 351–2; D. J. Doughty, 'The presence and future of salvation in Corinth', *ZNW* 66 (1975) 61–90, here 66–7.

16 Cf. C. K. Barrett, *The First Epistle to the Corinthians* (New York: Harper & Row, 1968) 155–6.

17 ἐχέτω does not refer to marriage apart from its consummation or, apparently, to the consummation alone, but to co-habitation and that which it normally involves. Cf. BAG, 332; Orr and Walther, *1 Corinthians*, 206; LSJ, 749. It is hard to decide whether or not this advice is directed to those already married. Cf. A. Robertson and A. Plummer, *A Critical and Exegetical Commentary on the First Epistle of St Paul to the Corinthians* (ICC; 2nd ed.; Edinburgh: T. and T. Clark, 1914) 133, says that ἐχέτω does not mean 'keep' and that ἄνθρωπος in v. 1 indicates the unmarried are in view. The difficulty with this view is that Paul addresses the unmarried in v. 8, and if both vv. 2 and 8 address the same group, then the advice seems to conflict.

18 This statement is not to be taken as an abstract remark about humanity in general. There was at least one case of πορνεία (5.1) and perhaps more in the Christian church in Corinth, and Paul is referring to their problem and the proper solution for these Christians in v. 2.

19 Cf. Orr and Walther, *1 Corinthians*, 206.

20 The Jews did not usually place such a duty equally on the male and female; cf. Ben Witherington, *Women in the Ministry of Jesus* (SNTSMS; Cambridge: Cambridge University Press, 1984) 1ff.

21 Here Paul actively stresses male and female equality in marriage. Cf. Barrett, *First Corinthians*, 156. Further, if it had been Paul's view that marriage merely served as a prophylactic to prevent immorality, then he did not need to go beyond v. 3 to say what he does in vv. 4–5.

22 Paul does not say that a person's sexual nature might lead to temptation; rather, the source of the temptation is said to be ὁ Σατανᾶς. διὰ τὴν ἀκρασίαν ὑμῶν need not imply anything negative or sinful about the married person. Paul adds that continence is a χάρισμα ἐκ θεοῦ (cf. n. 26 below).

23 Cf. elsewhere in 1 Corinthians 7 on the use of καλός to mean 'right', 'proper', or possibly here 'well'. Cf. n. 11 above.

24 Pace E.-B. Allo, *Saint Paul – Première Épître aux Corinthiens* (2nd ed.; Paris: Gabalda, 1956) 159; cf. Barrett, *First Corinthians*, 157–8; J. Héring, *The First Epistle of Saint Paul to the Corinthians* (London: Epworth, 1962) 50. Paul does not equate liberation with asexuality, but with sexuality under control (either in a monogamous marriage, or in a unmarried, continent person). Pace, Cartlidge, '1 Corinthians 7', 232.

25 There is a textual problem in v. 7, but δέ is preferred over γάρ for it has strong support in p⁴⁶, ℵ*, A, C, etc. Cf. Metzger, *TC*, 554. Later scribes, thinking that Paul was conceding marriage in v. 6, may have changed the δέ to γάρ, thus making v. 7 an explanation of why Paul conceded marriage. The δέ here is not adversative, but a simple connective. Paul is not opposing his own concession.

26 That Paul is giving advice, not commands, here is clear only in light of what he says about having a χάρισμα, but also in light of v. 35 (οὐκ ἵνα βρόχον ὑμῖν), and v. 40 (κατὰ τὴν ἐμὴν γνώμην, cf. v. 25).

Thus, while the present tense of θέλω indicates that Paul sees this as realizable in some cases, he knows it is not in all cases and cannot be commanded. But cf. Barrett, *First Corinthians,* 158. The χάρισμα probably is in refrence to the gift which allows one to remain single or married. Paul is not referring to marriage or singleness *per se* as a χάρισμα. Cf. Héring, *First Corinthians*, 50; Conzelmann, *1 Corinthians*, 118; Kähler, *Die Frau*, 208, n. 35.

27 It seems likely that Paul was a widower. This is so since Paul considered himself a good Jew, 'extremely zealous for the traditions of my ancestors' (Gal 1.14; cf. Rom 11.1; 2 Cor 11.22). Further, he was a rabbi and a good Pharisee (Acts 22.6; Phil 3.4–6), a member of mainstream Judaism. Unlike Jesus, he had no special mission or Messianic consciousness which might cause him to diverge from the rabbinic dictum that Jewish men were obligated to marry and procreate. On this issue, cf. J. Jeremias, 'War Paulus Witwer?', *ZNW* 28 (1929) 321–3; J. M. Ford, 'Levirate marriage in St Paul', *NTS* 10 (1964) 351–5, here 351; A. Peters, 'St Paul and marriage – a study of 1 Corinthians chapter 7', *AER* (1964) 214–24, here 218–19. In light of Paul's views on the indissolubility of marriage prior to death (1 Cor 7.11, 39; Rom 7.2–3), 1 Cor 9.5 would seem to favor the interpretation that Paul's wife was dead.

28 Cf. Barrett, *First Corinthians*, 160–2; Héring, *First Corinthians*, 51; Robertson and Plummer, *First Corinthians*, 138.

29 So H. Lietzmann, *An die Korinther I, II* (HNT; Tübingen: J. C. B. Mohr, 1969) 31; Kähler, *Die Frau*, 25. Orr and Walther, *1 Corinthians,* 219; J. M. Ford, 'St Paul, the philogamist (I Cor VII in early patristic exegesis)', *NTS* 11 (1965) 326–48, here 331, n. 2. ἄγαμος occurs in 7.11, 32, 34 only. The following points favor the translation 'widowers' here: (1) in v. 11 the adjectival form is applied to a woman who has been married but is now separated; (2) in v. 34 the ἄγαμος woman is distinguished from the virgin (cf. below on textual problem); (3) the reference to ἄγαμος in v. 32, coming as it does in the midst of several verses about what married people do (vv. 27, 39, 44), may refer to the behavior of one who has also been married though it could refer to all the unmarried whether single or widowed; (4) the masculine noun counterpart to χήρα is not found in the LXX or NT; ἄγαμος then is the most likely word to be used in its place; (5) if Paul is addressing widowers and widows in vv. 8–9, then vv. 25–38 begin a different discussion where Paul is addressing those who have never been married, but he uses illustrations from the state of those presently or formerly married to make his point, i.e., those who are or have been married can testify that being married allows one more time to devote to the Lord's service (cf. v. 34) – if so, then Paul is addressing different groups, each in turn, though he refers to the state of other groups already discussed to make his point (vv. 25–38); (6) cf. MM, 1; LSJ, 5; BAG, 4; A–S, 3; the word itself is not a technical term for widow(er), but in 1 Corinthians 7 it appears to be used specifically of those once married.

30 Verse 29 is too far removed to connect it to this verse.
31 Cf. *TEV*; *NIV*; Moffatt; *RSV*; *NEB*; Phillips.
32 Cf. M L. Barre, 'To marry or to burn: πυροῦσθαι in 1 Cor 7:9', *CBQ* 36 (1974) 193–202. Bruce, *1 and 2 Corinthians*, 68, cites several possible rabbinic parallels that may support this view.
33 Cf. Eph 6.16; 2 Pet 3.12; Rev 1.14, 3.18; and with the noun, 1 Pet 4.12; Rev 18.9, 18. 2 Cor 11.29 is the only other verse in the NT that might support the usual translation. There is no precedent for it in the Hebrew OT, though some parallels can be found in secular Greek and possibly the Maccabean literature. Cf. Barre, 'To marry or to burn', 194–5; F. Lang, 'πυρόω', *TDNT* 6 (1968) 948–50; LSJ, 1555, 1558.
34 Barre, 'To marry or to burn', 199; cf. Robertson, 1007–8; MHT III, 115; Paul knows this is happening.
35 Cf. B. Vawter, 'Divorce and the New Testament', *CBQ* 39 (1977) 527–42, here 536–7 and n. 16.
36 So BAG, 125; A–S, 71; LSJ, 290; Bultmann, 'ἀφίημι', *TDNT* 1 (1964) 510. The passage usually cited from Herodotus does not seem to use this verb of divorce. The phrases in question read, τὴν μὲν ἔχεις γυναῖκα ... ἔξεο, and τὴν ἔχει γυναῖκα ἐοῦσαν. In both cases Godley translates it 'send away'. Cf. Herodotus 5.39, LCl (1971) 42–3.
37 Witherington, *Women*, ch. 2–3.
38 So von Allmen, *Pauline Teaching*, 55.
39 BDF, sec. 373, p. 190.
40 Cf. Rom 8.35, 39; Phlm 15; Heb 7.26; or, as in Acts 1.4, 18.1–2, 'to leave'. Cf. J. K. Elliott, 'Paul's teaching on marriage in 1 Corinthians: some problems considered', *NTS* 19 (2, 1973) 219–25, here 223. So Vawter, 'Divorce', 526, against R. L. Roberts, 'The meaning of *chorizō* and *douloō* in 1 Corinthians 7:10–17', *ResQ* 8 (3, 1965) 179–84. Even if separation is referred to, it need not be thought of in legal terms or be equated with later ideas and practices of separation of 'bed and board'.
41 Cf. Robert, 'Meaning', 179–80; MM, 696; A–S, 486; BAG, 898; LSJ, 2016.
42 If the reference is to the action of an interfering party, whether one of the marriage partners or an outsider, then the word cannot be translated 'divorce' since it is impossible for anyone but the two marriage partners to divorce the other. The verb must be translated so that it could refer to the activity of anyone involving a third party.
43 Cf. Eph 2.3; 1 Thess 4.13, 5.6; Robertson and Plummer, *First Corinthians*, 141; P. Dulau, 'The Pauline privilege − is it promulgated in the First Epistle to the Corinthians?', *CBQ* 13 (1951) 146–52, here 50.
44 As Peters, 'St Paul and marriage', 221, rightly says, 'It is difficult to see how Paul could have written these words if for him marriage were not more than a mere *remedium concupiscentiae.*'
45 Note the following: (1) when Paul refers to the marriage bond in v. 39 he uses the verb δέω (cf. vv. 27, 39), not δουλόω as here;

as Robertson and Plummer (*First Corinthians*, 143) note, it seems natural to see peace as opposed to bondage in v. 15; (3) Roberts ('Meaning', 182) notes that δουλόω is seldom used to refer to the marital bond, and says, 'The force, then, of οὐ δεδούλωται is that the believer is not obligated to prevent the divorcing at the cost of losing all liberty, which is exactly what enslavement would be in this case' (181). Cf. Dulau, 'Pauline privilege', 151–2. Paul is not referring to marriage as bondage, but to situations where a Christian feels obligated to maintain a relationship at the price of his or her Christian peace.

46 Note that peace is associated with order (1 Cor 14.33). Disorder is produced when someone tries to restrain someone else from leaving when they are determined to go.

47 Cf. J. Jeremias, 'Die Missionarische Aufgabe in der Mischehe (1 Cor 7.16)', *Neutestamentliche Studien für Rudolf Bultmann zu seinem siebsigsten Geburtstag* (BZNW 21; Berlin: A. Töpelmann, 1954) 255–60; C. Burchard, 'Ei nach einem Ausdruck des Wissens oder Nichtwissens Joh 9.25, Ac 19.2, 1 Cor 1.16', *ZNW* 52 (1961) 73–82; and espec. Epictetus 2.20, 28–31, 2.22.31, LCL (1926) 1.380–1, 402–3.

48 S. Kubo, 'I Corinthians VII.16: optimistic or pessimistic?' *NTS* 24 (4, 1978) 539–44, here 542. I owe most of the arguments in this section to Kubo.

49 Cf. n. 46 above; with Robertson and Plummer, *First Corinthians*, 143–4; Conzelmann, *1 Corinthians*, 123–4, n. 48.

50 Kubo, 'I Corinthians VII.16', 544.

51 Barrett, *First Corinthians*, 166–7; contrast J. Weiss, *Der erste Korintherbrief* (KEK 5; Göttingen: Vandenhoeck and Ruprecht, 1910) 183.

52 Since this is advice for all the churches (by which Paul may mean all his churches), it is not given in reaction to a specific problem (e.g., persecution) that one church or group of churches in a certain area was facing.

53 So Lietzmann, *An die Korinther I, II*, 32.

54 This may be a point against seeing the discussion that follows as involving spiritual marriage or some sort of celibate relationship, or it may mean that Paul did not know Matt 19.10–12 or did not think it applied to the present situation.

55 It is possible that this was a Corinthian slogan which Paul accepts but qualifies. Cf. Jeremias, 'Zur Gedankenführung', 151. On the other hand, Paul uses the phrase or its variants as if it were his own (vv. 17–24).

56 Pace Conzelmann, *1 Corinthians*, 132, n. 19.

57 συστέλλω is taken from nautical usage where it means to shorten a sail. It is used in the NT only here and at Acts 5.6 where it has a somewhat transferred sense of 'wrapped up tight' ('shortened' or 'contracted' is more likely). Cf. Allo, *Première Épître aux Corinthians*, 179. Weiss, *Der erste Korintherbrief*, 196, rightly notes that Paul says ἐνεστῶσαν ἀνάγκην, not μέλλουσαν ἀνάγκην, and

yet he wrongly equates their meaning. Elsewhere Paul contrasts the
meaning of these two words; cf. Rom 8.38, 1 Cor 3.22. Cf. also
3 Mac 1.16 and Delling, *Paulus' Stellung*, 77, n. 141 ('ἐνεστώς heisst
gegenwärtig im Ausdrücklichen Gegensatz zur Zukunft').
58 In the Pauline corpus τὸ λοιπόν is used to introduce a sentence (cf.
Phil 3.1, 4.8; 2 Thess 3.1). It is disputed whether the sense is 'now'
or 'from now on' (henceforth). Cf. Barrett, *First Corinthians*, 176;
Turner, MHT III, 336; MHT IV, 92; BDF, sec. 168, p. 88 and sec.
451.6, p. 235; Moule, *I–B*, 34, 39, 161–2, 207.
59 'The outward form (or pattern) of this world is passing away.'
According to Barrett (*First Corinthians*, 178), '... Paul's point is
not the transiency of creation as such, but the fact that its outward
pattern in social and mercantile institutions, for example, has no
permanence.' Cf. Doughty, 'Presence and future', 69. There is a
possibility that παράγει here means 'is misleading (or deceiving)'.
Cf. Epictetus, 2.7.14, LCL (1925) 1.258–9 (παράγεις parallels
διαφθείρεις), and 2.20.7, LCL (1925) 1.372 (παράγεσθε parallels
ἐξαπατάσθε and means 'leads astray'). The point in 1 Corinthians
7 would be that the form of this world may seem to indicate a
permanent order of things, but this is misleading.
60 The problem in Corinth is that both ascetics and libertines
misunderstood the nature of salvation in Christ in both its present
and future aspects. The Corinthians are still shaping their lives with
reference to the world and material existence as such. The libertines
disdain the world, the ascetics renounce it, but in both cases their
lifestyle is being determined more by what they reject than by real
Christian principles. In neither case do they realize that the world
and the human body which is a part of this material existence have
a place in God's salvation plan. In 1 Corinthians 7 Paul sets out
to correct their misunderstandings about the nature of salvation,
and in the process he corrects both their 'already' and 'not yet'. The
Christian existence he advocates, and the imperatives he gives, are
determined not by what is not yet true about Christians (a defensive
posture), but as a result of what Christ has done and what is true
about this 'time', and about Christians in this eschatological time.
Paul's view does not amount to an endorsement of the status quo;
he is not indicating any sort of endorsement for any ethnic group,
social class, sex, or economic position. He is advocating that
Christians have a Christian attitude to their situation no matter what
it is. He does state his preference for the single life over the married
state, but again his reasons for doing so have more to do with his
belief that in the Christian era a single person can better give
undivided attention to God. This amounts to a sort of religious
pragmatism, not a sociological program that argues that singleness
is inherently better than marriage, maleness better than femaleness,
abstaining from sex better than having sexual relations, being
circumcised better than not being circumcised, etc. (cf. v. 19).
61 Cf. J. Christian Beker, *Paul's Apocalyptic Gospel. The Coming
Triumph of God* (Philadelphia: Fortress, 1982) 48–9.

62 Cf. von Allmen, *Pauline Teaching*, 19–20.
63 J. K. Elliott, 'Paul's teaching on marriage in 1 Corinthians: some problems considered', *NTS* 19 (2, 1973) 219–25, argues well for the second option.
64 παρθένος in v. 25 could refer to unmarried men as well as women (cf. Rev 14.4). More likely Paul is primarily addressing men and telling them what to do about their betrothed virgins (vv. 25ff.). Elsewhere in the NT παρθένος is used of a betrothed girl. Cf. Luke 1.27; Matt 1.23; possibly 25.1–3; 2 Cor 11.2. It is also possible that while in vv. 25–35 παρθένος is used simply in a non-technical sense of a girl who has never married, in vv. 36ff. Paul uses the term to refer to an engaged girl, a fact indicated not by a technical use of παρθένος, but by the addition of the possessive adjective (cf. vv. 36, 37, 38); but cf. Elliott, 'Paul's teaching', 220–1. Notice in v. 39 that a woman's husband is described as ὁ ἀνὴρ αὐτῆς.
65 Doughty, 'Presence and future', 67. It is unwarranted to import a ('already') into the second half of each of these dialectical statements.
66 Doughty, 'Presence and future', 72, n. 50. Cf. H. J. Schoeps, *Paul – The Theology of the Apostle in Light of Jewish Religious History* (trans. H. Knight; Philadelphia: Fortress, 1961) 211, who states, 'The Stoic solution of ἀταραξία may sound similar but has quite different roots. Paul's detachment from the world springs entirely from his relation to Christ ...' Cf. Diogenes Laertius 6.29, LCL (1925) 2.30–1.
67 Noting the change from ἀγοράζοντες to κατέχοντες. κατέχω means 'to keep (in one's possession)' here. Cf. BAG, 424; LSJ, 926; A–S, 241.
68 Doughty, 'Presence and future', 71, n. 47, says the nuance between χράομαι ('to use') and καταχράομαι ('to take full advantage of') is slight but significant. LSJ, 921; Barrett, *First Corinthians*, 178; Hering, *First Corinthians*, 59; AS, 240.
69 Doughty, 'Presence and future', 72.
70 On the face of it, ἄγαμος here could mean unmarried rather than widower (v. 32). If so, v. 33 would balance v. 32; however, v. 34 distinguishes between a woman who has yet to be married (παρθένος) and ἡ γυνὴ ἡ ἄγαμος which is probably a reference to the formerly married. In v. 34 the reading μεριμνᾷ is to be preferred; following Metzger, *TC*, 555–6; Elliott, 'Paul's teaching', 221.
71 It may be a point against Elliott's view that παρθένος means 'betrothed woman' throughout vv. 25–38, that here it is said the παρθένος *is* concerned about the things of the Lord. Clearly, a betrothed woman in Paul's day was not completely free from concern for her husband-to-be, especially in view of the serious and binding character of betrothal in various parts of the first-century world.
72 Cf. W. G. Kümmel, 'Verlobung und Heirat bei Paulus (I Cor 7, 36–38)', *Neutestamentliche Studien für Rudolf Bultmann*, 275–95, here 277–8. On the current defenders of this view, cf. Hering,

First Corinthians, 63—5; R.H.A. Seboldt, 'Spiritual marriage in the early church – a suggested interpretation of 1 Cor. 7.36—38', *CTM* 30 (1959) 176—89; cf. Delling, *Paulus' Stellung*, 85—91.

73 The evidence sometimes cited from the Shepherd of Hermas, Similitude 9, 11, 3, *Apostolic Fathers* (London: Macmillan and Co. 1907) 381, 468, does not support the spiritual marriage view. In the explanation of this similitude (9, 13, 2—3, pp.383, 469) it is said that the virgins are powers of the Son of God, and Hermas is made to pass the night with them ('as a brother, not a husband') as a part of his enlightenment. As D.E.H. Whiteley, *The Theology of St Paul* (Philadelphia: Fortress, 1972) 218, says, 'It would appear wholly gratuitous to imagine that Hermas is making an oblique reference to customs at Rome in his own day.' As J.M. Ford, 'Paul the philogamist', 326—48, shows, not until the second or third century do we have any real references in Christian literature to consecrated virginity, much less a spiritual marriage. Nor is there any clear evidence that 1 Corinthians 7 was used in this regard until the mid third century.

74 As Kümmel, 'Verlobung und Heirat', 289, says, the word does not seem to have any special ascetical sense here.

75 Cf. Rom 1.27, 1 Cor 12.23. At 1 Cor 13.5 it appears to have a somewhat more general sense, though it is possible even here that Paul is saying 'love is not (sexually) improper' – a piece of advice the Corinthians need to hear. Cf. Kümmel, 'Verlobung und Heirat', 280, and n.15.

76 Cf. BDF, sec. 101, p.51; MHT II, 409—10; MHT III, 57; Lietzmann, *Korinther I, II*, 350—6. Contrast, Allo, *Première Épître aux Corinthiens*, 185, and especially Kümmel, 'Verlobung und Heirat', 288, and n.48, who notes Paul's use of γνωρίζω in Phil 1.22 in the same sense as his regular use of γινώσκω.

77 Cf. the examples cited by Kümmel, 'Verlobung und Hierat', 270, n.12, and 280.

78 Cf. Witherington, *Women*, ch. 2; Kümmel, 'Verlobung und Hierat', 283—6. If Colossians is Pauline, then Col 3.21 would tend to argue against the view that father and daughter are being referred to in 1 Cor 7.36—38.

79 Ford, 'Levirate marriage', 362—4, argues that Levirate marriage is in view here, but overlooks that Levirate marriage was probably in disuse even in Israel at this time. It seems improbable that it was being practised in the Corinthian Christian community at any time. Cf. Witherington, *Women*, 101, and n.185.

80 ὑπέρακμος can equally well refer to the man as to the woman; probably the former.

81 On εἰ plus the present tense of the verb, cf. n.34 above; Turner, MHT III, 115, says of 7.36: 'Paul knows this is actually happening'.

82 This seems to be the meaning of 'his virgin' in these verses; cf. Barrett, *First Corinthians*, 184.

83 τηρεῖν τὴν ἑαυτοῦ παρθένον probably means 'to keep his virgin (as she is)', not 'to support his virgin', or 'to keep his virgin (for

himself)' (with the implication of marriage). Cf. Barrett, *First Corinthians*, 185; Robertson and Plummer, *First Corinthians*, 160; Kümmel, 'Verlobung und Heirat', 293–4.

84 Pliny the Younger, Letter I.9, LCL (1923) 1.30–1, says 'sponsalia aut nuptia frequentavi'. Cf. Conzelmann, *1 Corinthians*, 135, n. 4, for examples from Greek literature.

85 Cf. Kümmel, 'Verlobung und Heirat', 290–4.

86 Cf. Rom 7.1–2. It is possible that the use of δέω of the marital bond is not a technical usage but Paul's way of indicating an irreversible obligation to a relationship whether it be to one's marriage partner as here or, as seems possible in v. 27, to one's betrothed. Note that in v. 27 δέω is used only once and the parallel positive statement speaks of seeking a woman, not marrying one. This would be natural if 'being bound' in v. 27 refers to engagement which is the first step involving real commitment that one takes if one is seeking a wife.

87 Héring, *First Corinthians*, 65; Orr and Walther, *1 Corinthians*, 225; Bruce, *1 and 2 Corinthians*, 77; but cf. Barrett, *First Corinthians*, 186; Robertson and Plummer, *First Corinthians*, 161.

88 M. Dibelius, *An die Kolosser, Epheser an Philemon* (HNT; Tübingen: J. C. B. Mohr, 1913); K. Weidinger, *Die Haustafeln, ein Stück urchristliche Paränese* (UNT; Leipzig: J. C. Henrich, 1928).

89 J. E. Crouch, *The Origin and Intention of the Colossian Haustafel* (Göttingen: Vandenhoeck and Ruprecht, 1972); E. Lohse, *A Commentary on the Epistles to the Colossians and to Philemon* (trans. W. R. Poehlmann and R. J. Karris; Philadelphia: Fortress, 1971). W. Lillie, 'The Pauline house-tables', *ET* 86 (1975) 179–83. E. Schweizer, 'Traditional ethical patterns in the Pauline and post-Pauline letters and their development (lists of vices and housetables)', *Text and Interpretation* (ed. E. Best and R. Mcl. Wilson; Cambridge: Cambridge University Press, 1979) 195–209.

90 K. H. Rengstorf, 'Die neutestamentlichen Mahnungen an die Frau, sich dem Manne unterzuordnen', *Verbum Dei Manet in Aeternum* (ed. W. Foerster; Witten: Luther, 1953) 131–45; D. Schroeder, 'Die Haustafeln des Neuen Testaments (ihre Herkunft und Theologischer Sinn)', (Ph.D. dissertation; Hamburg: Mikrokopie, 1959); also Schroeder, 'Lists, ethical', *IDB Suppl.*, 546–7.

91 D. L. Balch, *Let Wives Be Submissive: The Domestic Code in 1 Peter* (SBLMS 26; Chico: Scholars, 1981).

92 M. Hengel, *Judaism and Hellenism* (2 vols.; Philadelphia: Fortress, 1974).

93 Cf. G. E. Cannon, *The Use of Traditional Materials in Colossians* (Macon: Mercer University, 1983) 100ff.

94 Cf. pp. 45–7 below.

95 Balch, *Let Wives Be Submissive*, 1–80, has more than adequately demonstrated this.

96 This might suggest that NT household tables were only addressed to those financially able to have slaves – except for two factors: (1) clearly the material is included in letters that are addressed to Christian communities; (2) since slaves, wives, and children are also

addressed directly, it follows that this is not merely material for the well-to-do household owner. Various families had children that could not have slaves, and slaves who were addressed were not themselves well-to-do of course. This is an ethic attempting to cover all the basic stations of life.

97 Aristotle, *Politics* 1253b.8, LCL (1944) 12–13.
98 Aristotle, *Politics* 1254a.22–24, LCL (1944).
99 Balch, *Let Wives Be Submissive*, 34.
100 Ibid., 6.
101 Epictetus, *Discourses* 3.2.4, LCL (1928) 2.22–23 on duties as father, brother, etc.
102 Seneca, *On Benefits* 2.18.1, *Moral Essays*, LCL (1935) 3.84–5; Horace, *Ars Poetica* 1.310, LCL (1929) 476–7; Cicero, *De Officiis* 17.58, LCL (1961) 21:52–61.
103 Plato, *Laws* 7.793, LCL (1926) 11:18–19; Xenophon, *Memorabilia* 4.19–24, LCL (1965) 322–2; Sophocles, *Antigone* 450, LCL (1968) 348–9.
104 Crouch, *Origin*, 72ff.
105 Philo, *Decalogue* 165–167, LCL (1937) 7:88–9; *Special Laws* 2.225–227 and 3.169–171, LCL (1937) 7:446–9, 580–3; Philo, *The Posterity of Cain* 181, LCL (1929) 2:434–5 on the loving care of a wife.
106 Philo, *Apology for the Jews* 7.3, 5–6, LCL (1941) 9.424–5.
107 Josephus, *Against Apion* 2.199, LCL (1926) 1.372, and n. 4. Various scholars suspect this material to be a Christian insertion into Josephus.
108 Plutarch, *Advice to Bride and Groom* 142, E, *Moralia*, LCL (1928) 2:322–3.
109 Cf. articles in both the 1st and 2nd editions of *Oxford Classical Dictionary* on Pseudo-Callisthenes, *Der griechische Alexanderorum.*
110 Cf. Lillie, 'The Pauline house-tables', 179–83, who also rightly points out the quotation of the fifth commandment in Eph 6.2–3, and the reference to Sarah's attitude at 1 Pet 3.6.
111 C. F. D. Moule, *Epistles to the Colossians and to Philemon* (CGTC; Cambridge: Cambridge University Press, 1968) 127–8.
112 But cf. Schweizer, 'Traditional ethical patterns', *Text and Interpretation*, 201–2.
113 Schroeder, 'Die Haustafeln', 10ff; and 'Lists', *IDB Suppl.*, 547.
114 Cf. Lohse, *Colossians*, 156ff.; Cannon, *Traditional Materials*, 96ff.
115 But cf. E. Selwyn, *The First Epistle of St Peter* (London: Macmillan, 1947) 420ff.
116 Cf. F. F. Bruce, *The Epistles to the Colossians, to Philemon, and to the Ephesians* (Grand Rapids: Eerdmans, 1984) 162; Selwyn, *1 Peter*, 419ff.; Schroeder, 'Lists', *IDB Suppl.*, 546–7; P. Carrington, *The Primitive Christian Catechism* (Cambridge: Cambridge University Press, 1940).
117 R. P. Martin, *Colossians and Philemon* (London: Oliphants, 1974) 117–18.

118 Moule, *Colossians*, 126; E. Schweizer, *The Letter to the Colossians* (Minneapolis: Augsburg, 1982) 213.
119 Cannon, *Use of Traditional Materials*, 98.
120 Ibid., 131.
121 Cf. pp. 84–6 on Gal 3.28.
122 Kähler, *Die Frau*, 7ff.
123 E. G. Hinson, 'The Christian household in Colossians 3.18–4.1', *RevExp* 70 (1973) 495–506.
124 Cf. pp. 46–7 above, and P. T. O'Brien, *Colossians, Philemon* (Waco: Word, 1982) 221.
125 Cf. p. 46 above.
126 BAG, 855; G. Delling, 'τάσσω', *TDNT* 8 (1972) 41–6.
127 Delling, 'τάσσω', *TDNT* 8 (1972) 45.
128 Nevertheless, that all Christian wives are expected to submit to all Christian husbands without exception (apparently), seems to suggest that at least in the case of the Christian husband and wife, gender is the determining factor deciding the order of the relationship. Cf. pp. 54ff. below on Eph 5.21–22.
129 Cf. pp. 52–3 below defining ὑποτάσσω.
130 Cf. O'Brien, *Colossians*, 222; H. Schlier, 'καθηκω', *TDNT* 3 (1965) 437–40; and the citation of the relevant texts from Stoicism in Lohse, *Colossians*, 158, n. 23.
131 Cf. Robertson, 887; BDF, 358.2, p. 181; MHT III, 90.
132 Cf. Col 3.20, 4.7, 17; and for other domestic usages, cf. 1 Cor 7.22, 39; Eph 6.1; Phlm 16.
133 Moule, *Colossians*, 129. While it is true that the phrase at least means 'as is fitting within the Christian fellowship', ἐν κυρίῳ may be an example of Paul's incorporation of language which refers frequently to the personal union one has with Christ in His Body. If this is implied here, then Schweizer may be right (*Colossians*, 216) that it means the Lord is the criterion of what is fitting.
134 Cf. Lohse, *Colossians*, 158.
135 Lohse, *Colossians*, 158, n. 28; W. Schrage, 'Zur Ethik der neutestamentlichen Haustafeln', *NTS* 21 (1974–75) 1–22, here 12–13.
136 Bruce, *Colossians*, 164, n. 179.
137 Cf. O'Brien, *Colossians*, 223.
138 Cf. the discussion of Plutarch, *On the Control of Anger* 457a, in Schweizer, *Colossians*, 222, n. 43, though Bruce rightly points out that Plutarch uses the compound form of the verb διακραίνονται. This sort of exhortation is also known in Judaism; cf. B. T. Babba Mei'a 59a in Str-B III, 631.
139 Cf. BAG, 567; W. Michaelis, 'πικρός', *TDNT* 6 (1968) 122–5, seems to be going too far in suggesting that unprovoked bitterness and anger is in view.
140 Cf. O'Brien, *Colossians*, 227.
141 Hinson, 'Christian household', 499–500.
142 Cf. Crouch, *Origin*, 114; Cannon, *Traditional Materials*, 117.
143 Cf. W. Foerster, 'ἀρεστός', *TDNT* 1 (1964) 456; BAG, 378.

144 O'Brien, *Colossians*, 224–5.
145 i.e., 0198, 81 al: Clement of Alexandria.
146 Cf. MHT III, 263.
147 Cf. O'Brien, *Colossians*, 225; Bruce, *Colossians*, 165; Lohse, *Colossians*, 159.
148 G. Schrenk, 'πατήρ', *TDNT* 5 (1967) 950–1; Philo, *Apology for the Jews* 7.2, LCL (1941) 9.422–3; *Special Laws* 2.232, LCL (1937) 7.450–3; Josephus, *Against Apion* 2.206, LCL (1926) 1.376–7; *Antiquities* 4.264, LCL (1930) 4.602–3.
149 Notice Cannon's (*Traditional Materials*, 120) conclusion: 'In spite of the weaknesses in the arguments of Rengstorf and Schroeder, they nevertheless draw attention to a distinctly Christian situation for the use of the Haustafel in primitive Christianity.'
150 We will not deal with the material in 1 Tim 2.8–15 and 6.1–10 or Titus 2.1–10 at this point for several reasons. (1) We have only fragments of any sort of table in this material; e.g., in 1 Tim 6.1ff. and Titus 2.9–10 slaves are admonished without any admonition for masters. The direct address format is also lacking. (2) It appears that at least in 1 Tim 2.8–15 what we have is a specific discussion about behavior in worship, not just general household advice. (3) 1 Tim 6.1–10 does not refer to women or wives as such, only to servants and their relation to their masters. (4) Most scholars judge at least 2 Timothy and Titus to be examples of Paulinism but not from Paul, though a good case can be made for 1 Timothy being Pauline. We will deal with 1 Timothy 2 in the next chapter, and Titus 2.9–10 as a later development (whether of or by Paul). 1 Pet 3.1–9 will be dealt with in passing in this section. Cf. J. P. Sampley, *And the Two Shall Become One Flesh* (SNTSMS 16; Cambridge: Cambridge University Press, 1971) 22.
151 Cf. Sampley, *And the Two*, 21ff.
152 Barth, *Ephesians 4–6*, 632.
153 Sampley, *And the Two*, 25.
154 Cf. E. Best, *One Body in Christ* (London: SPCK, 1955) 172ff.
155 Cf. H. Conzelmann, *Der Brief an die Epheser* (NTD 8; Göttingen: Vandenhoeck & Ruprecht, 1976) 118–19.
156 Cf. our text and 2 Cor 11.2; note the close parallel between παραστῆσαι τῷ Χριστῷ and παραστήσῃ αὐτὸς ἑαυτῷ. This factor also argues against seeing some allusion to a *hieros gamos* already 'made in heaven' and in effect now, much less a Gnostic celestial marriage. Cf. E. Percy, *Die Probleme der Kolosser und Epheserbriefe* (Lund: C. W. K. Gleerup, 1946) 395ff.
157 Cf. F. Stagg, 'The domestic code and the final appeal, Ephesians 5.21–6.24', *RevExp* 76 (1979) 541–52: 'The Ephesian code was developed to bring existing structures, including slavery and their customs, under Christian impact.' What we see here and elsewhere in the NT is the attempt to reform these structures *from the inside out*. The structures are neither repudiated nor endorsed, but reformed in light of the new creation brought about by and in Christ. Cf. E. Fiorenza, 'Marriage and disciple', *Bible Today* (April, 1979) 2027–34.

158 J. M. Robinson, 'Die Hodajot – Formel in Gebet und Hymnus des Früchristentums', *Apophoreta: Festschrift für Ernst Haenchen* (Berlin: A. Töpelmann, 1964) 194–235; cf. Sampley, *And the Two*, 115ff.

159 D. Daube, 'Participle and imperative', in Selwyn, *First Peter*, 467–88. This may suggest a Jewish-Christian author here which with other pieces of evidence might support Pauline authorship of Ephesians.

160 Cf. Sampley, *And the Two*, 114ff.

161 H. Schlier, *Der Brief an die Epheser* (Düsseldorf: Patmos, 1962) 252.

162 C. Masson, *L'Épître de Saint Paul aux Ephesiens* (Neuchâtel/Paris: Delachaux and Niestlé, 1953) 211, says the sense of ὑποτάσσω here is 'subordinate yourself', not 'be subordinate', and thus refers to a voluntary act accomplished by the wife. It is significant that ὑπακούω, not ὑποτάσσω, is used of slaves and children but not wives.

163 Sampley, *And the Two*, 121–3.

164 Cf. Metzger, *TC*, 608–9.

165 Barth, *Ephesians* 4–6, 612; T. K. Abbott, *Epistles to the Ephesians and to the Colossians* (Edinburgh: T. and T. Clark, 1897) 165.

166 Kähler, *Die Frau*, 101ff.

167 Cf. pp. 84–5; also S. Bedale, 'The meaning of κεφαλή in the Pauline epistles', *JTS* n.s. 5 (1954) 211–15; BAG, 431; LSJ, 945.

168 Aristotle, *Politics* 1254ab, 1255b, LCL (1932) 21: cf. Plutarch, *Advice to Bride and Groom* 142E, *Moralia*, LCL (1928) 2: Apparently Chrysippus called God head of administration of the world. Cf. Best, *One Body*, 222–3; E. Bevan, *Later Greek Religion* (London/New York: Dent/Dutton, 1927) 4, 13, 32.

169 M. Dibelius, *An Die Kolosser, Epheser an Philemon* (HGNT 12; Tübingen: J. C. B. Mohr, 1953) 93.

170 Bruce, *Colossians*, 384; Best, *One Body*, 1955, 179.

171 Cf. Barth, *Ephesians* 4–6, 617–18 and notes.

172 Barth, *Ephesians* 4–6, 619.

173 Codex Sinaiticus, the mss. of the Antiochian group, and the Syro-Palestinian version all omit καί but it is included in p⁴⁶, and various of the major codices including Vaticanus. Cf. Barth, *Ephesians 4–6*, 630, n.80.

174 Cf. J. A. Robinson, *St Paul's Epistle to the Ephesians* (London: Macmillan, 1904) 28.

175 Barth, *Ephesians 4–6*, 629–30; Bruce, *Colossians*, 391.

176 Sampley, *And the Two*, 30ff., who points out the evidence for Lev 11.18 being used as an exhortation to husbands about their response to wives.

177 There is some significant evidence for the term 'body' being used of the state or of a cosmic body of which we are all a part, outside the NT in the first century. Cf. Seneca, *Epistulae Morales* 95.51ff, LCL (1953) 6.90–1 ('membra summus corporis magni'). Cf. W. L. Knox, *St Paul and the Church of the Gentiles* (Cambridge: Cambridge University Press, 1979) 160–3, citing Dionysius of

Halicarnassus, *Ant. Rom.* III, II.5. While this may have significant bearing on the discussion of the Christ/Church pair, it seems an unlikely source for or influence on the husband/wife, head/body discussion, since the latter does not involve any corporate entity.

178 Cf. pp. 35ff. above, and pp. 62ff. below. The person who separates is to remain unmarried presumably because the initial union is still in force in Paul's view. This also seems to have been Jesus' view; cf. Witherington, *Women* 27–8.

179 Cf. chapter 4, pp. 78ff.

180 Cf. R. E. Brown, 'The Semitic background of the New Testament "Mysterion" II', *Bib* 40 (1959) 70–87, and von Allmen, *Pauline Teaching*, 35.

181 Robinson, *Ephesians*, 209.

182 Kähler, *Die Frau*, 126ff.; Bruce, *Colossians*, 395.

183 Kähler, *Die Frau*, 134; cf. J. Cambier, 'Le grand mystère concernant le Christ et son Eglise, Ephesiens 5, 22–33', *Bib* 47 (1966) 143–90, 223–42, here 146. Cambier also points out that the Jews did not use the term 'head' of the husband.

184 Sampley, *And the Two*, 86ff., says that the use of ἐγὼ δὲ λέγω was traditional when one wanted to offer an interpretation of an OT text *different* from the prevailing opinion in Judaism.

185 On the background here, see R. Batey, 'The ΜΙΑ ΣΑΡΞ union of Christ and the Church', *NTS* 13 (1966–67) 270–81; and his 'Jewish Gnosticism and the "Hieros Gamos" of Eph. v.21–33', *NTS* 10 (1963–64) 121–7.

186 Barth, *Ephesians 4–6*, 618ff.

187 BDF, 449.2, p. 234.

188 Barth, *Ephesians 4–6*, 647.

189 Ibid.

190 Kähler, *Die Frau*, 135.

191 Barth, *Ephesians 4–6*, 649–50.

192 Cf. E. Käsemann, *An Die Römer* (HNT 8; 3rd ed.; Tübingen: J. C. B. Mohr, 1974) 179; cf. C. E. B. Cranfield, *A Critical and Exegetical Commentary on the Epistle to the Romans* (ICC; Edinburgh; T. and T. Clark, 1975) 331.

193 H. Schlier, *Der Römerbrief* (HTKNT 6; Freiburg: Herder, 1977) 214 ('captatio benvolentiae'). Cf. D. Hans Lietzmann, *Einführung in die Textgeschichte der Paulusbriefe and die Römer* (HNT 8; Tübingen: J. C. B. Mohr, 1933) 72.

194 Pace O. Kuss, *Der Römerbrief* (Regensburg: F. Pustet, 1959) 2.435. C. K. Barrett, *A Commentary on the Epistle to the Romans* (HNTC; New York: Harper and Row, 1957) 135–6, rightly remarks of v. 2, 'This states fairly the position of the Jewish wife, not of the Roman.' Pace C. H. Dodd, *The Epistle of Paul to the Romans* (MNTC; London: Hodder and Stoughton, 1932) 100.

195 On those who think law in general, or a legal principle without specifying its source is meant, cf. H. Ridderbos, *Paul, An Outline of His Theology* (Grand Rapids: Eerdmans, 1975) 106; Käsemann,

An die Römer, 179. Most commentators think the Mosaic law is in view. Cf. F. J. Leenhardt, *The Epistle to the Romans* (London: Lutterworth, 1961) 177; J. D. M. Derrett, 'Romans vii.1–4. The relationship with the resurrected Christ', *Law in the New Testament* (London: Darton, Longmann and Todd, 1970) 461–71; W. G. Kümmel, *Römer 7 und das Bild des Menschen im Neuen Testament – Zwei Studien* (Munich: Chr. Kaiser, 1974) 38, n. 1. Cf. Rom 3.19, 5.13; 1 Cor 9.8–9, 14.21, 34; Gal 3.10, 19. Also, O. Michel, *Der Brief an die Römer* (KEK; 10th ed., Göttingen: Vandenhoeck and Ruprecht, 1955) 142.

196 On Jesus' view of the bond of marriage, cf. Witherington, *Women*, 18ff.

197 For those who see a parable or allegory (or allegorical analogy) in vv. 2–3, or connect vv. 2–3 closely with v. 4, cf. Barrett, *Romans*, 136; Lietzmann, *Römer*, 71; Dodd, *Romans*, 101; Schlier, *Römerbrief*, 216.

198 Cf. Kümmel, *Römer 7*, 41; Cranfield, *Romans I*, 331–3; A. W. Meyer, *A Critical and Exegetical Handbook to the Epistle to the Romans I* (Edinburgh: T. and T. Clark, 1881) 317; A. Schlatter, *Gottes Gerechtigkeit. Ein Kommentar zum Römerbrief* (5th ed.; Stuttgart: Calwer, 1975) 225; 'Käsemann, *Römer*, 179–80.

199 The very diversity of suggestions about what is represented by the first husband and wife, counts against any of them being right. Cf. A. Nygren, *Commentary on Romans* (London: SCM, 1952) 271. Those who insist on a sort of allegorical analogy here create their own difficulties, which disappear if vv. 2–3 are seen as an illustration (corollary) to the principle stated in v. 1.

200 Cf. Ephesians 5.

201 Kümmel, *Römer 7*, 41, argues that even if marriage imagery is in view in v. 4, it is the marriage of the individual through baptism with Christ. But Paul nowhere else speaks of the marriage of the individual believer to Christ.

202 Käsemann, *Römer*, 179–80, translates 'juridically valid'. On the Jewish principle that death frees one from the obligation to fulfill the law's commands, cf. Str-B III, 234.

203 J. B. Lightfoot, *Epistles of St Paul from Unpublished Commentaries* (London: Macmillan, 1895) 300, says the translation 'to her husband as long as she lives' is misleading. Meyer, *Romans I*, 318, also insists on the translation 'living husband'. τῷ ζῶντι correlates with ζῇ in v. 1.

204 One cannot be certain about this for the compound form is not used in Numbers. In Prov 6.24, 29 and Sirach 9.9, 41.23, we have the compound form, but it appears that it means 'married'. In the extra-biblical Greek, Polybius, *The Histories* 10.26.3, LCL (1925) 4:162–3, we have the compound form where the meaning is 'married women' as distinguished from widows. In Plutarch, *Pelopidas*, 9.2, *Pelopidas and Marcellus*, LCL (1961) 5.360–1, however, it appears to have the meaning 'women who are subject to men' (καὶ γύναικα τῶν ὑπάνδρων). Also, in Athenaeus,

The Deipnosophists 9. 388c, LCL (1930) 4.254–5, it appears to mean 'women under a man's authority' (τὰς ὑπάνδρους τῶν γυναικῶν). The word ὕπανδρος is Hellenistic and thus does not reflect classical views of a woman's position in marriage. Cf. LSJ, 1852; BAG, 845; Zerwick-Grosvenor II, 473; MM, 650, clearly affirm that in Rom 7.2, it means 'under the authority of a husband'.

205 Translating κατήργηται ἀπὸ νόμου is somewhat difficult if one is to distinguish it from ἐλευθέρα ... ἀπὸ τοῦ νόμου in v. 3. Derrett, 'Romans', 467, suggests 'rendered unanswerable to' or 'rendered inoperative in respect of'. Cranfield, Romans I, 333, suggests 'released from'; cf. K. Barth, The Epistle to the Romans (6th ed.; London: Oxford University, 1933) 232. On τοῦ νόμου τοῦ ἀνδρός meaning 'the law which binds the wife to the husband', cf. Lietzmann, Römer, 72–3; Kuss, Der Römerbrief II, 435; Schlier, Der Römerbrief, 216; Derrett, 'Romans', 470; Leenhardt, Romans, 177 (cf. Num 9.12).

206 Witherington, Women, 18ff.

207 Cf. BDF, sec. 349, p. 178; Robertson, 876; Michel, Römer, 142; Käsemann, Römer, 179–80.

208 M. Black, Romans (NCB; London: Oliphants, 1973) 99, says we have Hebraic usage here – 'becomes the property of' (hayah le ish). Cf. Deut 24.2 and Judg 15.2; Michel, Römer, 142; Kuss, Der Römerbrief II, 436; Cranfield, Romans I, 333, says it means 'to marry' citing Num 36.11, Deut 24.2, Hos 3.3 (LXX).

209 Derrett, 'Romans', 462, 468, says that γενέσθαι in vv. 3 and 4 means no more than 'consorts with'. Lightfoot, Epistles, 300, says ἐὰν γένηται ἀνδρὶ ἑτέρῳ means 'if she attaches herself to another man', comparing Hos 3.4.

210 von Allmen, Pauline Teaching, 53, rightly points out that a marriage ended by a (natural) death is marriage ended by God in His providence; cf. Whiteley, Theology of Paul, 217.

211 Paul's mentor, Rabbi Gamaliel, allowed a woman to remarry if her spouse died (M. Yebamoth 16.7, Danby, 244–5). Schoeps, Paul, 37, and n. 3, suggests that Paul derived his teaching in Rom 7.2–3 from his mentor.

212 G. Friedrich, Der Erst Brief an die Thessalonicher (NTD 8; Göttingen: Vandenhoeck & Ruprecht, 1976) 237.

213 H. Baltensweiler, 'Erwägungen zu 1 Thess 4, 3–8', TZ 19 (1963) 1–13, argues a particular legal matter is in view, i.e., a dispute over an inheritance by a daughter in a family that has no sons when the head of the family died. The Greek law stipulated that the 'nearest male relative' had a right to marry this daughter and raise up an heir, even if the daughter had already married someone else. Such a marriage could be considered incestuous by the Jews, and Baltensweiler suggests that Paul has been asked whether or not it is appropriate for Christians to observe such a law. There are problems with this view even though it unites the content of vv. 3–8. (1) Baltensweiler assumes that what applied in Athens and elsewhere in Greece in regard to the law about heiresses would also apply in

Thessalonica; however, Thessalonica was a Macedonian city and the legal rights of women there were greater than in Greece. They were allowed more freedom and the right to property, unlike many Grecian women. (2) ἐν τῷ πράγματι is too general a phrase to be referring to the law of inheritance without further clear indications in the context that this is the issue. Cf. E. Best, *A Commentary on the First and Second Epistles to the Thessalonians* (London: A. & C. Black, 1972) 164; C. Maurer, 'πρᾶγμα', *TDNT* 6 (1968) 639. (3) Baltensweiler's arguments require a very specific and technical meaning for πλεονεκτεῖν and possibly also for πορνεία. At most, his argument shows that πλεονεκτεῖν was used for business fraud, but not that it was a legal term. (4) Would there really be a sufficient number of cases of this problem in the Thessalonian Christian community to warrant the phrase ἕκαστον ὑμῶν ... κτᾶσθαι in v. 4?

214 Cf. J. Frame, *A Critical and Exegetical Commentary on the Epistles of St Paul to the Thessalonians* (ICC; Edinburgh: T. and T. Clark, 1912) 153; B. Rigaux, *Saint Paul. Les Épîtres aux Thessaloniciens* (Paris: Gabalda, 1956) 510.

215 Cf. A. Plummer, *A Commentary on St Paul's First Epistle to the Thessalonians* (London: Robert Scott, 1918) 62; Zerwick– Grosvenor 618.

216 Cf. 2 Cor 12.21; Gal 5.19; Col 3.5; Rom 1.24.

217 Lightfoot, *Epistles*, 56, cf. 41 where he notes that the accusative τό can express the result or consequence. Cf. Frame, *Thessalonians*, 152. This is better than taking τό to indicate a new subject. Cf. M. Dibelius, *An die Thessaloniker I, II, An die Philipper* (HNT 2; 2nd ed.; Tübingen: J. C. B. Mohr, 1925) 19, says 'a caesura in speech indicating a new subject'. This is also better than simply taking τό μὴ ὑπερβαίνειν in apposition with ὁ ἁγιασμὸς ὑμῶν. Pace Robertson, 1059, 1078; Rigaux, *Thessaloniciens*, 509–10; MHT III, 140–1, calls it 'a mere infinitive'. Cf. BDF, sec. 279.3, 203–4. It is because Paul wants his listeners to abstain from πορνεία such as that mentioned in v. 6 (cf. v. 3) that he says what he does in v. 4.

218 Cf. BAG, 761–2; LSJ, 1607; A–S, 408: C. Maurer, 'σκεῦος', *TDNT* 7 (1971) 358–67; Lampe, *PGL*, 1236.

219 Rigaux, *Thessaloniciens*, 504–5, lists Theodore of Mopsuestia, Augustine, Thomas Aquinas, Wettstein, and more recently, Frame, Oepke, Findlay, and we may add Baltensweiler, Ridderbos, Best, Moore, Friedrich, Delling, and probably Lightfoot, favoring the view that σκεῦος alludes to the wife. For the view that the human body is in view, he lists John of Damascus, Theophylactus, Tertullian, Calvin, Beza, Bengel, Milligan, Dibelius, and himself. σκεῦος is translated 'body' by *JB* (margin has 'his own body' or 'his wife's body'); *NASB* (margin, 'wife'); *NIV* (margin, 'wife'); *NEB*; Phillips. For the translation 'wife', cf. Weymouth, Moffatt, *RSV* (margin 'body'), *TEV* (margin, 'body'). The *KJV* says his 'vessel'. Ridderbos, *Paul*, 308, n. 138, says that the ἑαυτοῦ in contrast to the preceding πορνεία (cf. vv. 3–4) argues for the translation 'wife'.

220 But cf. Lightfoot, *Epistles*, 55.
221 Cf. the list in Rigaux, *Thessaloniciens*, 506.
222 Cf. Lightfoot, *Epistles*, 55; G. Milligan, *St Paul's Epistles to the Thessalonians* (London: Macmillan, 1908) 49.
223 Cf. MM, 362, to Milligan, *Thessalonians*, 49; Plummer, *Thessalonians*, 60; Rigaux, *Thessaloniciens*, 505–6. Wettstein II, 302, says 'cum κτᾶσθαι significet acquirere, non potest σκεῦος significare corpus suum, sed uxorem.'
224 Lightfoot (*Epistles*, 54) says, strangely, that 1 Pet 3.7 is not a parallel because Peter is expressing the idea that the woman is a vessel, not of her husband, but of the Holy Spirit. Cf. Dibelius, *Thessaloniker*, 18. Against this view, the husband is being addressed in 3.7, and the Holy Spirit is nowhere mentioned in this context. The wife is being called the weaker vessel in relation to the husband.
225 (1) 1 Cor 7.2, τὰς πορνείας; 1 Thess 4.3, πορνείας;
   (2) 1 Cor 7.2, ἕκαστος τὴν ἑαυτοῦ; 1 Thess 4.4, ἕκαστον ὑμῶν τὸ ἑαυτοῦ;
   (3) possibly ἐχέτω in 1 Cor 7.2, and κτᾶσθαι in 1 Thess 4.4 have similar meanings and connotations;
   (4) the idea that the wife's body belongs to the husband (1 Cor 7.4; cf. Thess 4.4, τὸ ἑαυτοῦ σκεῦος; Eph 5.28, τὰ ἑαυτῶν σώματα);
   (5) cf. 1 Cor 7.9, πυροῦσθαι, to 1 Thess 4.5, πάθει ἐπιθυμίας;
   (6) the idea of sanctification related to marital life and relations when one or two believers are involved, cf. 1 Cor 7.14 and 1 Thess 4.4;
   (7) God's call, cf. 1 Cor 7.15 and 1 Thess 4.7;
   (8) impurity: ἀκάθαρτά in 1 Cor 7.14 and ἀκαθαρσίᾳ in 1 Thess 4.7; contrasted with holiness: ἅγια in 1 Cor 7.14 and ἐν ἁγιασμῷ in 1 Thess 4.7.

Some of these parallels are not exact, but they are better than or equal to those cited by Rigaux, *Thessaloniciens*; cf. n.221 above.
226 We may also compare Str-B II, 394, where the woman is taken by the man in engagement with a coin and through the pronouncement of the betrothal formula in the presence of two witnesses. Baltensweiler, 'Erwägungen', 4, is probably right that the one-time act of marrying is not in view.
227 Cf. Str-B III, 632; Baltensweiler, 'Erwägungen', 4, n.13.
228 εἰδέναι should probably not be separated from κτᾶσθαι as though we had two separate clauses here ('each of you respect his own wife; acquire or keep her in holiness and honor'). Cf. Plummer, *1 Thessalonians*, 60. We do not have here the verb used to speak of 'sexual knowledge' in Paul and generally in the NT. Cf. Best, *Thessalonians*, 163; Delling, *Paulus' Stellung*, 58, n.1.
229 It would seem that 1 Cor 6.12–20 would be a more appropriate context for Paul to use σκεῦος than just about any other place in the Pauline corpus, for at 1 Cor 6.19 he comes closer to speaking of the body as a vessel. The use of σκεῦος in 2 Cor 4.7 includes a reference to the human body, but it is clearly a metaphor and it is probably not a reference to the body apart from the rest of the human personality. Notice that in 2 Cor 4.6 it is ἐν ταῖς καρδίαις ἡμῶν that God has shown His light, and the reference in 4.7 to the

'treasure' surely reflects back to the φωτισμόν τῆς γνώσεως τῆς δόξης. The use of σκεῦος in Romans 9, besides being a metaphor, intending to express the fact that God has created and shaped man like a potter does clay, is a reference to the whole person – not simply the human body. Notice how ἐπὶ σκεύη ἐλέους in v. 23 parallels and leads into ἡμᾶς in v. 24. In 2 Tim 2.21 σκεῦος refers to the whole person in so far as he is an instrument of either honorable purposes (εἰς τιμήν) or dishonorable ones (εἰς ἀτιμίαν). Cf. v. 20 where the metaphor arises. The point is that a person can be either an instrument of God's purposes (v. 21) or of ignoble purposes.

230 Lightfoot, *Epistles*, 55.

231 Lightfoot, *Epistles*, 54, traces this translation back to Chrysostom, but adds, 'This interpretation introduces a new difficulty as ἐν ἁγιασμῷ is not adapted to such a meaning of κτᾶσθαι.' Despite Dibelius' advocacy of this view (*Thessaloniker*, 19); cf. Baltensweiler, 'Erwägungen', 4, n. 12; LSJ, 1001; BAG, 456.

232 In 1 Thess 4.3–8 we have σκεῦος without the qualifiers we find in 2 Corinthians 4 and Romans 9, and it is not at all clear that if Paul is using it of the body, he is using it in a purely metaphorical way. Thus, it raises the question: vessel full of what, the Spirit? Cf. v. 8.

233 Cf. C. Maurer, 'σκεῦος', *TDNT* 7 (1971) 366: 'The fact that *baal* and κτᾶσθαι are parallel suggests that Paul, who spoke both Hebrew and Greek, would translate the Hebrew T. T. *baal ishah* ("to possess a woman sexually") by κτᾶσθαι γυναῖκα, thus imparting a durative sense to the Greek phrase. Under the influence of the Jewish euphemism *shamash kuli* he is led then to the new expression σκεῦος κτᾶσθαι ...' Best, *Thessalonians*, 163–4, who follows Maurer at this point, adds that the Hebrew idiom can be used both of entrance into marriage (Deut 21.13, 24.1) and of its continuance (Isa 54.1). In both cases there is reference to sexual relations. There may be a parallel to this in 1 Cor 7.2 where 'have' may imply 'have sexually'. Dibelius, *Thessaloniker*, 19, says that πρᾶγμα (or its Hebrew equivalent) can be used euphemistically of sexual intercourse, and he points to M. Berakoth 2.5. Cf. Danby, 3; Baltensweiler, 'Erwägungen', 6. On the other hand, πρᾶγμα seems nearer to the use of *dabar* in Deut 23.1. Cf. Rigaux, *Thessaloniciens*, 510; Frame, *Thessalonians*, 152–3.

234 τιμήν in 1 Peter 3 may be another indication of some relationship of 1 Pet 3.1–7 to 1 Thess 4.3–8, for these are the only two NT texts where honoring wives is mentioned (but cf. 1 Tim 5.3).

235 The knowledge of God should lead to the proper acknowledgement of God's creatures – male and female. The phrase πάθει ἐπιθυμίας probably is not an indication of Paul's familiarity with Stoic thought. Cf. Baltensweiler, 'Erwägungen', 5. Contrast Rigaux, *Thessaloniciens*, 509; W. Michaelis, 'πάθος', *TDNT* 5 (1967) 926; V. P. Furnish, *Theology and Ethics in Paul* (Nashville: Abingdon Press, 1968) 86.

236 πορνεία can refer to various sorts of sexual immorality, though sometimes it can be used in almost a technical sense to refer to a particular sin such as incest. Paul's views seem quite clear and consistent throughout his writings – any sort of extra-marital intercourse or sexual relationships is forbidden. This includes: (1) relations with a prostitute (cf. 1 Cor 6.12–20 where perhaps a ἑταίρα is involved; religious prostitution is ruled out; (cf. 1 Cor 10.1–15 where fornication and idolatry are associated); (2) homosexual relationships (cf. Rom 1.26–27; 1 Cor 6.9–10); (3) adulterous relationships (1 Cor 6.9–10); (4) incestuous relationships (1 Cor 5.1); (5) pre-marital relationships between an engaged couple (cf. 1 Cor 7.36–38). That Paul does not explicitly mention pre-marital sex between a man and woman not engaged, is probably because he did not think he needed to warn against it. On the basis of 1 Cor 7.36–38 (cf. 7.9), it is obvious what he would have said.

237 It is very unlikely Paul means 'neighbor', whether or not Christian, by 'brother' here, since he nowhere else in his letters uses ἀδελφός in this sense. Pace J. Calvin, *The Epistles of Paul the Apostle to the Romans and to the Thessalonians* (Edinburgh: T. and T. Clark, 1961) 359; Lightfoot, *Epistles*, 57; Plummer, *Thessalonians*, 62. The advice could apply to a Christian's behavior toward a non-Christian *mutatis mutandis*, but Paul is focusing on the Christian community here. Cf. Best, *Thessalonians*, 166; Frame, *Thessalonians*, 153.

238 This would comport with the use of κτάομαι in Ruth 4.10, Eccles 36.24 (LXX), and we may compare Xenophon, *Symposium* 2.10, LCL (1932) 392–3 (ταύτην κέκτημαι). BAG, 456, is wrong to say that we have κτᾶσθαι γυναῖκα at this point in Xenophon. Cf. Sirach 36:24 – 'he that gets a wife (gets) the choicest possession'. We have suggested that it is more likely that κτᾶσθαι is a euphemism for 'possess sexually'.

239 Pace Delling, *Paulus' Stellung*, 58–61.

240 Cf. Friedrich, *Thessalonicher*, 237–8.

241 Ibid., 239.

242 Lightfoot, *Epistles*, 58, argues that the change of prepositions in v. 7 (ἐπί to ἐν) is significant – 'not for uncleanness, but in sanctification.' Cf. Best, *Thessalonians*, 168; BDF, sec. 235.4, p. 123.

243 Cf. n. 236 above; V. P. Furnish, *The Moral Teaching of Paul* (Nashville: Abingdon, 1979) 48; A. L. Moore, *1 and 2 Thessalonians* (NCB; London: Nelson, 1969) 63.

244 For those who see this as a non-Pauline fragment, possibly inserted by Paul or a later Christian redactor of the Pauline corpus, cf. the excellent summary of the various views (to 1956) in E.-B. Allo, *Saint Paul – Seconde Épître aux Corinthiens* (2nd ed.; Paris: Gabalda, 1956) 189–93, and J. A. Fitzmyer, 'Qumran and the interpolated paragraph in 2 Cor 6,14–7,1', *CBQ* 23 (3, 1961) 271–81; J. Gnilka, '2 Cor. 6:14–7:1', *Paul and Qumran – Studies in New Testament Exegesis* (ed. J. Murphy-O'Connor; London: G. Chapman, 1968) 48–68. Fitzmyer and Gnilka both note the similarities of our text with portions of the Qumran and other Jewish literature, and argue

for the author of our fragment having drawn on such writings. H. D. Betz, '2 Cor 6:14–7:1: an anti-Pauline fragment?' *JBL* 92 (1973) 88–108, goes further in seeing this fragment as having arisen out of the viewpoint of Paul's opponents in Galatia. There is also the view that 2 Cor 6.14–7.1 is part of the pre-canonical letter referred to in 1 Cor 5.9. Cf. J. C. Hurd, *The Origin of 1 Corinthians* (London: SPCK, 1968) 44–6, 236–7.

245   Cf. Gordon Fee, 'II Corinthians vi.14–vii.1 and food offered to idols', *NTS* 23 (1976–77) 140–61, here 157, who says that the clue to the passage lies not in the metaphor itself (the use of yoke) but in the rhetorical questions that follow. Our passage seems too general to be referring solely or primarily to mixed marriages and the Corinthians engaged in them. Thus, a primary allusion to Lev 19.19a seems unlikely. Our text has nothing to do with 'breeding', unlike Lev 19.19a. More likely, Deut 22.10 is in the background. Cf. J. D. M. Derrett, '2 Cor 6,14ff. A midrash on Dt 22.19', *Bib* 59 (2, 1978) 231–50, here 234–45; A. Plummer, *A Critical and Exegetical Commentary on the Second Epistle of St Paul to the Corinthians* (ICC; Edinburgh: T. & T. Clark, 1915) 206; Lietzmann, *Korinther I, II*, 129.

246   Cf. C. K. Barrett, *A Commentary on the Second Epistle to the Corinthians* (New York: Harper & Row, 1973) 196; Bruce, *Corinthians*, 214. The association of idolatry and religious prostitution is also well known; thus, if Lev 19.19a is in the background, religious prostitution might be alluded to by ἑτεροζυγοῦντες. Cf. J.-F. Collange, *Énigmes de la deuxième Épître de Paul aux Corinthiens – Étude Exégétique de 1 Cor 2:14–7:4* (SNTS; MS 18; Cambridge: Cambridge University Press, 1972) 306. The verb ἑτεροζυγέω occurs first in 2 Cor 6.14.

247   Cf. Plummer, *2 Corinthians*, 206: 'St. Paul does not assert that such things have taken place. He says "Become not incongruously yoked with unbelievers ..."' BDF, sec. 355, p. 180, says, 'Γίνεσθαι (in various tenses) with a present or perfect participle is sometimes also used as an analogous way to denote the beginning of a state or condition: 2 Cor 6.14 ... ("do not lend yourselves to ...").' Cf. Robertson, 375. Betz, '2 Cor. 6.14–7:1', 89–90, believes that the yoke of the Torah is in view and that there are two different yokes. This is improbable and is dependent on his view that we have here a statement of Paul's opponents.

248   P. E. Hughes, *Paul's Second Epistle to the Corinthians* (NICNT; Grand Rapids: Eerdmans, 1962) 245; Fee, 'II Corinthians', 145.

249   As Betz, '2 Cor 6:14–7:1', 97–8, points out, 6.18 has υἱοὺς καὶ θυγατέρας while its source, 2 Sam 7.14 (LXX), has only υἱόν. Betz rightly says, 'A striking and undoubtedly intended addition is καὶ θυγατέρας. This addition accounts for a clear distinction from Qumran literature, with which the text otherwise has so much in common.' Perhaps we have here an intimation of Paul's view of the nature of the Christian community (the equality of male and female as joint heirs of grace) in contrast to the views of the Qumran community and some rabbis.

250 Col 3.21 – μὴ ἐρεθίζετε τὰ τέκνα ὑμῶν – seems to imply that the father is expected to rebuke or discipline his child. Eph 6.4 – παροργίζετε – seems to have a similar idea in mind. By contrast (ἀλλὰ) the father is expected to 'bring up his child in the discipline and instruction of the Lord'. He is thus responsible for their Christian training. Cf. Lohse, *Colossians*, 159.

251 That ὑπακούω not ὑποτάσσω is used in Ephesians and Colossians of the child's relationship to his parents probably implies that the author(s) intend to distinguish the way the wife and children relate to the head of the household. Cf. Barth, *Ephesians 4–6*, 710, n. 392.

252 Eph 6.2b does not correspond to the Hebrew text of either Exod 20.12 or Deut 5.16. Cf. Robinson, *Ephesians*, 210. Though the injunction to honor parents was common in extra-biblical literature, Paul specifically draws on a scriptural injunction and reaffirms it as valid for the Christian community. That Paul does so is perhaps significant since there were various rabbis who insisted that the father was to be honored above the mother.

253 The phrase ἐν κυρίῳ is absent from various important mss and patristic references (B, D*, G it ᵈⁱᵍ, Marcion, Clement, Tertullian, Cyprian, Ambrosiaster). It is, however, likely to be original since, if it were an addition based on 5.22, it would probably have been ὡς τῷ κυρίῳ. Cf. Metzger, *TC*, 609.

3 Women and the family of faith in the Pauline epistles

1 Cf. Ben Witherington, 'Rite and rights for women – Galatians 3.28', *NTS* 27:5 (1981) 593–604.

2 Betz, *Galatians*, 185ff.; F.F. Bruce, *Galatians* (Grand Rapids: Eerdmans, 1982) 187ff.

3 Betz, *Galatians*, 182ff. On the practice of Jewish proselyte baptism and other ritual washings, cf. W. S. LaSor, 'Discovering what Jewish miqva'ot can tell us about Christian baptism', *BAR* 13:1 (1987) 52–9.

4 Cf. Jervell's argument in nn. 47–48 below.

5 Witherington, 'Rite and rights', 594–604.

6 Barrett, *First Corinthians*, 4–5; Conzelmann, *1 Corinthians*, 13.

7 Cf. W.O. Walker, Jr, '1 Corinthians 11:2–16 and Paul's views regarding women', *JBL* 94 (1975) 94–110; L. Cope, '1 Cor. 11:2–16: one step further', *JBL* 94 (1975) 94–110; L. Cope, '1 Cor. 11:2–16: one step further', *JBL* 97 (1978) 435–6; G. W. Trompf, 'On attitudes toward women in Paul and Paulinist literature: 1 Corinthians 11:3–16 and its context', *CBQ* 42 (1980) 196–215.

8 G. Bornkamm, *Early Christian Experience* (New York: Harper and Row, 1969) 161, n. 2; 176.

9 J.B. Hurley, *Man and Woman in Biblical Perspective. A Study in Role Relationships and Authority* (Leicester: InterVarsity, 1981) 176.

10 Cf. J. Murphy-O'Connor, 'The non-Pauline character of 1 Corinthians 11.2–16'; *JBL* 45 (1976) 615–27, for a careful refutation of Walker, '1 Corinthians 11:2–16', J. P. Meir, 'On the veiling of hermeneutics (1 Cor 11.2–16)', *CBQ* 40 (1978) 212–26.

11 G. Thiessen, *The Social Setting of Pauline Christianity* (Philadelphia: Fortress, 1982) 99ff.; W. A. Meeks, *The First Urban Christians* (New Haven: Yale University, 1984) 75ff.

12 Thiessen, *Social Setting*, 75–6.

13 See ch. 1, pp. 10–12.

14 Meeks, *First Urban Christians*, 78ff.

15 Thiessen, *Social Setting*, 100–1, 124ff.; Meeks, *First Urban Christians*, 50ff.

16 J. Painter, 'Paul and the pneumatikoi at Corinth', *Paul and Paulinism. Essays in Honor of C. K. Barrett* (ed. M. D. Hooker and S. G. Wilson; London: SPCK, 1982) 237–50, here 245.

17 Cf. A. Oepke, 'κατακαλύπτω', *TDNT* 3 (1965) 561–2. E. Schüssler Fiorenza 'Women in the pre-Pauline and Pauline churches', USQR 33 (1978) 153–66, and her analysis of Tibullus 1, 3, 20–32 and the archaeological evidence. Cf. also, S. Kelley Heyob, *The Cult of Isis Among Women in the Greco-Roman World* (Leiden: E. J. Brill, 1975) 60.

18 Apuleius, *The Golden Ass (Metamorphoses)* 11.10, LCL (1915) 555.

19 C. M. Galt, 'Veiled ladies', *AJA* 35 (1931) 373–93.

20 Cf. Galt, 'Veiled ladies', 376, 381 (the statues from Corinth and the archaic painted tablet), 387, 390 (bronze statue with phial apparently engaged in a religious act). Remember that we are talking about adult women, not maidens who commonly were bareheaded. Paul, however, is addressing his adult congregation in Corinth who could follow his argument; thus, the evidence is particularly relevant.

21 Galt, 'Veiled ladies', 390, citing evidence from coins and reliefs: Cf. Valerius Maximus, *Factorum et Dictorum Memorabilium* 6.3.10, pp. 289–90; Cicero, *De Legibus* 2.59, LCL (1928) 444–5; and Nonnos M542 (arica worn by priestesses; aricinium = mourning veil). Tertullian (*Virg.* 8,8 and *Corin.* 4) indicates that even as late as his day, the Corinthian woman is striking because she wears a veil.

22 Plutarch, *Roman Questions* 267a, LCL (1936) 4: 27.

23 Plutarch, *Roman Questions* 266f., 267a, LCL (1936) 4:27. Plutarch indicates that even Roman men wore a head-covering at such sacrifices. Paul, of course, has theological reasons for distinguishing between what men and women did in regard to the head-covering.

24 Cf. J. Jeremias, *Jerusalem in the Time of Jesus* (Philadelphia: Fortress, 1969) 359ff.; E. Marmorstein, 'The veil in Judaism and Islam', *JJS* 52 (1954–55) 1–11.

25 A. Oepke, 'κατακαλύπτω', *TDNT* 3 (1965) 562.

26 Ibid., 563; Delling, *Paulus' Stellung*, 96–105; Conzelmann, *1 Corinthians*, 184–5, and notes.

27 Metzger, *TC*, 562.

28 LSJ, 1369; A–S, 354–5; BAG, 652.

29 Licht, *Sexual Life*, 357, quoting a fragment from Aristophanes.
30 MM, 505; BAG, 652.
31 On ἀντί = instead or against, cf. Moule, *I–B*, 71; Robertson, 574.
32 Rightly noted by O. Motta, 'The question of the unveiled woman (1 Cor 11.2–16)', *ET* 44 (1932) 137–9.
33 But cf. Hurley, *Man and Woman*, 176ff. and the forthcoming book by P. B. Payne, *Man and Woman: One in Christ* (Grand Rapids: Zondervan, 1987).
34 Galt, 'Veiled ladies', 379.
35 Cf. Bruce, *1 & 2 Corinthians*, 108; Barrett, *First Corinthians*, 258; Rom 16.4, 16; 1 Cor 4.17, 7.17, 14.33, 16.1, 19.
36 O. Cullmann, 'Paradosis et kyrios, le problème de la tradition dans le paulinisme', *RHPR* 30 (1950) 12–30.
37 Cf. H. Schlier, 'κεφαλή', *TDNT* 3 (1965) 674–6; C. Brown, 'Head', *DNTT* 2 (1976) 156–63; Kähler, *Die Frau*, 47ff.
38 S. Bedale, 'The meaning of kephale in the Pauline epistles', *JTS* n.s. 5 (1954) 211–15.
39 Payne, *Man and Woman*, 39ff., in the original draft which the author has kindly lent to me.
40 As Robertson, 781, and Héring, *First Corinthians*, 102–3, indicate, κεφαλή in each case means something a little different when predicated of Christ or of Adam.
41 The evidence cited by Hurley (*Man and Woman*, 170ff.) to show that women removed their veil to pray bare-faced in some Jewish contexts, is probably irrelevant here because we are not discussing veils but head-coverings. Further, interpreting ἀκατακαλύπτῳ to mean 'with the hair let down' is straining the term beyond its normal meaning. We might expect Paul to use κατὰ κεφαλῆς ἔχων of the women if that were the case. Cf. BAG, 412; A–S, 234; LSJ, 893 on the meaning of κατακαλύπτω. On κατὰ κεφαλῆς as 'down upon' or 'down from', cf. Moule, *I–B*, 60; BDF, 225, p. 120.
42 Note Paul says nothing about long hair (κομᾷ) as a covering for men until v. 14. Hairlength is not the subject of vv. 4–5, but the head-covering *simpliciter*.
43 On women of Paul's day convicted of adultery having their heads clipped or shaved, cf. Hurley, *Man and Woman*, 169, and Héring, *First Corinthians*, 105 and nn. 9, 10. This was apparently the Jewish practice upon expelling a woman from the synagogue. But, in view of the fact that he is attempting to accentuate the visible difference between male and female, might Paul have in mind the practice in some parts of Greece (esp. Sparta) of women with closely cropped hair? Cf. Lucian, *The Runaways* 27, LCL (1936) 5: 85, who criticizes the Spartan women who looked masculine due to their close cropped hair. Cf. Tacitus, *Germania* 19, LCL (1970) 1:158–61; Aristophanes, *Thesmophoriazusae* 838, LCL (1924) 3:204–5. Conzelmann, 1 Corinthians, 186, n. 48, indicates this may also have been ancient Athenian practice; cf. Héring, *First Corinthians*, 105, and n. 9.
44 MHT III, 21; BDF, 131, p. 73.

45 Verse 5b could be a *double entendre* if we are talking about wives here; but would it make sense to say the head or source of a woman is man in general (or is Adam the head of all women?).

46 W. Foerster, 'ἐξουσία', *TDNT* 2 (1964) 574.

47 Cf. J. Jervell, *Imago Dei, Gen. 1:26f im Spätjudentum, in der Gnosis und in den paulinischen Briefen* (Göttingen: Vandenhoeck and Ruprecht, 1960), 294–6.

48 Ibid., 293, n. 405.

49 ὑπάρχων may refer to the beginning of creation, or time, or history, or all three. Cf. Mark 10.6 (ἀπὸ ἀρχῆς κτίσεως); Matt 19.8 (ʼαπʼ ἀρχῆς). This appeal seems to follow the logic, 'the earlier the more authoritative'. The appeal to the creation order and its intended purpose appears to have been a common Jewish technique. Cf. Jervell, *Imago Dei*, 37–40, 300; Witherington, *Women*, p. 26 and n. 129.

50 But on the OT background, cf. A. Feuillet, 'L'homme "gloire de dieu" et la femme "gloire de l'homme" (1 Cor. XI,7b)', *RB* 81 (1974) 161–80; and 'La dignité et le rôle de la femme d'après quelques textes Pauliniens: comparison avec l'ancien testament', *NTS* 21 (1974–75) 157–91.

51 What they *do* in worship is the same as what men do; but what they *wear* in worship is not the same as what men wear.

52 Cf. Barrett, *First Corinthians*, 255; Robertson and Plummer, *First Corinthians*, 231.

53 BDF 452.3, p. 236.

54 Cf. Robertson, 565, 583–4.

55 All this is carefully analyzed by Payne, *Man and Woman*, 49 (draft copy).

56 W. M. Ramsay, *The Cities of St Paul* (Minneapolis: James Family Christian Pub., repr. n.d.) 202ff.

57 M. D. Hooker, 'Authority on her head: an examination of 1 Cor XI.10', *NTS* 10 (1963–64) 410–16. In what follows I am indebted to Prof. Hooker. On the OT background to ἐξουσία, cf. G. Schwarz, 'ἐξουσίαν ἔχειν ἐπὶ τῆς κεφαλῆς? (1 Korinther 11.10)', *ZNW* 70 (1979) 249.

58 Cf. A. Feuillet, 'Le signe de puissance sur la tête de la femme, I Cor. 11,10', *NRT* 95 (1973) 945–9; A. Jaubert, 'Le voile des femmes (1 Cor. 11.2–16)', *NTS* 18 (1971–72) 419–30. On the mistranslation of ἐξουσία as 'veil', cf. B. K. Waltke, '1 Corinthians 11.2–16: an interpretation', *BSac* 135:53 (1978) 46–57, here 50, n. 9.

59 Payne, *Man and Woman*, 50ff. (draft copy).

60 Hooker, 'Authority on her head', 413.

61 Witherington, *Women*, 6–10, and notes.

62 Barrett, *First Corinthians*, 150; contra N. Weeks, 'Of silence and head coverings', *WTJ* 35 (1, 1972) 21–7.

63 Cf. H. J. Cadbury, 'A Qumran parallel to Paul', *HTR* 51 (1958) 1ff.; J. A. Fitzmyer, 'A feature of Qumran angelology and the New Testament', *NTS* 4 (1957–58) 48–58, citing 1QSa II,8f. – IQM VII,4–6; 4QDb.

64 Cf. R. Perdelwitz, 'Die ἐξουσία auf dem Haupt der Frau, 1 Kor. 11.10', *TSK* 86 (1913) 611–13; Meir, 'On the veiling', 220.

65 Cf. G.B. Caird, *Principalities and Powers* (Oxford: Clarendon, 1956) 15–22; Hooker, 'Authority on her head', 412, and n.5; Orr and Walther, *1 Corinthians*, 264.

66 Robertson and Plummer, *1 Corinthians*, 233–4, make the interesting suggestion that διὰ τοὺς ἀγγέλους means 'because the angels do', i.e., according to Isa 6.2, the angels cover themselves in God's presence.

67 Cf. Hooker, 'Authority on her head', 415: '... her head must be covered, not because she is in the presence of man, but because she is in the presence of God and his angels – and in their presence the glory of man must be hidden.'

68 Cf. BAG, 675; Robertson, 1187, indicates it singles out the main point.

69 Robertson, 562.

70 Cf. ch.3, pp.54–6.

71 J. Kurzinger, 'Frau und Mann nach 1 Kor 11,11f', *BZ* 22:2 (1978) 270–5.

72 *JB, TEV,* Moffatt ('as'); *NIV* (ἀντί = 'as'); *RSV* ('for' – this is acceptable if 'for' = 'instead of' or 'as a substitute for'); *NEB, NASB* ('for'); *KJV* ('instead of'); Phillips ('long hair is the cover').

73 Cf. BAG, 797; LSJ, 1715; MM, 607.

74 Barrett, *First Corinthians*, 258.

75 Cf. Witherington, *Women*, 6–10, and notes.

76 Cf. Barrett, *First Corinthians*, 332–63; Conzelmann, *1 Corinthians*, 246; E. Schweizer, *Church Order in the New Testament* (London: SCM, 1961) n.783.

77 Cf. Metzger, *TC*, 565.

78 W. Grudem, 'The gift of prophecy in 1 Corinthians' (Ph.D. dissertation: Cambridge University, 1978) 247, n.16.

79 Conzelmann, *1 Corinthians*, 246, n.56.

80 E.E. Ellis, *Prophecy and Hermeneutic in Early Christianity* (Grand Rapids: Eerdmans, 1978) 27, n.25.

81 Robinson, 'Die Hodajot', 224.

82 S. Aalen, 'A rabbinic formula in 1 Cor. 14,34', *Studia Evangelica* (ed. F.L. Cross; Berlin: Akademie, 1964) 2:513–25.

83 Cf. espec. Tos. Yeb. 8.1 = Nid. 6.1 as discussed in Aalen, 'Rabbinic formula', 514, n.2.

84 Conzelmann, *1 Corinthians*, 246, n.53.

85 I am not contending that women were the sole cause of the problems in the Corinthian worship; indeed, both 1 Cor 11.17ff. and 14.1ff. would suggest otherwise. In the former case, it appears to have been a problem caused by the well-off not waiting for or being sensitive to the poor (not a gender-specific problem). In the latter case, it appears possible that Paul first deals with the problem caused by the men at Corinthian worship, then at 14.33b begins to discuss the problems created by the women.

86 G. L. Almie, 'Women's church and communion participation', *CBR*
    33 (1982) 41–55 (available to me only in *NTA*), has argued that in
    1 Corinthians 11–14 we have two chiastic units: 11.2–34 and
    12.1–14.40 (the περὶ δὲ at 12.1 introducing the second). Almie
    argues that 1 Corinthians 14 has to do with a separate teaching
    meeting in which only a limited number of men participated. But
    Paul gives no hint that he is addressing a smaller audience or a
    different sort of worship context in 1 Corinthians 14 than in 1
    Corinthians 11. This distinction must be read into the text; indeed,
    it involves ignoring such general phrases as ἐν ἐκκλησίᾳ which
    surely means 'in the church meeting'. The argument that 1 Cor
    11.2ff. is in a private setting also founders on the fact that Paul
    addresses *all* the Corinthians concerning what they all had received
    (v. 2) and shared in common with the customs of all the churches
    (v. 16). It also fails to explain the reference to the angels.
87 Cf. Grudem, *Gift of Prophecy*; Ellis, *Prophecy*, 23–71, 129–44;
    D. H. Hill, *New Testament Prophecy* (London: Marshall, Morgan
    and Scott, 1979) 110–18; J. D. G. Dunn, *Jesus and the Spirit*
    (Philadelphia: Westminster, 1975) 212–300.
88 Dunn, *Jesus and the Spirit*, 227.
89 Notice how the 'revelation' Paul reports in 2 Cor 12.1–10 in all
    likelihood did not lead to prophecy but was a personal communi-
    cation to Paul which he at a much later time shares with the
    Corinthians.
90 Cf. the fruitful comparison by Dunn, *Jesus and the Spirit*, 228.
91 Hill, *NT Prophecy*, 121ff.
92 Grudem, *Gift of Prophecy*, 55ff.; Hill, *NT Prophecy*, 135ff.
93 Hill, *NT Prophecy*, 132.
94 Dunn, *Jesus and the Spirit*, 127.
95 Barrett, *First Corinthians*, 326.
96 Dunn, *Jesus and the Spirit*, 230.
97 Hill, *NT Prophecy*, 137.
98 G. Friedrich, 'προφήτης', *TDNT* 6 (1968) 855.
99 Hill, *NT Prophecy*, 126.
100 Grudem, *Gift of Prophecy*, 238ff.
101 Dunn, *Jesus and the Spirit*, 212; cf. Grudem, *Gift of Prophecy*,
    263ff.
102 Hill, *NT Prophecy*, 133; Conzelmann, *1 Corinthians*, 245.
103 Dunn, *Jesus and the Spirit*, 234.
104 Grudem, *Gift of Prophecy*, 40ff.
105 Bruce, *I & II Corinthians*, 135.
106 F. W. Grosheide, *The First Epistle to the Corinthians* (Grand
    Rapids: Eerdmans, 1953) on 1 Cor 14.33b.
107 Héring, Bruce (with hesitation), Conzelmann, *RSV, NIV, JB*, Good
    News, all concur that v. 33b goes with what follows. If we establish
    that 1 Cor 14.33bff. belongs with 1 Cor 14.34, then important
    hermeneutical questions are raised. It is often asserted that Paul's
    imperatives here to women are to be seen purely as ad-hoc asser-
    tions that arose from and are only meant for a very particular, local

situation, and thus are not to be seen as normative beyond the Corinthian situation. If ἐν πάσαις ταῖς ἐκκλησίας goes with what follows, then this cannot be the case. It has been mentioned before that Paul was trying to get Corinthian practice to fall in line with that of the rest of the churches. He is not endorsing or reinforcing their particular local practice or trying to give them some off-the-cuff advice that would only apply to them. Rather, he has a rule, a tradition, which all the churches are to follow – and he is applying it. Note that the very points where he invokes this or a similar phrase are points where he is seemingly 'baptizing' the status quo. This appears to be the case when he says: (1) that each one is to lead the life which the Lord has assigned (7.17); (2) that woman are to wear head-coverings (11.16); and (3) that women are to be silent (14.33b).

108 K. L. Schmidt, 'ἐκκλησία', *TDNT* 3 (1965) 506.
109 A. Oepke, 'γυνή', *TDNT* 1 (1964) 786.
110 Verse 36 does have some affinities in intent and content with v. 33b. It apparently is a summary statement that applies to *all*, not just women, for he uses the word μόνους instead of μόνας probably to indicate a mixed audience.
111 D. W. Odell-Scott, 'Let the women speak in church, an egalitarian interpretation of 1 Cor 14.33b–36', *BTB* 13:3 (1983) 90–3.
112 Odell-Scott, 'Let the women speak in church', 90, citing support from Robertson, Funk, Thayer, BAG, LS, among others.
113 Cf. 1.12, 6.12, 10.23, 7.1. Actually, the case that in vv. 34–35 we have a quotation is made most cogently by N. M. Flanagan and E. A. Snyder, 'Did Paul put down women in 1 Cor 14.34–36?', *BTB* 11:1 (1981) 10–12.
114 As quoted by Conzelmann, *1 Corinthians*, 246, n. 53. Would this be another incident of Paul's own rule? Cf. 4.17.
115 BAG, 303; MHT III, 58.
116 Héring, *First Corinthians*, 154.
117 James Moffatt, *The First Epistle of Paul to the Corinthians* (London: Hodder and Stoughton, 1938) 233–4.
118 Barrett, *First Corinthians*, 332.
119 Grosheide, *First Corinthians*, on 14.34ff.
120 Whiteley, *Theology of Paul*, 224; cf. Barrett, *First Corinthians*, 331.
121 Conzelmann, *1 Corinthians*, 331–2.
122 Whiteley *Theology of Paul*, 225.
123 This is a very normal use of γάρ as all the grammars point out; cf. BAG, 151; BDF, sec. 475.
124 Cf. BAG, 855 to G. Delling, 'ὑποτάσσω', *TDNT* 8 (1972) 41–6.
125 Barrett, *First Corinthians*, 331.
126 Hurley, *Man and Woman*, 185–94.
127 Conzelmann, *1 Corinthians*, 246, n. 53.
128 I take the καί before ὁ νόμος as ascensive, as it is used in 1 Cor 2.10 and elsewhere in Paul. Cf. BAG, 394. The law is not being appealed to as the ultimate authority; rather, the point is that 'even the law' could have informed the Corinthians on this matter.

129 R. Banks, *Paul's Idea of Community* (Grand Rapids: Eerdmans, 1980) 32–42.
130 Meeks, *First Urban Christians*, 75.
131 Ibid., 75–6.
132 Thiessen, *Social Setting*, 107–9.
133 Meeks, *First Urban Christians*, 76.
134 Banks, *Paul's Idea*, 52–62.
135 Ibid., 59–61.
136 Barrett, *First Corinthians*, 115.
137 Ibid., 23–26, 115ff.; 273ff.
138 Chapple, *On Community in Paul*, 74–5.
139 Barrett, *First Corinthians*, 84; and *Romans*, 238.
140 Meeks, *First Urban Christians*, 78.
141 LSJ, 1711–2; G. Bertram, 'συνεργός', *TDNT* 7 (1971) 871ff.; MM, 605.
142 Meeks, *First Urban Christians*, 78.
143 Ibid., 80.
144 Ibid., 81.
145 Ibid., 134.
146 Thiessen, *Social Setting*, 99ff.
147 R. Scroggs' correspondence with W. Meeks reported in Meeks, 'Image of the androgyne', 203, n. 153.
148 Ellis, *Prophecy*, 3–22.
149 Ibid., 7.
150 Lightfoot, *Philippians*, 158.
151 Cf. R. P. Martin, *Philippians* (London: Oliphants, 1976) 152–3; G. F. Hawthorne, *Philippians* (Waco: Word, 1983) 178–81.
152 The older argument that these women were not quarreling is ably refuted by J. Hastings and J. A. Beet in response to J. C. Watts. Cf. J. Hastings, 'Notes of recent exposition', *ET* 5 (1893–94) 102–4; J. A. Beet, 'Did Euodia and Syntyche quarrel?' *ET* 5 (1893–94) 179–80; J. C. Watts, 'The alleged quarrel of Euodia and Syntyche', *ET* 5 (1893–94) 286–7.
153 Cf. Lightfoot, *Philippians*, 158–9; Martin, *Philippians*, 152–3; M. Hajek, 'Comments on Philippians 4.3 – who was Gnesios Syzygos?', *Communio Viatorum* 7 (3–4, 1964) 261–2. On the old 'allegory' of the Tübingen school which saw Euodia and Syntche as symbols for Jewish and Gentile Christians respectively, cf. C. H. Van Rhijn, 'Euodia en Syntyche', *TS* 21 (1903) 300–9.
154 Hawthorne, *Philippians*, 180.
155 In fact, Hawthorne (*Philippians*, 180) goes so far as to say, 'It implies a united struggle in preaching the Gospel.' On the sort of collaboration these women were involved in, as intimated by this passage and Romans 16, cf. M. Adinolfi, 'Le collaboratrici ministeriali di paolo nelle lettre ai Romani eai Filippesi', *BeO* 17:1 (1975) 21–32, here 31–2.
156 See above, pp. 12–13.
157 See below, pp. 147–9.
158 Bruce, *Philippians*, 115; F. W. Beare, *A Commentary on the Epistle*

to the *Philippians* (New York: Harper and Bros., 1959) 144; G. H. Gilbert, 'Woman in the churches of Paul', *BW* 2 (1893) 38–47, here 39–40. There is no indication in this letter that the problem here was caused by Gnostic agitation when these women allowed Gnostics into the assembly. Pace W. Schmithals, *Paul and Gnostics* (Nashville: Abingdon, 1972) 112–14.

159 Cranfield, *Romans* II, 780, noting the presence of δέ in 16.1; cf. W. Sanday and A. C. Headlam, *The Epistle to the Romans* (ICC: Edinburgh: T. and T. Clark, 1902) 417ff; Barrett, *Romans*, 281–2.
160 Cf. K. P. Donfried, 'A short note on Romans 16', *JBL* 89 (1970) 441–9; and espec. J. I. H. McDonald, 'Was Romans XVI a separate letter', *NTS* 16 (1969–70) 369–72, who demonstrates that there is evidence from the letters of antiquity that a letter could be mainly (60% or more of the content) devoted to greetings. Even if Romans 16 was a separate letter of recommendations and greetings, it had a much more serious purpose than modern postcards or greeting cards.
161 Cf. Käsemann, *Romans*, 409ff., who casts considerable doubts about a Roman destination, but contrast Barrett, *Romans*, 281ff.
162 Käsemann, *Romans*, 409.
163 Donfried, 'Short note', 443ff.
164 Cf. Adinolfi, 'Collaboratrici', 21–6; above, pp. 149–51.
165 Cranfield, *Romans* II, 781.
166 BAG, 726; Sanday-Headlam, *Romans*, 417.
167 Cranfield, *Romans* II, 782; Käsemann, *Romans*, 411.
168 MM, 551; Sanday-Headlam, *Romans*, 417.
169 M. D. Gibson, 'Phoebe', *ET* 23 (1911–12) 281; Cranfield, *Romans*, II: 783.
170 Käsemann, *Romans*, 411.
171 Cf. pp. 153–6 on Priscilla and Aquila, and pp. 111–13 on συνεργός.
172 Cf. Cranfield, *Romans* II, 787; E. G. Sihler, 'A note on the first Christian congregation at Rome', *CTM* 3 (1932) 180–4.
173 Witherington, *Women*, pp. 6–10 and notes.
174 Ibid.
175 Ellis, *Prophecy*, 3–22.
176 Compare and contrast Robertson, 172; BAG, 381; MM, 306; BDF, 125.2, p. 68; MH II, 155; Sanday-Headlam, *Romans*, 422–3; and espec. Cranfield, *Romans* II, 788–9.
177 Cranfield, *Romans* II, 789, n. 4 (quotation from Chrysostom).
178 Rom 9.3, 16.7, 11, 21; BAG, 780; MM, 595.
179 Cranfield, *Romans* II, 788–9; Sanday-Headlam, *Romans*, 423.
180 Should we read τοῖς πρὸ ἐμοῦ (DG) or οἳ καὶ πρὸ ἐμοῦ γέγοναν (most mss.)? The best witnesses clearly support the latter reading; cf. Metzger, *TC*, 539.
181 BAG, 298; MM, 243; LSJ, 656; A–S, 173.
182 MM, 243,
183 The examples in BAG, 258, specifically include the words εν οφθαλμοῖς τινος, though ἔν τινι apparently came to have the same meaning. Cf. Cranfield, *Romans* II, 789.

184 Apparently, all the patristic witnesses took it to mean 'outstanding among the apostles', Cf. Barrett, *Romans*, 283.

185 C.K. Barrett, *The Signs of an Apostle* (Philadelphia: Fortress, 1972) 23ff.; R. Schnackenburg, 'Apostles before and during Paul's time', *Apostolic History and the Gospel* (ed. W. Gasque and R.P. Martin; Grand Rapids: Eerdmans, 1970) 287–303, here 293–4.

186 Schnackenburg, 'Apostles', 294; C.K. Barrett, 'Shaliah and apostle', *Donum Gentilicium* (E. Bammel, *et al.*, eds.; Oxford: Oxford University Press, 1978) 88–102, here 98–101.

187 Käsemann, *Romans*, 414; Cranfield, *Romans* II, 789.

188 J. Jeremias, 'Paarweise Sendung im NT' *Abba. Studien zur neutestamentlichen Theologie und Zeitgeschichte* (Göttingen: Vandenhoeck and Reprecht, 1966) 132–9, here 136; Käsemann, *Romans*, 414.

189 Käsemann, *Romans*, 413.

190 Though there is no way to be certain about this; cf. Cranfield, *Romans* II, 793; Sanday-Headlam, *Romans*, 426.

191 Cranfield, *Romans* II, 793.

192 See chapter 1, pp. 16–23.

193 W.G. Kümmel, *Introduction to the New Testament* (17th rev. ed.; London: SCM, 1975) 371, n.10, including Jeremias, Schlatter, Kelly, Spicq, Guthrie, Metzger, Ellis, Michaelis, and now Gordon Fee, *1 & 2 Timothy, Titus* (New York: Harper & Row, 1984).

194 A.T. Hanson, *The Pastoral Epistles* (NCB; Grand Rapids: Eerdmans, 1982) 2ff.; M. Dibelius and H. Conzelmann, *The Pastoral Epistles* (Philadelphia : Fortress, 1972) 2–5, who recognize the clear allusion to various of Paul's 'capital' letters. By Paulinist I mean one who knew some of Paul's letters and practices and sought to consolidate or use that material as well as other materials for a new and later situation.

195 Cf. J. Jeremias, *Die Briefe an Timotheus und Titus* (Göttingen: Vandenhoeck & Ruprecht, 1975) 21. The parallels with 1 Pet 3.1ff. are primarily because there, as in our text, behavior and apparel are not purely an in-house matter – the world is watching. In 1 Pet 3.1ff. the husband is a non-believer and must be witnessed to in behavior and in apparel. Likewise, the advice to women here has one eye on the effect their behavior was having on the watching world and Christianity's credibility in the City. There is, of course, an overlap between appropriate behavior in the family (which is what 1 Pet 3.1ff. is about) and in the family of faith especially at worship (which is what 1 Tim 2.8ff. is about).

196 J. Murphy-O'Connor, 'Community and apostolate', *Bible Today* 11 (1973) 1260–6.

197 J.N.D. Kelly, *The Pastoral Epistles* (BNTC; London: A. and C. Black 1963) 12; C. Spicq, *Les Epitres Pastorales* (Paris: Gabalda, 1969) 91–117; Hanson, *Pastoral Epistles*, 25. The genealogies in 1 Tim 1.4, Titus 3.9 certainly seem to point in this direction.

198 Ephesus still seems the most likely location of the audience whether or not Paul wrote these letters. Cf. A. Besancon Spencer, 'Eve at

Ephesus', *JETS* 17:4 (1974) 215–22, here 219. Cf. Hanson, *Pastoral Epistles*, 14; Fee, *Timothy/Titus*, xv–xvii; Spicq, *Epitres Pastorales*, 47ff.

199 P.B. Payne rightly points out the parallels between 1.3, 6, 8, and 6.3 as well as the parallels between 5.13–15, 4.1 and 6.20–21, in his helpful article, 'Libertarian women in Ephesus: a response to Douglas Moo', *Trinity Journal* n.s.2 (1981) 169–97, here 185.

200 Cf. Fee, *Timothy/Titus*, 34; notice also the absence of an article in the phrase αὐθεντεῖν ἀνδρός as well as in διδάσκειν ... γυναικὶ οὐκ, cf. R. Falconer, '1 Tim 2.14, 15. Interpretive notes', *JBL* 60 (1941) 375–9.

201 Cf. Hanson, *Pastoral Epistles*, 70–1; W. Lock, *The Pastoral Epistles*, (ICC; Edinburgh, T. & T. Clark, 1924) 30.

202 Lock, *Pastoral Epistles*, 30; C.K. Barrett, *The Pastoral Epistles* (New Clarendon Bible; Oxford: Clarendon, 1963) 54: 'This is no mere literalism, for in Jewish usage 'place' meant 'meeting-place', 'place of prayer', and there is evidence (especially 1 Cor 1.2; 1 Thess 1.8) that it became Christian usage too'.

203 Lock, *Pastoral Epistles*, 31, citing Chrysostom in support; with Barrett, *Pastoral Epistles*, 55. I suggest that since vv.9–10 have no main verb, we should supply 'to pray'. Simply supplying βούλομαι (as Lock suggests) does not explain the use of ὡσαύτως here which implies some sort of comparison between the men and the women. Cf. Dibelius/Conzelmann, *Pastoral Epistles*, 45.

204 Hurley, *Man and Woman*, 199; the extensive documentation can be found in his '*Man and woman in 1 Corinthians*' (Ph.D. thesis; Cambridge University, 1973). Cf. Spicq, *Epitres Pastorales*, 421ff.; D.M. Scholer, 'Women's adornment', *Daughters of Sarah* 6:1 (1980) 3–6. For examples of a similar critique, cf. Juvenal, *Satire* 6, LCL (1918) 121ff.; D.M. Scholer, 'Exegesis: 1 Timothy 2:8–15', *Daughters of Sarah* 1:4 (May, 1975) 7–8.

205 Hurley, *Man and Woman*, 199.

206 This appears to be the usual meaning of the word in the NT in any case. Cf. 2 Thess 3.12; Ac 22.2; the translations; Payne, 'Libertarian women', 169–70, but cf. BAG, 350. Outside the NT the word usually means peaceful, quiet, still, or at rest. Cf. LSJ, 779; MM, 281.

207 On Jewish attitudes about teaching Torah, cf. Witherington, *Women*, 6–10 and notes. Not too much should be made of the imperative since what is being commanded is not simply learning, but learning in quietness and submission.

208 Once again, we do not have a personal object for ὑποταγῇ (cf. 1 Cor 14.34b). What is being inculcated is a proper attitude and behavior in worship and not merely in relationship to men or husbands. The text says they are to learn in all submissiveness, not that they are to submit to all men. It entails submission to the teaching and, by transference, to the one giving the faithful teaching

whom one is to show respect for. Cf. D. Guthrie, *The Pastoral Epistles* (TNTC; Grand Rapids: Eerdmans, 1957) 76.

209 Payne, 'Libertarian women', 172–3; Fee, *Timothy/Titus*, 39.

210 Cf. pp. 90–8 and D. J. Moo, '1 Timothy 2:11–15: meaning and significance', *Trinity Journal* n.s. 2 (1980) 62–83, and his response to Payne's rebuttal, 'The interpretation of 1 Timothy 2:11–15: a rejoinder', *Trinity Journal* n.s. 2 (1981) 198–222.

211 Payne, 'Libertarian women', 172–3.

212 Pace Moo, '1 Timothy 2:11–15', 65ff.; cf. Guthrie, *Pastoral Epistles*, 76 ('public teaching'); Spicq, *Épîtres Pastorales*, 379–80.

213 Cf. C. O. Osburn, 'ΑΥΘΕΝΤΕΩ (1 Timothy 2:12)', *ResQ* 25 (1982) 1–12, here 2; N. J. Hommes, 'Let women be silent in church', *CTJ* 4 (1969) 5–22, here 18–19; Dibelius/Conzelmann, *Pastoral Epistles*, 47, n. 19.

214 G. W. Knight, 'ΑΥΘΕΝΤΕΩ in reference to women in 1 Timothy 2.12', *NTS* 30 (1984) 143–57; C. C. Kroeger, 'Ancient heresies and a strange Greek verb', *RJ* 29 (1979) 12–15, offers a very strained and sexual interpretation of αὐθεντέω which is rightly refuted by Osburn, 'ΑΥΘΕΝΤΕΩ', 1–12.

215 Cf. Knight, 'ΑΥΘΕΝΤW', 145.

216 Lampe, *PGL*, 262; Chrysostom, *Homily 10 on Colossians* (NPNF XIII; ed, Phillip Schaff; Grand Rapids: Eerdmans, 1976 repr.) 304.

217 LSJ, 275.

218 MM, 91; Falconer, '1 Tim 2.14, 15', 375.

219 Hommes, 'Let women be silent', 5–22.

220 Robertson, 433, 1189–91; BDF, 452, p. 236; MHT III, 331.

221 So Payne, 'Libertarian women', 176.

222 On this exposition as haggada, cf. Hanson, *Pastoral Epistles*, 72–3; on traditional Jewish exposition of Genesis 2–3, cf. 2 Enoch 31.6, 4 Macc 18.6–8, B. T. Yebamoth 103b, and Philo, *Questions on Genesis* 1.33.46. In some cases it is suggested that Eve succumbed because she was weaker than Adam; others suggest that the serpent is engaging in sexual seduction. Cf. Fee, *Timothy/Titus*, 40; Str-B III, 256ff.

223 The curse is not in Eve desiring Adam, but in the fact that a fallen Adam will rule over Eve in a way that will not always reflect the love of God. The word translated 'rule' or 'lord it over' in Gen 3.16 is κυριεύσει (LXX) which has the same root as κυρίος. It is derived from the Hebrew word *mashal* meaning 'to rule or to have dominion over'. Cf. the helpful expositions by J. Coppens, 'Miscellanies Bibliques I, La soumission de la femme à l'homme d'après Gen. III, 16b', *ETL* 14 (1937) 632–41, and S. Foh, 'What is the woman's desire?' *WTJ* 37 (1975) 376–83.

224 Strictly speaking, the Genesis narrative only says that Adam was 'made', Cf. Payne, 'Libertarian women', 174ff.; Barrett, *Pastoral Epistles*, 56.

225 παράβασις means 'overstepping' or 'transgression' and can refer to a violation of a law (here commandment). Cf. Gal 3.19 where

it does not have any specific sexual connotation; BAG, 617; MM, 480; and contrast, Hanson, *Pastoral Epistles*, 73.

226 Cf. Witherington, *Women*, pp. 1ff. and n. 222.

227 Cf. Barrett, *Pastoral Epistles*, 56; Fee, *Timothy/Titus*, 37; Kelly, *Pastoral Epistles*, 69.

228 So Payne, 'Libertarian women', 117, citing Ignatius; Justin, *Dialogue*; Tertullian; Theophylact; and Lock, *Pastoral Epistles*, 32–3.

229 See n. 228 above; Moule, *I–B*, 56.

230 Cf. Moffatt (translation); Guthrie, *Pastoral Epistles*, 76–7; Jeremias, *Timotheus/Titus*, 22. As Fee, *Timothy/Titus*, 31, says, the author 'uses an entirely different word for the idea of being kept safe throughout his letters (see e.g. 2 Tim 3.11 and 4.18)'.

231 As pointed out to me by Dr A. T. Lincoln (Sheffield, England).

232 So S. Jebb, 'A suggested interpretation of 1 Tim 2.15', *ET* 81 (1969–70) 221–2. Cf. Moo, '1 Timothy 2:11–15', 71–3.

233 Cf. the quotation and interpretation of B. T. Berakoth 17a in Jeremias, *Timotheus/Titus*, 22; Chrysostom and Jerome thought children were in view here. Cf. Lock, *Pastoral Epistles*, 33, but compare Guthrie, *Pastoral Epistles*, 78–9, and Dibelius/Conzelmann, *Pastoral Epistles*, 48.

234 Barth, *Ephesians 4–6*, 661: 'The cult of the Great Mother in the Artemis Temple stamped the city more than others as a bastion and bulwark of women's rights.'

235 Cf. R. M. Lewis, 'The women' of 1 Timothy 3:11, *BSac* 136 (1979) 167–75.

236 Lewis, '1 Timothy 3:11', 168; cf. Barrett, *Pastoral Epistles*, 62, who rightly points to Pliny (Letters 10.96) in his reference to two 'ancillae quae ministrae dicebantur', written at a time that was perhaps not far from the date of these epistles.

237 C. K. Barrett, *Galatians: Freedom and Obligation* (Philadelphia: Westminster, 1985).

238 Cf. the conclusions of E. Schüssler Fiorenza, 'Women in the pre-Pauline and Pauline churches', *USQR* 33 (1978) 153–66, here 161–2; J. Nolland, 'Women in the public life of the Church', *Crux* 19:3 (1983) 17–23.

4 Women and the third evangelist

1 On all this, cf. H. Flender, *St Luke – Theologian of Redemptive History* (London: SPCK, 1967) 9–10, and J. Drury, *Tradition and Design in Luke's Gospel – A Study in Early Christian Historiography* (London: Darton, Longman and Todd, 1976) 71.

2 Flender, *St Luke*, 10.

3 Cf. Frederick W. Danker, *Jesus and the New Age According to St Luke* (St Louis: Clayton Pub. House, 1972) 209; Taylor, *Mark*, 497.

4 Cf. Witherington, *Women*, 100–3; and B. Witherington, 'On the road with Mary Magdalene, Joanna, Susanna, and other disciples: Luke 8.1–3', *ZNW* 70 (3–4, 1979) 242–8.

5 I. Howard Marshall, *The Gospel of Luke, A Commentary of the Greek Text* (NIGTC; Exeter: Paternoster, 1978) 486.
6 Witherington, *Women*, 35ff.
7 C. F. Evans, *Resurrection and the New Testament* (London: SCM, 1970) 103; cf. Luke 8.1–3, 23.55. Luke omits Mark's promised appearance in Galilee, probably because of his Jerusalem schema.
8 This sort of remembering may be seen as the prolegomenon to a faith response, but it is not clear that 'to remember' is equivalent to 'to respond in faith'. But cf. Danker, *Jesus*, 247; John M. Creed, *The Gospel According to St Luke* (London: Macmillan and Co., 1930) 294; E. L. Bode, *The First Easter Morning – The Gospel Accounts of Women's Visit to the Tomb of Jesus* (Rome: Biblical Institute, 1970) 62, 67; O. Michel, 'μιμνῄσκομαι', *TDNT* 4 (1967) 677.
9 This feature, probably not derived from Mark's (lost) ending, may reflect Luke's tendency to maximize the visibility and importance of the women's roles.
10 Cf. Evans, *Resurrection*, 104; Danker, *Jesus*, 247.
11 I. H. Marshall, 'The resurrection of Jesus in Luke', *TynB* 24 (1973) 55–98; X. Léon-Dufour, *Resurrection and the Message of Easter* (New York: Holt, Rinehart, Winston, 1974) 151, suggests that the list is here in order to link the death, burial, and resurrection. The placement of the list and at least part of its contents appears to be derived from Luke's special source. Cf. R. H. Fuller, *The Formation of the Resurrection Narratives* (New York: Macmillan and Co., 1971) 95.
12 Cf. Léon-Dufour, *Resurrection*, 153.
13 It seems likely that the juxtaposition of τοῖς λοιποῖς and αἱ λοιπαί is meant to imply a group of men in the former instance and a group of women in the latter. Cf. Marshall, 'Resurrection', 74.
14 Cf. Léon-Dufour, *Resurrection*, 159. Luke may add these other women at this point to create the impression of numerous witnesses of the empty tomb who went to the Apostles, and thus rule out the Eleven's excuse that it was only an idle tale of one or two hysterical women. The translation in the *JB* probably best conveys Luke's meaning. The reading ἦν δέ in K and other mss. is also probably a later correction and, interestingly, it singles out Mary Magdalene for special mention.
15 Joanna may be Luke's addition. Cf. Marshall, 'Resurrection', 74.
16 Cf. P. Schubert, 'The structure and significance of Luke 24', *Neutestamentliche Studien für Rudolf Bultmann* BZNW 21 (Berlin: A. Töpelmann, 1957) 168, and n. 12, cf. p. 174.
17 Cf. Marshall, 'Resurrection', 71; Bode, *First Easter Morning*, 67, 71.
18 Alfred Plummer, *A Critical and Exegetical Commentary on the Gospel According to S. Luke* (ICC; 5th ed.; Edinburgh: T. and T. Clark, 1922) 550; William Manson, *The Gospel of Luke* (MNTC; London: Hodder & Stoughton, 1930) 265.
19 Assimilation might be a possible reason for omitting vv. 6 and 12.

This does not, however, outweigh the following considerations: Lukan male—female parallelism, Luke's stress on Peter, and Luke's point that faith only comes from an appearance of Jesus who instructs His disciples on the basis of the Word, all argue for seeing v. 12 as Lukan and an original part of our text. Cf. Metzger, *TC*, 184; A. R. C. Leaney, 'The resurrection narratives in Luke (xxiv.12—53)', *NTS* 2 (1955—56) 110—14 Bode, *First Easter Morning*, 68—9; E. E. Ellis, *The Gospel of Luke* (NCB: Greenwood: Attic, 1974 rev. ed.) 272—3.

20 Cf. Marshall, *Luke*, 888.

21 Cf. A. Feuillet, 'La découverte du tombeau vide en Jean 20, 3—10 et la foi au Christ ressuscité', *EspV* 87 (1977) 273—4. Further, only Peter may be mentioned in 24.12 in order to stress the irony or reversal involved in having the chief Apostle confirm the women's message. Cf. P. Benoit, 'Marie Madeleine et les disciples au tombeau selon Joh 20, 1—18', *Judentum Urchristentum Kirche. Festschrift für Joachim Jeremias*. ZNW 26 (ed. W. Eltester; Berlin: A. Töpelmann, 1960) 148.

22 Cf. Léon-Dufour, *Resurrection*, 116.

23 Schubert, 'Structure', 172, concludes that the traditional empty tomb has little or no significance on the basis of the critique of 24.24. This fails to recognize that Luke is not devaluing the women's witness in 24.24 but rather is depicting the obtuseness of the followers to whom the women reported.

24 These parallels are suggested by J. D'Arc, 'Catechesis on the road to Emmaus', *LV* 32:2 (1977) 143—56. Various scholars have conjectured that the unnamed disciple was a woman, perhaps Cleopas' wife. Cf. G. B. Caird, *The Gospel of St Luke* (PNTC; Harmondsworth: Penguin, 1963) 259; Marshall, *Luke* 894. This may be so, but Luke makes nothing of the fact and thus the conjecture deserves no more than a passing mention.

25 So D'Arc, 'Catechesis', 151—3; cf. Marshall, *Luke*, 896; J. Reiling and J. L. Swellengrebel, *A Translator's Handbook on the Gospel of Luke* (Leiden: E. J. Brill, 1971) 753.

26 It is possible that Luke means to imply Peter's precedence over these two disciples in receiving an appearance. Cf. vv. 24, 34; Evans, *Resurrection*, 106. This might be an attempt to restore Peter to his pre-eminent place after he experiences less at the empty tomb than the women.

27 By this term Luke is making clear that Mary had no intimate sexual relations before the confrontation with Gabriel (so Danker, *Jesus*, 10). G. Delling, 'παρθένος', *TDNT* 5 (1967) 826—36, is probably right that, as in Matthew, the focus is on the specialness of Jesus and His birth, and that παρθένος is not used for ascetic or docetic reasons. The birth in the narrative is depicted as a normal human birth (Luke 2.23). Elizabeth conceives and gives birth through the natural agency, but with God's help, since she and Zechariah are old. Mary, the παρθένος, conceives by an act of God alone. Cf. C. H. Dodd, 'New Testament translation problems I', *BT* 27

(3, 1976) 301–5, and the reply by J. Carmignac, 'The meaning of *parthenos* in Luke 1.27 – a reply to C. H. Dodd', *BT* 28 (3, 1977) 327–30.

28 Metzger, *TC*, 129; Plummer, *Luke*, 22.

29 On the parallels and the usual form of annunciations and call narratives, cf. G. S. Prabhu, '"Rejoice, Favored One!"' Mary in the annunciation story of Luke', *Biblebhashyam* 3 (4, 1977) 259–77; John McHugh, *The Mother of Jesus in the New Testament* (London: Darton, Longman and Todd, 1975) 31–52. Pace Raymond Brown and K. P. Donfried, *et al.*, eds. *Mary in the New Testament* (Philadelphia: Fortress, 1978) 130–2; Marshall, *Luke*, 65. The view that χαῖρε is the ordinary Greek greeting fails to explain why Luke portrays Mary as wondering what sort of greeting she had just received. The standard blessing formula ὁ κύριος μετὰ σοῦ is not likely to be intended as the source of the confusion.

30 Danker, *Jesus*, 11.

31 Cf. Plummer, *Luke*, 22; Raymond Brown, *The Birth of the Messiah* (London: Geoffrey Chapman, 1977) 326–7; R. L. Humenay, 'The place of Mary in Luke: a look at modern biblical criticism', *AER* 5 (1974) 291–303. The phrase εὖρες γὰρ χάριν παρὰ τῷ θεῷ is equivalent to a common OT phrase (Gen 6.8; Judg 6.17; 1 Sam 1.18; 2 Sam 15.25) and as such signifies the free, gracious choice of God, rather than human acceptability. Cf. Marshall, *Luke*, 66. Pace McHugh, *Mother of Jesus*, 48.

32 Luke does not say specifically that Mary names Him (cf. 2.21). Cf. Gen 16.11, 30.11; Judg 13.24; 1 Sam 1.20; Brown, *Birth of the Messiah*, 289. Here it should be noted that God through the angel gives the name; thus, Mary and/or Joseph are instructed what to call Him.

33 Brown, ed., *Mary in the NT*, 114–5, nn. 244–5.

34 Cf. M. Zerwick, '... quoniam virum non cognosco (Lc I, 34)', *VD* 37 (1959) 212–24, 276–88, esp. 286–8.

35 In any case, to say 'I have had no relations', and 'I know no man immediately', are virtually equivalent. Cf. Brown, *Birth of the Messiah*, 289; Danker, *Jesus*, 12, on Gen 19.8, Judg 11.30, and our text. Cf. H. Guy, 'The virgin birth in St Luke', *ET* 68 (1957) 157–8.

36 Note the connection between 'handmaiden' in Luke 1.38 and Acts 2.18; cf. Brown, ed., *Mary in the NT*, 137.

37 Cf. Plummer, *Luke*, 24; Creed, *Luke*, 20; S. Schulz, 'ἐπισκιάζω', *TDNT* 7 (1971) 400, thinks divine generation is meant, but admits that this word is never used as a euphemism for sexual relations.

38 So LSJ, 657; cf. BAG, 298; Psa 91.4, 141.8.

39 McHugh, *Mother of Jesus*, 132–3.

40 We do not have mere resignation here. Cf. Marshall, *Luke*, 72: 'γένοιτό μοι ... a wish expressed by the optative' (i.e., 'may it be to me'). Also, McHugh, *Mother of Jesus*, 64–7.

41 Plummer, *Luke*, 25; cf. Luke 12.49–53, 14.25–27.

42 Danker, *Jesus*, 13.

43 Note how Luke maintains his focus on Mary rather than Joseph by important passing remarks (2.19, 51).

44 The ὅτι clause which follows is in all likelihood causal and thus the focus is on the ground of Mary's blessedness, i.e, her faith, not the content of that faith. Cf. Creed, *Luke*, 22; but cf. Marshall, *Luke*, 82 and Acts 27.25.

45 Brown, ed., *Mary in the NT*, 136, n.302.

46 Brown, *Birth of the Messiah*, 333, is correct that εὐλογημένος here has a comparative, not a superlative, value. Cf. Judg 5.24.

47 Cf. Danker, *Jesus*, 15; Creed, *Luke*, 22–4.

48 Ellis, *Luke*, 75.

49 Cf. Brown, *Birth of the Messiah*, 350–5.

50 Creed, *Luke*, 303–4; Plummer, *Luke*, 30–1.

51 Cf. M. Luther, 'The Magnificat', *Luther's Works*, vol.21 (ed. J. Pelikan; St Louis: Concordia Publishing House, 1956) 321.

52 Cf. J.T. Forestell, 'Old Testament background of the Magnificat', *MS* 12 (1961) 205–44; A. Richardson, *An Introduction to the Theology of the New Testament* (London: SCM, 1958) 176–8.

53 W. Grundmann, 'ταπεινός', *TDNT* 8 (1972) 21.

54 Cf. Brown, *Birth of the Messiah*, 349.

55 Ibid., 252, 342.

56 On the male–female parallelism in the Lukan infancy narrative in particular, cf. Brown, *Birth of the Messiah*, 248–53.

57 One should be careful not to make too much of this act since Elizabeth calls her son by the name the angel gave her. The naming ritual is an important rite of exercising authority by a Jewish parent, but in this case the woman is merely passing on the name the angel had given.

58 Cf. P. Benoit, 'L'Enfance de Jean-Baptiste selon Luc I', *NTS* 3 (1956–57) 194.

59 The text does not say that Mary was of the line of David, though several mss. try to insert such an idea. Cf. Plummer, *Luke*, 53; Creed, *Luke*, 33.

60 Cf. Str-B II, 124–6; Marshall, *Luke*, 118.

61 οἱ γονεῖς (Luke 2.27) is the natural term for Luke to use of Mary and Joseph without resorting to circumlocution. As Marshall, *Luke*, 119, says, '... it is hypercritical to find here a tradition that did not know of the virgin birth'. Pace Brown, ed., *Mary in the NT*, 144, n.320 and 158, n.356. Cf. Luke 2.5, 27, 33, 41, 48.

62 Cf. Brown, *Birth of the Messiah*, 462–3, who enumerates most of the well-known views. Also, P. Benoit, '"Et toi-même un glaive transpercera l'âme!" (Luc 2, 35)', *CBQ* 25 (3, 1963) 251–61.

63 So Marshall, *Luke*, 123. The key to a proper interpretation here would seem to be found by asking what negative factor affected both Jesus and Mary causing them anguish. The answer would be: the rejection of Jesus by most of Israel (He was the sign spoken against).

64 Anguish, doubt, sorrow, or suffering are not what the sword represents; they are the results of the sword's work (cf. Ezek 14.17).

The rejection of Jesus, not Mary's reaction to her son's rejection, is what the sword represents. Cf. McHugh, *Mother of Jesus*, 106–12.

65 Brown, *Birth of the Messiah*, 446, 466.
66 Cf. Creed, *Luke*, 43; Marshall, *Luke*, 124; Str-B II, 141.
67 So G. Stählin, χήρα', *TDNT* 9 (1974) 451, states: 'She is a prophet and is thus granted to see the child Jesus (v. 38). She is a witness, and is as such a model of the full-scale witness of the woman in the Christian community. She is unwearying in prayer ... And in virtue of her witness and prayer she stays continually in the temple, cf. v. 49. In this regard, too, this prophetess is a model for the first community of disciples, Lk 24:53, Ac 2:46.'
68 Who was also devout, did not remarry, and lived to approximately the same age (105). Cf. Judith 16.23: Danker, *Jesus*, 36.
69 Marshall, *Luke*, 115.
70 Plummer, *Luke*, 71.
71 Luke stresses that Mary and Joseph are good Jews; cf. 2.21, 22, 23–24, 39. As Brown, *Birth of the Messiah*, 327, notes, '... if the birth were conceived as miraculous, no purification should have been needed'. Apparently, Joseph and Mary did not see the birth as other than normal, and thus the διανοῖγον μήτραν of Luke 2.23 is fatal to the view that Mary gave birth to Jesus with the preservation of her virginity. So Plummer, *Luke*, 65; Creed, *Luke*, 39; Brown, ed., *Mary in the NT*, 153, n. 344.
72 Brown, ed., *Mary in the NT*, 150–1.
73 Ibid., 161–2.
74 It has been suggested that by having Mary as the spokeswoman for the family, Luke prepares the reader for the eclipse of Joseph who will not appear again in Luke–Acts except at Luke 3.23. Cf. Brown, ed., *Mary in the NT*, 160.
75 Brown, ed., *Mary in the NT*, 161, n. 367. Note also that Jesus' reproach is directed to both Joseph and Mary (αὐτούς, 2.49); Mary is not singled out for rebuke.
76 Cf. Danker, *Jesus*, 29.
77 We have an elliptical sentence and there is no need to include Damaris in the list of male converts. Cf. F. F. Bruce, *Commentary on the Book of Acts* (NICNT; Grand Rapids: Eerdmans, 1954) 341; Ernst Haenchen, *The Acts of the Apostles, A Commentary* (Philadelphia: Westminster Press, 1971) 527; Kirsopp Lake and H. J. Cadbury, *The Acts of the Apostles*, vol. 4 (London: Macmillan and Co., 1933) 120.
78 C. F. Parvey, 'The theology and leadership of women in the New Testament', *Religion and Sexism, Images of Woman in the Jewish and Christian Tradition*, (ed. R. R. Ruether; New York: Simon and Schuster, 1974) 117–49, here 145.
79 While some rabbis insisted that a woman is not to serve a meal to men or to eat with men, it is questionable whether or not the rabbis' ruling applied to the serving of women (here widows) or to homes without servants or sons. Cf. Leonard Swidler, *Women in Judaism:*

The Status of Women in Formative Judaism (Metuchen: Scarecrow, 1976): Str-B I, 480, 882. Neither the Greeks nor the Romans had any scruples about women waiting on tables, though it was normally only a woman who was of the servant class whom they would expect to perform such a task in any but the poorest of homes. Cf. Cato's list of a housekeeper's duties in *On Agriculture*, 143, LCL (1934) 124—5.

80 Cf. Witherington, *Women*, 100ff.

81 In Jewish circles the term was bestowed on benefactresses or was simply an honorary title. So far as I know, a Jewess never had a synagogue in her own home, and in this respect she differed from her Christian counterparts. My use of the term of John Mark's mother and Lydia not only includes the idea of benefactress, but also the idea of being a house mother to a church. Cf. O. Michel, 'οἶκος', *TDNT* 5 (1967) 130.

82 This is carefully detailed by H. J. Cadbury, 'Lexical notes on Luke—Acts, III — Luke's interest in lodging', *JBL* 45 (1926) 305—22. Cf. the following examples which involve or turn on matters of hospitality or lodging: Luke 7.36—50, 10.38—42, 19.1—10, 16.19—31, 14.7—14, 10.25—34, 16.1—13, 24.29—30, 13.36—43; Acts 1.13, 12.12—17, 2.46, 21.8, 21.16, 28.7, 17.5—9, 9.11, 10.5—6, etc.

83 D. W. Riddle, 'Early Christian hospitality: a factor in the gospel transmission', *JBL* 57 (1938) 141—54.

84 Ibid., 152.

85 There are intimations elsewhere in the NT that women played an important part in the establishment or maintenance of house churches. Cf. Rom 16.3—5; 1 Cor 16.19; and possibly Col 4.15. The elect lady of 2 John may be Lady Eclecta who has a church in her house, but v. 13 probably militates against this suggestion.

86 Though παιδίσκη is literally a diminutive of girl, in the NT it is always used of someone of servant class. Cf. BAG, 609; Matt 26.69; Mark 14.66, 69; Luke 22.56; Acts 16.16, and espec. John 18.17. Contra H. Burton, 'The house of Mary', *Exp* 2nd ser 1 (1881) 313—18.

87 Burton, 'The house of Mary', 317—18, suggests this is an all-female prayer meeting but the gender of ἱκανοί probably rules this out. If 'the brethren' means the Twelve, then Peter's words do not imply this is an all-female meeting.

88 Ibid., 316.

89 A. Oepke, 'γυνή', *TDNT* 1 (1964) 785, notes that this text indicates women's full membership in the early Christian community.

90 T. F. Torrance, 'St Paul at Philippi: three startling conversions. Acts 16:6—40', *EvQ* 13 (1941) 62—74.

91 Y. Redalié, 'Conversion ou libération? Notes sur Actes 16, 11—40', *Bulletin du Centre Protestant d'Études* 26 (7, 1974) 7—17.

92 Cf. Homer, *The Iliad* 4.141—143, LCL (1924) 1:162—3, who refers to this as a woman's task. Cf. J. Hastings, 'Women in the Acts of the Apostles', *ET* 4 (1892—93) 434—6.

93 Cf. W. D. Thomas, 'The place of women in the church at Philippi', *ET* 83 (1971–72) 117; Haenchen, *Acts*, 499.
94 Thus, Lydia is not seen as a full proselyte of Judaism. Cf. Bruce, *Acts*, 215; K. G. Kuhn, 'προσήλυτος', *TDNT* 6 (1968) 744.
95 Though παρεκάλεσεν here may mean 'encourage' or 'invite'; in view of the repetition of the plea, it seems that 'beg' or 'plead' is a more likely translation. Cf. BAG, 622; A–S, 340; At 16.40 the same word means 'encourage', but the context is different.
96 Whether she is portrayed as unmarried or widowed, it would be scandalous in Jewish circles for Paul to stay with Lydia. W. M. Ramsay, 'The denials of Peter – section III: the house in the New Testament', *ET* 27 (1915–16) 471–2, suggests that Lydia was able to entertain men without violating local custom because her house was large enough to allow the men to have one section to themselves.
97 There is evidence that women continued to be prominent in the Philippian church after Paul's time. Cf. Thomas, 'Place of women', 119–20, on Polycarp.
98 Cf. J. Daniélou, *The Ministry of Women in the Early Church* (Leighton Buzzard, England: Faith, 1974) 20; R. Gryson, *Le ministère des femmes dans l'Église ancienne* (Gembloux; Duculot, 1972) 19–33; G. G. Blum, 'Das Amt der Frau im Neuen Testament', *NovT* 7 (1964) 142–61, concentrating especially on the Pauline corpus. H. W. Beyer, 'διάκονος', *TDNT* 2 (1964) 93, says, 'It is indisputable, however, that an order of deaconesses did quickly arise in the Church. A particular part was played here by widows who, on the strength of their chaste conduct on the one side and their loving service on the other, already received official recognition in 1 Tim 5.3ff.'
99 This probably indicates that Luke's audience was not Aramaic speaking. Dorcas or Tabitha means 'gazelle'. Cf. Lake and Cadbury, *Acts* IV, 109–10; BAG, 810; MM, 169, 624. Does this name indicate that Luke portrays this woman as originally a slave or freed woman? Cf. Lake and Cadbury, *Acts* IV, 110.
100 Cf. Haenchen, *Acts*, 339, n. 1; Bruce, *Acts*, 212; K. H. Rengstorf, 'μαθήτρια', *TDNT* 4 (1967) 460–1. J. Viteau, 'L'institution des diacres et des veuves – Actes vi.1–10, viii.4–40, xxi.8', *RHE* 22 (1926) 513–37, argues that Tabitha's being called disciple indicates Luke portrays her as having had formal instruction in Christian religion, perhaps in preparation for being a 'spiritual widow'. That Luke calls Tabitha a disciple indicates he had no difficulties in calling women Christians and thus it is unlikely that Luke is trying to exclude the widows from the group of believers in 8.41. Cf. Acts 9.41. The phrase τοὺς ἁγίους καὶ τὰς χήρας on the surface might imply that the widows were not among the saints (Christians). Alternatively, if there was a semi-official order of widows at this time, then χήρα may be a technical term for a certain group within the community who had duties involving funeral preparations and mourning (cf. v. 39). G. Stählin, 'χήρα', *TDNT* 9 (1974) 451, n. 107, and 452, n. 108 (cf. n. 144),

mentions the possibility that we do have an order of widows here and this is why they are mentioned.

101 Cf. Barclay M. Newman, and Eugene A. Nida, *A Translator's Handbook on the Acts of the Apostles* (London: United Bible Societies, 1972) 200; Bruce, *Acts*, 212; G. Delling 'πλήρης', *TDNT* 6 (1968) 286, objects to the translation 'full of good works', but at least in English it is an accurate idiomatic way of saying 'continually involved in doing good'.

102 ἐλεημοσυνῶν ὧν ἐποίει refers to Tabitha's donations. Haenchen, *Acts*, 339, says it is added to forestall the idea that Tabitha had received good works. In the NT this phrase always refers to benevolent activity to the poor or needy. Cf. R. Bultmann, 'ἐλεημοσύνη', *TDNT* 2 (1964) 486.

103 Cf. M. Shabbath 23.5, Danby, 120.

104 For the view that she is part of an order of widows, cf. Viteau, 'L'institution des diacres', 532–3; Parvey, 'Theology and leadership', 145.

105 Thus Tabitha probably is not the Tabitha referred to in the 'Historia Josephi'. Cf. E. Nestle, 'Schila et Tabitha', *ZNW* 11 (1910) 240; W. E. Crum, 'Schila und Tabitha', *ZNW* 12 (1911) 352. Also, though Tabitha was perhaps a widow, she probably was not part of an order of widows, for her deeds seem to be more in line with a diaconal ministry, though perhaps our knowledge on this subject is too meagre to permit such a distinction. Cf. Richard B. Rackham, *The Acts of the Apostles, An Exposition* (Westminster Commentaries; 10th ed.; London: Methuen and Co., 1925) 145, and n. 4. It should be noted that the good deeds of the widows in 1 Tim 5.10 belong to the widows' past, and that 1 Tim 2.10 indicates that good deeds were not the task of widows alone. Probably 1 Tim 5.10 is a general description, not a list of widow's official functions.

106 By my count, there are eighty-five or more references to prophets and prophesying in Luke–Acts, evenly distributed between the two volumes (approximately forty-two in Luke, and forty-three or -five in Acts).

107 Cf. E. E. Ellis, 'The role of the Christian prophet in Acts', *Apostolic History and the Gospel* (ed. W. Ward Gasque and R. P. Martin; Grand Rapids: Eerdmans, 1971) 55–6.

108 Ibid.

109 Ibid., 56, 62. It should be noted that Luke says προφητεύουσαι, not 'they prophesied about this or that'. He thus is referring to their functions in general, not to a particular prophecy for which they were noted. It was this which was distinctive about their ongoing activities.

110 So Viteau, 'L'institution des diacres', 523. Such an order of virgins or spiritual widows appears to have existed at least by the early decades of the second century. Cf. Ignatius, *Smyrnaeans* 13.1, *The Apostolic Fathers*, LCL (1912) 1:266–7.

111 Parvey, 'Theology and leadership', 145. παρθένοι may simply mean 'unmarried' with no technical sense at all, and it is possible that

Luke mentions this because he thinks it is a good example for his audience to follow. Cf. G. Delling, 'παρθένος', *TDNT* 5 (1967) 834, and n. 52, to 1 Cor 7.5. Cf. Newman and Nida, *Translator's Acts*, 405; BAG, 632; Lampe, *PGL*, 1037–40.

112 It is to be noted that in both examples of prophetesses in Luke–Acts (Anna, Philip's daughters) there seems to be a relationship between abstinence from marriage and the gifts they have. Cf. G. Stählin, 'χήρα', *TDNT* 9 (1974) 451, n. 98; contrast Eusebius, *Ecclesiastical History* 3.30.1, 5.18.3–4, LCL (1926) 1.268–9, 486–7.

113 BAG, 708.

114 A. von Harnack, 'Über die Beiden Rezensionen der Geschichte der Prisca und des Aquila in Act Apost. 18, 1–17', *Studien zur Geschichte des Neuen Testaments und der Alten Kirche* (Berlin/Leipzig: W. De Gruyter, 1931) 54–6.

115 BAG, 708; also, Bruce, *Acts*, 369; E. H. Plumptre, 'Aquila and Priscilla', *Biblical Studies* (E. H. Plumptre, ed.; London: Griffith, Farran, Okeden and Welch, 1885) 423.

116 Haenchen, *Acts*, 550; Sanday and Headlam, *Romans*, 418–20.

117 von Harnack, 'Über die Beiden Rezensionen', 48–61.

118 Haenchen, *Acts*, 533; n. 4; cf. Plumptre, 'Aquila and Priscilla', 421; Rackham, *Acts*, 324; C. S. C. Williams, *A Commentary on the Acts of the Apostles* (London: A. and C. Black, 1957) 209.

119 Haenchen, *Acts*, 539; cf. J. Schneider, 'προσέρχομαι', *TDNT* 2 (1964) 684; H. Conzelmann, *History of Primitive Christianity* (Nashville: Abingdon, 1973) 98–9; E. Schweizer, 'Die Bekehrung des Apollos, Apg 18, 24–26', *Beiträge zur Theologie des Neuen Testaments – Neutestamentliche Aufsätze (1955–1970)* (Zurich: Zwingli, 1970) 71–9.

120 W. Michaelis, 'ὁδός', *DNT* 5 (1967) 89–90; B. T. D. Smith, 'Apollos and the Twelve Disciples at Ephesus', *JTS* 16 (1914–15) 245–6; Haenchen, *Acts*, 551; Lake and Cadbury, *Acts* IV, 233; Williams, *Acts*, 216.

121 Lake and Cadbury, *Acts* IV, 233–4; BDF, sec. 244, p. 127; MHT I, 78, all agree that we likely have an elative here. The elative comparative is still a comparative implying that more complete information was given. Cf. Robertson, 665; BAG, 32.

122 Cf. G. B. Stevens, NPNF XI (1975) 245, n. 2, commenting on Homily XL of John Chrysostom. On the basis of Chrysostom's text of Acts 18.26 which possibly reads, '... πρισκιλλα προσελάβετο αὐτόν καὶ ἀκριβέστερον αὐτῷ ἐξέθεντο τὴν ὁδὸν τοῦ κυρίου', F. W. Blass ('Priscilla und Aquila', *TSK* 74 [1901] 124–6) conjectured that the name Aquila originally may have been an interpolation at this point. Cf. R. Schumacher, 'Aquila und Priscilla', *TGl* 12 (1920) 97.

123 This is to read twentieth-century concerns back into the text. προσλαμβάνω seems to mean 'to take aside', or possibly 'to take home'. Cf. BAG, 724; G. Delling, 'προσλαμβάνω', *TDNT* 4 (1967) 15.

124 Stevens, NPNF XI (1975) 245. On Paul's view of Priscilla and

Aquila and their work, cf. E. A. Leonard, 'St Paul on the status of women', *CBQ* 12 (1950) 311–20.

5. Women in the churches of Matthew, Mark and John

1 Cf. Witherington, *Women*, pp. 28ff.
2 I do not believe that in all texts Mark means no more than the Twelve when he uses the term disciples. Women are intimated to be disciples at various points (cf. below on Mark 15.40–41).
3 Witherington, *Women*, pp. 6–10 and notes.
4 Ibid., pp. 118ff.
5 Ibid., pp. 118–23.
6 H. Schlier, 'Die Osterbotschaft aus dem Grab (Markus 16.1–8)', *KG* 27 (1, 1971) 4; L. Brun, 'Der Auferstehungsberichte des Markusevangeliums', *TSK* 87 (1914) 350 (346–88).
7 É. Dhanis, 'L'ensevelissement de Jésus et la visite au tombeau dans l'évangile de Saint Marc (Mc. XV, 40–XVI, 8)' *Greg* 39 (2, 1958) 367–410.
8 Bode, *First Easter Morning*, 5.
9 W. R. Farmer, *The Last Twelve Verses of Mark* (SNTSM 25; Cambridge: Cambridge University Press, 1974); cf. Z. C. Hodges, 'The women and the empty tomb', *BSac* 123 (October, 1966) 301–9.
10 Metzger (*TC*, 126) says, 'No one who had available as the conclusion of the Second Gospel the twelve verses 9–20, so rich in interesting material, would have deliberately replaced them with four lines of a colorless and generalized summary.'
11 Cf. vv. 9–11 to John 20.1–2; vv. 12–13 to Luke 24.13–35; v. 15 to Matt 28.19; v. 19 to Acts 1.9 in C. F. D. Moule, *The Gospel According to Mark* (CBC; Cambridge: Cambridge University Press, 1965) 133. Cf. G. W. Trompf, 'The first resurrection appearance and the ending of Mark's Gospel', *NTS* 18 (3, 1972) 327.
12 These verses may date to the first half of the second century and may originally be a catechetical summary; cf. William L. Lane, *The Gospel According to Mark* (Grand Rapids: Eerdmans, 1974) 601–11.
13 H. J. Cadbury, 'Mark 16.8', *JBL* 46 (1927) 344–5. These examples are important because they date both before and after the first century AD and their vernacular character makes them close to Mark in form and style. Cf. R. H. Lightfoot, *The Gospel Message of St Mark* (Oxford: Oxford University Press, 1962) 80–97, 106–16; F. F. Bruce, 'The end of the Second Gospel', *EvQ* 17 (1945) 169–81.
14 Cf. R. R. Ottley, 'ἐφοβοῦντο γάρ Mark xvi.8', *JTS* 27 (1925–26) 407–9.
15 Cf. Lightfoot, *Gospel Message*, 87ff.; K. Tagawa, *Miracles et Évangile. La pensée personnelle de l'évangeliste Marc* (Études d'histoire et de philosophie religieuses 62; Paris: Universitaires de France, 1966) 99–122; D. Catchpole, 'The fearful silence of the women at the tomb – a study in Markan theology', *JTSA* 18 (1977)

3–10; R.P. Meye, 'Mark 16:8 – the ending of Mark's Gospel', *BR* 14 (1969) 33–43.
16 There is a parallel structure in 16.8:

a – and they went out and fled from the tomb
b – for trembling and astonishment had come upon them
a' – and they said nothing to anyone
b' – for they were afraid

Cf. R.H. Smith, 'New and old in Mark 16:1–8', *CTM* 43 (1972) 518–27, here 525–6. The γάρ is explanatory in each case. Cf. Taylor, *Mark*, 609.
17 It is difficult to see how Fuller, *Formation*, 64, can maintain that the women's silence is part of Mark's secrecy motif since the scene takes place after the resurrection, and in the Marcan redaction the women are told explicitly to bear witness (v. 7).
18 Cf. Lane, *Mark*, 601–11.
19 So Taylor, *Mark*, 609–10; Cranfield, *Mark*, 470–1; E. Klostermann, *Das Markusevangelium* (HNT 3; 2nd rev. ed.; Tübingen: J.C.B. Mohr, 1926) 190. The argument that Mark is presenting only that which is accessible to all Christians (i.e., the word about the risen Lord, the empty tomb, etc.) fails to take into account that the Fourth Evangelist goes out of his way to present his material as that which is accessible to all generations by faith in the word of testimony, yet he does not omit resurrection appearances.
20 We cannot go into the vexed question of how Mark's original ending became lost except to say that it is probable that Mark's Gospel was mutilated at this point, since 16.8 may have been at the end of a column, and since the end of a scroll would be outermost once it had been read. Apparently, it was left this way after reading, and often the title and author of a scroll would be put at the end, not the beginning, of a scroll. Cf. F.G. Kenyon, 'Papyrus rolls and the ending of St Mark', *JTS* 40 (1929) 56–7. Further, once Matthew and Luke came into circulation (documents which included almost all of Mark), the need for replacing a lost ending of Mark would not be felt for a time except in an area where Mark was the only available Gospel (perhaps Italy?). Cf. E.J. Goodspeed, 'The original conclusion of the Gospel of Mark', *AJT* 9 (1909) 484–90, espec. 486.
21 Cf. Goodspeed, 'Original conclusion', 484–90. The conjectures of C.F.D. Moule, 'St Mark xvi.8 – once more', *NTS* 2 (1955–56) 58–9, and A. Farrer, *St Matthew and St Mark* (Westminster: Dacre Press, 1954) 144–59, both of whom propose that Mark had only a short concluding phrase after 16.8, are worth consideration, but fail to solve the dilemma since the phrases they suggest do not include references to any resurrection appearances.
22 Goodspeed, 'Original conclusion', 488; cf. E. Klostermann, *Das Mattäusevangelium* (HNT 4; 2nd rev. ed.; Tübingen: J.C.B. Mohr, 1927) 229.
23 C.E.B. Cranfield, 'St Mark 16.1–8', *SJT* 5 (1952) 287.

24 Cf. J. Calvin, *A Harmony of the Gospels* III (ed. D. W. and T. F. Torrance; Edinburgh: St. Andrews, 1972) 221.
25 Perhaps Mark was not excluding the women from the promised appearance since they are addressed here. Contrast R. Brown, 'The resurrection and biblical criticism', *Commonweal* 87 (8, 1967) 232–6, here 234, to F. Neirynck, 'Les femmes au tombeau: étude de la rédaction Matthéenne (Matt. xxviii.1–10)', *NTS* 15 (1968–69) 181–2.
26 Pace Lightfoot, *Gospel Message*, 92; G. Mangatt, 'At the tomb of Jesus', *Biblebhashyam* 3 (2, 1977) 91–6, here 94–5.
27 Smith, 'New and old in Mark 16:1–8', 525–6; Witherington, *Women*, 118–19.
28 Moule, 'St Mark xvi.8', 58–9, argues that the women's trembling and amazement made them run straight to the disciples and tell them only, and not stop along the way to give normal Eastern greetings or proclaim the Easter message. T. Horvath, 'The early Markan tradition on the resurrection – Mk 16, 1–8', *RUO* 43 (3, 1973) 445–8, suggests that the women were frightened because their task of instructing men was unheard of among the Jews.
29 Catchpole, 'Fearful silence', 6.
30 Notice how Matthew has enhanced and altered the Marcan account in this and in other respects.
31 The ms. tradition which has been said to refer to Joseph as Jesus' father will bear another interpretation. Cf. B. Metzger, 'On the citation of variant readings of Matt. 1:16', *JBL* 77 (1958) 361–3.
32 Indeed, as Brown, *Birth of the Messiah*, 50, argues, it is likely that Matthew composed his infancy narratives as an integral part of his Gospel, not as an afterthought.
33 K. Stendahl, 'Quis et unde? An analysis of Mt 1–2', *Judentum Urchristentum Kirche. Festschrift für Joachim Jeremias* (BZNW 26; ed. W. Eltester; Berlin: A. Töpelmann, 1960) 94–105, here 102 says 'vv. 18–25 are the enlarged footnote to the crucial point in the genealogy'. Brown, *Birth of the Messiah*, 52–4, points out that Matthew 1 is about who and how (i.e., the virginal conception), and that Matthew 2 is about where and whence.
34 Cf. R. E. Brown, *The Virginal Conception and Bodily Resurrection of Jesus* (New York: Paulist Press, 1973) 27, nn. 30–1. H. von Campenhausen, *The Virgin Birth in the Theology of the Ancient Church* (Naperville, Il: A. R. Allenson, 1964) rightly points out that Mary's immaculate conception, perpetual virginity, assumption, and sinlessness are to be seen as concepts that arose after the NT was written.
35 It was not normal to list women in a genealogy though it was done: (1) when the father was unknown; (2) to distinguish various sons that came from one patriarch but several different wives; and (3) if they were related to or were famous figures. Cf. M. D. Johnson, *The Purpose of Biblical Genealogies with Special Reference to the Setting of the Genealogies of Jesus* (SNTSM 8; Cambridge: Cambridge University Press, 1969) 152; Gen 22.20–24; Exod 6.23.

36 View (2) is the suggestion of Johnson, *Purpose of Biblical Genealogies*, 152ff., and has the advantage that it is based on something all four women share in common, but it is based on Jewish debates on the women in the genealogy that are considerably later in date than Matthew's Gospel. Cf. Brown, ed., *Mary in the NT*, 80, nn. 161–2. View (4) is doubtful since it seems unlikely that the Evangelist would try to argue in such a negative fashion, or to prove that Jesus, David, and Solomon had something unseemly in their past. Similarly, '... dubious is an apologetics which answers (assumed) Jewish charges of Mary's sinfulness by pointing to other sinful women – Would that make Jesus' suspected origins less objectionable?' (Brown, ed., *Mary in the NT*, 81–2). View (3) has the advantage that it is able to find something unseemly, but focuses rather on the divine plan involved in these irregularities. Cf. Stendahl, 'Quis et unde?', 101.

37 H. Wansbrough, 'Event and interpretation: VIII. The adoption of Jesus', *Clergy Review* 55 (12, 1970) 921–8.

38 Of course, legal paternity was a possibility in first-century Judaism; cf. Brown, *Birth of the Messiah*, 138–9.

39 Cf. X. Léon-Dufour, 'Le juste Joseph', *NRT* 81 (3, 1959) 225–31. This picture of Joseph is very much in keeping with the Jewish view of the family structure and its patriarchal dominance. If Brown, *Birth of the Messiah*, 45, is right in seeing the First Evangelist's audience as including both Jewish and Gentile disciples, or even if R. Walker, *Die Heilsgeschichte im ersten Evangelium* (FRLANT 91; Göttingen: Vandenhoeck and Ruprecht, 1967) 9–10, 120–7, is correct that the author's main point is that the Jews have had their chance and thus the mission of the Church is to be directed towards Gentiles, then the Evangelist, by setting up Joseph as a model disciple, could be affirming that male headship and female subordination have their place in the *new* covenant community even if predominantly Gentile in character.

40 Cf. MHT III, 322.

41 Cf. BAG, 796; LSJ, 1712; David Hill, *The Gospel of Matthew* (NCB; Greenwood: Attic Press, 1972) 78; Alan Hugh M'Neile, *The Gospel According to St Matthew* (London: Macmillan and Co., 1965) 7; Brown, *Birth of the Messiah*, 124; J. Schneider, 'συνέρχομαι', *TDNT* 2 (1964) 634, n.1; MM, 606. The word γινώσκω may mean sexual union here; cf. BAG, 159ff.

42 I. Broer, 'Die Bedeutung der "Jungfrauengeburt" im Mattäusevangelium', *BibLeb* 12 (4, 1971) 248–60.

43 McHugh, *Mother of Jesus*, 37–48, 78–9; cf. Luke 11.27.

44 Since Matt 1.18 is probably the Evangelist's editorial comment, the ἐκ πνεύματος ἁγίου should not be taken as a statement about Joseph's initial understanding of the circumstances. Also, the δέ here seems to be continuative rather than adversative.

45 A formal procedure was necessary since betrothal was seen as legally binding. Cf. Jeremias, *Jerusalem*, 359ff.; M. Kiddushin 1.1, Danby, 321.

46 McHugh, *Mother of Jesus*, 204; A. Vögtle, 'Mt. 1, 25 und die Virginitas B.M. Virginis post partum', *TQ* 147 (1, 1967) 28–39.
47 M'Neile, *Matthew*, 10, says, 'In the New Testament, a negative followed by ἕως οὗ (e.g., xvii.9) ... always implies that the negated action did, or will, take place after the point of time indicated by the participle ...'
48 The meaning of ἕως without οὗ is not relevant here. BDF, sec. 485, p.237. Moule, *I–B*, 85, says that ἕως οὗ in the NT is strictly equivalent to 'until such time as' (cf. LSJ, 751). As BAG, 335, shows, the translation 'while' of ἕως οὗ is found only when the verb is in the subjunctive. The punctiliar sense of the aorist indicative ἔτεκεν when coupled with the οὐκ indicates the duration of Joseph's not knowing. Thus, while ἕως οὗ may not in itself imply anything about what happened after the limit of the 'until' (so Brown, ed., *Mary in the NT*, 87–7, n.177), when it precedes an aorist indicative such as ἔτεκεν and following ἐγίνωσκεν, it is hard to escape the conclusion that Joseph knew her after the child was born.
49 Cf. Brown, *Birth of the Messiah*, 231; R.R. Ruether, *Mary – The Feminine Face of the Church* (London: SCM, 1979) 26.
50 Witherington, *Women*, 18–21.
51 Cf. B. Witherington, 'Matthew 5.32 and 19.9 – exception or exceptional situation?' *NTS* 31:4 (Oct., 1985) 571–6.
52 Witherington, *Women*, 28–32.
53 Ibid., pp.41–4, for a detailed exegesis.
54 Cf. Hill, *Matthew*, 359; Fuller, *Formation*, 74–5; Cranfield, 'St Mark 16.1–8', 411–2; Martin Dibelius, *From Tradition to Gospel* (London: Ivor Nicholson and Watson, 1934) 297–8.
55 Cf. Neirynck, 'Les femmes au tombeau', 175–6; Taylor, *Mark*, 604.
56 Cf. Fuller, *Formation*, 74–5.
57 Neirynck, 'Les femmes au tombeau', 171–3; M'Neile, *Matthew*, 431.
58 Cf. Trompf, 'First resurrection appearance', 315–19, on how closely Matthew follows Mark in his passion narrative.
59 BAG, 724, notes, 'The Risen Lord is esp. the object of worship: Mt 28:9, 17; Lk 24:52 t.r.' As Hill, *Matthew*, 359, says, the Evangelist's addition of προσκυνέω 'may well reflect a liturgical setting for the development of the tradition'.
60 Zerwick, sec. 7, p.3, argues that the 'they' in 28.9 is a plural of category referring only to Mary Magdalene. Cf. MHT III, 26; D. Wenham, 'The resurrection narratives in Matthew's Gospel', *TynB* 24 (1973) 21–54.
61 Cf. Neirynck, 'Les femmes au tombeau', 178; Fuller, *Formation*, 79.
62 Cf. Neirynck, 'Les femmes au tombeau', 179; H. Greeven, 'προσκυνέω', *TDNT* VI (1968) 764; K. Weiss, 'πούς', *TDNT* VI (1968) 630.
63 E. Schweizer, *Das Evangelium nach Matthäus* (NTD 2; eds. P. Althaus and J. Behm; Göttingen: Vandenhoeck and Ruprecht, 1950) 342.
64 Witherington, *Women*, 80–5, for detailed exegesis.

65 Ibid., 92–8.
66 Ibid., 110ff.
67 J. Daniélou, 'The empty tomb', *Month* n.s. 39 (1968) 215–22, here 217; M. Hengel, 'Maria Magdalena und die Frauen als Zeugen', *Abraham Unser Vater, Festschrift für Otto Michel, zum 60. Geburtstag* (Leiden: E. J. Brill, 1963) 243–56, here 151–6; Bode, *First Easter*, 75. R. Brown, 'Roles of women in the Fourth Gospel', *TS* 36 (4, 1975) 688–99, here 692, argues, 'The phenomenon of giving a quasi-apostolic role to a woman is even more apparent in chap. 20.' Brown points out that on the Pauline criterion for apostleship (having seen the risen Jesus and having been sent to proclaim Him) and in view of the fact that what Mary proclaims is the standard apostolic proclamation ('I have seen the Lord') Mary comes close to meeting the requirements for, or functioning as, an apostle. Interestingly, in Gnostic quarters it is Mary Magdalene, not Peter, who became the most prominent witness to the teaching of the risen Lord. Rabanus Maurus in his famous ninth-century life of Mary Magdalene calls Mary one 'like an apostle'. Cf. C. Journet, 'L'apparition à Marie de Magdala', *NVet* 40 (2, 1965) 147.
68 Cf. Raymond Brown, *The Gospel According to John*, vol. I (Anchor Bible; Garden City: Doubleday and Company, 1966) 512–13; Leon Morris, *The Gospel According to John* (NICNT; Grand Rapids: Eerdmans, 1971) 833–4; Brooke Foss Westcott, *The Gospel According to St John: The Authorised Version* (London: John Murray, 1882) 290–1.
69 Such contrasts are made by A. Feuillet, 'La découverte du tombeau vide en Jean 20,3–10 et la Foi au Christ ressuscité', *EspV* 87 (19, 1977) 273–84. P. S. Minear, ' "We don't know where ..." John 20:2', *Int* 30 (1976) 127, rightly points out that the function of the two disciples in vv. 3–10 is a dual corroboration of Mary's report. He ably refutes the usual view that the beloved disciple believed Jesus was risen.
70 Cf. Fuller, *Formation*, 136–42.
71 Cf. C. K. Barrett, *The Gospel According to St John* (London: SPCK, 1955) 469; Morris, *John*, 839. As Brown, 'Roles of women', 695, points out, '... John has no hesitation in placing a woman in the same category of relationship to Jesus as the Twelve would be placed if they are meant "by his own" in 13:1.',Cf. 10.3. Here Mary is depicted as one in the process of becoming a fully-fledged disciple. It is not enough to recognize the Shepherd's voice, one must go on to understand His word and work and obey His commands.
72 Cf. Minear, ' "We don't know where" ', 137.
73 Morris, *John*, 838.
74 P. Benoit, 'Marie-Madeleine et les disciples au tombeau selon John 20,1–18', *Judentum Urchristentum Kirche. Festschrift für Joachim Jeremias* (BZNW 26; ed. W. Eltester; Berlin: A. Töpelmann, 1960) 144–6, 150–2.
75 Edwyn C. Hoskyns, *The Fourth Gospel*, vol. II (ed. F. N. Davey; London: Faber and Faber, 1940) 646–8, and Morris, *John*, 839,

probably are wrong to see the title 'Rabboni' as a declaration of faith paralleling Thomas' exclamation. Cf. Raymond Brown, *The Gospel According to John*, vol. II (1970) 991–2; R. H. Lightfoot, *St John's Gospel, A Commentary* (ed. C. F. Evans; Oxford: Oxford University Press, 1957) 334–5.

76 Cf. T. H. Farmer, '"Touch me not"', *ET* 28 (1916–17) 92–3; T. Nicklin, '"Noli me tangere"', ET 51 (1939–40) 478; C. H. Dodd, *The Interpretation of the Fourth Gospel* (Cambridge: Cambridge University Press, 1953) 443, n. 2. A. Shaw, 'The breakfast by the shore and the Mary Magdalene encounter as Eucharistic narratives', *JTS* 25 (1974) 12–26.

77 Cf. Brown, *John* II, 1012; C. K. Barrett, *The Gospel According to John* (London: SPCK, 1978) 565.

78 Cf. C. Spicq, 'Noli me tangere', *RSPT* 32 (1948) 226–7; D. C. Fowler, 'The meaning of "Touch me not"' in John 20:17', *EvQ* 47 (1, 1975) 16–25; Journet, 'L'apparition', 146.

79 Cf. Barrett, *John* (1955) 470; Zerwick, sec. 476, 160.

80 Cf. MHT III, 63; Robertson, 869–70. Alternatively, it might be a way of expressing something about to happen. Cf. BDF, sec. 323, p. 168; Barrett, *John* (1978) 566; 1 Cor 15.32.

81 Minear, '"We don't know where"', 132; C. F. Evans, 'I will go before you into Galilee', *JTS* n.s. 5 (1, 1954) 16–17.

82 The Johannine context probably rules out any reference to Jesus' physical family (v. 18).

83 Possibly, a technical usage may be in mind here, i.e., proclaiming the Good News. Cf. J. Schniewind, 'ἀγγέλλω', *TDNT* I (1964) 61. It has been argued that πορεύομαι in John 20.17 is used as a technical term to refer to the missionary command or activity. Cf. F. Hauck and S. Schulz, 'πορεύομαι', *TDNT* VI (1968) 575.

6 Trajectories beyond the New Testament

1 Since I am not an expert in the post-NT, pre-Nicene period, I have relied more heavily on secondary sources in this chapter than in the other chapters. Like the first chapter, what is included here is intended to be a representative sample of material, not a definitive or exhaustive study. I am especially grateful for the assistance of Dr E. Ferguson of Abilene Christian University.

2 The example of the *Acts of Paul and Thecla* being included in a list of NT books, Codex Claromontanus (sixth century), may suggest that this list goes back to a time prior to the Gelasian Decree which may have originated in part in the time of Pope Damascus (AD 366–84). Alternatively, it may suggest that E. von Dobschütz was right that the Decree dates to the early sixth century. In any event, Codex Claromontanus is an insufficient warrant for the suggestion that the *Acts of Paul and Thecla* was widely accepted as a 'canonical' document. Cf. E. Schüssler Fiorenza, *In Memory of Her* (New York: Crossroad, 1983) 300ff. and notes.

3 Ben Witherington, 'Anti-feminist tendencies of the "Western" text in Acts', *JBL* 103:1 (1984) 82–4.
4 Ibid.
5 F. Blanke and F. J. Leenhardt, *Die Stellung der Frau in Neuen Testament und der alten Kirche* (Zurich: Zwingli, 1949). Blanke is responsible for the study of 'der alten Kirche'. Cf. R. Gryson, *The Ministry of Women in the Early Church* (trans. J. Laporte and M. L. Hall; Collegeville, MN: Liturgical Press, 1976); Leipoldt, *Die Frau*; Daniélou, *Ministry of Women*; Swidler, *Biblical Affirmations*, 339ff.; Fiorenza, *In Memory of Her*, 270ff., 285ff.; G. H. Tavard, *Woman in Christian Tradition* (South Bend: University of Notre Dame, 1973).
6 I say 'trajector*ies*' precisely because in some cases no *one* developing trend can be traced, but rather a variety of practices and views develop in various parts of the Empire simultaneously.
7 Cf. pp. 190–2 below on Gnosticism.
8 *1 Clement* 33.5–6, *Apostolic Fathers*, LCL I (1977 repr.) 64.
9 Whether or not Rhoda is a type of the church in Rome, the very first two verses locate the main character in Rome.
10 *Shepherd of Hermas, Mand.* 4.1.3–11, *The Apostolic Fathers*, Loeb 2 (1970 repr.) 78.
11 *Shepherd of Hermas, The Apostolic Fathers*, Loeb 2 (1970 repr.) 79, n. 1.
12 Whether or not this material was originally Jewish in origin, in its present form it seems to be a Christian document dating to the latter part of the second century or beginning of the third. Cf. M. de Jonge, *Pseudepigrapha Veteris Testamentis Graece*, vol. 1 (Leiden: E. J. Brill, 1964).
13 Clement of Alexandria, *Exhortation to the Greeks* 11, LCL (1939 repr.) 236, n. 2 (Butterworth follows Schwartz in his translation).
14 Ibid., 254–55 (cf. Butterworth's notes).
15 There is some real debate as to whether or not Clement of Alexandria was responsible for this work.
16 Clement of Alexandria, *Stromata* 2.23, *The Ante-Nicene Fathers* 1 (trans. A. Robert and S. Donaldson; Grand Rapids: Eerdmans, 1975 repr.) 378.
17 J. Ferguson, *Clement of Alexandria* (New York: Twayne Publishers, 1974) 131.
18 Cf. Tavard's translation of *Comm. Mt.* 17.33 in *Woman in Christian Tradition*, 67.
19 H. Crouzel, *Virginité et Mariage selon Origene* (Paris: Bruges, 1962) 142, n. 1.
20 Ibid., 63ff., commenting on Origen's *Lukan Homily* 24.
21 Cf. Tavard, *Woman in Christian Tradition*, 68.
22 Everett Ferguson (Abilene Christian University), personal letter dated 9 June 1986.
23 Cf. M. Smith, *Studies in Early Mysticism in the Near and Middle East* (London: Sheldon, 1931) 35–6.
24 Ibid.; cf. Swidler, *Biblical Affirmations*, 340–1.

25 Cf. E. H. Pagels, *The Gnostic Gospels* (New York: Random House, 1979), and her article, 'What became of God the Mother? Conflicting images of God in early Christianity', *Signs* 2 (1976) 293–303. Pagels seems intent on emphasizing the egalitarian views of some of the Gnostics, especially the Valentinians, despite her disclaimer not to advocate any side. R. E. Brown is surely right in his perceptive critique of her work when he says, 'But about nine-tenths of the discussion of each topic in the book consists of her sympathetic efforts to try and understand the gnostic's side, which will leave the reader cheering for them and wishing that the narrow-minded orthodox had not won.' R. E. Brown, 'The Christians who lost out', *New York Times* book review (20 January 1980) 3, 33, here 3. Cf. the heated responses of Pagels and Brown in the *New York Times* letter section (17 February 1980), 27. For a much more balanced view on the Gnostic data by a feminist scholar, cf. Fiorenza, *In Memory of Her*, 270–4 and passim.

26 Cited in Epiphanius, *Panarion* 45.2.1. Cf. Fiorenza, *In Memory of Her*, 274ff.

27 Clement of Alexandria, *Stromata* 3.45. For another translation cf. J. E. L. Oulton and H. Chadwick, eds., *Alexandrian Christianity* (Philadelphia: Westminster, 1954) 61.

28 Clement of Alexandria, *Stromata* 3.92; cf. Oulton and Chadwick, eds., *Alexandrian Christianity*, 83. Cf. *Gospel of Thomas* log. 23; *Martyrdom of Peter* 9. There is some question whether the garment of shame refers to the human body or the act of sexual intercourse.

29 Clement of Alexandria, *Stromata* 3.63; cf. Oulton and Chadwick, eds., *Alexandrian Christianity*, 69.

30 Cf. the translation in Tavard, *Woman*, 63–4.

31 Cf. the helpful survey of all the Gnostic texts dealing with andronization by M. W. Meyer, 'Making Mary male: the categories "male" and "female" in the Gospel of Thomas', *NTS* 37 (1985) 554–70.

32 Clement of Alexandria, *Stromata* 3.6; cf. Oulton and Chadwick, eds., *Alexandrian Christianity*, 43.

33 R. A. Baer, *Philo's Use of the Categories Male and Female* (Leiden: E. J. Brill, 1970) 71.

34 Fiorenza, *In Memory of Her*, 274.

35 Ibid.; here and elsewhere in this chapter I am indebted to Fiorenza for her helpful analysis.

36 Cf. *ODCC*, 300; J. Quasten, *Patrology* 1 (Utrecht: Spectrum Pub., 1966) 53–4.

37 Could this be what Paul has in mind in 1 Cor 11.10? Women must have a head-covering for the angel of the prophetic spirit will be falling on and filling them; during such a time human glory must not be seen.

38 Cf. chapters 3 and 4.

39 Cf. R. R. Ruether and E. McLaughlin, eds., *Women of Spirit – Female Leadership in the Jewish and Christian Traditions* (New York: Simon and Schuster, 1979) 37ff.

40 *ODCC*, 1049.

41 *Acts of Paul and Thecla* 5–6, NTAp II, 354. On the relationship of this material to the Pastorals, cf. Dibelius/Conzelmann, *Pastoral Epistles*, 48–9 and nn. 29–30.

42 On the didactic character of some Christian prophecy, cf. chapter 4.

43 Cf. the thesis of S. Davies, *The Social World of the Apocryphal Acts* (Philadelphia: Temple University, 1978), and his *The Revolt of the Widows* (Carbondale, Il: S. Illinois University, 1980) which state that these documents were written by and for women, in particular, the Church's 'widows'. This thesis has been ably refuted by D. R. MacDonald, 'The role of women in the production of the Apocryphal Acts of the Apostles', *Iliff Review* 40 (3, 1983) 21–38, who notes that the stress on virginity could be a result of the general interest in asceticism and the romance genre of this period. He also adds that women were involved in early Christian social conflicts over Church roles and functions, and would be written about in any case.

44 *Kerygma of Peter, NTAp* II (1965) 110–11; G. Strecker dates it c. AD 200 and suggests a Syrian audience.

45 Ibid., 107.

46 *ODCC*, 1070. One must be careful to distinguish between the *Kerygma Petrou* which Clement of Alexandria quotes, and 'Ebionite' *Kerygmata Petrou* in the Pseudo-Clementines.

47 *Kerygma of Peter* H.2.15, *NTAp* II, 117–18.

48 Hippolytus, *Refutation of All Heresies* 8.12; cf. *Ante-Nicene Fathers* I, 123. Fiorenza, *In Memory of Her*, 302, is wrong in saying, 'Hippolytus acknowledged that the doctrine of the Montanists and of the great Church were the same …'

49 R. B. Eno, 'Authority and conflict in the early Church', *ETh* 7 (1967) 41–50, here 47–8.

50 Origen, frag. 74 on 1 Corinthians.

51 It is possible (cf. *ODCC*, 1064) that Tertullian edited the *Acts of Perpetua and Felicitas*, in which case it would be very early in origin, perhaps even an eye-witness testimony. For another female martyr, Blandina ('Martyrs of Lyon'), cf. Eusebius, *Ecclesiastical History* 5, LCL 1 (1926).

52 Fiorenza, *In Memory of Her*, 302.

53 Didymus the Blind, *On the Trinity* 3.41.3, PG 30.988c–989a. The dating of the *Dialogue Between a Montanist and an Orthodox*, apparently cited by Didymus, is difficult, but appears to be from the fourth century (before Didymus). Cf. Gryson, *Ministry of Women*, 75–7.

54 To borrow the book title of R. R. Ruether and E. McLaughlin, *Women of Spirit – Female Leadership in the Jewish and Christian Traditions* (New York: Simon and Schuster, 1979).

55 Fiorenza, *In Memory of Her*, 285, rightly notes that studies of Church offices have been inconclusive. One does get the feeling from reading the primary sources, however, that as the structure of the Church became more universally fixed, they also became more gender-specific – with women allowed to be deaconesses, widows,

ascetics, and teachers (of women), and perhaps even prophetesses in the Church (but not elders or bishops).

56 Cf. chapter 4.
57 Pliny the Younger, *Letters* 10.96—97, LCL 2 (1969) 404—5.
58 Cf. *ODCC*, 653; Daniélou, *Ministry of Women*, 22ff.
59 This is the translation in *Ante-Nicene Fathers* 7 (1975) 492.
60 Cf. Tavard, *Woman in Christian Tradition*, 94, for a discussion of deaconesses among the Kanoni.
61 Cf. Swidler, *Biblical Affirmations*, 314—15.
62 Hippolytus, *Apostolic Tradition* 10 (cf. 30), (ed. B. Botte; Münster: Aschendorff, 1963) 30, cf. 60, which mentions widows fasting often and praying for the Church.
63 C. Osiek, 'The widow as altar: the rise and fall of a symbol', *Second Century* 3 (3, 1983) 159—69.
64 Ibid., 166—7.
65 Ibid., 168—9.
66 Cf. Tavard, *Woman in Christian Tradition*, 78—9.
67 Cf. pp. 134ff.
68 Cf. pp. 151—2.
69 Tavard, *Women in Christian Tradition*, 92. On virgins and the Church Fathers of the late fourth century, cf. R.R. Ruether, 'Misogynism and virginal feminism in the Fathers of the Church', *Religion and Sexism* (New York: Simon and Schuster, 1974) 150—83.
70 Cf. the different translation in Eusebius, *Ecclesiastical History* 7.30 LCL 2 (1932).
71 Methodius of Lycia, *Banquet, Discourse* 1.1, *Ante-Nicene Fathers* 6 (trans. W.R. Clark; 1975) 310.
72 Ibid., 311—12.
73 Tavard, *Woman in Christian Tradition*, 81.
74 Witherington, *Women*, 85—100.
75 *NTAp* 1, 344—5. This material seems to be from the late second century and adds little or no information as to how the Gnostics actually viewed Mary other than as a source of secret revelation.
76 The term ἀειπάρθενος however, comes from Athanasius, slightly later than our period.
77 Cf. J.-M. Salgado, 'La présentation de Marie au temple', *PalCler* 51 (1972) 469—74.
78 *NTAp* I, 425.
79 Ephraem Syrus (AD 306—373) at least seems to claim he found this idea in the Diatesseron. Cf. the discussion in *NTAp* I, 428—9.
80 Cf. E. Testa, 'Lo sviluppo della "Dormitio Marie" nella litteratura, nella teologia e nella archeologia', *Marianum* 44 (3—4, 1982) 316—89, available to me only in *NTA* 28 (1984) 72. The idea of Mary's assumption seems to develop sometime after AD 325.
81 Cf. the slightly different translation in *Ante Nicene Fathers* 1 (1975) 249.
82 Witherington, *Women*, 116ff.; pp. 177—80.
83 This has been helpfully chronicled by F. Bovon, 'Le Privilège Pascal de Marie-Madeleine', *NTS* 30 (Jan. 1984) 50—62, espec. 52—3, to whom I am indebted for what follows.

84 Cf. E. Clark and H. Richardson, *Women and Religion* (New York: Harper and Row, 1977) 281, n. 15.
85 *NTAp* I, 278.
86 *Gospel of Philip* 2.63.30–35; cf. *The Nag Hammadi Library* (ed. J. M. Robinson; San Francisco: Harper and Row, 1977) 138.
87 Bovon, 'Le Privilège Pascal', 56.
88 On Clement's exegesis of the Rahab traditions, Cf. A. T. Hanson, 'Rahab the harlot in the early Christian tradition', *JTNT* 1 (1978) 53–60.
89 Tavard, *Woman in Christian Tradition*, 52–3.

Conclusions

1 R. L. Wilken, *The Christians as the Romans Saw Them* (New Haven: Yale University, 1984) 63.
2 Meeks, *First Urban Christians*, 9ff.
3 Cf. R. MacMullen, *Christianizing the Roman Empire, AD 100–400* (New Haven: Yale University, 1984), 39, and 137, n. 33.
4 Could it be significant that wives were usually much younger than their husbands, in fact barely teenagers in many of the first-century cultures in which Paul came in contact? Cf. MacMullen, *Christianizing the Roman Empire*, 39.
5 Wilken, *Christians as the Romans Saw Them*, 31ff.
6 Here and in what follows I will be interacting with some of the stimulating essays of E. Käsemann collected in *New Testament Questions of Today* (trans. W. J. Montague, *et al.*; Philadelphia: Fortress, 1969). Quote, p. 237.
7 R. N. Longenecker, *New Testament Social Ethics for Today* (Grand Rapids: Eerdmans, 1974) 92.
8 Käsemann, *NT Questions of Today*, 136–7.
9 Ibid., 211–12.

BIBLIOGRAPHY

Introduction

Boldrey, R. and J. *Chauvinist or Feminist? Paul's View of Women.* Grand Rapids: Baker, 1976.

Foh, S. *Women and the Word of God. A Response to Biblical Feminism.* Philadelphia: Presbyterian and Reformed, 1979.

Goldberg, S. *The Inevitability of Patriarchy.* New York: W. Morrow, 1973–74.

Knight, G. W. *The New Testament Teaching on the Role Relationship of Men and Women.* Grand Rapids: Baker, 1977.

Stagg, E. and F. *Women in the World of Jesus.* Philadelphia: Westminster, 1978.

Stendahl, K. *The Bible and the Role of Women.* Philadelphia: Fortress, 1966.

Swidler, L. *Biblical Affirmations of Woman.* Philadelphia: Westminster, 1979.

Trible, P. *God and the Rhetoric of Sexuality.* Philadelphia: Fortress, 1978.

1 Women in the first-century Mediterranean cultures

Adcock, F. E. 'Women in Roman life and letters', *Greece and Rome* 14 (1945) 1–22.

Altheim, F. *A History of Roman Religion.* London: Methuen and Co., 1938.

Arthur, M. B. 'Early Greece: the origins of the Western attitude toward women', *Arethusa* 6:1 (1973) 7–58.

Balsdon, J. P. V. D. *Roman Women: Their History and Habits.* London: Bodley Head, 1962.

Blackman, A. M. 'On the position of women in ancient Egyptian hierarchy', *BA* 7 (1921) 8–30.

Bonner, R. J. 'Did women testify in homicide cases in Athens?' *Classical Philology* 1 (1906) 127–32.

Carcopino, J. *Daily Life in Ancient Rome.* London: George Routledge, 1941.

Compernole, R. van. 'Le mythe de la gynécocratie – doulocratie argienne', *Hommages à Claire Préaux.* Ed. J. Bingen. Brussels: Brussels University, 1975. 355–64.

Cornish, F. W. and Bacon, J. 'The position of women', in *A Companion to Greek Studies.* Ed. L. Whibley. Cambridge: Cambridge University, 1931. 610–17.

Delling, Gerhard, *Paulus' Stellung zu Frau und Ehe.* Stuttgart: Kohlhammer, 1931.

Donaldson, James. *Woman: Her Position and Influence in Ancient Greece and Rome, and Among Early Christians.* London: Longmans, Green and Co., 1907.

Dover, K.J. 'Classical Greek attitudes to sexual behavior', *Arethusa* 6:1 (1973) 59–73.

Farnell, L.R. *The Cults of the Greek States.* 5 vols. Oxford: Oxford University Press, 1896–1909.

Flacelière, Robert. *Love in Ancient Greece.* Trans. J. Cleugh. London: F. Muller, 1962.

Gaudemet, J. 'Le statut de la femme dans l'empire Romain', in *Recueils de la Société Jean Bodin.* Vol.XI: *La Femme.* Brussells: Éditions de la Librarie Encyclopédique, 1959. 191–222.

Gomme, A.W. 'The position of women in Athens in the fifth and fourth centuries BC', in *Essays in Greek History and Literature.* Ed. A.W. Gomme. Oxford: Oxford University Press, 1973. 89–115.

Goodwater, L. *Women in Antiquity: An Annotated Bibliography.* Metuchen: Scarecrow, 1974.

Hadas, M. 'Observations on Athenian women', *Classical Weekly* 19:13 (1926) 97–100.

Hallett, J.P. 'The role of women in Roman elegy: counter-cultural feminism', *Arethusa* 6:1 (1973) 103–24.

Hopkins, M.K. 'The age of Roman girls at marriage', *Population Studies* 18 (1965) 309–27.

Leipoldt, J. *Die Frau in der antiken Welt und im Urchristentum.* Leipzig: Koehler and Amelang, 1955.

Licht, H. *Sexual Life in Ancient Greece.* Ed. L.H. Sawson. Trans. J.H. Freese. London: George Routledge, 1932.

Loane, H.J. *Industry and Commerce of the City of Rome (50 BC – AD 200).* Baltimore: Johns Hopkins University, 1938.

Macurdy, G.H. 'Queen Eurydice and the evidence for woman power in early Macedonia'. *AJP* 48 (1927) 201–14.

Marshall, F.H. 'The position of women', in *A Companion to Latin Studies.* Ed. J.E. Sandys. Cambridge: Cambridge University Press, 1910. 184–90.

Meeks, Wayne, 'The image of the androgyne: some uses of a symbol in earliest Christianity'. *HR* 13:3 (1974) 165–208.

Mohler, S.L. 'Feminism in the Corpus Inscriptionum Latinarum'. *Classical Weekly* 25 (Feb. 15, 1932) 113–17.

Nilsson, Martin. *A History of Greek Religion.* Oxford: Clarendon, 1925.
Die Religion der Griechen. Tübingen: J.C.B. Mohr, 1927.
The Dionysiac Mysteries of the Hellenistic and Roman Age. Lund: C.W.K. Gleerup, 1957.
Greek Folk Religion. New York: Harper and Row, 1961.

Peck, H.T., ed. *Harper's Dictionary of Classical Literature and Antiquities.* New York: Harper and Bros., 1897.

Pirenne, Jacques. 'Le statut de la femme dans l'ancienne Égypte', in *Recueils de la Société Jean Bodin.* Vol.XI: *La Femme.* Brussells: Éditions de la Librarie Encyclopédique, 1959. 63–77.

Pomeroy, Sarah. *Goddesses, Whores, Wives, and Slaves.* London: Robert Hale, 1975.

'Selected bibliography on women in Antiquity', *Arethusa* 6:1 (1973) 125–57.

Préaux, Claire. 'Le statut de la femme à l'époque hellénistique principalment en Égypte', *Recueils de la Société Jean Bodin*. Vol. XI: *La Femme*. Bruxelles: Éditions de la Librarie Encyclopédique, 1959. 127–75.

Richter, D. C. 'The position of women in classical Athens', *Classical Journal* 67 (1971) 1–8.

Ste. Croix, G. E. M. de. 'Some observations on the property rights of Athenian women', *Classical Review* 20 n.s. (1970) 273–8.

Smith, A. H. 'Notes on a tour of Asia Minor'. *JHS* 8 (1887) 216–67.

Tarn W. W. and Griffith, G. T. *Hellenistic Civilisation*. 3rd ed. London: Edward Arnold, 1952.

Treggiari, S. 'Domestic staff at Rome in the Julio-Claudian period: 27 BC – AD 68', *Histoire Sociale: Revue Canadienne* 6 (1973) 241–55.

Villers, R. 'Le statut de la femme à Rome jusqu'à à la fin de la République', in *Recueils de la Société Jean Bodin*. Vol. XI: *La Femme*. Brussells: Éditions de la Librarie Encyclopédique, 1959. 177–89.

Wender, D. 'Plato: misogynist, paedophile, and feminist', *Arethusa* 6:1 (1973) 75–90.

White, R. E. 'Women in Ptolemaic Egypt'. *JHS* 18 (1898) 238–66.

2 Women and the physical family in the Pauline epistles

Allmen, J. J. von. *Pauline Teaching on Marriage*. London: Faith, 1963.

Balch, D. L. 'Backgrounds of 1 Cor. VIII: sayings of the Lord in Q; Moses as ascetic ΘΕΙΟΣ ANHP in II Cor. III'. *NTS* 18 (1972) 351–64.

Let Wives Be Submissive: The Domestic Code in 1 Peter. SBLMS 26. Chico: Scholars, 1981.

Baltenzweiler, H. 'Erwägungen zu 1 Thess 4, 3–8'. *TZ* 19 (1963) 1–13.

Barre, M. L. 'To marry or to burn: πυροῦσθαι in 1 Cor 7:9'. *CBQ* 36 (1974) 193–202.

Bartchy, S. Scott. MAΛΛON XPHΣAI: *First-Century Slavery and the Interpretation of 1 Corinthians 7.21*. SBLDS. Missoula: University of Montana, 1973).

Batey, R. 'The MIA ΣAPΞ union of Christ and the Church'. *NTS* 13 (1966–67) 270–81.

'Jewish Gnosticism and the "Hieros Gamos" of Eph. V.21–33'. *NTS* 10 (1963–64) 121–7.

Bedale, S. 'The Meaning of κεφαλή in the Pauline epistles'. *JTS* n.s. 5 (1954) 211–15.

Beker, J. Christian. *Paul's Apocalyptic Gospel. The Coming Triumph of God*. Philadelphia: Fortress, 1982.

Best, E. *One Body in Christ*. London: SPCK, 1955.

Betz, H. D. '2 Cor 6:14–7:1: an anti-Pauline fragment?' *JBL* 92 (1973) 88–108.

Bevan, E. *Later Greek Religion*. London/New York: Dent/Dutton, 1927.

Brown, R. E. 'The Semitic background of the New Testament "Mysterion" II'. *Bib* 40 (1959) 70–87.

Burchard, C. 'Ei nach einem Ausdruck des Wissens oder Nichtwissens Joh 9.25, Ac 19.2, 1 Cor 1.16'. *ZNW* 52 (1961) 73–82.

Butler, C. 'Was Paul a male chauvinist?' *New Blackfriars* 56 (1975) 174–9.

Caird, G. B. 'Paul and women's liberty'. *BJRL* 54 (1972) 268–81.

Cambier, J. 'Le grande mystère concernant le Christ et son Eglise, Ephesiens 5, 22–33'. *Bib* 47 (1966) 143–90, 223–42.

Cannon, G. E. *The Use of Traditional Materials in Colossians*. Macon: Mercer University, 1983.

Carrington, P. *The Primitive Christian Catechism*. Cambridge: Cambridge University Press, 1940.

Cartlidge, D. R. '1 Corinthians 7 as a foundation for a Christian sex ethic'. *JR* 55 (1975) 220–34.

Chadwick, H. '"All things to all men" (1 Cor. IX.22)'. *NTS* 1 (1954–55) 261–75.

Chapple, Allan. 'Local leadership in the Pauline churches: Theological and social factors in its development − a study based on I Thessalonians, I Corinthians and Philippians' Ph.D. dissertation, University of Durham, 1985.

Collange, J.-F. *Énigmes de la deuxième Épître de Paul aux Corinthiens − Étude Exegétique de 1 Cor 2:14–7:4*. SNTSMS 18. Cambridge: Cambridge University Press, 1972.

Crouch, J. E. *The Origin and Intention of the Colossian Haustafel*. Göttingen: Vandenhoeck and Ruprecht, 1972.

Derrett, J. D. M. 'Romans vii.1–4. The relationship with the resurrected Christ', *Law in the New Testament*. London: Darton, Longmann and Todd, 1970. pp. 461–71.

'2 Cor 6, 14ff. A midrash on Dt 22.19'. *Bib* 59 (2, 1978) 231–50.

Doughty, D. J. 'The presence and future of salvation in Corinth'. *ZNW* 66 (1975) 61–90.

Dubarle, A.-M. 'Paul et l'antifeminisme'. *RSPT* 60 (1976) 261–80.

Dulau, P. 'The Pauline privilege − is it promulgated in the First Epistle to the Corinthians?' *CBQ* 13 (1951) 146–52.

Elliott, J. K. 'Paul's teaching on marriage in 1 Corinthians: some problems considered'. *NTS* 19 (2, 1973) 219–25.

Fee, Gordon. 'II Corinthians vi.14–vii.1 and food offered to idols'. *NTS* 23 (1976–77) 140–61.

Fiorenza, 'Marriage and disciple'. *Bible Today* (April, 1979) 2027–34.

Fischer, J. A. 'Paul on virginity'. *Bible Today* 72 (1974) 1633–8.

Fitzmyer, J. A. 'Qumran and the interpolated paragraph in 2 Cor 6, 14–7, 1'. *CBQ* 23 (3, 1961) 271–81.

Ford, J. M. 'Levirate marriage in St Paul'. *NTS* 10 (1964) 351–5.

'St Paul, the philogamist (1 Cor VII in early patristic exegesis)'. *NTS* 11 (1965) 326–48.

Furnish, V. P. *Theology and Ethics in Paul*. Nashville: Abingdon Press, 1968.

The Moral Teaching of Paul. Nashville: Abingdon Press, 1979.

Gnilka, J. '2 Cor. 6:14–7:1'. *Paul and Qumran − Studies in New Testament Exegesis*. ed. J. Murphy-O'Connor. London: G. Chapman, 1968. 48–68.

Graham, R. W. 'Women in the Pauline churches: a review article', *LTQ* 11 (1976): 25–34.

Hengel, M. *Judaism and Hellenism*. 2 vols. Philadelphia: Fortress, 1974.

Hinson, E. G. 'The Christian household in Colossians 3:18–4:1'. *RevExp* 70 (1973) 495–506.

House, H. W. 'Paul, women, and contemporary feminism'. *BSac* 136 (1979) 40–53.

Hurd, J. C. *The Origin of 1 Corinthians*. London: SPCK, 1968.

Jeremias, J. 'Zur Gedankenführung in den Paulinischen Briefen', *Studia Pauline in honorem Joannis de Zwaan Septuagenarii*. Haarlem: De Erven F. Bohn, 1953, 146–62.

'War Paulus Witwer?' *ZNW* 28 (1929) 321–3.

'Die Missionarische Aufgabe in der Mischehe (1 Cor 7.16)'. *Neutestamentliche Studien für Rudolf Bultmann zu seinem siebsigsten Geburtstag*. BZNW 21. Berlin: A. Töpelmann, 1954. 255–60.

Jewett, P. K. *Man as Male and Female*. Grand Rapids: Eerdmans, 1975.

Kähler, E. *Die Frau in den paulinischen Briefen unter besonderer Berücksichtigung des Begriffes der Unterordnung*. Zurich: Gotthelf, 1960.

Knox, W. L. *St Paul and the Church of the Gentiles*. Cambridge: Cambridge University Press, 1979.

Kubo, S. '1 Corinthians VII.16: optimistic or pessimistic?'. *NTS* 24 (4, 1978) 539–44.

Kümmel, W. G. 'Verlobung und Heirat bei Paulus (I Cor 7, 36–38)'. *Neutestamentliche Studien für Rudolf Bultmann zu seinem siebsigsten Geburtstag*. BZNW 21. Berlin: A. Töpelmann, 275–95.

Römer 7 und das Bild des Menschen im Neuen Testament – Zwei Studien. Munich: Chr. Kaiser, 1974.

Leonard, E. A. 'St Paul on the status of women'. *CBQ* 23 (1950) 311–20.

Lietzmann, D. Hans. *Einführung in die Textgeschichte der Paulusbriefe an die Römer*. HNT 8. Tübingen: J. C. B. Mohr, 1933.

Lillie, W. 'The Pauline house-tables'. *ET* 86 (1975) 179–83.

Mollenkott, V. R. *Women, Men, and the Bible*. Nashville: Abingdon, 1977.

Osborne, R. G. 'Hermeneutics and women in the Church'. *JETS* 20 (1977) 337–47.

Percy, E. *Die Probleme der Kolosser und Epheserbrief*. Lund: C. W. K. Gleerup, 1946.

Peters, A. 'St Paul and marriage – a study of 1 Corinthians chapter 7'. *AER* (1964) 214–24.

Raurell, F. 'Saint Paul fut-il misogyne et antifeministe?' *Etudes Franciscaines* 15 (1965) 66–73.

Rengstorf, K. H. 'Die neutestamentlichen Mahnungen an die Frau, sich dem Manne unterzuordnen'. *Verbum Dei Manet in Aeternum*. ed. W. Foerster. Witten: Luther, 1953, 131–45.

Ridderbos, H. *Paul, An Outline of His Theology*. Grand Rapids: Eerdmans, 1975.

Roberts, R. L. 'The meaning of *chorizō* and *douloō* in 1 Corinthians 7:10–17'. *ResQ* 8 (3, 1965) 179–84.

Robinson, J. M. 'Die Hodajot – Formel in Gebet und Hymnus des

Frühchristentums', *Apophoreta: Festschrift für Ernst Haenchen*, Berlin: A. Töpelmann, 1964, 194–235.

Sampley, J.P. *And the Two Shall Become One Flesh*. SNTSMS 16. Cambridge: Cambridge University Press, 1971.

Schoeps, H.J. *Paul – The Theology of the Apostle in Light of Jewish Religious History*. Trans. H. Knight. Philadelphia: Fortress, 1961.

Schrage, W. 'Zur Ethik der neutestamentlichen Haustafeln'. *NTS* 21 (1974–75) 1–22.

Schroeder, D. 'Die Haustafeln des Neuen Testaments (ihre Herkunft und Theologischer Sinn)'. Ph.D. dissertation. Hamburg: Mikrokopie, 1959.

Schweizer, E. 'Traditional ethical patterns in the Pauline and post-Pauline letters and their development (lists of vices and housetables)'. *Text and Interpretation*. ed. E. Best and R. Mcl. Wilson. Cambridge: Cambridge University Press, 1979, 195–209.

Scroggs, R. 'Paul and the eschatological woman'. *JAAR* 40 (1972) 283–303.

Seboldt, R.H.A. 'Spiritual marriage in the early Church – a suggested interpretation of 1 Cor. 7:36–38'. *CTM* 30 (1959) 176–89.

Stagg, F. 'The domestic code and the final appeal, Ephesians 5.21–6.24'. *RevExp* 76 (1979) 541–52.

Stein, D. 'Le statut des femmes dans les lettres de Paul'. *Lumière et Vie* 27 (1978) 63–85.

Vawter, B. 'Divorce and the New Testament'. *CBQ* 39 (1977) 527–42.

Weidinger, K. *Die Haustafeln, ein Stück urchristliche Paränese* UNT. Leipzig: J.C. Henrich, 1928.

Whiteley, D.E.H. *The Theology of St Paul*. Philadelphia: Fortress, 1972.

Witherington, Ben. *Women in the Ministry of Jesus*. SNTSMS. Cambridge: Cambridge University Press, 1984.

3 Women and the family of faith in the Pauline epistles

Aalen, S. 'A rabbinic formula in 1 Cor. 14, 34'. *Studia Evangelica*. ed. F.L. Cross. Berlin: Akademie, 1964, 2:513–25.

Adinolfi, M. 'Le collaboratrici ministeriali di paolo nelle lettre ai Romani eai Filippesi'. *BeO* 17:1 (1975) 21–32.

Almie, G.L. 'Women's church and communion participation'. *CBR* 33 (1982) 41–55.

Banks, R. *Paul's Idea of Community*. Grand Rapids: Eerdmans, 1980.

Barrett, C.K. *The Signs of an Apostle*. Philadelphia: Fortress, 1972.

'Shaliah and apostle'. *Donum Gentilicium*. ed. E. Bammel, *et al.* Oxford: Oxford University Press, 1978, 88–102.

Galatians: Freedom and Obligation. Philadelphia: Westminster, 1985.

Bedale, S. 'The Meaning of Kephale in the Pauline Epistles'. *JTS* n.s. 5 (1954) 211–15.

Beet, J.A. 'Did Euodia and Syntyche quarrel?' *ET* 5 (1893–94) 179–80.

Bornkamm, G. *Early Christian Experience*. New York: Harper and Row, 1969.

Cadbury, H.J. 'A Qumran parallel to Paul'. *HTR* 51 (1958) 1–2.

Caird, G.B. *Principalities and Powers*. Oxford: Clarendon, 1956.

Cope, L. '1 Cor. 11:2–16: one step further'. *JBL* 97 (1978) 435–6.

Coppens, J. 'Miscellanies Bibliques I, La soumission de la femme a l'homme d'après Gen. III, 16b'. *ETL* 14 (1937) 632–41.

Cullmann, O. 'Paradosis et kyrios, le problème de la tradition dans le paulinisme'. *RHPR* 30 (1950) 12–30.

Donfried, K. P. 'A short note on Romans 16', *JBL* 89 (1970) 441–9.

Dunn, J. D. G. *Jesus and the Spirit*. Philadelphia: Westminster, 1975.

Ellis, E. E. *Prophecy and Hermeneutic in Early Christianity*. Grand Rapids: Eerdmans, 1978.

Falconer, R. '1 Tim. 2:14, 15. Interpretive notes'. *JBL* 60 (1941) 375–9.

Feuillet, A. 'L'homme "gloire de Dieu" et la femme "gloire de l'homme" (1 Cor. XI, 7b)'. *RB* 81 (1974) 161–80.

'Le signe de puissance sur la tête de la femme, I Cor. 11, 10'. *NRT* 95 (1973) 945–9.

'La dignité et le rôle de la femme d'après quelques textes Pauliniens: comparison avec l'ancien testament'. *NTS* 21 (1974–75) 157–91.

Fiorenza, F. Schüssler, 'Women in the pre-Pauline and Pauline churches'. *USQR* 33 (1978) 153–66.

Fitzmyer, J. A. 'A feature of Qumran angelology and the New Testament', *NTS* 4 (1957–58) 48–58.

Flanagan, N. M. and Snyder, E. A. 'Did Paul put down women in 1 Cor 14.34–36?' *BTB* 11:1 (1981) 10–12.

Foh, S. 'What is the woman's desire?' *WTJ* 37 (1975) 376–83.

Galt, C. M. 'Veiled ladies'. *AJA* 35 (1931) 373–93.

Gibson, M. D. 'Phoebe'. *ET* 23 (1911–12) 281.

Gilbert, G. H. 'Women in the churches of Paul'. *BW* 2 (1893) 38–47.

Grudem, W. 'The gift of prophecy in 1 Corinthians'. Ph.D. dissertation. Cambridge University, 1978.

Hajek, M. 'Comments on Philippians 4.3 – who Was Gnesios Syzygos?' *Communio Viatorum* 7 (3–4, 1964) 261–2.

Hastings, J. 'Notes of recent exposition'. *ET* 5 (1893–94) 102–4.

Heyob, S. Kelley. *The Cult of Isis Among Women in the Greco-Roman World*. Leiden: E. J. Brill, 1975.

Hill, D. H. *New Testament Prophecy*. London: Marshall, Morgan and Scott, 1979.

Hommes, N. J. 'Let women be silent in church'. *CTJ* 4 (1969) 5–22.

Hooker, M. D. 'Authority on her head: an examination of 1 Cor XI.10'. *NTS* 10 (1963–64) 410–16.

Hurley, J. B. *Man and Woman in Biblical Perspective. A Study in Role Relationships and Authority*. Leicester: InterVarsity, 1981.

'Man and woman in 1 Corinthians'. Ph.D. dissertation. Cambridge University, 1973.

Jaubert, A. 'Le voile des femmes (1 Cor. 11.2–16)'. *NTS* 18 (1971–72) 419–30.

Jebb, S. 'A suggested interpretation of 1 Tim 2.15'. *ET* 81 (1969–70) 221–2.

Jeremias, J. *Jerusalem in the Time of Jesus*. Philadelphia: Fortress, 1969.

'Paarweise Sendung im NT'. *Abba. Studien zur Neutestamentlichen Theologie und Zeitgeschichte*. Göttingen: Vandenhoeck and Ruprecht, 1966, 132–9.

Jervell, J. *Imago Dei, Gen. 1:26f im Spätjudentum, in der Gnosis und in den paulinishchen Briefen*. Göttingen: Vandenhoeck and Ruprecht, 1960.

Knight, G. W. 'ΑΥΘΕΝΤΕΩ in reference to women in 1 Timothy 2.12'. *NTS* 30 (1984) 143–57.

Kroeger, C. C. 'Ancient heresies and a strange Greek verb'. *RJ* 29 (1979) 12–15.

Kümmel, W. G. *Introduction to the New Testament*. 17th rev. ed. London: SCM, 1975.

Kurzinger, J. 'Frau und Mann nach 1 Kor 11, 11f'. *BZ* 22:2 (1978) 270–5.

LaSor, W. S. 'Discovering what Jewish miqva'ot can tell us about Christian baptism'. *BAR* 13:1 (1987) 52–9.

Lewis, R. M. 'The "women" of 1 Timothy 3:11'. *BSac* 136 (1979) 167–75.

Marmorstein, E. 'The veil in Judaism and Islam'. *JJS* 52 (1954–55) 1–11.

McDonald, J. I. H. 'Was Romans XVI a separate letter?' *NTS* 16 (1969–70) 369–72.

Meeks, W. A. *The First Urban Christians*. New Haven: Yale University, 1984.

Meir, J. P. 'On the veiling of hermeneutics (1 Cor 11.2–16)'. *CBQ* 40 (1978) 212–26.

Moo, D. J. '1 Timothy 2:11–15: meaning and significance'. *Trinity Journal* n.s. 2 (1980) 62–83.

'The interpretation of 1 Timothy 2:11–15: a rejoinder'. *Trinity Journal* n.s. 2 (1981) 198–222.

Motta, O. 'The question of the unveiled woman (1 Cor 11.2–16)'. *ET* 44 (1932) 137–9.

Murphy-O'Connor, J. 'The non-Pauline character of 1 Corinthians 11.2–16?' *JBL* 45 (1976) 615–27.

'Community and apostolate'. *Bible Today* 11 (1973) 1260–6.

Nolland, J. 'Women in the public life of the church'. *Crux* 19:3 (1983) 17–23.

Odell-Scott, D. W. 'Let the women speak in church, an egalitarian interpretation of 1 Cor 14.33b–36'. *BTB* 13:3 (1983) 90–3.

Osburn, C. O. 'ΑΥΘΕΝΤΕΩ (1 Timothy 2:12)'. *ResQ* 25 (1982) 1–12.

Painter, J. 'Paul and the pneumatikoi at Corinth'. *Paul and Paulinism. Essays in Honor of C. K. Barrett*. ed. M. D. Hooker and S. G. Wilson. London: SPCK, 1982, 237–50.

Payne, P. B. *Man and Woman: One in Christ*. Grand Rapids: Zondervan, in press.

'Libertarian women in Ephesus: a response to Douglas Moo'. *Trinity Journal* n.s. 2 (1981) 169–97.

Perdelwitz, R. 'Die ἐξουσία auf dem Hapt der Frau, 1 Kor. 11.10'. *TSK* 86 (1913) 611–13.

Ramsay, W. M. *The Cities of St Paul*. Minneapolis: James Family Christian Publication, repr. n.d.

Rhijn, C. H. Van. 'Euodia en Syntyche'. *TS* 21 (1903) 300–9.

Schmithals, W. *Paul and the Gnostics*. Nashville: Abingdon, 1972.

Schnackenburg, R. 'Apostles before and during Paul's time'. *Apostolic History and the Gospel*. ed. W. Gasque and R. P. Martin. Grand Rapids: Eerdmans, 1970, 287–303.

Scholer, D. M. 'Women's adornment'. *Daughters of Sarah* 6:1 (1980) 3–6.

'Exegesis: 1 Timothy 2:8–15'. *Daughters of Sarah* 1:4 (May, 1975) 7–8.

Schwarz, G. 'ἐξουσίαν ἔχειν ἐπὶ τῆς κεφαλῆς? (1 Korinther 11.10)'. *ZNW* 70 (1979) 249.
Schweizer, E. *Church Order in the New Testament*. London: SCM, 1961.
Sihler, E.G. 'A note on the first Christian congregation at Rome'. *CTM* 3 (1932) 180–4.
Spencer, A. Besancon. 'Eve at Ephesus'. *JETS* 17:4 (1974) 215–22.
Thiessen, G. *The Social Setting of Pauline Christianity*. Philadelphia: Fortress, 1982.
Trompf, G.W. 'On attitudes toward women in Paul and Paulinist literature: 1 Corinthians 11:3–16 and its context'. *CBQ* 42 (1980) 196–215.
Walker, W.O. Jr. '1 Corinthians 11:2–16 and Paul's views regarding women'. *JBL* 94 (1975) 94–110.
Waltke, B.K. '1 Corinthians 11:2–16: an interpretation'. *BSac* 135:53 (1978) 46–57.
Watts, J.C. 'The alleged quarrel of Euodia and Syntyche'. *ET* 5 (1893–94) 286–7.
Weeks, N. 'Of silence and head coverings'. *WTJ* 35 (1, 1972) 21–7.
Witherington, Ben. 'Rite and rights for women – Galatians 3.28'. *NTS* 27:5 (1981) 593–604.

4 Women and the third evangelist

Benoit, P. 'Marie Madeleine et les disciples au tombeau selon Joh 20, 1–18'. *Judentum Urchristentum Kirche. Festschrift für Joachim Jeremias*. BZNW 26. Berlin: A Töpelmann, 1960, 141–52.
'L'Enfance de Jean-Baptiste selon Luc I'. *NTS* 3 (1956–57) 169–94.
'"Et toi-même un glaive transpercera l'âme!" (Luc 2, 35)'. *CBQ* 25 (3, 1963) 251–61.
Blass, F.W. 'Priscilla und Aquila'. *TSK* 74 (1901) 124–6.
Blum, G.G. 'Das Amt der Frau im Neuen Testament'. *NovT* 7 (1964) 142–61.
Bode, E.L. *The First Easter Morning – The Gospel Accounts of the Women's Visit to the Tomb of Jesus*. Rome: Biblical Institute, 1970.
Brown, Raymond and Donfried, K.P. *et al.*, eds. *Mary in the New Testament*. Philadelphia: Fortress, 1978.
Brown, Raymond. *The Birth of the Messiah*. London: Geoffrey Chapman, 1977.
Burton, H. 'The House of Mary'. *Exp.* 2nd ser 1 (1881) 313–18.
Cadbury, H.J. 'Lexical notes on Luke–Acts, III – Luke's interest in lodging'. *JBL* 45 (1926) 305–22.
Carmignac, J. 'The meaning of *parthenos* in Luke 1.27 – a reply to C.H. Dodd'. *BT* 28 (3, 1977) 327–30.
Conzelmann, H. *History of Primitive Christianity*. Nashville: Abingdon, 1973.
Crum, W.E. 'Schila und Tabitha'. *ZNW* 12 (1911) 352.
Daniélou, J. *The Ministry of Women in the Early Church*. Leighton Buzzard: Faith, 1974.
Danker, Frederick W. *Jesus and the New Age According to St Luke*. St Louis: Clayton Publishing House, 1972.
D'Arc, J. 'Catechesis on the road to Emmaus'. *LV* 32:2 (1977) 143–56.

Dodd, C. H. 'New Testament translation problems I'. *BT* 27 (3, 1976) 301–11.

Drury, J. *Tradition and Design in Luke's Gospel – A Study in Early Christian Historiography*. London: Darton, Longman and Todd, 1976.

Ellis, E. E. 'The role of the Christian prophet in Acts'. *Apostolic History and the Gospel*. ed. W. Ward Gasque and R. P. Martin. Grand Rapids: Eerdmans, 1971, 55–6.

Evans, C. F. *Resurrection and the New Testament*. London: SCM, 1970.

Feuillet, A. 'La découverte du tombeau vide en Jean 20, 3–10 et la foi au Christ ressuscité'. *EspV* 87 (1977) 273–4.

Flender, H. *St Luke – Theologian of Redemptive History*. London: SPCK, 1967.

Forestell, J. T. 'Old Testament background of the Magnificat'. *MS* 12 (1961) 205–44.

Fuller, R. H. *The Formation of the Resurrection Narratives*. New York: Macmillan and Co., 1971.

Gryson, R. *Le ministère des femmes dans l'Église ancienne*. Gembloux: Duculot, 1972.

Guy, H. 'The virgin birth in St Luke'. *ET* 68 (1957) 157–8.

Harnack, A. von. 'Über die Beiden Rezensionen der Geschichte der Prisca und des Aquila in Act Apost. 18, 1–17'. *Studien zur Geschichte des Neuen Testaments und der Alten Kirche*. Berlin/Leipzig: W. De Gruyter, 1931, 54–6.

Hastings, J. 'Women in the Acts of the Apostles'. *ET* 4 (1892–93) 434–6.

Humenay, R. L. 'The place of Mary in Luke: a look at modern biblical criticism'. *AER* 5 (1974) 291–303.

Leaney, A. R. C. 'The resurrection narratives in Luke (xxiv.12–53)'. *NTS* 2 (1955–56) 110–14.

Leonard, E. A. 'St Paul on the status of women'. *CBQ* 12 (1950) 311–20.

Léon-Dufour X. *Resurrection and the Message of Easter*. New York: Holt, Rinehart, Winston, 1974.

Luther, M. 'The Magnificat'. *Luther's Works*, vol. 21. St Louis: Concordia Publishing House, 1956.

Marshall, I. H. 'The resurrection of Jesus in Luke'. *TynB* 24 (1973) 55–98.

McHugh, John. *The Mother of Jesus in the New Testament*. London: Darton, Longman, & Todd, 1975.

Nestle, E. 'Schila et Tabitha'. *ZNW* 11 (1910) 240.

Parvey, C. F. 'The theology and leadership of women in the New Testament'. *Religion and Sexism, Images of Woman in the Jewish and Christian Tradition*. ed. R. R. Ruether. New York: Simon and Schuster, 1974, 117–49.

Plumptre, E. H. 'Aquila and Priscilla'. *Biblical Studies*. ed. E. H. Plumptre. London: Griffith, Farran, Okeden, and Welch, 1885, 423–4.

Prabhu, G. S. '"Rejoice, Favored One!" Mary in the annunciation story of Luke'. *Biblebhashyam* 3 (4, 1977) 259–77.

Ramsay, W.M. 'The denials of Peter – section III: the house in the New Testament'. *ET* 27 (1915–16) 471–2.

Redalié, Y. 'Conversion ou libération? Notes sur Actes 16, 11–40'. *Bulletin du Centre Protestant d'Études* 26 (7, 1974) 7–17.

Richardson, A. *An Introduction to the Theology of the New Testament.* London: SCM, 1958.

Riddle, D.W. 'Early Christian hospitality: a factor in the Gospel transmission'. *JBL* 57 (1938) 141–54.

Schubert, P. 'The structure and significance of Luke 24'. *Neutestamentliche Studien für Rudolf Bultmann.* BZNW 21. Berlin: A. Töpelmann, 1957, 165–86.

Schumacher, R. 'Aquila und Priscilla'. *TGl* 12 (1920) 86–99.

Schweizer, E. 'Die Bekehrung des Apollos, Apg 18, 24–26'. *Beiträge zur Theologie des Neuen Testaments – Neutestamentliche Aufsätze (1955–1970).* Zurich: Zwingli, 1970, 71–9.

Smith, B.T.D. 'Apollos and the Twelve Disciples at Ephesus'. *JTS* 16 (1914–15) 241–6.

Swidler, Leonard. *Women in Judaism: The Status of Women in Formative Judaism.* Metuchen: Scarecrow, 1976.

Thomas, W.D. 'The place of women in the church at Philippi'. *ET* 83 (1971–72) 117–20.

Torrance, T.F. 'St Paul at Philippi: three startling conversions. Acts 16.6–40'. *EvQ* 13 (1941) 62–74.

Viteau, J. 'L'institution des diacres et des veuves – Actes vi.1–10, viii.4–40, xxi.8'. *RHE* 22 (1926) 513–37.

Witherington, Ben. 'On the road with Mary Magdalene, Joanna, Susanna, and other disciples: Luke 8.1–3'. *ZNW* 70 (3–4, 1979) 242–8.

Zerwick, M. '... quoniam virum non cognosco (Lc I, 34)'. *VD* 37 (1959) 212–24, 276–88.

5 Women in the churches of Matthew, Mark and John

Broer, I. 'Die Bedeutung der "Jungfrauengeburt" im Mattäusevangelium'. BibLeb 12 (4, 1971) 248–60.

Brown, R. 'The resurrection and biblical criticism'. *Commonweal* 87 (8, 1967) 232–6.

The Virginal Conception and Bodily Resurrection of Jesus. New York: Paulist Press, 1973.

'Roles of women in the Fourth Gospel'. *TS* 36 (4, 1975) 688–99.

Bruce, F.F. 'The end of the Second Gospel'. *EvQ* 17 (1945) 169–81.

Brun, L. 'Der Auferstehungsbericht des Markusevangeliums'. *TSK* 87 (1914) 346–88.

Cadbury, H.J. 'Mark 16.8'. *JBL* 46 (1927) 344–5.

Campenhausen, H. von. *The Virgin Birth in the Theology of the Ancient Church.* Naperville, IL: A.R. Allenson, 1964.

Catchpole, D. 'The fearful silence of the women at the tomb – a Study in Markan theology'. *JTSA* 18 (1977) 3–10.

Cranfield, C.E.B. 'St Mark 16.1–8'. *SJT* 5 (1952) 282–98, 398–414.

Daniélou, J. 'The empty tomb'. *Month* n.s. 39 (1968) 215–22.

Dhanis, É. 'L'ensevelissement de Jésus et la visite au tombeau dans l'évangile de Saint Marc (Mc. XV, 40–XVI, 8)'. *Greg* 39 (2, 1958) 367–410.

Dibelius, Martin, *From Tradition to Gospel.* London: Ivor Nicholson and Watson, 1934.

Dodd, C. H. *The Interpretation of the Fourth Gospel*. Cambridge: Cambridge University Press, 1953.

Evans, C. F. 'I will go before you into Galilee'. *JTS* n.s. 5 (1, 1954) 3–18.

Farmer, T. H. '"Touch me not"'. *ET* 28 (1916–17) 92–3.

Farmer, W. R. *The Last Twelve Verses of Mark*. SNTSMS 25. Cambridge: Cambridge University Press, 1974.

Farrer, A. *St Matthew and St Mark*. Westminster: Dacre Press, 1954.

Feuillet, A. 'La découverte du tombeau vide en Jean 20, 3–10 et la Foi au Christ ressuscité'. *EspV* 87 (19, 1977) 273–84.

Fowler, D. C. 'The Meaning of "Touch me not" in John 20:17'. *EvQ* 47 (1, 1975) 16–25.

Goodspeed, E. J. 'The original conclusion of the Gospel of Mark'. *AJT* 9 (1909) 484–90.

Hengel, M. 'Maria Magdalena und die Frauen als Zeugen'. *Abraham Unser Vater, Festschrift für Otto Michel, zum 60 Geburtstag*. Leiden: E. J. Brill, 1963, 243–56.

Hodges, Z. C. 'The women and the empty tomb'. *BSac* 123 (October, 1966) 301–9.

Horvath, T. 'The early Markan tradition on the resurrection – Mk 16, 1–8'. *RUO* 43 (3, 1973) 445–8.

Johnson, M. D. *The Purpose of Biblical Genealogies with Special Reference to the Setting of the Genealogies of Jesus*. SNTSMS 8. Cambridge: Cambridge University Press, 1969.

Journet, C. 'L'apparition à Marie de Magdala'. *NVet* 40 (2, 1965) 143–7.

Kenyon, F. G. 'Papyrus rolls and the ending of St Mark'. *JTS* 40 (1929) 56–7.

Léon-Dufour, X. 'Le juste Joseph'. *NRT* 81 ((3, 1959) 225–31.

Mangatt, G. 'At the tomb of Jesus'. *Biblebhashyam* 3 (2, 1977) 91–6.

Metzger, B. 'On the citation of variant readings of Matt. I:16'. *JBL* 77 (1958) 361–3.

Meye, R. P. 'Mark 16:8 – the ending of Mark's Gospel'. *BR* 14 (1969) 33–43.

Minear, P. S. '"We don't know where ..." John 20:2'. *Int* 30 (1976) 125–39.

Moule, C. F. D. 'St Mark xvi.8 – once more'. *NTS* 2 (1955–56) 58–9.

Neirynck, F. 'Les femmes au tombeau: étude de la rédaction Matthéenne (Matt. xxviii.1–10)'. *NTS* 15 (1968–69) 168–90.

Nicklin, T. '"Noli me tangere"'. *ET* 51 (1939–40) 478.

Ottley, R. R. 'ἐφοβοῦντο γάρ, Mark xvi.8'. *JTS* 27 (1925–26) 407–9.

Ruether, R. R. *Mary – The Feminine Face of the Church*. London: SCM, 1979.

Schlier, H. 'Die Osterbotschaft aus dem Grab (Markus 16.1–8)'. *KG* 27 (1, 1971) 1–6.

Shaw, A. 'The breakfast by the shore and the Mary Magdalene encounter as Eucharistic narratives'. *JTS* 25 (1974) 12–26.

Smith, R. H. 'New and old in Mark 16:1–8'. *CTM* 43 (1972) 518–27.

Spicq, C. 'Noli me tangere'. *RSPT* 32 (1948) 226–7.

Stendahl, K. 'Quis et unde? An analysis of Mt 1–2'. *Judentum Urchristentum Kirche. Festschrift für Joachim Jeremias*. BZNW 26. Berlin: A. Töpelmann, 1960, 94–105.

Tagawa, K. *Miracles et Évangile. La pensée personnelle de l'évangeliste Mark.* Études d'histoire et de philosophie religieuses 62. Paris; Universitaires de France, 1966.

Trompf, G. W. 'The first resurrection appearance and the ending of Mark's Gospel'. *NTS* 18 (3, 1972) 308–30.

Vögtle, A. 'Mt. 1, 25 und die Virginitas B.M. Virginis post partum'. *TQ* 147 (1, 1967) 28–39.

Walker, R. *Die Heilsgeschichte im ersten Evangelium.* FRLANT 91. Göttingen: Vandenhoeck and Ruprecht, 1967.

Wansbrough, H. 'Event and interpretation: VIII. The adoption of Jesus'. Clergy Review 55 (12, 1970) 921–8.

Wenham, D. 'The resurrection narratives in Matthew's Gospel'. *TynB* 24 (1973) 21–54.

Witherington, B. 'Matthew 5.32 and 19.9 – exception or exceptional situation?'. *NTS* 31:4 (Oct. 1985) 571–6.

6 Trajectories beyond the New Testament era

Baer, R. A. *Philo's Use of the Categories Male and Female.* Leiden: E. J. Brill, 1970.

Blanke, F. and Leenhardt, F. J. *Die Stellung der Frau in Neuen Testament und der alten Kirche.* Zurich: Zwingli, 1949.

Bovon, F. 'Le Privilège Pascal de Marie- Madeleine'. *NTS* 30 (Jan. 1984) 50–62.

Brown, R. E. 'The Christians who lost out'. *New York Times* book review (20 January 1980) 3, 33.

Clark, E. and Richardson, H. *Women and Religion.* New York: Harper & Row, 1977.

Crouzel, H. *Virginité et Mariage selon Origene.* Paris: Bruges, 1962.

Davies, S. *The Social World of the Apocryphal Acts.* Philadelphia: Temple University, 1978.

The Revolt of the Widows. Carbondale, Il: S. Illinois University, 1980.

de Jonge, M. *Pseudepigrapha Veteris Testamentis Graece*, vol. 1. Leiden: E. J. Brill, 1964.

Eno, R. B. 'Authority and conflict in the early Church'. *ETh* 7 (1967) 41–50.

Ferguson, J. *Clement of Alexandria.* New York: Twayne Publishers, 1974.

Fiorenza, E. Schüssler, *In Memory of Her.* New York: Crossroad, 1983.

Gryson, R. *The Ministry of Women in the Early Church.* Collegeville, MN: Liturgical Press, 1976.

Hanson, A. T. 'Rahab the harlot in the early Christian tradition'. *JTNT* 1 (1978) 53–60.

MacDonald, D. R. 'The role of women in the production of the Apocryphal Acts of the Apostles'. *Iliff Review* 40 (3, 1983) 21–38.

Meyer, M. W. 'Making Mary male: the categories "male" and "female" in the Gospel of Thomas'. *NTS* 37 (1985) 554–70.

Osiek, C. 'The widow as altar: the rise and fall of a symbol'. *Second Century* 3 (3, 1983) 159–69.

Oulton, J. E. L. and Chadwick, H., eds. *Alexandrian Christianity.* Philadelphia: Westminster, 1954.

Pagels, E. H. *The Gnostic Gospels*. New York: Random House, 1979.
'What became of God the Mother? Conflicting images of God in early Christianity'. *Signs* 2 (1976) 293–303.

Ruether, R. R. and McLaughlin, E., eds. *Women of Spirit – Female Leadership in the Jewish and Christian Traditions*. New York: Simon & Schuster, 1979.

Ruether, R. R. 'Misogynism and virginal feminism in the Fathers of the Church'. *Religion and Sexism*. New York: Simon and Schuster, 1974, 150–83.

Salgado, J-M. 'La presentation de Marie au temple'. *PalCler* 51 (1972) 469–74.

Smith, M. *Studies in Early Mysticism in the Near and Middle East*. London: Sheldon, 1931.

Tavard, G. H. *Woman in Christian Tradition*. South Bend: University of Notre Dame, 1973.

Testa, E. 'Lo sviluppo della "Dormitio Marie" nella litteratura, nella teologia e nella archaelogia'. *Marianum* 44 (3–4, 1982) 316–89.

Witherington, B. 'Anti-feminist tendencies of the "Western" text in Acts'. *JBL* 103:1 (1984) 82–4.

Conclusions

Käsemann, E. *New Testament Questions of Today*. Philadelphia: Fortress, 1969.

Longenecker, R. N. *New Testament Social Ethics for Today*. Grand Rapids: Eerdmans, 1974.

MacMullen, R. *Christianizing the Roman Empire, AD 100–400*. New Haven: Yale University, 1984.

Wilken, R. L. *The Christians as the Romans Saw Them*. New Haven: Yale University, 1984.